AUTHENTIC VICTORIAN GHOST STORIES

✄ THE LOCHLAINN SEABROOK COLLECTION ✄

AMERICAN CIVIL WAR
Abraham Lincoln Was a Liberal, Jefferson Davis Was a Conservative: The Missing Key to Understanding the American Civil War
Confederacy 101: Amazing Facts You Never Knew About America's Oldest Political Tradition
Confederate Blood and Treasure: An Interview With Lochlainn Seabrook
Everything You Were Taught About African-Americans and the Civil War is Wrong, Ask a Southerner!
Everything You Were Taught About the Civil War is Wrong, Ask a Southerner!
Give This Book to a Yankee! A Southern Guide to the Civil War For Northerners
Heroes of the Southern Confederacy: The Illustrated Book of Confederate Officials, Soldiers, and Civilians
Lincoln's War: The Real Cause, the Real Winner, the Real Loser
Seabrook's Complete Battle Book: War Between the States, 1861-1865
The Great Yankee Coverup: What the North Doesn't Want You to Know About Lincoln's War!
The Hampton Roads Conference: The Southern View
The Ultimate Civil War Quiz Book: How Much Do You Really Know About America's Most Misunderstood Conflict?
Women in Gray: A Tribute to the Ladies Who Supported the Southern Confederacy

CONFEDERATE MONUMENTS
Confederate Monuments: Why Every American Should Honor Confederate Soldiers and Their Memorials

CONFEDERATE FLAG
Confederate Flag Facts: What Every American Should Know About Dixie's Southern Cross
What the Confederate Flag Means to Me: Americans Speak Out in Defense of Southern Honor, Heritage, and History

SECESSION
All We Ask Is To Be Let Alone: The Southern Secession Fact Book

RECONSTRUCTION
Twelve Years in Hell: Victorian Southerners Debunk the Myth of Reconstruction, 1865-1877

SLAVERY
Everything You Were Taught About American Slavery is Wrong, Ask a Southerner!
Slavery 101: Amazing Facts You Never Knew About America's "Peculiar Institution"
The Bittersweet Bond: Race Relations in the Old South as Described by White and Black Southerners

NATHAN BEDFORD FORREST
A Rebel Born: A Defense of Nathan Bedford Forrest - Confederate General, American Legend (winner of the 2011 Jefferson Davis Historical Gold Medal)
A Rebel Born: The Screenplay (film about N. B. Forrest)
Forrest! 99 Reasons to Love Nathan Bedford Forrest
Give 'Em Hell Boys! The Complete Military Correspondence of Nathan Bedford Forrest
I Rode With Forrest! Confederate Soldiers Who Served With the World's Greatest Cavalry Leader
Nathan Bedford Forrest and African-Americans: Yankee Myth, Confederate Fact
Nathan Bedford Forrest and the Battle of Fort Pillow: Yankee Myth, Confederate Fact
Nathan Bedford Forrest and the Ku Klux Klan: Yankee Myth, Confederate Fact
Nathan Bedford Forrest: Southern Hero, American Patriot - Honoring a Confederate Icon and the Old South
Saddle, Sword, and Gun: A Biography of Nathan Bedford Forrest For Teens
The God of War: Nathan Bedford Forrest As He Was Seen By His Contemporaries
The Quotable Nathan Bedford Forrest: Selections From the Writings and Speeches of the Confederacy's Most Brilliant Cavalryman

QUOTABLE SERIES
The Alexander H. Stephens Reader: Excerpts From the Works of a Confederate Founding Father
The Quotable Alexander H. Stephens: Selections From the Writings and Speeches of the Confederacy's First Vice President
The Quotable Jefferson Davis: Selections From the Writings and Speeches of the Confederacy's First President
The Quotable Nathan Bedford Forrest: Selections From the Writings and Speeches of the Confederacy's Most Brilliant Cavalryman
The Quotable Robert E. Lee: Selections From the Writings and Speeches of the South's Most Beloved Civil War General
The Quotable Stonewall Jackson: Selections From the Writings and Speeches of the South's Most Famous General
The Unquotable Abraham Lincoln: The President's Quotes They Don't Want You To Know!

CIVIL WAR BATTLES
Encyclopedia of the Battle of Franklin - A Comprehensive Guide to the Conflict that Changed the Civil War
Nathan Bedford Forrest and the Battle of Fort Pillow: Yankee Myth, Confederate Fact
Seabrook's Complete Battle Book: War Between the States, 1861-1865
The Battle of Franklin: Recollections of Confederate and Union Soldiers
The Battle of Nashville: Recollections of Confederate and Union Soldiers
The Battle of Spring Hill: Recollections of Confederate and Union Soldiers

CONSTITUTIONAL HISTORY
America's Three Constitutions: Complete Texts of the Articles of Confederation, Constitution of the United States of America, and Constitution of the Confederate States of America
The Articles of Confederation Explained: A Clause-by-Clause Study of America's First Constitution
The Constitution of the Confederate States of America Explained: A Clause-by-Clause Study of the South's Magna Carta

CHILDREN
Honest Jeff and Dishonest Abe: A Southern Children's Guide to the Civil War
Saddle, Sword, and Gun: A Biography of Nathan Bedford Forrest For Teens

VICTORIAN CONFEDERATE LITERATURE
I, Confederate: Why Dixie Seceded and Fought in the Words of Southern Soldiers
Rise Up and Call Them Blessed: Victorian Tributes to the Confederate Soldier, 1861-1901
Support Your Local Confederate: Wit and Humor in the Southern Confederacy
The Bittersweet Bond: Race Relations in the Old South as Described by White and Black Southerners
The God of War: Nathan Bedford Forrest As He Was Seen By His Contemporaries
The Old Rebel: Robert E. Lee As He Was Seen By His Contemporaries
Victorian Confederate Poetry: The Southern Cause in Verse, 1861-1901
We Called Him Jeb: James Ewell Brown Stuart As He Was Seen By His Contemporaries

ABRAHAM LINCOLN
Abraham Lincoln: The Southern View - Demythologizing America's Sixteenth President
Lincolnology: The Real Abraham Lincoln Revealed in His Own Words - A Study of Lincoln's Suppressed, Misinterpreted, and Forgotten Writings and Speeches
Lincoln's War: The Real Cause, the Real Winner, the Real Loser
The Great Impersonator! 99 Reasons to Dislike Abraham Lincoln
The Unholy Crusade: Lincoln's Legacy of Destruction in the American South
The Unquotable Abraham Lincoln: The President's Quotes They Don't Want You To Know!

NATURAL HISTORY
North America's Amazing Mammals: An Encyclopedia for the Whole Family
The Concise Book of Owls: A Guide to Nature's Most Mysterious Birds
The Concise Book of Tigers: A Guide to Nature's Most Remarkable Cats

FAMILY HISTORIES
The Blakeneys: An Etymological, Ethnological, and Genealogical Study - Uncovering the Mysterious Origins of the Blakeney Family and Name
The Caudills: An Etymological, Ethnological, and Genealogical Study - Exploring the Name and National Origins of a European-American Family
The McGavocks of Carnton Plantation: A Southern History - Celebrating One of Dixie's Most Noble Confederate Families and Their Tennessee Home

MIND, BODY, SPIRIT
Authentic Victorian Ghost Stories: Genuine Early Reports of Apparitions, Wraiths, Poltergeists, and Haunted Houses
Autobiography of a Non-Yogi: A Scientist's Journey From Hinduism to Christianity (Dr. Amitava Dasgupta, with Lochlainn Seabrook)
Britannia Rules: Goddess-Worship in Ancient Anglo-Celtic Society—An Academic Look at the United Kingdom's Matricentric Spiritual Past
Carnton Plantation Ghost Stories: True Tales of the Unexplained from Tennessee's Most Haunted Civil War House!
Christ Is All and In All: Rediscovering Your Divine Nature and the Kingdom Within
Christmas Before Christianity: How the Birthday of the "Sun" Became the Birthday of the "Son"
Jesus and the Gospel of Q: Christ's Pre-Christian Teachings As Recorded in the New Testament
Jesus and the Law of Attraction: The Bible-Based Guide to Creating Perfect Health, Wealth, and Happiness Following Christ's Simple Formula
Mysterious Invaders: Twelve Famous 20th-Century Scientists Confront the UFO Phenomenon
Seabrook's Bible Dictionary of Traditional and Mystical Christian Doctrines
Sea Raven Press Blank Page Journal: For Reflections, Notes, and Sketches
Secrets of Celebrity Surnames: An Onomastic Dictionary of Famous People
The Bible and the Law of Attraction: 99 Teachings of Jesus, the Apostles, and the Prophets
The Book of Kelle: An Introduction to Goddess-Worship and the Great Celtic Mother-Goddess Kelle, Original Blessed Lady of Ireland
The Goddess Dictionary of Words and Phrases: Introducing a New Core Vocabulary for the Women's Spirituality Movement
The Greatest Jesus Mystery of All Time: Where Was Christ Between the Ages of 12 and 30?
The Martian Anomalies: A Photographic Search for Intelligent Life on Mars
UFOs and Aliens: The Complete Guidebook
Victorian Hernia Cures: Nonsurgical Self-Treatment of Inguinal Hernia
Vintage Southern Cookbook: 2,000 Delicious Dishes From Dixie
Your Soul Lives Forever: Documented Victorian Case Studies Proving Consciousness Survives Death

WOMEN
Aphrodite's Trade: The Hidden History of Prostitution Unveiled
Princess Diana: Modern Day Moon-Goddess - A Psychoanalytical and Mythological Look at Diana Spencer's Life, Marriage, and Death (with Dr. Jane Goldberg)
Women in Gray: A Tribute to the Ladies Who Supported the Southern Confederacy

REPRINTS
A Short History of the Confederate States of America (author Jefferson Davis; editor Lochlainn Seabrook)
Prison Life of Jefferson Davis (author John J. Craven; editor Lochlainn Seabrook)
Life of Beethoven (author Ludwig Nohl; editor Lochlainn Seabrook)
The New Revelation (author Arthur Conan Doyle; editor Lochlainn Seabrook)
The Rise and Fall of the Confederate Government (author Jefferson Davis; editor Lochlainn Seabrook)

Lochlainn Seabrook does not author books for fame and glory, but for the love of writing and sharing his knowledge.

SeaRavenPress.com

Authentic Victorian
GHOST STORIES

Genuine Early Reports of Apparitions, Wraiths, Poltergeists, and Haunted Houses

CONCEIVED, COLLECTED, EDITED, ARRANGED, & DESIGNED WITH AN INTRODUCTION BY

LOCHLAINN SEABROOK

AWARD WINNING AUTHOR ON THE MYSTERIOUS AND THE PARANORMAL

Diligently Researched and Generously Illustrated by the Author for the Elucidation of the Reader

2024

Sea Raven Press, Park County, Wyoming, USA

AUTHENTIC VICTORIAN GHOST STORIES

Published by
Sea Raven Press, Cassidy Ravensdale, President
Park County, Wyoming, USA
SeaRavenPress.com

Copyright © all text and illustrations Lochlainn Seabrook 2024
in accordance with U.S. and international copyright laws and regulations, as stated and protected under the Berne Union for the Protection of Literary and Artistic Property (Berne Convention), and the Universal Copyright Convention (the UCC). All rights reserved under the Pan-American and International Copyright Conventions.

PRINTING HISTORY
1st SRP paperback edition, 1st printing, May 2024 • ISBN: 978-1-955351-44-7
1st SRP hardcover edition, 1st printing, May 2024 • ISBN: 978-1-955351-45-4

ISBN: 978-1-955351-44-7 (paperback)
Library of Congress Control Number: 2024938004

This work is the copyrighted intellectual property of Lochlainn Seabrook and has been registered with the Copyright Office at the Library of Congress in Washington, D.C., USA. No part of this work (including text, covers, drawings, photos, illustrations, maps, images, diagrams, etc.), in whole or in part, may be used, reproduced, stored in a retrieval system, or transmitted, in any form or by any means now known or hereafter invented, without written permission from the publisher. The sale, duplication, hire, lending, copying, digitalization, or reproduction of this material, in any manner or form whatsoever, is also prohibited, and is a violation of federal, civil, and digital copyright law, which provides severe civil and criminal penalties for any violations.

Authentic Victorian Ghost Stories: Genuine Early Reports of Apparitions, Wraiths, Poltergeists, and Haunted Houses, by Lochlainn Seabrook. Includes an introduction, illustrations, index, endnotes, appendix, and bibliography.

ARTWORK
Front and back cover design and art, book design, layout, font selection, and interior art by Lochlainn Seabrook.
All images, image captions, graphic design, and graphic art copyright © Lochlainn Seabrook.
All images selected, placed, manipulated, cleaned, colored, tinted, and/or created by Lochlainn Seabrook.
Cover image: "Haunted Poltergeist House, Stirling, Scotland"

All persons who approve of the authority and principles of Colonel Lochlainn Seabrook's literary work, and realize its benefits as a means of reeducating the world about facts left out of mainstream books, are hereby requested to avidly recommend his titles to others and to vigorously cooperate in extending their reach, scope, and influence around the globe.

The views documented in this book concerning the paranormal and spirituality are those of the publisher.
WRITTEN, DESIGNED, PUBLISHED, PRINTED, & MANUFACTURED IN THE UNITED STATES OF AMERICA

DEDICATION

To the many ghosts, goblins, wraiths, and angels that have visited me throughout my life, forever reminding me—through mysterious apparitions, sounds, and lights—of the immortality of the soul and the Better World that awaits us beyond the veil.

Lochlainn Seabrook, 2024

EPIGRAPH

There comes a time to every mortal being,
Whate'er his station or his lot in life,
When his sad soul yearns for the final freeing
From all this jarring and unceasing strife.

There comes a time, when, having lost its savor,
The salt of wealth is worthless; when the mind
Grows wearied with the world's capricious favor,
And sighs for something that it cannot find.

There comes a time, when, though kind friends are thronging
About our pathway with sweet acts of grace,
We feel a vast and overwhelming longing
For something that we cannot name or place.

There comes a time, when, with earth's best love by us,
To feed the heart's great hunger and desire,
We find not even this can satisfy us;
The soul within us cries for something higher.

What greater proof need we that we inherit
A life immortal in another sphere?
It is the homesick longing of the spirit
That cannot find its satisfaction here.

Ella Wheeler Wilcox, 1888

CONTENTS

Introduction, by Lochlainn Seabrook ❧ page 11

CHAPTER 1 ❧ page 13
CHAPTER 2 ❧ page 33
CHAPTER 3 ❧ page 55
CHAPTER 4 ❧ page 77
CHAPTER 5 ❧ page 99
CHAPTER 6 ❧ page 121
CHAPTER 7 ❧ page 143
CHAPTER 8 ❧ page 165
CHAPTER 9 ❧ page 187
CHAPTER 10 ❧ page 203
CHAPTER 11 ❧ page 223
CHAPTER 12 ❧ page 245
CHAPTER 13 ❧ page 265
CHAPTER 14 ❧ page 285
CHAPTER 15 ❧ page 307

Appendix: Six Proofs That Ghosts Are Real ❧ page 329
Notes ❧ page 331
Bibliography ❧ page 341
Index ❧ page 347
Meet the Author-Editor ❧ page 365
Learn More ❧ page 367

SEA RAVEN PRESS

was founded for the express purpose of publishing and circulating such books as are calculated to store the mind with useful knowledge. We therefore publish only books of a high moral tone and tendency—such works as will be welcomed in every home and at every fireside as valuable family treasures.

L. Seabrook

INTRODUCTION

"If a man die, shall he live again?" — Job 14:14

FROM MY EARLIEST MEMORIES I have experienced paranormal phenomena on an almost daily basis, a wide variety that includes many of those described in the following pages. All have been positive in some way; never truly frightening, but always emotionally moving and spiritually enlightening.

Thus, naturally, I have always been drawn to ghost stories, and as a child enjoyed nothing more than settling down before sleep with a good book of hair-raising supernatural tales, particularly *Victorian* supernatural tales. It is in this spirit that I assembled this book: for the pleasure of those, like myself, who never tire of reading accounts regarding the Other Side.

However, this is *not* a speculative book of ghostly myths and legends (though I have included a few of these types out of sociological interest). In fact, the majority—though not all—of the following 19th-Century stories and images were well researched and documented by both scientifically-minded groups, such as England's prestigious Society for Psychical Research, *and* a host of brilliant individuals, including Sir Arthur Conan Doyle (British physician and creator of "Sherlock Holmes"), Sir Oliver Lodge (British physicist), Sir William Crookes (British chemist), and Alfred Russel Wallace (British biologist)—all who were firm believers in the After Life and supporters of Spiritualism: the doctrine that Spirit is the primary reality, that Spirit is immortal, and that spirits of the deceased regularly interact with the living.

Out of respect for my topic and my original 19th- and early 20th-Century informants, in editing this work I have retained all Victorian spellings and the word-for-word transcriptions of the original stories. My comments are in brackets, my emphasis (italics) is marked, and, for those interested, I have recorded the source of each entry in my Notes section.

While we still do not have definitive scientific answers concerning ghosts and the World Beyond—or *anything* supernatural, paranormal, or spiritual, for that matter—and probably never will (Romans 11:33), it must be clear to all but the most narrow-minded skeptics that a multitude of mysterious dimensions exist outside the one we are familiar with here on earth. And this book easily demonstrates this plain fact, as many scientists themselves are beginning to discover.

May *Authentic Victorian Ghost Stories* bring my readers years of enjoyment and illumination, for this is a subject that is not only emotionally comforting, it is intellectually revolutionizing as well.

Lochlainn Seabrook
Park County, Wyoming USA
May 2024

"Books invite all; they constrain none."
Hartley Burr Alexander (1873-1939)

CHAPTER ONE

SHROPSHIRE FARM POLTERGEIST
☞ A series of occurrences which have caused great excitement in the neighbourhood of Leebotwood, and no small speculation and wonder in the adjacent town of Shrewsbury, have just taken place. At a secluded farm called "The Woods," which is about a mile and a half from Toppington and nine or ten from Shrewsbury, resides a farmer, named Hampson, and about four o'clock one afternoon, at the latter end of last week, the servants were in the kitchen of the farmhouse, preparing tea.

On the fire was a saucepan in which were some eggs boiling, and this "jumped," as the girls declared, off the fire, while the tea things were thrown from the table and smashed. Some of the hot cinders were also thrown out of the grate, and set fire to some clothes in a basket. So far, the explosion of some material in the grate might have been sufficient to account for the occurrence; but what is said to have occurred subsequently will not bear such an explanation.

On the table was a paraffin lamp, with a globe, and the globe was "lifted" off the stand and thrown across the room, the lamp itself being left on the table. A mat under the lamp took fire, and the inmates of the house becoming alarmed, they ran out for the neighbours. Among others who went to the house was a Mr. Lea, an adjacent farmer, who states that when he approached the house it seemed as if all the upstairs rooms were on fire, "as there was such a light in the windows." Mr. Hampson consequently went upstairs and made an examination, but everything there was safe, and in the usual order.

As things were continuing to jump about the kitchen in a manner which was altogether inexplicable, and many were getting damaged, Hampson decided to remove everything that was in that apartment outside. He accordingly took down a barometer from the wall, when something struck him on the leg, and a loaf of bread

Victorian photograph of a female ghost.

which was on the table was thrown by some invisible means and hit him on the back. A volume of *Pilgrim's Progress* was thrown or "jumped" through the window, and a large ornamental seashell went through in a similar fashion. In the parlour a sewing machine was thrown about and damaged, and has had to be sent to be repaired. The nurse-girl was nursing the baby by the fire when some fire leapt from the grate, and the child's hair was singed and its arms burnt. The girl was so alarmed that she set off to a neighbour's, and on the way there her clothes took fire, and had to be torn from her body. During the evening, while the girl was at the neighbour's, a plate which she touched while having her supper was apparently thrown on the floor, and the pieces were picked up by some unseen agency, and put in the centre of the table. Other occurrences are said to have taken place in the neighbour's house while the nurse-girl was there, the whole lasting considerably over half an hour.

As no one could explain the cause of what they witnessed, the police were communicated with, and made full inquiries from the inmates of the house and others, the result being that they ordered the coal to be consumed in the open air, believing it to contain some explosive substance, but it burnt quietly away. Those who witnessed these occurrences tell a marvellously straightforward story, and curiously enough none of them attributed it to any supernatural cause, as might have been expected in a quiet country locality, but they say it was "something in the coal or in the air," while one or two fancy it was some electrical phenomena.

Subsequently [our] Shrewsbury correspondent telegraphs that he paid another visit to Weston Lullingfield yesterday, and was informed that on Saturday and Sunday there were more extraordinary manifestations in connection with the girl Emma Davies. Police-constable Taylor, of the Shropshire Constabulary, remained in the house until late on Saturday. During the time he was there the fender moved from the fireplace into the middle of the room, and on being replaced came forward a second and third time. A cushion placed at the back of a chair on which the girl sat several times flew across the room, and all the stitches in her apron came undone, followed later on by the buttons upon her dress being wrenched off.

Miss Maddox, the village schoolmistress, made a statement to the correspondent to the effect that she called to see the girl, a former pupil, on Saturday evening, and had not long been seated when she observed both the chair and the girl rise from the floor. She took the girl on her lap and sat in the chair herself, and immediately the girl's boots flew off, and although replaced the circumstance was twice repeated. On Sunday a box in a bedroom was hurled across the room, and a number of cups and saucers smashed.[1] — AN UNNAMED SHROPSHIRE NEWSPAPER, 1883

THE VIENNA DISTURBANCES
☛ Unaccountable [poltergeist] disturbances, very similar to those at Weston Lullingfield [England], have recently occurred in a house in Vienna [Austria]. The *Daily News* gave a brief description of what took place, and a fuller account, translated from the *Neues Wiener Tagblatt*, appeared in *Light* for February 16th. The disturbances were investigated on January 19th by a "commission of the district magistracy," and no assignable cause could be found by the three commissioners.[2] — JOURNAL OF SOCIETY FOR PSYCHICAL RESEARCH, UK, 1884

A CASE OF BILOCATION BETWEEN INDIA & ENGLAND
☛ Mr. E. D. Ewen, of Chattisgarh, Central Provinces, India, stated that he had . . . a few days ago (on Friday, May 23rd [1884], at about 10 p.m.), received a visit from Mr. Damodar ["Secretary to the Theosophical Society, and a Brahmin of high caste"] in the astral body. He, Mr. Ewen, had gone to an upstairs room, at 77, Elgin-Crescent, W. [London, England], to replenish his tobacco-pouch. He was in the act of doing so from a store of tobacco in a drawer, when he suddenly perceived Damodar standing beside him.

He recognised Damodar distinctly, having previously known him personally in India. His first impression was that Damodar had come to see Colonel Olcott, who was in the house at the time. He (Mr. Ewen) rushed out on to the landing, and called to Colonel Olcott. As he stood on the landing, just outside the door of the room in which he had seen Damodar, Damodar appeared to pass through him, to emerge from the room without sensible contact, although the door was not wide enough to admit of a normal exit, while Mr. Ewen stood in front of it, without a collision, which Mr. Ewen must have felt. After thus apparently passing through him, the form of Damodar descended the stairs for some little way and then seemed to disappear through a closed window.[3] — JOURNAL OF SOCIETY FOR PSYCHICAL RESEARCH, UK, 1884

THE COLD HAND OF A DEATH-WRAITH

☛ During the great French war, when Napoleon I was overrunning Holland and after the unfortunate Walcheren expedition, our fleet was ordered to the [Battle of the] Scheldt, I believe in the severe winter of 1813. The sailors and marines from the various ships were landed in parties to man and defend the dykes. So severe was the cold that long wooden sheds were erected, and large fires kept up for the watch parties. All the officers in turn landed to keep the men to their posts.

On one night when my father, Captain Peter Heywood, landed with his men from the *Montague*, the line of battle ship he commanded, and the watch had been set, the officers stretched themselves down on some mattresses, the first lieutenant near him, then the Master of Marines. All was quiet, when the last mentioned officer cried out that some one had laid a cold hand on his cheek! Silence was ordered. Again in a few minutes he made the same complaint and challenged the lieutenant, who peremptorily ordered silence. A third time he made the same outcry, jumped up and rushed from the spot in terror. The whole party were thoroughly roused, and my father considered the circumstance so peculiar that he noted it, with the date and the precise hour at which it had occurred.

Weeks after, when the despatches and letters arrived from England, the Master of Marines received the news of his father's death, and the hour of his departure, which tallied exactly with the note which Captain Heywood had made. Up to the period of my dear father's death I have heard him mention the fact, but he never reasoned on it. He possessed a calm judgment and a very religious mind. I remain, dear sir, yours very truly.[4] — AS TOLD BY LADY DIANA BELCHER, 25 CUMBERLAND TERRACE, REGENT'S PARK, LONDON, ENGLAND, APRIL, 1884

FACE OF *TITANIC* VICTIM APPEARS IN MASSACHUSETTS

☛ On Sunday, April 14 [1912] at about 10 o'clock p. m. I saw, being positively awake at the time, the face of a person. The face was entirely strange to me. It was that of an old man with hair and beard. The hair and beard were outlined in white, clear as light, and the features had a darker appearance. Marked lines between the eyes and an appearance of great suffering which had been smoothed away so as to give repose but somehow indicating an unbroken spirit were the features about this face that were most impressive. The face appeared to be below the level of my sight at arm's length. It was this that surprised me, this being the solitary instance in which a face appeared.

I have seen many faces, flesh tinted, beautifully peaceful in expression, but they have all appeared erect and very near my own face. Nothing ever came of these manifestations last referred to, tho at the time they seemed rarely gracious, leaving a feeling of great peace.

Entirely different in every way has been the sequel to the appearance of this face on last Sunday evening, and I write of it now because I feel that I ought to record a remarkable experience.

On Monday, April 15th [1912] the evening papers were brought in, in part describing the wreck of the *Titanic*. They proved incorrect. I knew intuitively that other news differing in character was to come.

On Tuesday morning a friend telephoned the news of the loss of 1500 passengers. I then told my daughter of the singular occurrence of Sunday night and described to her as well as I was able to the appearance of the face floating, altho the word "floating" poorly fits. I remember my thought at the time was like this. "At least this face is different and what under the sun is it?" And I tried to forget it in an effort to see the funny side of my varied "appearance."

I believe I am a normal person. I know I was planning hard work for a week of pretty strenuous going on in the house beside dressmaking. I hadn't a thought of "them that go down to sea in ships," and my only worries at that moment were of the weekly wash and the planning of breakfast and the hope that I could sleep well so as to be ready for the day's work. Indeed I recall all these thoughts as sordid, much so.

With no warning, with seemingly no connection whatever with anything near or far, there came this appearance! It was not startling but it was pitiful and I didn't know enough to give pity, tho, as I once said in answer to Mrs. Gerrish's questions as to how I received these facts, that I rather bade them all welcome. I didn't feel like welcoming this one, because it was so different. It was no spook though, I'm sure.

Just visible ghost captured on film, seen at center.

Immediately following the telephone message mentioned I said to my daughter "I wish I could know any individual among the *Titanic* passengers who was elderly and had a face like the one I saw." In the afternoon she bought the *Boston American* of Tuesday the 15th and on the fourth page was the face I had seen, except that the hair and beard were not quite as heavy and the face seemed younger. The other Boston papers followed with the same pictured face, that of Mr. Stead, and in tonight's *Globe* the copy of Mr. Stead's photograph makes me willing to state positively that this is the face I saw, tho it does not, of course, reveal the trace of suffering which I plainly saw. (I also saw a look of surprise.) Might it not have been a wireless photograph? I think it was just that.

If asked to give my explanation of it, I should say that the mind of this individual acting with great force, like any other mechanism, had projected an image and I happened to catch it. Here in Groton, Mass., the time around 10 p.m. would indicate a considerably later hour in the longitude of the vessel. I shall be glad to add any other information, should you desire, and also make affidavit. Very truly yours.[5] — HENRIETTA M. CHASE, GROTON, MASS., APRIL 17, 1912

VISITING SPIRIT OR A DREAM?

☞ I awoke on the morning of June 10th, and was lying on my back with my eyes fixed on the ceiling, when I heard the door open and felt some one come in and bend over me, but not far enough to come between my eyes and the ceiling; knowing it was only [my friend] C. I did not move, but, instead of kissing me, she suddenly drew back and going towards the foot of the bed, crouched down there. Thinking this very strange, I closed and opened my eyes several times, to convince myself that I was really awake, and then turned my head to see if she had left the door open, but found it still shut.

Upon this a sort of horror came over me and I dared not look towards the figure which was crouching in the same position, gently moving the bedclothes from my feet. I tried to call to the occupant of the next room, but my voice failed. At this moment she touched my bare foot, a cold chill ran all over me and I knew nothing more till I found myself out of bed looking for C., who must, I felt, be still in the room.

I never doubted that she had really been there until I saw both doors fastened on the inside. On looking at my watch it was a few minutes past 5.

Although I am accustomed to have very vivid dreams, I have never had one of this kind before. When I found my friend was not in the room, and that the doors were securely fastened on the inside, [again,] I looked at my watch; it was a few minutes past 5. I have never, I believe, walked in my sleep. There are two doors to my bedroom. One was locked on the inside; the handle was broken off the other on the outside. Thus it was impossible for anyone to open it except from the inside.[6] — MISS K. E., LANCASTER GATE, ENGLAND, JUNE 1883

DOCTOR RECEIVES THREE SPIRIT VISITATIONS

☛ I shall endeavor to give you as clear and accurate an account of the incidents of a lifetime. A medical practice of 40 years in the city of New York, an additional study of Physics, Chemistry, Physiology and Psychology will make the average physician a good observer and a fair judge of the normal and abnormal phenomena of life.

The incident that is most important happened on the night of November 4th, 1914. Myself and family at that time occupied the large cottage, 1967 Grand Concourse, in Bronx County. The house was surrounded by a garden. I had two rooms for myself: one was fitted up and used as an office, and in the rear of this I had my bedroom. Partition and drapery separated the two rooms. When the shutters were closed at night and the shades drawn down not a ray of light could enter this room. It was pitch dark.

On the night stated above, I had been soundly asleep for some hours and had gradually fallen into that stage which you may call a very light sleep, when instantaneously a bright light came to my vision and I beheld a beautiful apparition picture of my cousin, "Anna Kloss." I was now in a condition in which you may say I was not fully awake but perfectly conscious. I remember distinctly how I called out, "Oh, Anna! you look beautiful." My cousin, A. K., died 15 years ago at the age of 50, in a town located in an eastern part of Germany. The last time I had seen her alive was 46 years ago. She was at that time a young lady of 18 years. She appeared to me now in full figure. I recognized her at once.

She was in a sitting posture leaning against a wall. Her brown hair was glossy. Her eyes were sparkling. The prominent high forehead and face had the natural color as in life. Her chin and face were somewhat longer than when I had seen her last when she was 18 years of age. She looked to me now like a woman of 50 years of age. She was dressed in a silk garment of a color between crimson and blue. The gloss of this apparent silk dress was of a brilliancy which surpassed any silk that I had ever seen before: it seemed to vibrate. There was a large collar about two or three inches wide around the neck over the silk dress and lace around each sleeve. Her hands were of natural color. The long tapering fingers, a characteristic feature of her, had the same natural color as in life time.

The face, though calm, showed intense attentiveness. The eyes were searchingly kept on me. Was the picture a true reproduction, image of my cousin's present attitude, then her face was the source of the deepest intellectual sounding to which I had ever been exposed. Nothing on earth could have been stranger and no one more surprised than I was. I had positively been on trial.

The wall she was leaning against was apparently that of the interior of a small house or hut. The part of the rear wall on the right side of the figure was a streaming mass of light of a yellow color. The light emitted on the left side of the figure was of a golden yellow tint. Here and there the light was interrupted by gray shades. The side wall radiated light not quite so strong: the color of the rays emitted were between infra-red and golden yellow. There was a peculiar shaped apparatus standing in front and at the left side of the figure. I cannot compare it with anything I have seen before.

The front wall of this little house or hut was missing. Had it been removed to give a full view into the little room? I am not willing to give an opinion on it. Between the side wall and the rear wall was an opening like a door casing, but no door. Looking through this opening I could see it was dark outside.

The phantom picture lasted about 45 or a few more seconds. It then disappeared instantaneously. It was like turning off an electric light. By this time I was fully awake and found myself sitting up in bed. I was in a condition of agreeable excitement, but my senses were perfectly calm and tranquil. The experience of a lifelong medical practice had trained and hardened them for sudden and unexpected occurrences. I reasoned thus:

This phantom picture has been carried by rays of high rapidity, electric currents, ether vibrations, call it what you may, through the house-wall to my brain cells. A common dream cannot show such light, such abundance of light and brilliant colors as these had been. The light in a dream can be a dim light only to the conception of a resting brain. It might be at its best equivalent to the production of a faded out moving picture film. A light of great brilliancy of such volume and color can be produced only by highly intensified molecular activity in the brain cells ergo, vibrations of its molecules. It is impossible to conceive of vibrations without supposing a medium that makes the molecules vibrate. Such a medium can consist of small particles—electrons—only, which are carried in by electric currents known as ether vibrations, X-rays or radium rays. There was no electricity, X-ray apparatus or radium in the house. Where did these rays carrying such a brilliant picture come from? Who produced them, directed them and shut them off instantaneously?

Many years ago I visited a camera obscura. The little room measured about 8 by 10 feet. I saw demonstrated here how one ray of light entering through a pinhole in the wall could carry a picture of the surrounding landscape. In it was a much-frequented road with many people going about. This ray of light after entering the camera had been thrown by a reflector down upon a white table, where I saw the entire picture in front of me. The light in this picture was a mild one. It could not compare with the phenomena in the vision of my cousin as far as intensity of light and brilliancy of colors are concerned. As an object like a landscape or figure must exist to make up a picture in a ray of light, so my cousin Anna must exist.

This incident put me into a happy state of mind. My cousin had always been a very clever woman. She had been a teacher in a college for young women. Her letters proved her to be of great strength and nobility of mind. She always took a great interest in me besides. I quite felt the desire in me to see her once more or hear from her. Somebody suggested mediums. But I knew none. Moreover I was not experienced enough to try one.

Accidentally, however, I was looking over the advertisements of a daily paper. I came across the following advertisement:

German American Spiritualists' Church.
Pabst Building, 59th St. and 8th Ave.
Service every Sunday night at 8 P.M.

Something urged me to go there. I went next Sunday. I arrived in the large hall on the top floor shortly after the service had commenced. The hall was filled. I saw one chair at the center aisle, last row, which was not occupied, and sat down. Organ playing and singing was going on and gave me time to make observations. On the platform way off in front were three persons. The center chair was occupied by a certain Rev. Mrs. E. M. Cahoon as I found out later on. The service had gone on with a sermon about Spiritualism and its connection with the Bible. Later on the medium, a short man, gave consolation to a number of bereaved family members, with some success I thought. Later Mrs. Cahoon got up and addressed the congregation thus:

"I see two spirits here tonight. One is a very bright light. She tells me her name is Anna K." She listened. "I cannot get the entire name. She says she is a relation of the gentleman in the last row of the center aisle. She pointed at me. "You know her?" looking at me.

"The other spirit tells me." She listened again. "That he is a friend of the same gentleman," pointing me out again. " He says that he died suddenly; that he goes to see this gentleman in his office (how would she know I had one); that the spirit was stroking his hair caressing him late at night while he is reading the books that his dead friend, the spirit, had given him."

She was then making motions with her hands to show to the congregation how the spirit died. Then Mrs. Cahoon asked me if I have had a friend who had died suddenly. "Madam," I said, "I cannot deny it, but may I ask you the name of the one you are speaking about?" Her answer was: "No, I cannot. He did not give his name."

At this the stout woman who was sitting in front of me turned round and said to me: "Excuse me, sir, when you asked for the name of your spirit friend, the name of Charles came to me." I thanked her. A few minutes later I was informed by another woman who was seated not very far off that the letters "P R B S T" had come to her. "Can you make it out?" she said. "I will try to," I answered, thanking her.

Then it dawned upon me that this spirit was my friend Charles Probst. He had been dead then 12 years. C. Probst was an artist painter who had lived in his villa surrounded by a garden in New Jersey. He was a philosophical genius, an accomplished literary man, a perfect stranger in New York and a dear friend. He left me in his will his books, some pictures and some other articles.

After the service I was lingering in the hall. I made sure of the fact that nobody in the congregation had ever seen me and that I knew none of them.

To return to my cousin, Anna Kloss. I had never known any other Anna K., dead or alive. She had been a very accomplished and clever woman, had gone through examinations for a college teacher and had always taken a great interest in me up to the last days of her life.

I come now to another incident. Shortly after my marriage in 1886, I took notice that my wife was burdened with telepathic and psychic endowments. She could foretell in the morning the visitors who were going to, or had intentions of calling on her in the afternoon. We had no telephones in the houses at that time. I paid little attention to such powers, considering telepathy a purely physical phenomenon, and asked myself: "Do we know all the laws of nature?" Besides I was a very busy man. But weeks later on she informed me that she could see her dead father and sometimes her dead sister, and gave me an accurate description of the phenomenon. I began to get interested. But I was a busy man.

It was in 1907 that we made our second trip to Europe. Taking the Mediterranean route, we arrived in Rome after seeing Naples. We stayed in Rome from the 9th to the 21st of May. It was on May 17th when my wife came down to the breakfast table of the hotel and was in a nervous flutter. Her face was flushed and she complained of a dull headache. She had been through a very restless night. On repeated inquiry, she came out finally and made the following statement. She had seen her dead father and with him a friend of his by the name of Ferdinand Ehrhardt. The two were talking together. "When we left New York three weeks ago, I know," she said, "that Mr. Ehrhardt was alive and in good health," and added: "It is probably this fact that made me restless and awakened me so that I was unable to go to sleep again." I was very much puzzled. Finally I made a note of this incident and the date, to end the matter.

We returned from our European trip about October 8th. A few days later I made a call on my friend, Herman Klotz, who lives now in the Bronx. After some parleying I said: "Mr. Klotz, may I ask you how your friend F. Ehrhardt is?" He looked at me surprised. "Don't you know that Ehrhardt is dead?" I said: "How could I know? We have just arrived from Europe."

I asked him then for the exact date of E.'s death. He brought out his Masonic journal and informed me that Ferdinand Ehrhardt had died May 16th, thus confirming the vision in Rome which my wife had in the night between the 16th and 17th of May.

The third incident happened in the year 1897. I do not remember the exact date. At that time we occupied a private house in East 7th Street. The parlor floor consisted of a front and rear parlor. One evening late my wife and myself were sitting in the front parlor in conversation when the clock on the mantel piece struck eleven. The house was very quiet. A small light was burning in the hall of the parlor floor.

Suddenly we heard repeated knocking on the door leading from the parlor to the hall. We both jumped up surprised. I ran to the door, throwing it open. There was no one outside. I began a thorough examination. The door leading to the basement was locked. The servants had gone to their rooms an hour before. I searched the rear parlor and then the upper floors, but could find nothing out of order and no one about. The street doors were both locked the inner door was chained besides.

After I had come back to the parlor, my wife said to me quietly: "Have you heard from Mr. Schultz lately?" I said, "No." Since he left this neighborhood and moved up town three years before, I had not seen him or heard anything about him. "But," I continued, "what is it that sets you to thinking of Mr. Schultz?" And asked some such questions.

Mr. Schultz had been a patient of mine before he left the neighborhood. My wife had seen him in the waiting room (rear parlor) about half a dozen times. I paid no further attention to the incident, although the knocking had been very loud and distinctly audible to both of us. I had suspected burglars, but saw no sign of them. There was no opportunity for such to get into the house.

Next morning I was called to a patient living far up town. Walking from the elevated to the patient's house, somebody gave me a tap on the shoulder. Turning around, I looked into the sad face of young Schultz, the son of the man, the Schultz we had spoken about the previous night. "Hello," I said, "what is the news?" "Doctor," he said, "I want to tell you that my father died last night at about eleven o'clock." I was staggered at the time. Nothing can surprise me today.[7] — RICHARD L. HOELGER, M.D., NEW YORK, FEBRUARY 13TH, 1918

FATHER'S SPIRIT APPEARS IN DAUGHTER'S DREAMS

☞ In accordance with my promise I write to you regarding the dream I had of my father, who departed this life in 1909. This dream convinced me of the survival of the individual and of the constant watchfulness over the affairs of their loved ones on earth, and I am most anxious to further pursue the study of psychology.

Last December my husband, a young man not quite forty-two years of age, was attacked by acute inflammatory rheumatism. During his illness, one night, I dreamed of my father, but, tho I knew it was my father, he in no way looked like himself. He looked young, clean shaven, gaily dressed and was in a jolly mood, in fact in every way he fully represented my husband: for my father was 69 years old when he died, was a much more heavily built man and wore side whiskers like the late Emperor Francis Joseph of Austria, and was moody and frequently cross.

Ghost of a Victorian monk photographed in an old English manor house.

I woke next morning with a keen recollection of my dream, and a depression as if something was impending. Thereafter for days and weeks I was impressed with the desire to leave New York and go South with my husband; so much so that I actually gave up my apartment on March 1st, but unfortunately my husband's dentist had to do over some work that did not fit, and delayed our departure during the first three weeks of March.

My husband was taken with pneumonia the fourth week in March and died on April 1st. I cannot rid myself of the remorse I feel in failing to obey my impulse to leave New York during March. My husband might have been alive and with me today.

One night in May I could not sleep and yet toward morning I

dozed. Immediately I dreamed of my father, and again he did not look like himself. This time too he was smooth shaven, but now he was stout and careless in his dress. As I saw him coming towards me, through a long hall, he was reeling as if intoxicated. When he reached the door he stumbled into the room and then I awoke.

The strange part of this dream was, when a few hours later I went down town to a business building I own. I learned that one of my tenants was in bankruptcy, and as a result I might have a vacancy and suffer financial loss. This tenant bears out in every detail the appearance and characteristics my father represented to me in my dream.[8] — (MRS.) FRANK COHEN, NEW YORK, SEPTEMBER 13TH, 1918

FEMALE APPARITIONS MANIFEST TO FAMILY MEMBER

☛ Both your letters have been received, but owing to illness I have been unable to answer either of them, but will try and get this off to you today.

I am glad to state the experience to which you refer, but will be unable to permit the use of the names of either of those seen in the apparition or my own. The narrative is as follows, as nearly as I can recall:

My sister passed away some sixteen years ago and about eight years ago my favorite Aunt was taken seriously ill. I was with her at the time of her shock which occurred about March 7th or 8th, 1911. She lay in a comatose state for two days. I spent much of that time with her. The third night I returned to my home and retired about midnight, falling into a sound sleep. After being in bed only a short time my body seemed to be suspended in mid-air and yet I seemed conscious too of my body on the bed. I floated sometime and then a spark of light seemed to come toward me until it resembled a huge ball of fire. It came very close to my eyes and then burst, revealing the face of my departed sister, and resting on her shoulder, as if beaming upon her, was the face of my Aunt who was ill. Both were smiling and then faded away.

I awoke crying and nervous. I did not mention this to any one except my husband, who was a witness to my waking and crying. The following morning my Aunt passed away.

I might state that I have had the floating sensations several times, and the night my mother died a panel of light appeared to me, but I shook myself awake as I did not want to see what might appear. These experiences seem to make me nervous and I try not to allow myself to fall into this state for that reason. I hope these experiences may be of some little help, but as I know nothing of

this study, I do not know whether they mean anything or not.⁹ —
A. G. U., CIRCA 1918

FRIEND'S SPIRIT RETURNS FOR ONE LAST CHESS MATCH
☛ I will now fulfill my promise to write for *The Religio-Philosophical Journal* a statement of some which are usually called "tests" of the soul's identity beyond the grave. Being so constitutionally conscious of my own self existence and of the impossibility apparent to me of subtracting anything from or adding anything to the infinite system of which my identity is an intelligent factor, I have never been a special "test" seeker in that direction, yet I am always more than willing to help others differently constituted to gather the proof they require to convince them of their own self existence and its self-perpetuating necessities and certainties. I will give a few experiences in as few words as I can present them.

While residing in Baltimore my husband had a very dear friend with whom he had been in the habit of playing chess every evening nearly for several years. By experts at the game they were considered very skillful and evenly-matched players. I often sat beside them with my writing and reading to recall them to their normal state whenever their extreme concentration of mind upon the game caused them involuntarily to hypnotise themselves into materializing too forcibly their ideals of castle taking and knight capturing; yet I never interested myself in the game, nor even became in the slightest degree acquainted with either the principles or details of its movements.

In 1880 our friend passed from the outer form, yet he still continued to visit us quite as constantly as before he ascended to a higher plane of consciousness, as was most clearly proved, not only through the seership of my daughter, my sister and myself, but through the agency of the table which served in giving us intelligent messages from him whenever we chose to seek communion with him in that manner.

On the occasion to which I shall now especially refer, as we were conversing with him at the table, my husband asked him if it would not be a pleasure to him to play another game of chess with his old friend, and whether he could do so. He gave us to understand that it would, and that he could do so if I would follow his directions by the signals he could give me through the table, [my husband] Mr. Hyzer arranging the pieces on the board and proceeding with his side of the game in the usual manner. I consented most willingly, and after more than an hour of the closest application of skill on my husband's part and the most faithful obedience that ignorance could yield to persistent and unquestioned authority on my own, the game, which Mr. Hyzer admitted was one of the closest tests of his skill that he had ever played, was won by our friend, to his apparent great delight, as the unusual dancing and tipping of the table bore evidence.

Who played the game with Mr. Hyzer? I surely was as ignorant of the nature of every movement made on the board as the board itself. Intelligence directed the movements on both sides. Mr. Hyzer surely did not play with such all-absorbing intensity of mental concentration against himself, and if "magnetic force" or "electric currents" can of themselves prove such skillful chess players, I am sure our immortality of individual mind and its future possibilities of usefulness and beauty are raised upward on these evidences of the grandeur and magnificence of the universe, to which we must be most undeniable factors, to an incomparable height of imagination. At this point, with my poetical wings freed by such a concession, I am quite sure I should soon more than ever deserve the charge of being not only a "transcendental," but a "mathematical" Spiritualist. I leave the simple and true statement of the facts of this experience with those whom it may concern to consider it. The only object I have in stating them is a desire to aid those who still require such proof of individual identity beyond the grave.

In the spring of 1876 a very dear friend of mine, residing with his wife and two beautiful little children in Philadelphia, left his home very suddenly, as was supposed by his friends under the influence of a very intense mental excitement resulting from the loss of his entire property, a loss which his excessive mental efforts for months had failed to prevent, and which, as it seemed, had produced in his brain a state of temporary aberration or insanity.

I received a telegram from his friends informing me of his departure from home and the inquiry if he had visited my home in Baltimore, as his friends thought his warm friendship and that of his wife for myself might have led him to seek me. I replied that I had not seen him.

On the same night, as I was lying in my bed, feeling quite too much interested in the fate of my friend to be at all inclined to sleep, my psychic vision was suddenly quickened, and the missing friend, accompanied by two other spirits, stood before me. He seemed to be very eager to reach me, and to have me know that he had arisen from the outer form, while his companions seemed as anxious to induce him to go with them in another direction. His clothing appeared quite disarranged, his hair disheveled and apparently dripping with water, and altogether his appearance impressed me that he had left the body in a very unhappy state of mind and under unfavorable conditions in relation to his transition.

He and his friends very soon disappeared, leaving me in a state of physical chilliness and excitability quite unpleasant to bear. Immediately my guardian father stood before me, and thus addressed me:

> "I have just learned that a dear friend of yours was born to the higher plane of life last evening. As soon as he fully recovered consciousness he wished to communicate the fact of his new birth to his sorrowing wife and friends. His first thought in so desiring was to appeal to you to send or bear her the message, as he could not directly impress her. It is quite true that his mind did become unbalanced ere he left his home, and he had wandered he can not now remember where or how long after he left his home, till he found himself in the water of a lake or river, not so far from shore but that he could easily reach it, when once more his bewilderment of mind set in upon him, and he recalls nothing further until he found himself released from his weary earth form and surrounded by his loving, care-taking friends in the higher life. His influence upon your atmosphere was too oppressive, owing to his overwrought emotional state, and I requested his guardian friends to assist in aiding his withdrawal from your presence, promising them and him to instruct you of his condition and of his wishes to have you communicate with his wife."

I promised my father that I would do so, but on the following morning when I sat down to write to his wife, my heart became so sorrowful for her that I could not persuade myself to give her the details of the scene that had been presented to me regarding her husband's transition, and I yielded so far to the influence of sorrowful sympathy as to only say to her that I was deeply impressed with the conviction that her husband was in the higher atmosphere, and would no more be her companion save as an a risen, liberated spirit.

I soon received a letter from her telling me what efforts she had made and was still making to find her husband through consultations with the best mediums of whom she could learn, and through advertisements in many daily papers in different cities. I might say many things in relation to all the details of our correspondence and her sorrowful search for her husband, but I will only pass directly to the test spirit communion involved in the narrative under consideration.

In three weeks from the time when my friend informed me of his transition, his wife learned by information received from the mayor of New York City that a person answering in every particular to her advertisement of her lost husband had registered on the books of one of the city hotels on such an evening—I have forgotten the day of the month, just three days I think from the time he left his home—and that his lifeless body was found in his room on the following morning; that he seemed to have fallen carelessly across his bed, still wearing his overcoat and other street clothing, proving that he passed from the body soon after reaching his chamber. The clerk of the office remembered that he presented a somewhat singular appearance, as his dress was quite disorderly and his hair seemed wet and almost dripping, though the weather was dry, and that his manner was wholly free from any appearance of an abnormal character.

His friends immediately went to New York, identified his clothing, watch and pocketbook, which were still in charge of the superintendent of the morgue where his form had been kept for several days for identification ere it was interred in the cemetery of strangers. His body was removed by his friends to Laurel Hill, Philadelphia. As it proved, upon comparison of details, our friend gave me the call

Photograph of a 19th-Century experiment in levitation.

on the evening following his departure from the earth form, and my father's statement to me was wholly correct regarding the time of his birth. I have since learned from his spirit friends that on the evening of his departure from the body, ere he sought the hotel, he fell into the river near the New York and Jersey City ferry and was rendered temporarily sane again by the shock of coming in contact with the cold water, and in that condition of physical chill and mental excitement he had reached the hotel, registered his name, taken a room and had passed from the body very soon after having entered it [the room]. I leave the plain statement of the facts to those who may be interested to reflect upon it.[10] — MRS. F. O. HYZER, CIRCA 1890

GHOST OF DYING SISTER REACHES OUT

☛ In May 1871, I was away from home for a change, leaving a sick sister behind, who had been ill for many months from mesenteric decline. I was to go to a ball at Willis' Rooms on May 11th, and left some friends in Kensington to stay with an old schoolfellow at Denmark Hill. I heard that my sister was worse, but concluded it was one of the usual spasmodic attacks of sickness that accompany the disease—how could I ever have been so blind!

It was a Thursday; my new dress had come, and dinner time came—a large family circle, and I the only stranger, as I had never stayed in the house before. I could hardly swallow my dinner, and felt a chillness all over me. When the time came to dress I went upstairs and slowly began. As I bent down to pick my dress up I stopped. I felt an unseen presence, and a terrible chillness, which, even as I write, returns only too vividly. I rang the bell. When the servant came, I could only say faintly, "Ask Miss Emily to come to me." When my friend came, I could explain nothing; I merely said I could not go to the ball.

I have often wondered how I looked at the time, for I know how I felt, even to my lips. The next morning came the news that my sister had died on the previous morning, longing and calling for me to the last.[11] — MISS AGNES M. A. S., WHEPSTEAD RECTORY, BURY ST. EDMUNDS, ENGLAND, 1871

DYING MOTHER'S GHOST APPEARS AT SCHOOL

☛ About the year 1834 or 1835, I was in a boarding school at Cadogan Place, Chelsea, kept by ladies named Horn, where, amongst other pupils, there were two sisters with whom I was very intimate. These girls came from a distance, their home being in the North of England, I believe, and travelling then being very different to what it is in these days of railways, they did not always go home for their holidays, and consequently were not impressed by the critical state of their mother's health.

We slept in a large dormitory, in which were several beds, the two sisters occupying a double bed. On a certain night, most of the girls being asleep, and myself in the next bed to one of the sisters, who was already in bed, and, like myself, anxious to be quiet, and allowed to go to sleep; but we were hindered by the frolicsomeness of the younger sister, who sat outside the bed and facing the door at the end of the room, which, I remember, was not quite dark, either owing to moonlight or the time of year.

As the elder sister was urging her to be quiet and to get into bed, the younger one suddenly exclaimed, and, putting her hands over her face, seemed greatly agitated. As there seemed no cause for this sudden excitement, we, thinking it was only another form of her nonsense, and fearing the noise would bring up the governess, who also slept in the room, scolded her well, upon which she got into bed. Turning again to look towards the door, she uttered another cry, directing her sister's attention to the door; but she saw nothing, and still thought the younger one was joking. But the latter buried her head under the clothes, and I, being very tired, went to sleep and thought no more about this disturbance.

Next morning no notice was taken of it, and no impression seems to have been made on my mind or that of the other girls, probably, as I now think, owing to our being accustomed to the volatile disposition of the younger sister. However, about two days afterwards, the sisters were summoned into the room of the ladies of the school to receive letters. Shortly after I was sent for, and found them in floods of tears, having just heard the news of their mother's death. Being their chief friend, I was excused from lessons that I might be with them, and try to console them.

As we were approaching our room the younger sister stopped us suddenly, and grasping my arm with violence, she said, "Oh, do you remember the other night when I was frightened? I believe it was dear mamma that I saw. Let us go back and ask more about it," or words to that effect. We went back to Miss Horn's apartment, and on referring to the letter, we found that their mother had died, as nearly as we could calculate, at the same hour that the incident in the dormitory occurred.

This is what the girl said she saw: A tall, slight figure in white, resembling her mother, as she now thought, though she did not recognise features, who, with outstretched arms, seemed to beckon to her.

Talking it over on the same day, she remarked, "Ah, I think I see now why dear mamma appeared to me. She had often reproved me for my giddiness, and as she was dying, she wished to give me one more look and reproof. I will try and be very different. I shall never forget her warning," etc. She appeared deeply impressed, but as the sisters and I were soon parted, and did not correspond, I lost sight of them.

This is a true account, and I believe clearly remembered by me, though so many years ago. Neither I nor the sister saw the appearance, but witnessed the effect on the girl who did see it, both being quite awake.[12] — MRS. RICHARDS, SPRING WOOD, GODALMING, ENGLAND, 1884.

Chapter Two

SPIRIT OF BROTHER APPEARS TO BRITISH GENERAL

☛ The late Sir John Sherbrooke and Gen'l [George] Wynyard were early friends, and as young men, officers in the 33rd Regt., which, at the time referred to in the following narrative, was employed on foreign service, and their respective companies quartered in the Island of Cape Breton in Nova Scotia. The frost of that winter had been longer and more intense than for many previous ones, and they had consequently been deprived for a proportionate length of time of any intercourse with England; and amongst other requisites of which they were in need were their regimental hats, and several of the officers, amongst whom were the two above mentioned, had caps made of fur, or the skins of the wild animals they had killed. And they were encamped (if it may be so termed) in the log houses used in that country, which generally consisted of two apartments, opening one into the other, the inner one being used as a bedroom, the outer apartment as a sitting-room.

Gen'l Wynyard had sprained his ankle so as to prevent his dining with the Mess, and immediately after dinner Sir John Sherbrooke withdrew from thence and came to sit with his friend.

It was still daylight, and neither of the young men had drunk any wine. Whilst they were conversing together Capt. Sherbrooke (for that was his rank at the time) became sensible of the appearance of a figure which suddenly presented itself a seemingly tall youth about 20 years of age, looking extremely ill and emaciated, but who was to him a perfect stranger. Struck with so singular an object, standing near the outer door (which had not been opened), he immediately drew the notice of Capt. Wynyard to their unexpected visitor, who on turning his eyes upon the figure, became suddenly agitated. "I have heard," exclaimed Capt. Sherbrooke, "of a man being as pale as death, but I never saw a living man look so like a corpse as you Wynyard." But his friend seemed deprived of speech, and Sherbrooke perceiving his agitation, felt no inclination to address the figure, who looked silently and mournfully upon Wynyard (and with a fixed gaze).

Still keeping its eyes upon him it proceeded slowly (passing the table at which they were sitting) into the inner apartment, from which there was no possible egress, except thro' the door, which apparently opened of itself to admit this extraordinary vision. The windows both of the bedchamber and the outer room were double glass, well secured to prevent the entrance of the frost.

The feeling of oppression excited in both gentlemen by this appearance, was no sooner relieved than Wynyard seized his friend by the arm and in extreme astonishment and emotion, muttered in a low voice, "Sherbrooke, that is my brother."

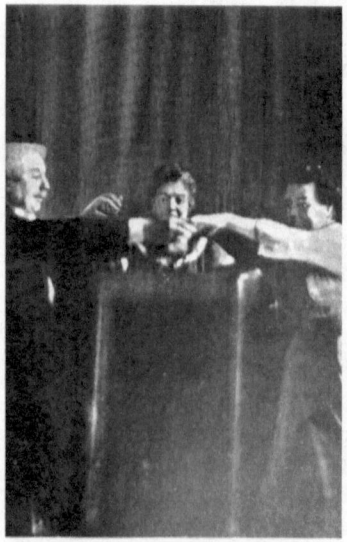

Table being lifted off the floor by unseen forces.

"Your brother," repeated Sherbrooke, "what can you mean? There must be some deception, but we will soon discover it," and giving his arm to assist his lame friend, they immediately proceeded into the small bedroom, but their astonishment was great at finding the place empty.

Wynyard's mind had received an impression from the first moment that the figure which had appeared to them was the spirit of his brother. Sherbrooke still persevered in asserting that some delusion had been practiced. They, however, took a note of the day and hour in which this event happened, and to prevent the possibility of its being lost, or any mistake arising, a copy of the memorandum was locked up in the Regimental chest with other papers of importance, and so unwilling were they to believe in any supernatural appearance that they tried to persuade themselves that they had been imposed upon by some trick, tho' they could not by any means account for it.

Wynyard, however, could not help dwelling on the occurrence and feeling great anxiety respecting his young brother, whom he had left well in England, and having recently entered one of the Regiments of the Guards, of which the figure appeared to wear the uniform, and Sherbrooke, in talking it over afterwards with his friend, particularly remarked, "What a good hat he had on, and how different from theirs." Under these circumstances it may be supposed that they awaited the arrival of letters from England with intense anxiety, but by the first ships no intelligence relating to this circumstance could be received, for they had all left England previous to the time of its occurrence.

At length the long wished for vessel arrived, all the officers had letters except Wynyard, but after all the others had been read, without any tidings that could explain the mystery, Sherbrooke found one that he had at first overlooked (or rather he had read all from his own family the first), and this letter was from a mutual friend requesting that he would break to Wynyard "the death of his favorite and most beloved brother," who it appeared (on comparing the account transmitted of his death with the time when his spirit so mysteriously appeared in America) had expired in London on the day and hour (allowing for the difference of longitude, etc.) which the two friends had been sitting together in their cantonment in Cape Breton.

From that moment Wynyard ceased to doubt the fact that his brother had appeared to him in the moment of dissolution; but tho' Sherbrooke's mind was convinced of the reality of the appearance, he was so reluctant to believe the possibility of any preternatural intercourse with the departed that he was still disposed to doubt the evidence of his senses.

Some years afterwards when they had all returned to England, and Sherbrooke was walking with a brother officer in London, he saw on the other side of the street a gentleman with whom he was so struck that he stopped short, exclaiming to his companion "That man is the very image of the ghost of Wynyard's brother which I saw in Nova Scotia." To which his companion replied:

> "That is most extraordinary, for the gentleman you see is a Mr. Eyre (afterwards Lord Newburgh), and who so strongly resembled the younger Wynyard that they were frequently taken the one for the other, and moreover Mr. Eyre had once had money paid to him by the same misapprehension."

Thus ends the account of the apparition.

I will now add a very extraordinary circumstance which is considered by all who have heard it as a most complete corroboration, but I believe it is known only to our own family and the particular friends to whom my uncle occasionally but rarely related it.

When my late uncle, then General Sherbrooke, was in the

Peninsula, and second in command of our Army, then in Portugal, which was encamped on the banks of the Duoro, a compact which he and Wynyard had mutually framed when in America, was suddenly and awfully recalled to his mind. It was that "if the spirits of the departed were really permitted to return to earth, which ever of them died the first would appear to the other to warn him of the event." General Sherbrooke, on the night to which this refers, was suddenly awoke with the painful conviction that General Wynyard (whom he had left in England) had just expired. He was dreadfully agitated and affected. He neither saw any appearance nor heard anything, but he was convinced his friend was no more, and with the most powerful effort of his reason he could not shake off the distressing impression.

Contrary to his usual custom when his servant came into his tent early in the morning he found his master dressed, but looking so wretched that he could not help asking if he was ill. In fact his reason was so shook that he could not bear to see any one, and sending for the officer next in command, he took a boat and crossed the river to a sequestered place and spent the day alone. Of course he did not fail to note the time of this occurrence, and his forebodings were but too soon confirmed—Gen'l Wynyard, the companion and friend of his early days, and for whom he entertained the affection of a brother, had expired that very night.

The above narrative was copied by me from the original memorandum taken down from the lips of Sir John Sherbrooke by his niece Miss Oates. The original account is now in the possession of her nephew, [Mr.] Oates, Esq., of Hesthrope, W. Newark.[13] — CHAS. S. WAKE, NOV. 18, 1863

LIVING SISTER'S GHOST APPEARS FROM 4,000 MILES AWAY

☛ [On the] anniversary of my mother's death [January 6th, 1897] . . . I had been thinking of my sister, recently gone to America (I then being in London, England), and regretting we should be parted on such a sad occasion as this. Went to bed thinking of her.

About 2 a.m. woke, and saw her standing at the foot of my bed, looking intensely sad. Was in her nightgown. Frightened, I called out "Oh! Go, go!" She went slowly, looking back at me regretfully as she passed out through the door.

My sister has no knowledge at all of this appearance, and did not will to appear. Was not particularly thinking of me. She and I were at this time ignorant of occultism.[14] — MRS. R. T. J., DE PERE, WISCONSIN, OCT. 28TH, 1908

ASTRAL-PROJECTING MOTHER IN THE SPIRIT BODY

☛ [From the same informant as above:] I woke one morning in July, 1906, and felt someone or something bending over me. The thought came, at the same moment, "I wish I could leave my body as Mr. D (a medium) once told me I should learn to do." With the thought I heard a distinct hiss, and then a snap, in the region of the solar plexus, and instantly, without knowledge of getting there, I found myself in light, white form, standing by the cot of my child (in the same room).

An elderly woman can be seen looking through the window at left. The house was empty at the time this Victorian family photograph was taken.

He was awake, and playing with the bed-clothes. I called him three times by name, but he evidently did not see or hear. As I stood there I could see plainly, think clearly. My body looked like a cloud cut in human shape. I stood erect, fully conscious of this thought: "Now I am in the spirit body."

The next thing I knew I was a gasping for breath as I (apparently) came back to my physical body on the bed.

When my breath became normal I questioned the child. He had not seen nor heard anything at his cot. He said: "I thought you were asleep: you were lying on the bed with your eyes shut."

Another night, a week or two later, I found myself in this same white, cloudlike form, human-shaped, in the back corridor of the house, a very large one. I had to walk two long passages before I could reach my bedroom door, and I knew it. I started, gliding slowly, finding that thought of movement produced movement. At last, feeling exhausted, I gained my bedroom door, when, as I was about to enter, I felt as if impelled to go into the half-open door of a bedroom on my right. I sighed, feeling intensely tired, but went in, and looked at the sleeping girl in the bed. The next thing I remembered, after taking a look at the bed, was gasping for breath in my own bed.[15] — MRS. R. T. J., DE PERE, WISCONSIN, OCT. 28TH, 1908

VANISHING SPECTER FOLLOWS COUPLE IN PARK

☛ We were walking home from Richmond [England], my husband and I, one bright July day about half-past five, having ordered the boat to meet us and take us up to our own steps. Between Richmond and Twickenham, on the Surrey side, is a splendid avenue of large trees; between the avenue and the river is a long and wide stretch of beach, and at the Twickenham end the ground is very open, and one sees the curve of the river and glimpses of some houses at Twickenham and Teddington; there is no bank or tree to intercept the view, and any one walking along the towing path can be seen for a long distance.

When a little way down the avenue, at the third tree, perhaps, a man passed stealthily behind me, to my left side, and went outside the trees—I was walking the furthest from the river. Two or three times he passed me thus, always in the same stealthy manner, as if not wishing to be seen. I did not draw my husband's attention to him, because, although the last man to commence a quarrel, he never submitted to an impertinence, and this stranger's movements appeared so spy-like.

I did not know my husband had seen him till he passed the third time; then R. said: "What is that fellow dodging about for? the avenue is open to all, why does he not keep in or out of it? he appears anxious to know what we are talking about; as it does not concern him, we will go out into the open." We were then about the seventh or eighth tree down.

As he spoke he stepped on to the open beach, and gave me his hand to help me over some obstruction in the path, a fallen branch, if I remember rightly. Both these movements were made in less time than it would take me to speak of them. As I put my hand in his, I looked round, and saw the stranger standing between the trees. It was the first full look we had, and I said, "He looks as if he had stepped out of an old picture!" We could only see his boots, his cloak, and hat. The boots were peculiar, high, and falling over at the knee, his cloak large and round, and thrown over his left shoulder, in the Spanish fashion, and his hat, apparently a soft felt, had a very wide drooping border, and was worn so much on one side we saw no face.

We both distinctly remember that in all the times we saw him that day, no face was visible. His whole costume was of one tone, and that of a dusty cobweb is the only thing I can liken it to. We stood looking at him, I wondering if he would resent my husband's speech, but he made no movement, and I put my hand in R.'s to step into the open. As my husband's fingers closed on mine, he started, and as I looked up to see the cause I saw his eyes fixed steadily on the open space at the remote end of the avenue.

There, clearly defined by the bright background of the towing path and the river, stood the figure that, less than an instant before, was by our side, and which we certainly thought to be that of a fellow creature (of rather ill-bred manners, utterly inconsistent with the decided dignity of his appearance).

Had he been shot out of a gun, he could not have gone faster.

The distance I have since measured; it is about 150 yards; the time occupied in traversing it I could not have counted a dozen in, however rapidly.

Now comes the most peculiar part of our experience, that which has made me very chary of telling it, for fear of ridicule.

When we saw the figure standing out there on the open ground, we were simply perplexed; no sensation of fear, or suspicion of the supernatural, entered our minds. We walked towards him with our eyes fixed on him.

There stood the figure, clearly defined, till we got within a certain distance; then it changed. It is so difficult to describe what did take place; the only way I can suggest it even is thus: You have seen a thick volume of smoke come out of a railway engine and gradually become thinner and thinner as it hovers over the ground, till you see through it the objects behind.

That is what took place. The figure stood there still, but, though it did not lose its shape, it gradually became transparent, till we saw the river and the bank and the distant trees through it! Still it was there. Then it got fainter and fainter, till there was not the least suggestion of it left; nothing but the large, bright, open space, without a single object behind which any one could have hidden.

We stood still, and I saw our boat coming. I got into it, feeling rather "dazed," like one does when waking from a too heavy sleep. As my husband pulled passed the place where the figure had stood, for the first time a feeling of horror came over me, and I said,

"What could it have been?"

He answered, "God only knows, darling, perhaps we never shall."

And so, I suppose, we must leave it.[16] — M. R. L., CIRCA 1884

AN UNCLE'S SPIRIT SHOVES, BREATHES, & GROANS
☞ [From the same informant as above:] London, Nov., 1900—On the three first Tuesdays of this month I was wakened at night, from deep sleep, by feeling a person get roughly on to my bed—a narrow one—and apparently push me in order to get sufficient room. I distinctly felt myself pushed, though I saw nothing. Then, for at least ten minutes on each occasion, and while lying fully and consciously awake, I heard heavy and rather stertorous breathing right by my head. [For] three weeks same thing happened.

Dec., 1900—One night near Xmas, (I cannot give exact date) while kneeling to say my prayers, I distinctly heard a heavy sigh, as if from a person standing just at the back of me. I paused; then began praying again. Instantly another sigh, almost a groan, came again. I saw nothing, and quitted my room. . . . In Jan., 1901, an uncle of mine died.[17] — MRS. R. T. J., DE PERE, WISCONSIN, RECORDED CIRCA 1919

LAUGHING GHOST MANIFESTS IN BEDROOM
☞ [From the same informant as above:] Oct., 1901. Dorking, Surrey, England: I was wakened one night this month by the feeling of someone having touched me. Looking up, I saw on the chair by the head of my bed the face and figure of a man. He was materialized to the waist perfectly, but the limbs were shadowy and dark. He was laughing, and seemed delighted to be seen. He was dressed in a navy serge sack coat, and had on collar and tie. (I think, red.) No one that I knew; and from his clothes, which were in style, must have recently passed over. For several moments I gazed; then he abruptly vanished.[18] — MRS. R. T. J., DE PERE, WISCONSIN, RECORDED CIRCA 1919

HUSBAND'S DECEASED SISTERS APPEAR AT BEDSIDE
☞ [From the same informant as above:] Dec., 1901. London—Just before Xmas: I was wakened one night to full consciousness, though I did not seem able to open my eyes. I felt a sensation of being wafted slightly upward, and turned to look at my husband. It seemed as if my sight came from within—not being caused by the normal, open eye.

Extremely haunted Victorian English bedroom.

From my husband I looked to the side of the bed. Two women were standing there. The younger was looking down rather sadly at my sleeping husband; the elder was looking at me. She smiled, and said "We've been looking at you such a long time." Then they instantly vanished.

Both were dressed in ordinary clothes, outdoor, hats and all. The clothes were somewhat out of date; the younger woman's especially. I woke my husband, and described my experience. He said "You have given an exact description of my two dead sisters. The younger died several years before the elder."

On coming to America, one year later, and entering the house of my husband's mother, I saw at once an enlarged photo of the elder dead woman, hanging on the wall. I recognized it at once as the woman I had seen in London, though she was not dressed in the same way.[19] — MRS. R. T. J., DE PERE, WISCONSIN, RECORDED CIRCA 1919

ANGEL VISITS A SICK HUSBAND

☛ [From the same informant as above:] Feb., 1902. London: During the early part of this month my husband was in poor health. One night, as I raised my head, after finishing my prayers by the side of the bed, I distinctly saw, standing on the opposite side of my bed, and looking down at my husband, the beautiful, white-robed form of a woman. With the exception of wings, she was exactly like the average idea of an angel, and had long bright hair hanging loosely to her waist. She took no notice of me, but steadfastly regarded my husband, (who was asleep), standing motionless, with hands linked in front of her, though apparently not clasped in prayer. I was awed. She was visible about three seconds.[20] — MRS. R. T. J., DE PERE, WISCONSIN, RECORDED CIRCA 1919

THE GHOST IN THE WHITE NIGHT-SHIRT

☛ [From the same informant as above:] I was lying in bed awake.

Very hot night. Room slightly lighted, lamp outside. My husband at my side had been restless. For a few minutes he had been quiet. I lay on my back with my head turned away from him.

I heard the bed creak and thought he is getting up and going downstairs where it is cooler. A man's figure in a white night-shirt crossed the end of the bed and walked across the room to a dormer window, stood looking out, peering very wistfully into the road below. He had a hand raised to the muslin curtain. I saw the hand move the muslin curtain slightly aside. The man leaned his elbows on the sill and the head and neck were craned forward so that the full height was not revealed while he was at the window. The extreme wistfulness as he looked out struck me and I watched at least for 20 seconds and probably 30.

Just as I was going to speak an elbow touched my side. My husband was in bed beside me, when I turned to look, and was just waking from a doze. He had not moved. I quickly looked back to the window but the figure had vanished. My first thought was as to time and I was going to rise and see, when the clock struck midnight.[21] — MRS. R. T. J., DE PERE, WISCONSIN, JUNE 28TH, 1916

ASTRAL-PROJECTING MAN RECEIVES NEWS ABOUT SHIPWRECK FROM ONE OF THE VICTIMS

☛ I had had a good night's sleep and woke suddenly, and got up and walked to the window. It was a clear sunrise and looking at my watch saw it was five o'clock and remembered it was the 4th of July. (I think it was 1892.) Finding it too early to dress I went back to bed and soon felt that my soul was leaving my body.

I found myself flying through space at a very rapid rate. I felt as if I was pressing my way among a crowd of beings as a fish might do through a shoal in water. Previous to this, when in this state, I had never been in communication with any one, but now as I was flying inconceivably quick I saw a human being approaching me as rapidly as I was moving. It was a woman in a nightgown with her hair disheveled and as she passed me she said distinctly: "Yes, the vessel was lost on the coast of Newfoundland. There were sixteen of us—nine were drowned," and she passed on.

I came back to my body and went to breakfast at the usual time where I met the party I was travelling with from Michigan. I asked if any one had heard of the loss of this vessel, repeating the dream I had just had. No one knew anything about it.

The next day we were coming near New York when the *Tribune* was brought in the [train] cars, and one of my party handed me an article to read. It was an account of the shipwreck of the *Peter Stuart* on the banks of Newfoundland at 5 o'clock July 4th. There had been sixteen on board and nine were drowned. Among them was the wife of the captain, the only woman on the vessel.

I cut out this account, and have it in my pocket:

BOSTON HERALD
July 5, 1892
14 OUT OF 27 MISSING
SHIP *PETER STUART* ASHORE NEAR YARMOUTH, N.S.
In a Fog She Runs on the Ledges, and Immediately Goes to Pieces. Over Half of Her Crew Lost, and Also the Wife and Child of the Captain.
(Special Dispatch to the *Boston Herald*.)

HALIFAX, N.S. July 4, 1892: Ship *Peter Stuart*. Capt. Hughes, from St. John for Liverpool, deal laden, struck on the ledges off Chebogue Point, Yarmouth, early this morning in a dense fog, and immediately went to pieces. The captain's wife and child were drowned before leaving the ship. The captain and mate, with 11 of the crew, succeeded in reaching the shore in safety, but in a very exhausted condition, being badly bruised. Four of the crew perished in the boat from exposure. The second mate is among the missing. In all 14 out of a total of 27 are missing. The injured men are all under medical treatment. The *Peter Stuart* was 1749 tons register, and owned in London. Her cargo and pieces of the hull are strewn along the shores of the sound and harbor.[22] — PROF. S. P. LANGLEY, OCTOBER 16, 1894

DECEASED WIFE APPEARS TO HUSBAND IN A VISION

☞ When my wife was dying I said to her, "You know what I believe as to the communication between spirits. Will you come?" She said, "I will, if the Good Father will let me."

Eleven months had passed away and not even a dream about the one I loved better than my soul. She had left me with four children, and at no time during that period was there a hint to my soul that she was interested in us at all. I had fussed over the thing, I had prayed over the thing, and I had wondered why nothing had come to me.

During our life we had a very extraordinary relation. We were exceedingly sensitive to each other's condition, and when she was in difficulty or ill and away from me I almost always knew it. I call it telepathy myself.

She died in May. The following April I was in the City of Philadelphia, in the Bingham House. I went to my room about twelve o'clock. There was a large chandelier with four or five lights in it in the center of the room and a push-button right at the head of the bed. I was lying with my eyes closed, not asleep—as truly awake as ever in my life. I was thinking of her. That was all I was doing in those days.

It didn't seem to come suddenly, it seemed to come naturally, the room was filled with her presence. I could see, tho my eyes were closed, her form, shadowy, with something that looked like the mist of the morning about it, and I said, "Darling, why have you not come before?"

A group picture at the Annual Meeting of the Society for the Study of Supernormal Pictures (S.S.S.P.), circa 1921. Its current vice president, Arthur Conan Doyle, creator of "Sherlock Holmes," can be seen at left, center row, tilting his head to the viewer's right. The photographer has captured the ghostly image of an unidentified man, who can be seen at the center "situated horizontally to the sitters."

She answered, "The Good Father would not permit me."

I said, "I have been so lonesome and so heartbroken that I have hungered for you. Where did you come from?"

"I have been up to see the children." (They were up near Lake Hopatcong [in New Jersey].) "They are lovely." She seemed to be sitting on the edge of the bed.

The vision was so real that I reached up and touched the button and made an attempt to put my arms about her, as the room was flooded with light. I saw nothing and felt nothing. I could have cried. "What have I done! What have I done! O Father, forgive me, let her come back!"

That was my prayer.

I do not know how long I waited praying earnestly and thinking intensely, when she was in the room again. I could see the smile on her face. My eyes were still closed. I never moved, never moved a hand or opened my eyes. I just let my soul do the talking. I was afraid to move and destroy it.

I could see her. I have never lost the vision at all. I can see her this second! She came in with a gentle laugh, said "Why did you do that? Don't you know you can't see me?"

I do not know how long we talked. I know I never slept a wink that night, and we talked of our life, of our children, of her father and brother that had passed on and whom she said she was instructing on the other side. God knows they needed it. She said that she was instructing them. That [she was educating a pair of truly terrible individuals] has destroyed my belief in hell as much as in hellfire. I have never preached hell since. And I have never feared death since. Death to me is only a little change. That's all.

That was our conversation, there wasn't a silly thing, there wasn't a trivial thing, nothing but what was of interest to her and me.

Now, here is the climax. She said, "I have come to you that you may stop your grieving, for it's making it impossible for you to do your work. That must be done."

I went back home, took the first train to my children, gathered them about me, and told them I had seen and talked with their mother and that she was watching over us. That had a powerful effect upon my children.

Once again she came to me, but that seemed more like a half-waking, half-sleeping dream, just as satisfactory to me as the other. But not so vivid or evidential. My little girlie of twelve did not appear to me for a year after her passing, but she came then in much the same fashion as the mother on the second occasion.

During that first occasion I could hear the rumble of the noises on the street but in addition I could hear this voice in my soul, it was real, like a sounding board. I could hear her little laugh and her voice. She was there to me tangibly and I felt that I could touch that button and grab for her. There was nothing different about my emotional state or my need for her at that time.[23] — REV. DR. V., JAN. 21, 1919

GHOST OF DECEASED JUDGE VISITS HIS OLD HOME

☛ The house I occupy at present, I bought from Judge Thacher, who had lived in it some twenty-odd years, and was very much attached to the place.

One night in the early part of November last, we retired as usual about 11 P.M. We were suddenly awakened from a sound sleep by a noise in the adjoining room, the door of which stood open, and which had been used by the Judge as a bed room, such a noise as would be made by a person moving slowly about the room. I immediately jumped up and lighted the gas, expecting to see one of the children or some one else there, but found everything quiet. We searched all through the rooms, and nothing out of the way was to be seen. The children were all asleep and the closets etc., vacant. In fact there was nothing visible to account for the noise. This was about 1:30 A.M.

I turned off the gas and got into bed.

After waiting a while I was beginning to get drowsy, both my wife and I were again very much startled by a repetition of the noise. It sounded distinctly, as though some one was feeling his way slowly about the room; a chair was apparently pushed gently aside, a drawer in the chiffonier opened, which is about four feet from our bed and close by the open door. Then something fell to the floor with a sound as of an apple or pear dropping.

Both of us jumped out of bed, I lighted the gas with a match I held in my hand ready. Everything was serene, except our nerves. We made another thorough search, and then left the gas burning for the rest of the night.

After going back to bed, surmising what the noise could possibly be, I jokingly said to my wife, probably the Judge is dead and his spirit is visiting his former bedroom. She replied that was nonsense as the old man was still alive.

Thinking no more about it, my wife came to the office the next day about 11 A.M. and said she had heard from a friend that Judge Thacher had died on the afternoon preceding; so that we regarded the event of that night as rather a peculiar coincidence, coming as it did on the night of his death. We have heard nothing peculiar since.[24] — H. B. CHANDLER, 34½ BEACON ST., BOSTON, MASS., JANUARY 21, 1894

ILL WOMAN HAS BEAUTIFUL NEAR-DEATH-EXPERIENCE

☛ On the afternoon of January 27, 1917, I was taken to the hospital after having been ill at home three days. For the greater part of the time during the next four months the physicians despaired of my recovery.

In order to leave no doubt as to the validity of the two experiences recounted below, I will state that as soon as I was able after the first experience and before the second, I questioned my nurse, who never left me, as to what had happened. She said that the first night no anesthetic had been administered, neither had I fallen asleep nor fainted, but had been fully conscious all of the time the doctors had been working over me. At the same time, while going through the experience I was not conscious of what was taking place around me or of being in the room at all. As I did not know exactly when the second one occurred, I was unable to question her about it, but assume that the physical circumstances were identical. I do know that I had no anesthetic. Until midnight the first night at the hospital, specialists and the nurse stayed by the bedside watching me closely, for I was sinking rapidly.

Suddenly, while broad awake, I was transported from my immediate surrounding and found myself traveling forwards, whither I did not know. A sense of the utmost security enveloped me and my way was made clear by a dim though radiant light shining from behind. I knew I was being led and felt a wonderful Presence behind me—too wonderful for me to dare to look upon.

After awhile we stopped.

I looked and saw just ahead a field—quiet, restful, with low hills in the background. There were beautiful restful undulations, no flowers, and no trees, but the impression remains of a soft yellowish green growth which was neither grass nor grain. There were shadowy places but over all the most peaceful yellow light, so nothing was hidden, but at the same time it did not mar the indescribable sense of Rest which took possession of my soul and body. No words can possibly convey the feeling of complete Rest which enveloped me—all cares, pains, detail, importance of physical existence dropped from me at once.

No words were spoken but after I had drunk in the wondrous scene before me, communication in the nature of understanding was established between me and my guide, who ever remained unseen. I was told I might step into that field and sleep undisturbed or I might go back to my earth duties. The temptation to sink into the beautiful spot was great, so great that I felt I had not the right to decide at once, for I would have lost sight of every duty, every opportunity for service to my loved and loving ones in the rapture of what lay before me. I communicated to my guide that I could not answer immediately for the decision must not be a thoughtless one.

I then found myself back again in my bed with the doctors and nurse beside me.

A period of time elapsed—just how long I do not know, but I imagine it was two or three days.

Again I trod the [heavenly] path with my [spirit] guide and again the joy was granted me of gazing upon that scene of indescribable beauty, the thrill of which had been with me constantly since the preceding occurrence. Once more I was told I might drop the shackles of earth life and rest in the gracious softness and lighted shadows, or that I might return from whence I came with a special undertaking for Him who is all wise and loving. This work was shown me and also that the way back would be long and difficult.

I bathed myself in the ecstasy of Rest and Peace and then retrod the path to earth.

The word rest is thoroughly inadequate to express the sense of complete removal of all burdens which emanated from that Place. Equally impossible is it to express the security felt in the Guidance and Light from the One behind. I felt it would be sacrilege to look back and that I might not be able to endure the Light.

During the interval between these two experiences, I was conscious of a Presence by my bedside, though I saw nothing. When my Guide communicated to me that the way back would be very hard, no detail was given, but during the months of physical and mental anguish which followed I was supported by the memory of the Glory I had witnessed and of the Promise which could not fail. No fear of death remained. "I know that my Redeemer liveth."[25] — MRS. USHER, MAY 26, 1919

GHOST OF DYING ENGLISH MOTHER VISITS HER SON IN AMERICA

☛ On the 29th or 30th of March, 1889, I was occupying with my two sons a room at 300 west 15th St. [New York City]. That night after we had all retired, leaving a lamp burning low on the table by my bed, I happened to look toward the ceiling and there in the circle of light cast up by the lamp through the chimney, I saw a faint shadowy picture like a photograph of a woman's bust and head which, on rising up in bed, I distinctly and clearly recognized to be the likeness of my wife who had died two years before. I called my sons' attention to it and they arose and Willie, the eldest, then aged sixteen, at once exclaimed "O there is Mamma!"

We gazed at it in wonder and astonishment for several minutes (cold shivers running up and down my back, and my eyes feeling as if they were bulging from their sockets). We slowly turned up the lamp, where upon the image disappeared.

The light was then turned low again, and we had all once more retired, when suddenly, possibly about half an hour later, another face began to form in the circle of light, but this time to our astonishment it was the likeness, not of my wife but of my mother, who was then in England, as distinct and clear as it had ever appeared to us in life.

The incident so upset me that I did not sleep that night, and the next day I wrote home to my folks in England relating the occurrence and inquiring concerning my mother.

About three weeks later I received a letter from my sister informing me of my mother's death on the very day and at the very hour, possibly instant, that I had seen the above vision. My mother died in my home in Hull, England, No. 23 Portland St.

Although I am not a believer in these things I must confess that this occurrence has mystified me. It can be substantiated by my two sons in America and by my sister in England who will remember receiving my letter. I was my mother's favorite child and it is possible that she was thinking of me strongly at the time of her death. I had been thinking of her all day, but what made me feel most apprehensive was that my dead wife's face appeared first.[26] — MR. W. STUART WRIGHT, MARCH 29TH, 1919

APPEARANCE OF DEATH-WRAITH TO SKEPTIC

☞ Many years ago I awoke suddenly in the middle of the night, as it appeared to me, with a distinct impression of a certain person. Next morning, early, I was informed that she had died during the night. Though it did not occur to me to fix the time of awaking, yet I felt compelled to admit (i.e., as afterwards explained, felt it strikingly probable) that the death coincided with my impression. The poor woman had been ill of cancer in the village where I was staying, and I had visited her at times, at the request of my aunts. I had thought little about her, the visit over, and certainly never dreamed of her.

I am not a believer in dreams, or rather, do not encourage attention to them, and I am in no sense credulous of the supernatural. The vividness of the impression I refer to is as strong to-day as it was the moment it happened, and I do not think it will ever be effaced from my memory. This must have occurred between the years 1851 and 1858. I was a sound sleeper at the time, rarely awaking through the night. I certainly never had such an impression of a person's presence as the one I wrote about, either before or since. But for the death following, I could have attached no meaning to it.[27] — MRS. CATHERINE WILSON, ENGLAND, 1884

DECEASED MAN APPEARS ON ROAD TO HIS BROTHER

☞ [On the occasion of the marriage of Mary Upcher to Edmund C.

Buxton, September 3rd, 1834, there were [to be] some festivities at Northrepps Cottage. [My brother and I were] to fire off [our cannon] there [in celebration].

I went to the Cottage on the night of Mr. Edward's birthday, together with my brother, the gamekeeper, as we had been asked to fire the guns [cannon], which we took with us. My brother was in excellent spirits, and talked and laughed all the way, and said what a pleasure it was to him to show respect to the family (the Buxtons).

When we arrived at the Cottage, we were told that positive orders had been given that no Cromer guns should be fired; so I returned home, and my brother, very much disappointed, said he should go to the Hall, to look to one of the horses' feet. When I got to Cromer, and was going into the Brick Hill field, opposite Mr. Gurney Hoare's house, I was surprised to see my brother coming to meet me. He had on his velveteen shooting jacket, and walked in his usual manner, was quite light, and I distinctly saw him. [I addressed him, but he did not answer.] I turned my eyes away for a moment to look at the gate, and then he was gone. It was so light that I saw a gentleman walking on the cliff, about 200 yards off, and recognised him as Mr. Gurdon.

I was much struck with the apparition, but I passed it off my mind, and went to the cliff, and heard some people singing for about half an hour—when a boy said to me, "Have you heard of the [exploding gun] accident to your brother at Northrepps Hall?" I replied, "No, but if an accident has happened to my brother, I know he is dead."[28] — SIR THOMAS FOWELL BUXTON, M.P., OF NORTHREPPS HALL, NEAR CROMER, ENGLAND, 1891

HAUNTED HOUSE MAKES EMPLOYEES ILL

☞ I never heard or saw anything in any way extraordinary until I went to be cook at _____ Lodge about December 18th, 1883. I had heard nothing whatever about the house. I was engaged by a Mrs. Bain, who had taken the house for 6 months from Mrs. Jackson, I believe.

As I came up to the front door of the house for the first time I saw a face looking out at me from the windows above the door. It seemed to be a woman's face, very serious and stern, with the hair close to the head. It did not smile when I came up, but still I thought it must be one of the maids, and I said to them, "I saw you were expecting me and looking out." They said that no one had been in the room or looked out of the window.

I was put to sleep in that same room, along with another maidservant. We went to bed and turned down the gas till only a little button of gas was alight. Then it seemed to me that the gas turned red and there came more light in the room than the gas would make. The wall opposite my side of the bed, a few feet away, seemed to disappear, and I saw a round table with a red cover and an old lady reading at it, and girls sitting round it. They seemed to be about 12 years old, in high dresses, but I could not see more than their heads and shoulders. They made no noise.

Then they disappeared, and then came men with daggers and hilts and girdles, and a sort of capes and plumes in their hats, and sandals on their feet, who seemed to fight. These made a loud noise. When one of them was struck he seemed to fall down. The fight seemed to take place in daylight. All this seemed to last about half an hour, then all vanished.

I was so terrified that I could not move or speak while it went on. I perspired so much with fear that the mattress was soaked on the side where I lay. This happened night after night about 20 times, the same figures appearing, except that sometimes there would be a man with spectacles reading at the table instead of the old lady. And one night a white figure seemed to leave the group of men who were fighting and to pass round by the end of the bed and disappear into the wall.

I told my fellow servant something of what I saw, and asked her to notice that the gas turned red as soon as it was turned low. But she could not see this, and laughed at me, and said that it was all nonsense, and always went to sleep before the figures came. I did not dare to say any more about the figures, and I got very ill with the fright. I could hardly eat anything, and was too weak to do my work.

A doctor was sent for and said that I had had some great mental shock. I did not dare to mention the figures, and I had had no other shock. I became a regular invalid and should have had to go to the hospital but that my mistress very kindly wished me to stay, though I could only sit down in the kitchen and direct the cooking, which the gardener's wife, Mrs. Hoe, did for me. But after the doctor came the gas was always left high all night, and I saw the figures no more.

I was seriously ill for four months, and it was more than a year before I got over it. I stayed in the place till Mrs. Bain left, in May, 1884. During my stay the gardener, who lived in a separate building a few yards from the house, repeatedly complained of noises in a lumber-room next to his bedroom and accused us girls of going there and playing tricks on him, which we did not do. The house is an old one, I believe of Queen Elizabeth's time [16th Century].

I have never seen or heard anything strange since then, and my health is now good. I have heard from Mrs. Judd, the wife of a former gardener at Lodge, that the house has long been haunted, and that a servant girl had to leave it from being made ill by fright, long before my time. Mrs. Wallace, an old inhabitant of Finchley, has also told me that the house was haunted. Of this I knew nothing when I went to the place.[29] — (Signed) MARY MORTLOCK, OXFORD HOUSE, NORTH FINCHLEY, ENGLAND, APRIL 12TH, 1888

GHOST CHILD VANISHES AT CEMETERY GATE

☛ The Rev. E. H. Newenham tells us that he saw the figure of a child at gate of churchyard. When he reached the gate, he spoke to the child, which immediately vanished. One or two persons to whom he mentioned the incident said the figure was probably the spirit of child supposed to have been buried alive some years before in that churchyard. No date given.[30] — SOCIETY FOR PSYCHICAL RESEARCH, UK, RECORDED FEBRUARY 1889

COUSIN'S GHOST APPEARS TO FAMILY MEMBERS

☛ M. A. de Rochas informs us in 1889 that his father and a child in different rooms saw the cousin of the former by their beds on the night after his death. This occurred in the house where the corpse was lying. No date given.[31] — SOCIETY FOR PSYCHICAL RESEARCH, UK, FEBRUARY 1893

TRANSPARENT GHOST MANIFESTS IN CHURCH

☛ Mr. F. Sidebottom sees in church during morning service appearance like "black clear mist" in outline of a man; transparent. It moved about the church for some time, and finally vanished. About a fortnight later, Miss Maclean told Mr. Sidebottom that she had seen the same thing, but we have not been able to procure this lady's account. No date given.[32] — SOCIETY FOR PSYCHICAL

RESEARCH, UK, RECORDED OCTOBER 1888

GHOST OF CORPSE WANDERS HOTEL
☛ 2nd hand. Lady B. in Continental hotel sees man in her bedroom at night. After repeated orders to retire he mysteriously disappears—certainly not by door or window. Next day Lady B. makes landlord prove that there is no secret exit from the room. In the course of the day she hears that a visitor died in the hotel during the past night. Getting permission to view the corpse, Lady B. immediately recognises it as that of the man seen in her room. Recorded in November, 1890, by gentleman who heard the matter discussed with Lady B. in the autumn of 1841, but he does not tell us the date of the events.[33] — SOCIETY FOR PSYCHICAL RESEARCH, UK, 1893

SPIRIT APPEARS, TOUCHES FRIEND ON SHOULDER
☛ Two or three years after death. Percipient, Lady Jenkinson. Mrs. V. appears to her in boudoir coming in from drawing-room and disappears. Lady J. then goes into drawing-room. As she passes a cabinet in which she used to keep letters from Mrs. V., which she believed she had destroyed, she feels a hand on her shoulder characteristic of Mrs. V.—feels impelled to look in cupboard, and finds an old letter from her. Date of record 1890, but that of experience not given.[34] — SOCIETY FOR PSYCHICAL RESEARCH, UK, 1893

Victorian scientist Sir William Crookes (pictured) obtained this psychic photograph of a face at his laboratory.

CHAPTER THREE

DEATH-WRAITH ANNOUNCES DEMISE OF BROTHER

☛ In the autumn of 1874 my elder brother, W. M., resided in Edinburgh with his wife and family. Taking advantage of the temporary absence of his household on a visit to Glasgow, he went to stay for a few days with a married sister who lived in the country, 18 miles east from town. Previous to this time he had been subject, at irregular intervals, to attacks of illness of a severe character, but, at the date at which I write, was in fair health, and attending to business.

Two or three days after his arrival at our sister's house he was quite unexpectedly seized, late one evening, with serious illness, hematemesis supervened, and within two or three hours from the first seizure he was a corpse. The late hour, and distance from the railway station, prevented any communication during the night with our household in Edinburgh. My brother's wife being also expected to join him in the country next day, it was judged advisable to convey the intelligence to her en route, in case after receipt of it she might be unable to make the journey. I mention these latter facts to show that on the night when my brother's death actually occurred, no intelligence of it could possibly have reached our Edinburgh house, where my aged father and mother at that time were residing, and also, for the night, my brother's wife on her way from Glasgow.

Between 11 and 12 o'clock that night my mother, aged then 72, but active and vigorous in body and mind, as indeed she is still, was alone in her bedroom and in the act of undressing. She occupied this room alone, and it was the only sleeping apartment on the dining-room flat which was in use that night, the only other bedroom there being the adjoining room, then untenanted, owing to my own absence in the North. My father, eldest brother, and sister-in-law occupied rooms on the flat above. The servants' accommodation was in the under, or sunk flat beneath, shut off

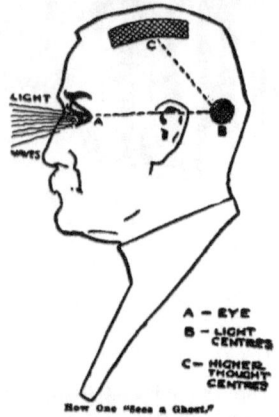

Believing ghosts to be nothing more than brain-generated "hallucinations," Victorian sceptics and scientists worked hard—and failed—to come up with rational explanations that would explain "how one sees a ghost." This is one of them.

from the upper by a swing door at the foot of a flight of steps. A small dog, the only other inmate of the house, slept that night, and indeed always, in the kitchen. My mother was in her usual good health, her faculties perfectly preserved, and her mind untroubled with any apprehensions of evil tidings.

She had read, as usual, a portion of her Bible, and was in the act of undressing, when she was suddenly startled by a most extraordinary noise at the door of her room, which opened directly into the inner lobby. It was as if made by a person standing directly outside and close to the door, but it was utterly unlike any ordinary summons or alarm. In her own words it was like nothing so much as the noise of someone hastily and imperiously lashing the door with a heavy riding whip, demanding admittance. It was loud, and repeated three or four times, as if insisting on attention, with brief intervals between. Then it ceased.

My mother, though possessed of considerable coolness, was startled, but with a resolution which many might envy, she proceeded to light a candle, knowing the hall lights were extinguished, the whole of the inmates having before retired for the night, and went to the door. "I knew," she said, "that it was no one in the house seeking admission. Such an imperative summons would never have been made at my door." On opening it nothing was visible, the various doors opening on the lobby were closed, and the fastening of the front door undisturbed. Much surprised, though retaining self-possession, my mother debated with herself as to rousing the other members of the family, but ultimately resolved not to do so unless the sound was repeated, which it was not. It was about midnight, but my mother did not note the precise hour and minute.

Early next forenoon, my father and sister-in-law having left, the news came that my brother had expired at midnight, 18 miles off by road from Edinburgh. It may be noted that nothing near or in the door could possibly have occasioned the noise in question, the material being old, well-seasoned timber not liable to warp or crack. It afterwards appeared that the noise in question had not been heard by anyone in the house save by my mother, which no one will wonder at who knows how perfectly "deafened" old-fashioned stone houses in Edinburgh invariably are.

Speaking for my own part, I would not have placed so much reliance on the narrative which I have from my mother's own lips, had it come from any other person in the house. The others might have been imaginative or nervous, or wise after the event, or possibly wholly mistaken. But with my mother's clear and balanced judgment, little affected by matters which powerfully sway others, I have no room for hesitation whatsoever. I believe, as firmly as I believe in the fact of my own existence, that the circumstances happened exactly as she narrated them, and also, in her instinctive feeling, at the time of their occurrence, that the sound in question was not accidental or caused by any agency of which we have present cognisance, I believe she was right.[35] — NAME OF EYEWITNESS WITHHELD BY THE S.P.R., 1884

SCREAMS & FOOTSTEPS IN HAUNTED HOUSE
☞ Miss E. G. A. Jackson and her father and mother lived in a new house for nearly three years, in which they were constantly troubled by unaccountable footsteps in the passage, staircase, and rooms. Once when sitting up nursing she heard a loud scream in the room, which was also heard by the patient and by a nurse upstairs. Date, "Some years ago."[36] — SOCIETY FOR PSYCHICAL RESEARCH, UK, RECORDED MARCH 1886

HAUNTED RECTORY DISTURBS INHABITANTS
☞ The Rev. W. M. H. Church and his family when living in a very old country rectory heard great crash like heavy chest of drawers being dashed down. After they left, caretaker's boy heard similar noise, and later the caretaker and his wife also heard it together. Other unexplained noises were also heard by the family and visitors. Date, about 1870.[37] — SOCIETY FOR PSYCHICAL RESEARCH, UK, RECORDED AUGUST 1886

SPIRIT OF DROWNED BROTHER APPEARS & SPEAKS
☞ Borderland. Miss M. W. P., who was in no anxiety about her brother, was wakened by hearing his voice call her several times. She sat up and saw him standing at the foot of her bed. Apparition said: "I could not go without telling you good-bye," and disappeared. Miss P.'s sister testifies that the above was mentioned to her and to several schoolfellows next day. About six weeks later,

news arrived of the brother's death by drowning, which occurred in Texas at about 2 p.m. on a Friday, while the dream took place in New York at about 1 a.m. on the Sunday. Date, April 1865.[38] — SOCIETY FOR PSYCHICAL RESEARCH, UK, RECORDED MARCH 1885

DECEASED MOTHER APPEARS TO DAUGHTER
☛ 2nd hand. Mr. Coulson Kernahan informs us that, some days after his mother's death, his sister, when kneeling at her bedside, looked up and saw her mother standing beside her. She smiled and vanished. There had been a promise to appear after death if possible. Date not given.[39] — SOCIETY FOR PSYCHICAL RESEARCH, UK, RECORDED JUNE 1887

AN ANGRY GHOST
☛ Through American Branch. Mrs. K. E. Alexander and her daughter, at different times, hear toilet set rattle, and daughter feels dress pulled. Subsequently, when in bed, Mrs. Alexander felt the bedclothes pulled and her face slapped. She concluded that dead relative to whom toilet set and dress had belonged was displeased about distribution of effects; she therefore addressed the supposed presence, explaining that no unfair division of property had been made. There were no more disturbances. Date of events, 1889.[40] — SOCIETY FOR PSYCHICAL RESEARCH, UK, RECORDED DECEMBER 1890

VANISHING WHITE GHOST COUPLE
☛ Collective. Mr. and Mrs. Morris at country house 3 miles from anywhere saw in the evening a man accompanied by a woman in white approach. Suddenly the figures unaccountably disappeared, and though carefully searched for could not be found. Date, September 1884.[41] — SOCIETY FOR PSYCHICAL RESEARCH, UK, RECORDED DECEMBER 1884

MYSTERIOUS LIGHT IN HAUNTED HOUSE
☛ Mr. H. M. L. sleeping at house near Leeds saw a patch of light on the ceiling. There was nothing to account for it—no gas or fire in room, foggy night, no moon. Mr. L. retired under the bed-clothes for 20 minutes, and when he looked up light had gone. He then heard footsteps cross the room. House reported haunted. No date.[42] — SOCIETY FOR PSYCHICAL RESEARCH, UK, RECORDED APRIL 1884

A DYING BOY'S SPIRIT CALLS OUT TO HIS COUSIN
☛ . . . on October the 9^{th,} 1874, at two or three minutes to 5 in the morning, I woke with the strange feeling that my cousin was dead and that he was in the room. I then saw a vision of him; it was quite momentary. The boy died at that time, calling for me, and saying that he must see me. I knew that my cousin would not recover from the illness he was suffering from, but his death was not expected so soon.^{43} — MISS THERESA THORNYCROFT, MORETON HOUSE, MELBURY ROAD, KENSINGTON, ENGLAND, 1884

HORSE SPOOKED BY CRIMINAL'S GHOST
☛ Returning home in [their horse and buggy] the evening after a long drive the Misses Leslie [sisters] passed through a valley. Here the "steady cob" [one of their Welsh ponies] suddenly jumped into the air, kicked violently, and destroyed the carriage. They afterwards discovered from guide-book that valley was regarded as haunted since a certain murder, travellers being warned not to venture through it at eventide. Date, October 1881.^{44} — SOCIETY FOR PSYCHICAL RESEARCH, UK, RECORDED AUGUST 1889

HAUNTED COTTAGE DRIVES OUT TENANTS
☛ 2nd hand. The Rev. W. K. W. Chafy—Chafy informs us that a young man-servant of his rented a cottage at Church Lench. Retiring tenants had stated that during past 40 years they frequently saw the ghost of a woman. Within the first week the new tenant saw the ghost two nights running; and refused to sleep there again. Persons who subsequently watched in the house saw nothing. Events, October 1886.^{45} — SOCIETY FOR PSYCHICAL RESEARCH, UK, RECORDED OCTOBER 1886

GHOST WOMAN PASSES THROUGH SOLID DOOR
☛ In April of last year, while the light was still good, I was returning home from a walk with my wife, and when within a few yards of the gate, which opens into a straight path leading to the house, both my wife and I saw a woman pass through the open gate and walk straight to the house, when, on reaching the door, she disappeared.

I ran to the door, opened it with my latchkey, and expected in my astonishment to find her inside, for she seemed to have walked through the door. It all seemed so real that I at once searched the house, but in vain. We were the only two people in the street, and did not see the figure until she entered the gate, when we simultaneously exclaimed, "Who is that?" She seemed to come out of space and go into space again in a most marvellous manner.

She wore a plaid shawl, and her bonnet was a grey-black with a bit of colour in it. We could not remember hearing any sound as she walked, but otherwise we have never seen anything more apparently substantial. It is impossible for us to conceive how she could have disappeared if she had been of flesh and blood. If only one of us had seen this figure, I should have thought little about it, as such cases of hallucination seem sufficiently common, and may be accounted for by some physical or mental disturbance; but the evidence in this case points to the existence of something exterior to ourselves. We are neither of us believers in ghosts or the like, but are two ordinary matter-of-fact people.[46] — REGINALD BARBER, 24 LORNE-GROVE, FALLOWFIELD, MANCHESTER, ENGLAND, JANUARY 21ST, 1891

GHOST OF OLD WOMAN GLIDES DOWN HALLWAY

☛I may say that I am not a believer in ghosts, and have no sympathy with Spiritualism in any form; am a member of a Baptist church in this city. I give the following facts, to the best of my recollection, for what they are worth, having never been able to find any satisfactory explanation thereof.

Our family was living in a large, comfortable house, called _____ Hall, which had recently been taken for a term of years by my father, F. M., of _____. There was a passage leading from the outside back door, past the pantry and cellar doors to the servants' hall. On the left hand side of the passage, looking towards the back door, there was an opening into the cellar, which was reached by steep stairs. At the time of which I write I was sixteen years of age, my sister, now Mrs. W., being one year older; the year probably being 1866 or 1867.

It was towards twilight; the time of the year I have forgotten. My sister and I were walking together down the passage towards the back door, when we distinctly saw the figure of an old woman, dressed in shawl and bonnet, coming towards us, and pass us. We immediately turned round, and saw the figure glide towards the cellar steps, where she disappeared, the impression left upon our minds being that she had gone down.

As far as my memory serves me, I believe the phantom, or whatever it was, was of a transparent, or, at any rate, of an ethereal nature, as she passed us without inconvenience in the narrow passage. We were surprised at seeing this strange figure, and followed her to look down the cellar steps, but saw and heard nothing. I cannot say certainly at this distance of time whether we were very much frightened, or whether we experienced any particular sensations: but what is very clearly stamped upon my mind is the ridicule heaped upon our story by any who heard it; for whenever we mentioned it we got so laughed at we soon ceased to speak of it at all.

I may say, in conclusion, my sister and I were in good health and spirits at this time, and that nothing was further from our thoughts than the possibility of seeing anything supernatural. The figure was that of a total stranger. I have never had a similar experience either before or since. The impression always remained upon my mind that I had seen an apparition, and I believe my sister shared that impression. I related this incident to my husband soon after we were married, and it is his interest in this story that has kept it in my mind. I declare the above to be correct to the best of my knowledge and belief.[47] — MRS. B., FEBRUARY 2ND, 1892

DECEASED AUNT PLAYS PIANO ONE LAST TIME

☛ It is nearly thirty years ago now, but it is as vividly impressed on her memory, as if it had happened yesterday. She was sitting in the dining-room (in a self-contained house), which was behind the drawing-room, with Jamie, my eldest brother, on her knee, who was then a baby scarcely two years old. The nurse had gone out for the afternoon, and there was no one in the house except the maid downstairs. The doors of the dining-room and drawing-room in both happened to be open at the time.

All at once she heard the most divine music, very sad and sweet, which lasted for about two minutes, then gradually died away. My brother jumped from mamma's knee, exclaiming "Papa! papa," and ran through to the drawing-room. Mamma felt as if she could not move and rang the bell for the servant, whom she told to go and see who was in the drawing-room. When she went into the room, she found my brother standing beside the piano and saying "No papa!" Why the child should have exclaimed these words was that papa was very musical, and used often to go straight to the piano when he came home.

Such was the impression on mamma that she noted the time to a minute, and six weeks after she received a letter saying her sister [Mary Sophia Ingles] had died at the Cape [Durban, Natal, South Africa], and the time corresponded exactly to the minute that she had heard the music. I may tell you that my aunt was a very fine musician.[48] — MISS EMILY M. HORNE, DECEMBER 11TH, 1890

GHOST OF FAMOUS BOSTON MUSICIAN GIVES FINAL PERFORMANCE

☛ In the year 1845 Mr. Herwig, a German, and a much esteemed musician, who had for several years resided in Boston, Massachusetts, died suddenly in that city. I was then a young girl, and knew him only through his high reputation, and my own great enjoyment of his delightful performances on the violin in public concerts. The only personal association I ever had with him was, that in the winter before his death, in returning to my home from that of a friend who was studying with me, I chanced for many weeks to meet Mr. Herwig almost daily on a certain part of Beacon Street. It seemed to be only an accident, but finally it became such a constant occurrence that he smiled on me kindly, and gave me a respectful little bow, which I ventured as respectfully to return.

An impressive but staged Victorian ghost photograph.

The following autumn he died, as I have said, very suddenly, and his funeral took place on November 4th, 1845, in Trinity Church—then on Summer Street, Boston. It was a solemn and touching service, attended by a crowd of musicians and other eminent citizens, for all mourned the loss of such an accomplished and valuable man. I was present with my sister, and, in the midst of the services, there came to me a most unaccountable and inexpressible feeling that he might then and there at once rise from the coffin and appear in life again among us. Hardly knowing what I did, I caught my sister's hand, exclaiming almost aloud, "Oh, he must, he must come to life again!" so very earnestly that she looked at me in wonder and whispered "Hush! hush!"

That evening my mother, my two sisters, a friend (Mr. S., from Cuba), and myself—five of us in all—were sitting in our dining-room, No. 4, H. Street, Boston, while my sister and I were describing the funeral. My sister had just told of my singular exclamation while there, and I was repeating the words, when suddenly the room was filled with a burst of glorious music, such as none of us had ever heard. I saw a look of astonishment and even fear on every face, and, in a sort of fright myself, I continued speaking incoherently when, once more, after a slight pause, came a similar full swell of harmony which then died softly away.

My sister and I at once rushed to the hall door, which was but a few steps from us, to discover if outside there were any music, but we heard not a sound save the hard drizzle of a dark rainy night.

I then ran upstairs to the parlour over the dining-room, where was only a Quaker lady reading. A piano was in that room, and, though it was closed, I asked, "Has anyone been playing?"

"No," she replied, "But I heard a strange burst of music. What was it?"

Now, let it be understood that, as a family, we had never been superstitious, but, on the contrary, had been educated to scoff at the idea of ghosts, omens, etc., so that none of us announced this occurrence as supernatural, but could only look at each other saying, "What was it?"

The Quakeress, however, we found more excited than ourselves. She related the experience to her daughters, who were absent at the time, and they spent much time in perambulating the neighbourhood to discover if there had been any music in the houses near ours; but it was distinctly proved that there had been none, nor had any been heard from the street. In fact, what we heard seemed to be close around ourselves, as we each described it, and unlike any we had ever heard.

It may seem strange that, after so many years, I should be able to describe so particularly this event. But I own [admit] it made a deep impression upon the minds of all the hearers. I have often narrated it, and heard the others narrate it in exactly the same way, and my sister, the only one now living of that little company, will verify my description word for word.

I add my replies to some questions which have been asked.

When we went to the hall door we looked up and down the street, which was well lighted. Street performers upon musical instruments were absolutely unknown in Boston at this period. Mrs. S., the Quaker lady of whom I have spoken, was staying in the house as a guest. I asked whether anyone had played upon the piano, not because the music bore any resemblance to that of a piano, but to connect it, if possible, with some natural cause.

The music appeared to all of us to be in the room where we

were sitting. It seemed to begin in one corner, and to pass round the room. I said that it was like a burst of sunshine in sound, and can give no better description of it. My mother and Mr. S. agreed that the music was utterly inexplicable. My sister and I, as well as the daughters of Mrs. S., made thorough inquiries at all the houses about us, but could hear nothing that could account for the phenomenon. (Miss Elizabeth Jenkins corroborates as follows: "I have carefully read the above account written by my sister, and testify to its accuracy.")[49] — SARAH JENKINS, 1893

GHOST OF LIVING PERSON APPEARS FROM 10,000 MILES DISTANCE

☛ I saw a very dear friend [Mr. Gunderson], about 70 years old, [then still] living in Christiania [Oslo, Norway], at 7 o'clock in the afternoon, when walking about a year ago with some Australian friends in one of the streets of Melbourne. I saw his face as in prayer, and quite suddenly and near, so I did almost touch him. I was talking of singing with my friends, as we were going to practice at the time. I was quite well and have never had hallucinations or anything like this before or later. It was daylight and quite full of passers-by and vehicles, etc., in the street.

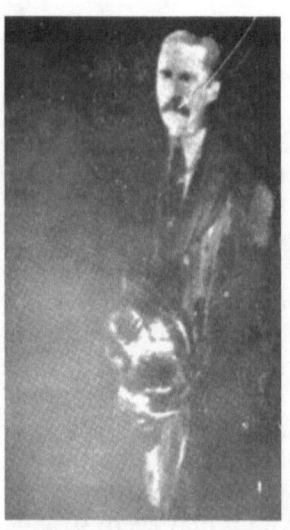

A Victorian psychic photograph, said to be created by impressing film with a mental image.

I had not seen him since a year before, but it struck me so vividly that I wrote home to Christiania, Norway, asking [my friend Gunderson if he was alright] at that [exact] hour (subtracting the 9 hours we are before here in Melbourne), and got the answer: "Praying very intensely for you and your mission in Melbourne." Two [other persons were present] who saw nothing and were quite outside the whole incident. I never studied "telepathy," but it occurs to me that this fact must be connected with such a thing.[50] — SÖREN PEDERSON, 282 WILLIAMS STREET, MELBOURNE, AUSTRALIA, JANUARY 12TH, 1892

DECEASED MAN TEASES BEST FRIEND

☛ I cannot give exact dates, but as near as I can now remember it was near the end of October 1870. I had a very affectionate friend, Robert Broome, Esq., Burbage House, near Buxton. My business and residence were in Manchester, but at that time I gave up my business and went to reside at Penrith, in Cumberland. I had a large farm at Castle Sowerby, about 9 miles from Penrith. I drove to this twice each week. I left Penrith at 7 a.m., and generally returned at 6 p.m.

On an occasion to which I wish to refer I remained later at the farm, as the harvest had been finished, and I stopped to take supper with the labourers. It was a temperance supper, as I was an abstainer.

I left the farm alone about 11 o'clock, driving a gig with a very steady horse. It was a cloudy night but moonlight. I met no one on the road till I came to the Greystoke pillar, about a mile from Penrith. There, driving slowly as I was about to turn into a narrow lane, I was deeply shadowed from behind, and upon looking back to see what caused the shadow I saw my friend Broome, bending over me with an expression of the most tender affection upon his countenance. I spoke to him, pulled up the horse, and alighted. I walked round the gig, called him by name, begged him not to play tricks at midnight, but to come to me and come home with me. I had, of course, to go without him.

At home I inquired if Mr. Broome had called. The answer was, No. I then told my wife that I had seen him near the Greystoke pillar, that he must be in the town, and would be sure to call in the morning.

Three days passed, when we received intelligence that Mr. Broome was [dead], and strange to tell he had died at the very hour at midnight at which I had seen him near the Greystoke pillar. This is the only experience [like this] I have ever had.[51] — MR. A. MCDOUGALL, F.C.S., 1893

GHOSTS OF IRISH MONKS HAUNT HOUSE
☛ Mr. J. M. Goold Adams, staying at his father's house, Co. Cork, [Ireland,] goes downstairs in the night to find boots, and through glass door sees kitchen lighted up and three monks seated round fire. He retreats in haste. House was adjacent to ruins of Abbey. Date uncertain, but earlier than 1877.[52] — SOCIETY FOR PSYCHICAL RESEARCH, UK, RECORDED 1888

DECEASED WIFE TENDS TO DYING HUSBAND
☛ 3rd hand, good as 2nd. Mrs. Beaumont heard her parents relate that their parents lay dying in adjoining rooms. The mother died,

and her death was kept secret from the father. An hour after her death he remarked that he was glad she was getting so much better, for she had been sitting by his bed for nearly an hour. Date, when Mrs. B. was about 10.[53] — SOCIETY FOR PSYCHICAL RESEARCH, UK, RECORDED 1886

GHOST LADY IN A BROCADE SKIRT
☛ Sent by Mr. C. H. Bowman. Mrs. G. and her three brothers and sister, when children, used every evening to see an apparition of a lady in a stiff brocade skirt, which rustled as she moved, pass through the garret where they played. She was always seen by all present and had also been seen by two ladies next door. The two houses had originally communicated through the garret. Other witnesses now dead, and no more evidence attainable. Date: 1846-1852.[54] — SOCIETY FOR PSYCHICAL RESEARCH, UK, DATE OF RECORD 1891

BEAUTIFUL FEMALE APPARITION ON CLIFF FOOTPATH
☛ Fixed local. Miss S. Moore (daughter of the late General Moore) walking back from church by footpath along cliff sees a beautiful woman in blue bathing dress. She meets, passes, and watches the figure walk out of sight. The figure is transparent—grass is visible through it. Miss M. hears that a light lady has been seen by others in the same neighbourhood. Date not stated.[55] — SOCIETY FOR PSYCHICAL RESEARCH, UK, RECORDED DECEMBER 1888

VIOLENT POLTERGEIST PROWLS GLASTON HOUSE
☛ Mrs. Ellicott (wife of Bishop of Gloucester) hears noises constantly in room overhead. Once hears terrific noise apparently in drawing-room, like the five windows being violently opened and closed and heavy bookcase falling. Governess sees motions in curtains as if by fingers behind. Violent noises in kitchen, and on kitchen table. The house (Glaston House, near Uppingham, Rutland) has no ghostly history. Date not given.[56] — SOCIETY FOR PSYCHICAL RESEARCH, UK, RECORDED OCTOBER 1888

HANGED MAN'S GHOST SEEN SITTING ON GATE
☛ Mr. Edmund Wilson, of Leeds, and two others see man sitting on gate in open country who mysteriously disappears as they approach. They hear afterwards that a man was once hanged close by, and that his ghost is said to sit on that gate. No confirmation. Date "4 or 5 years ago."[57] — SOCIETY FOR PSYCHICAL

RESEARCH, UK, RECORDED FEBRUARY 1888

THE GHOSTLY BILLIARD PLAYER
☛ Through Mr. E. Westlake. Mrs. Fry and other members of family hear unaccountable noises in their house at Darlington, especially billiard balls *cannoning* when no one is playing. No confirmation. Experiences since 1886.[58] — SOCIETY FOR PSYCHICAL RESEARCH, UK, RECORDED FEBRUARY 1888

UNHAPPY SPIRITS OF FATHER & DAUGHTER
☛ Second-hand. Fixed local. Through Lady Harrington. Mr. and Mrs. X., staying in old family house, hear footsteps about house at night, but no one is to be seen. Servants threaten to leave. Butler and clerk are put to watch with pistols. These two see figure of old-fashioned gentleman, and they fire without effect. Butler afterwards recognises ghost as grandfather of Mr. X. from portrait accidentally seen. Later, household is awakened by prolonged and piercing shrieks, which die away in one of the stalls of the stable.

Next day news comes that aunt of Mr. X. had died previous day in lunatic asylum. It transpired that this aunt had lost her reason through ill treatment: her father (the above ghost) surprised [her] secret meeting with a forbidden [male] lover; he beat her, dragged her to stables, and flung her in one of the stalls, where she became hysterical and lost her reason. After her death disturbances ceased. Date, "about 40 years ago."[59] — SOCIETY FOR PSYCHICAL RESEARCH, UK, NARRATED NOVEMBER 1888

GHOST OF DROWNED ABBESS APPEARS IN WINDOW
☛ Borderland. Miss Emma Maria Pearson, when a little girl, woke and saw evil face at window and hand offering letter. She rose to take letter, but fainted before she could do so. Learnt some years afterwards that tradition existed about abbess being drowned by remote ancestors of her family; she died predicting deaths by drowning for descendants of the family, and threatening that she would appear to each generation until the proffered letter was accepted. Several members of the family have since been drowned. Experience, 1836.[60] — SOCIETY FOR PSYCHICAL RESEARCH, UK, RECORDED ABOUT 1888

THE PHANTOM & THE POTATOES
☛ 3rd hand. Through Rev. A. T. Fryer. Mr. White, when washing his hands, sees former occupant of his house, who had died a short time before. Asked what troubled him, the apparition said that he

had buried some seed potatoes in a certain place, which he described exactly, and disappeared. Death occurred in 1855.[61] — SOCIETY FOR PSYCHICAL RESEARCH, UK, RECORDED 1891

SPECTER WARNS OF RECTOR'S DEATH

☛ I cannot, unfortunately, introduce you to a spectre, and it is difficult to convey an accurate impression of the mysterious annoyances at my old home, which appealed rather to touch and hearing than to sight. They were nonetheless real and distressing. It was difficult for my mother to keep her servants any length of time, and guests seldom renewed their visits to the rectory.

Phantom feet trod the passages at night and were heard ascending the staircases, locks turned, doors opened and closed, furniture appeared to be dragged about in unoccupied rooms, viewless hands rustled the bed-curtains and moved across the pillows. Sometimes weird, unearthly screams echoed through the house; and these manifestations were not confined to the hours of night. But these are generalities. I will now state a particular incident which appeared to point to influences beyond the ken of our philosophy.

My father was not the incumbent; he was only the curate-in-charge. The rector, a wealthy country squire of old family, although he drew nearly £1,200 a-year from the living, resided on his own estate, never did any church duty, and left the parish entirely in my father's hands, merely paying him a friendly visit now and then. On one of these visits, when he came accompanied by his wife, my mother eagerly invited the opinion of the latter about the noises which so often disturbed our rest, and proved a constant source of terror to the servants. "I have no opinion to offer," she replied; "all I know is that the house has so long enjoyed the reputation of being haunted

As a couple poses for the camera, a ghost imprint of the man's father was caught in the background in this Victorian spirit photograph.

that, in the case of servants, one might suggest superstition, working on an already excited and expectant imagination; but this easy solution is, of course, inapplicable either to strong-minded persons like yourself and Mr. V or to those who had never heard the reports, like your visitors.

One of the current legends you may some day have the opportunity of verifying, though I trust that that day is far distant. According to this tradition, no sooner does a rector of B_____ die, than a strange, incomprehensible sound proceeds from the landing of the front staircase. This noise, I am told, has been compared to the slashes of a cart-whip falling on a metal tube." This unromantic comparison excited more merriment than credulity, and the matter was soon forgotten.

A good many months had elapsed, when one autumnal evening, about 9 p.m., my mother was startled by a most unusual disturbance: the loud slashes of a whip on some metallic substance echoed through the passage and down the stairs. No one was to be seen anywhere, and the origin of the sound could not be traced. Two days later, my father received the tidings of his rector's sudden death. The day and hour of this quite unexpected event coincided with the predicted supernatural warning. At the time of the rector's sudden death he was on a visit to a country seat at least 50 miles from the rectory. He was apparently in his usual health and spirits until the moment of the seizure, which in half-an-hour ended fatally. Railways and telegraphs were not [in existence at the time], and the place was 16 miles from a coach-road.[62] — MRS. V., 1884

HAPPY CHILD SPIRIT RETURNS TO ASSURE MOTHER
☞ Through Rev. A. T. Fryer. Mrs. Mary Riffold sees her daughter a few days after her death. She [the daughter] clasps her [the mother] tightly round the waist and says: "I want to kiss you; I am so happy." Mrs. Riffold in consequence ceases to grieve. Date: a good many years ago.[63] — SOCIETY FOR PSYCHICAL RESEARCH, UK, RECORDED MARCH 1891

APPARITION OF NUN HAUNTS SCHOOLHOUSE
☞ Mrs. Beasley and her young son and daughter see, at different times, figures, especially of a nun, in an old school-house. Servants and school-children also see the nun. The family occupied the house from 1858 to 1879. The apparitions were seen during the last 3 years. The account, signed by Mrs. and Miss M. A. Beasley, was written about 1885, and sent to us in 1889.[64] — SOCIETY FOR

PSYCHICAL RESEARCH, UK, 1893

HAUNTED HOUSE FILLED WITH "GHOSTLY NOISES"
☛ The two Misses Beasley [named above] also saw female figures in the next house the family moved to—between 1879 and 1881—which had the reputation of being haunted. Footsteps and other ghostly noises were also heard here by all the family and servants. Miss Beasley adds that at an old convent on the Rhine they all saw a similar figure at different times.[65] — SOCIETY FOR PSYCHICAL RESEARCH, UK, 1893

BRIGHTON HOUSE GHOST LADY
☛ Mrs. S. informs us in 1889 that in 1850-1852 she several times saw a female figure in her house at Brighton, which could not have been a real person. Her young son once rushed from his bedroom at night saying that he had seen a woman leaning over his bed. Fifteen years afterwards a lady confided to Mrs. S. that she had seen the same figure when visiting her.[66] — SOCIETY FOR PSYCHICAL RESEARCH, UK, 1893

GRANDFATHER'S GHOST RELAXES IN FORMER ARMCHAIR
☛ 2nd hand, good as 1st. First printed in the *Phasmatological Papers*, last series. A lad aged 14, playing with his cousin, aged 13, in the garden of a country house, looked into library through window and observed that an old gentleman occupied armchair by fire. The cousin also looked but saw nothing. The lad's description of what he saw corresponded to aspect of cousin's maternal grandfather, who had constantly occupied this chair, and who had been dead about a year. The percipient did not know the old gentleman when alive. We have the cousin's account of the matter, and also letters from the percipient's mother, who heard of it soon after the occurrence. Date end of summer 1876.[67] — SOCIETY FOR PSYCHICAL RESEARCH, UK, RECORDED FEBRUARY 1885

HAUNTED HOUSE POLTERGEISTS FORCE OUT TENANTS
☛ Accounts of very remarkable noises heard by a family and friends in a house at Wandsworth in 1884. The tenants were obliged to leave in consequence of the disturbances—which consisted of heavy thumping noises, footsteps, snatching of bedclothes, touches, rocking of furniture, etc. We have accounts from 3 of the witnesses, written some months after the experiences. Upwards of a dozen members of the S.P.R. spent nights in the house in October and November, 1885, after the

tenants had left, but they observed nothing unusual.⁶⁸ — SOCIETY FOR PSYCHICAL RESEARCH, UK, 1893

LIVING FATHER'S SPIRIT WAVES HIS HAT TO DAUGHTERS
☛ On February 5th, 1887, my father, sister, and I went out hunting. About the middle of the day my sister and I decided to return home with the coachman, while my father went on. Somebody came and spoke to us, and delayed us for a few moments. As we were turning to go home, we distinctly saw my father, waving his hat to us and signing us to follow him. He was on the side of a small hill, and there was a dip between him and us.

My sister, the coachman, and myself all recognised my father, and also the horse. The horse looked so dirty and shaken that the coachman remarked he thought there had been a nasty accident. As my father waved his hat I clearly saw the Lincoln and Bennett mark inside, though from the distance we were apart, it ought to have been utterly impossible for me to have seen it. At the time I mentioned seeing the mark in the hat, though the strangeness of seeing it did not strike me till afterwards.

Fearing an accident, we hurried down the hill. From the ground we had to lose sight of my father, but seconds to reach the place where we had seen him. When we got there, there was no sign of him anywhere, nor could we see anyone in sight at all. We rode about for some time looking for him, but could not see or hear anything of him.

We all reached home within a quarter of an hour of each other. My father then told us he had never been in the field, nor near the field, in which we thought we saw him, the whole of that day. He had never waved to us, and had met with no accident.

From the nature of it took us very few. My father was riding the only white horse that was out that day.⁶⁹ — LOUISA BOURNE & H. M. BOURNE, 1893

CRYING APPARITIONS
☛ One evening in the early spring of last year (1883) as I was retiring to bed—but whilst I was in full enjoyment of good health and active senses—I distinctly saw my mother and my younger sister crying. I was here in Carmarthen [Wales], and they were away in Monmouthshire [Wales], 80 miles distant. They distinctly appeared to me to be giving away to grief, and I was at once positive that some domestic bereavement had taken place. I said to myself "I shall hear something of this in the morning."

When the morning came the first thing which was handed to

me was a letter from my father in Monmouthshire, stating that they had, on the day of writing, had intelligence that my nephew had just died. The little boy was the son of my elder sister, living in North Devon [England]. There was no doubt but that my mother and younger sister had both given way to grief on the day of my strange illusion, and it was in some mysterious manner communicated to my mind—together with a certain presentiment that I was on the eve of intelligence of a death in the family. I thought it most probable, though, that the imaginative faculty added—in a purely local manner—the idea of speedy intelligence to the communication which the mind received in some strange way from Monmouthshire. It was the only occurrence of the sort I have ever experienced.[70] — JOHN HOPKINS, 23 KING STREET, CARMARTHEN, WALES, MAY 2ND, 1884

SPIRIT OF LIVING LAND OWNER APPEARS & DISAPPEARS

☛ Pitsea Rectory, March 17th, 10:40 a.m. [1892]. Yesterday, at half-past eleven, N., the rat-catcher, came to see master [the land and house owner], who was out. We looked at the clock to tell N. when we thought he could see master, who had ordered luncheon at 12:15 [Note: He was actually over a mile away at that moment, L.S.]. We were both outside the door when N. came. He was in a cart and had with him two dogs.

He drove on, and Mrs. Watts, looking down the road, said, "Here comes the master!" Then I saw him too, his dog with him. N. had just got below the front gate. We watched to see them meet; wondered why N. did not stop to speak, as he wanted to see master. He drove right on.

About that time we lost master; couldn't think where he was, but fancied he must have gone to Wilson's house. Wilson himself was standing lower down, where the roads meet. We still watched, and when we couldn't see him (master) come out we went indoors.

When Mr. Hasted came home I wasn't going to say anything, but Mrs. Watts asked if he had seen N., who wanted to tell him about a puppy. He said he had been at Mr. Williams's, and all the story came out.[71] — ELIZA SMALLBONE & JANE WATTS, 1892

GHOST OF RECENTLY DECEASED WOMAN VISITS EARTHLY FRIENDS

☛ I was talking to my wife on the balcony, when I [heard the rustling of material and] saw the figure of a lady in a white dress, with her hair hanging down, come from the corridor, cross over the room, and disappear through the door leading into my study.

My attention was first called by a noise in the room. Place S. Joaode Itaborahy, Province of Rio [Brazil]. Vesper hour, one day in the month of September, 1860 or 1861.

I was talking to my wife on some ordinary topic. Age at time, 34. I am now 65. Health and spirits at time good—in all probability, though I was supposed at the time to have something the matter with my heart.

We were disposed on the occasion to suppose that our [negro] slave, Henriqueta, had crossed into the study, there being nobody else in the house but ourselves and this black woman. She was called, and denied having entered the room. Besides, she was dressed in dark clothes, and had the usual negro hair.

The form, stature, and manner of wearing the hair reminded me of a friend whom I had lost seven days before. I had been present at the mass said for her soul on that very day. I had spoken of her a short time before to my wife, but we had changed the subject of conversation. [The other persons present were] my son Eugenio and my wife, who both shared the experience. [I have had] no other experience [of this kind].[72] — DR. CANDIDO DA SILVEIRA RODRIGUES, PRAÇA DA PRINCEZA ISABEL, 8 NOVA FRIBURGO, RIO, BRAZIL, MARCH 28TH, 1892

TALL WHITE SPIRIT APPEARS TO TWO COUSINS

☛ Last summer [August 1891] I was paying a visit to some cousins, who were *en pension* with a German family, at Cassel [France]. My cousin L. V. [assumed initials] and I shared a room, known, from the stained [glass] window, as the "Ritterzimmer." Our beds occupied almost all one side of the room, of which I send a rough plan.

One night we were late going to bed, and were not in bed till after 11:30. We went on talking for some time. We were neither of us the least nervous, nor was our conversation such as to make us so. I remember we were talking about the opera *Robert der Teufel*, to which we were going next day. We had stopped talking for a few minutes, and I was lying with my face to the wall, when I was startled by a scream from my cousin, and, turning round, saw a tall white figure standing in the room, near L.'s bed.

I did not at the time feel frightened; my one idea was to find out what strange thing it was. It turned and came towards my bed, and I distinctly remember noticing that it made no sound on the polished wood floor. Its eyes were green and glistening, but the rest of the face seemed muffled up. As soon as it was close to my bed, I seized it, and seemed to take hold of something soft, like

Victorian psychic photograph.

flimsy drapery, but whatever it was seemed dragged from me by some invisible power, and the thing literally sank into the floor by my bedside.

L. was in a perfect terror, and her mother, and G. von T., and another friend were startled by the noise, and came to see what was the matter. We searched everywhere, but nothing was to be seen.

I cannot account for not feeling afraid of it, especially as afterwards I heartily wished the night were over. L. knew there was a legend about our room, and that this apparition was said to come that day once in ten years, but she did not believe in it, and I knew nothing at all of the story.

The people who had lived in the house before told Frau von T. that they had seen something twice in that room. They had lived there over 20 years; but Frau von T. had not been there long enough to test it before. No one could possibly have got into the room, as the door was a very noisy one, close to the foot of my bed. We slept in the room for some time, both before and after, but never saw anything more. As my cousin and I both saw the "thing," I am at a loss to account for it, but I should be extremely sorry to sleep in that room that day ten years.[73] — AGNES MCCASKILL, 4 SHAKESPEARE ROAD, BEDFORD, ENGLAND, JULY 25TH, 1892

FEMALE PHANTOM APPEARS TO TWO CLERGYMAN IN CHURCHYARD

☞ About six years ago I was walking one summer evening very late in my garden with the now rector of Kelvedon [England], and saw a dark female form in the churchyard. We carefully followed the figure, and saw it vanish. We could find no explanation for the phenomenon. No living person could have escaped us.

The churchyard has two gates, and we went to them and met half-way up the path. I went to the garden entrance and Mr. Peregrine to the path gate. We then joined, and the figure had disappeared. No one was about, and anyone would have been caught without a shadow of doubt.

I am interested in psychology and have my own ideas about the figure, but Mr. Peregrine is a non-believer in ghosts. I state the bare facts merely.[74] — REV. H. R. HARRISON, 66 BALNE VICARAGE, SNAITH R.S.O., YORKSHIRE, ENGLAND, MARCH 14TH, 1892

GHOST MIMICS VOICE OF LIVING FAMILY MEMBER

☞ I heard the voice of my sister-in-law calling me by name loudly and distinctly. I was standing at the gateway—a side entrance to the school—talking with a friend. This was in the Rua Santos Lima, S. Christovão, Rio. It was evening, and between nine and ten o'clock, on the 19th of the present month of October (1891). Two names were really pronounced, my own, Ulysses, and that of my brother-in-law, Bittencourt.

I was talking with my friend Dr. Silva Santos about hypnotism. I was in perfect health. Age 37 years.

The voice was that of my sister-in-law, who lives with me. We were moving from one house to another, and she was at the time in the old house, away from me. She was awake at the time and either talking or occupied in household duties. She neither

Italian Spiritualist Eusapia Palladino, circa early 1900s.

called nor felt any impression whatsoever. While talking she thought of me in relation to the difficulties of accommodation for that night.

Dr. Silva Santos was present and some sixteen of my boys. All heard the voice, and some of the latter ran along the street to see what had become of my sister-in-law. Her voice was recognised by all. The houses opposite were all shut up for the night.[75] — ULYSSES JOSÉ DA COSTA CABRAL, RUA ESCOBAR, 48 RIO, BRAZIL, OCTOBER 28TH, 1891

Mrs. Cora L. V. Richmond, famed Victorian medium and Spiritualist.

CHAPTER FOUR

GHOST OF GERMAN DROWNING VICTIM REVEALS LOCATION OF HIS BODY
☛ From Mr. U. von Ripperda. 3rd hand, or more remote. Some country people at Ratzeburg [Germany], where a fisherman had been drowned and his body not yet recovered, saw in the forest a sort of cloud, from which a voice issued, saying: "Up te dyb!"—the name of a part of the lake, where the body was found the next day. A full account of the facts is said to have been deposited in the archives of Ratzeburg. Date, early part of this century.[76] — JOURNAL OF SOCIETY FOR PSYCHICAL RESEARCH, UK, 1893

POLTERGEISTS OVERRUN HAUNTED HOUSE
☛ From Miss J., through Mr. O. Elton. Miss J. has reasons for withholding address of house, in the country, in which her sister is awakened by cold hand on her face; two servants and her brother have impression at different times of large bird flying about bedroom in the dark; footsteps and knockings are heard continually; two sisters saw door open mysteriously. Occurrences undated.[77] — JOURNAL OF SOCIETY FOR PSYCHICAL RESEARCH, UK, RECORDED 1892

"HORRIBLE APPARITION" MANIFESTS BEFORE TWO MEN
☛ Sent by Mr. Carmichael. Noises heard constantly. Horrible apparition seen one night by Mr. William Curtis and a friend together. Account given in letter from Mr. Curtis, saying that the events happened "three months ago." Undated, but certainly remote.[78] — JOURNAL OF SOCIETY FOR PSYCHICAL RESEARCH, UK, 1893

GHOST OF FORMER HOME-OWNER APPEARS TO TENANT
☛ From Mrs. Lewis Paine. Mrs. Thomson, living in Charles

Lamb's cottage at Edmonton [England], sees an apparition of a man in old-fashioned costume—knee breeches, etc.—standing in the passage one evening. Later on the same evening, she recognises a portrait of Charles Lamb, in a book her husband had bought that day, as representing the man she had seen. Date, "about 8 years ago."[79] — JOURNAL OF SOCIETY FOR PSYCHICAL RESEARCH, UK, 1893

LOUD BELL-RINGING GHOST DISTURBS FAMILY
☛ Through Rev. A. T. Fryer. An account of mysterious bell-ringing in Ewbank Cottage, Loughor, near Swansea [England], occupied by Mr. Richard James. Apparition of a "little grey man," seen twice by Mrs. James. The bells went on ringing in spite of their wires being cut, and swung about violently after they had been stuffed with cotton wool to stop the ringing. Date of events, 1850-1852.[80] — JOURNAL OF SOCIETY FOR PSYCHICAL RESEARCH, UK, RECORDED BY MR. JAMES, 1892

GHOST OF DECEASED YOUNG MAN CRIES OUT
☛ Mrs. Stanton, sleeping in American hotel some years ago, is twice disturbed by hand stroking her face and voice saying, "Oh, mother, mother!"

Next day she learns that young man had died in that room, crying "Oh, mother, mother!" and that his body had been carried out an hour before she took possession of the room.

Mr. Charles McLaren, Reform Club, tells us that he thinks he recollects "Mrs. Stanton relating the story in question at my table in the presence of the correspondent of the paper."[81] — JOURNAL OF SOCIETY FOR PSYCHICAL RESEARCH, UK, PRINTED IN THE *SHEFFIELD INDEPENDENT*, SEPTEMBER 6TH, 1890

HAUNTED HOUSE FILLED WITH RESTLESS SPIRITS
☛ Through Mr. O. Murray. Mrs. N. W. hears noises and sees a woman in grey in a small house in St. John's Wood [England]. (It was the last of a row of semi-detached houses in a *cul de sac* in the N.W. district.)

Her husband also heard noises and independently felt a presence, and told her that his dog was disturbed. A nurse, whose account we have, also saw a figure independently, but it does not appear to have been like that seen by Mrs. N. W. Noises and footsteps seem to have been heard by all.

Mrs. W. has on other occasions seen apparitions (twice of living people) of which the accounts are here given. One of these cases was perhaps veridical. Date of experiences, 1882.[82] — JOURNAL OF SOCIETY FOR PSYCHICAL RESEARCH, UK, RECORDED 1891

FEMALE GHOST IN WHITE STALKS HALLS OF HAUNTED HOUSE

☛ The family had lived in the house about 25 years. Several years ago [around 1:00 AM], when sleeping in the spare room, had heard footsteps as of a person passing the door, who tried the handle and then mounted to the floor above. The door in question was situated just at the top of the principal staircase, which is of stone, and, as would have been the case with any ordinary person, the steps were inaudible till they were on the boarded floor at the top. After trying the door, the wooden staircase to the next floor was heard to creak, accompanied by a peculiar sound of stumbling, as though the person had caught her foot in her dress.

At first Lady B. attributed the sounds to some living person. She, however, mentioned them to her sister, who said she had often heard them. Afterwards she looked out of her door when the sounds were heard, but saw nothing. The maids denied having been out of their rooms, though questioned several times. The walking upstairs and other noises were heard frequently, but sometimes with intervals of months. No importance was attached to them till after the visual experience. This occurred about a year and a half ago.

Lady B. was sleeping in her own room, which is next [to] the spare room, and Miss B. was sleeping in another bed at her side. In the middle of the night both ladies suddenly started up wide awake without any apparent cause, and saw a figure in a white garment, which might have been a nightdress, with dark curly hair. The room was not quite dark, although there was no artificial light except from the gas lamp in the square. No fear nor any physical sensation was experienced. The figure was standing in front of the fireplace, over which was a mirror. The position was such as to show the face in quarter profile

Victorian ghost photo (see arrow).

and to intercept its own reflection from the mirror. It was a female figure, with hair down the back. The face, so far as shown, was clearly visible.

The two ladies both spoke and sprang out of bed to the doors, which they found locked. On turning round again, the figure had disappeared. The maid-servant is said to have seen a figure in daylight in the same position but in a black costume. She took it for a burglar. Nothing since has been noticed except noises.[83] — LADY B., MISS B. (HER DAUGHTER), & MISS D. B. (HER NIECE), CIRCA 1894

SPLASHING GHOST HERALDS DROWNING VICTIM

☛ My mother had been superintending the bathing of her children, and had sent them up to bed. She washed her hands in the bath they had and turned half way back, and was drying her hands when she heard a great splash as if someone had fallen into the bath. She looked round hastily, and was amazed to find not a ripple on the water. She noted the time and date, and afterwards learned that her brother had been drowned at that very time, in a storm at sea. This my mother related to me herself, when I was a girl.[84] — NAME OF WITNESS WITHHELD BY THE S.P.R., AUGUST 1, 1884

A HAUNTED PATH, PALE GHOST, & BLUE LIGHTS

☛ The incident I am about to relate occurred on the 7th of May, 1892, between five and six in the afternoon.

Having gone for a walk, I was returning homewards by a road in the vicinity of St. Boswells [Scotland]. The greater portion of the way is quite level, but at one part a short incline terminates with a sharp corner at the end. From the top of this eminence the whole road is conspicuous, with a hedge and bank on either side. Upon reaching the specified point, and finding time limited, I thought I would expedite matters by running, and had not gone many steps when I came to a sudden halt, for just a few yards beyond I perceived a tall man dressed in black, and who walked along at a moderate pace.

Fancying he would think mine an extraordinary proceeding, I finally stopped altogether to permit of his getting on further, while at the same time watching him turn the corner and pass on where his figure was still distinctly defined between the hedges referred to. He was gone in a second—there being no exit anywhere—without my having become aware of it. Greatly surprised, I then myself passed the same corner and spot where I had seen the man vanish a few seconds before, and here, a short space onward, I saw one of my sisters standing and looking about everywhere in a bewildered manner.

When I came up to her I said: "Wherever has that man disappeared to?" and upon our comparing notes together it became evident that we had both experienced a similar sensation regarding the stranger, the only difference being that I had seen the apparition on in front, while she says he came facing her, and she, too, had noticed he vanished almost immediately. But here the strangest part of it all is that we found that when the man became invisible to her, he appeared to me between the part of the road where she and I were standing. I may also here add that at the time we saw the apparition neither sister knew the other was so near.

Our experience then ended, until some weeks later, for though we thought the encounter a strange one, we did not trouble much about it.

Towards the end of July, and at the same hour as before, another sister and myself were traversing the same spot, when not far distant I observed a dark figure approaching, and exclaimed: "Oh, I do believe that is our man. I won't remove my eyes from him!" and neither we did till he seemed to fade away towards the bank on our right. Not waiting a moment to consider, each rushed frantically to either side of the road, but, of course, saw nothing.

We questioned some boys who were on the top of a hay-cart in the opposite field, and to whom the expanse of road was clearly visible, but they declared no one had passed that way. This time I again viewed the entire figure, while my sister only saw the head and to below the shoulders.

The man was dressed entirely in black, consisting of a long coat, gaiters, and knee-breeches, and his legs were very thin. Round his throat was a wide white cravat, such as I have seen in old pictures. On his head was a low-crowned hat the fashion I am unable to describe. His face, of which I only saw the profile, was exceedingly thin and deadly pale.

Nearly eight months have elapsed since these incidents, but the figure has not appeared to us again, though we frequently have occasion to pass that way, both by daylight and darkness, so in conclusion I must just relate two experiences of others at about the same period as we had our visitations.

Two girls going from the village were attracted near the haunted walk by some wild strawberries growing on the bank. They stopped to gather them, and while thus employed they heard a thud or thump upon the ground beside them, but seeing no one they again continued their occupation. The sound was repeated.

Looking up, they then saw a tall man gazing intently, and they, being almost paralysed with fright at the awful expression of his countenance, clutched one another convulsively and fled precipitately, but after a time, venturing to look back, they saw the figure still standing, and while they looked he gradually faded away. These girls affirm that the man was dressed exactly as I have before described, that his face was white as death, and a white filmy sheet or vapour now enveloped his raiment.

It is [reported] that the same apparition appeared about two years ago to some boys, and, coming up close beside them, instantly melted into space.

Also for nearly a fortnight blue lights were seen after dark near the spot frequented by the ghost; these were not stationary, but moved about in varied directions. Many people followed them, but all attempts to solve the mystery have proved fruitless. No cause can be suggested for the strange proceedings, though legend hath it that a child was murdered close by, but this fact is quite beyond the recollection of the oldest inhabitant of the neighbourhood. The apparition has been visible to many, and few care to traverse his haunts after dark.[85] — MISS M. W. SCOTT (SUBMITTED BY MISS E. E. GUTHRIE, 4 BASK PLACE, ORME-SQUARE, LONDON, ENGLAND, FEBRUARY 20TH, 1893)

TERRIFYING PALLID SPECTER REAPPEARS ON ROAD

☛ [From the same informant as above:] I have again seen the ghost, and under the following circumstances.

On Sunday last, June 12th, at a few minutes before ten in the morning, having occasion to pass that way, I perceived far in front a dark figure, who at that distance was indistinguishable as to whether it were man or woman, but believing the person to be the latter, and one I was acquainted with and likely to meet at that hour, I determined to hurry on and overtake her.

I had not gone far, however, when I soon discovered it to be none other than the apparition we had looked for and failed to see for so many months. I did not then feel at all afraid, and, hoping to get a nearer inspection, boldly followed, running in close pursuit; but here the strangest part of it all is that, though he was apparently walking slowly, I never could get any closer than within a few yards, for in but a moment he seemed to float or skim away. Presently he suddenly came to a standstill, and I began to feel very much afraid, and stopped also. There he was!—the tall spectre dressed as I have described before.

He turned round and gazed at me with a vacant expression, and the same ghastly, pallid features. I can liken him to no one I have ever seen.

While I stood, he still looked intently at me for a few seconds, then resumed his former position. Moving on a few steps he again stood and looked back for the second time, finally fading from view at his usual spot by the hedge to the right. There was no one else on the road but myself, and here I solemnly state that what I have written is not at all traded upon by imagination, as I was not thinking of the apparition at the time, he not having been seen for months previous to this visitation.

This couple's deceased son's spirit image was captured in this Victorian psychic photograph. His actual photo is shown in upper right for comparison.

With this strange experience I now felt really terribly frightened, so much so that I beat a hasty retreat homewards, when further on I met a woman coming along who knew of the bad reputation of the road, and to her I related my adventure. She, too, was terrified, and declared she would go no further alone, so at last I agreed to accompany her onwards to see if we could perceive anything more of the man. We, however, reached our destination in safety, without the ghost becoming visible.

All I can say in conclusion is that I will never voluntarily pass along the same place alone.

The girls who saw the man last summer when gathering wild strawberries, have failed to give me their statements in writing, though I have long waited for them. Perhaps the reason is that being so young they may feel themselves unable to commit their experiences to paper. I am assured, however, that the description I gave of their sensations in my sketch to Miss Guthrie is absolutely correct in every detail.

I have had a splendid inspection of his appearance this time. He wears what is likely to be black silk stockings and shoe-buckles, short knee-breeches, and long black coat. The hat I cannot describe. The man is certainly dressed as a clergyman of the last century, and we have an old picture in the house for which he might have sat.[86] — MISS M. W. SCOTT, JUNE 28TH, 1893

PHANTOM HORSE & RIDER

☛ Three years ago [in 1881], when staying at Ems for my health, one morning after having my bath I was resting on the sofa reading. A slight drowsiness came over me and I distinctly saw the following: My husband, who was then in England, appeared to me riding down the lane leading from my father's house. Suddenly the horse grew restive, then plunged and kicked, and finally unseated his rider, throwing him violently to the ground. I jumped up hastily, thinking I had been asleep, and on my going down to luncheon, I related to a lady who was seated next me what I had seen and made the remark, "I hope all is well at home." My friend, seeing I was anxious, laughed and told me not to be superstitious, and so I forgot the incident, until two days afterwards I received a letter from home saying my husband had been thrown from his horse and had dislocated his shoulder. The time and place of the accident exactly agreed with my vision.[87] — LAURA FLEMING, ENGLAND, 1884

A PROMISE KEPT

☛ Mr. J. R. S. when a boy saw an old schoolfellow, B. M., standing in his bedroom. They had agreed some years previously that whichever of them died first should appear to the other. The apparition was seen by gaslight. B. M. died at the time, Mr. S. not knowing that he was ill. Date about 1880.[88] — JOURNAL OF SOCIETY FOR PSYCHICAL RESEARCH, UK, RECORDED 1889

GHOST OF HUSBAND SEEN TWICE

☛ Repeated apparitions of the same person. Mr. G. A. K. [deceased] is seen twice by his wife—on both occasions out of doors in the evening, once "a year ago," and once since—(she has had other hallucinations of a similar kind); once by his mother-in-law in a room, in November, 1888; once by Mrs. B., 6 or 7 years ago; and once by another lady (no details given).[89] — JOURNAL OF SOCIETY FOR PSYCHICAL RESEARCH, UK, RECORDED MARCH 1889

LIVING ATTEMPTS TO VISIT OTHERS IN SPIRIT

☛ Through American Branch. (1) Dr. Adele Gleason, having arranged with Mrs. E. A. Conner that she should try to appear to her, makes many unsuccessful attempts. One evening Mrs. Conner has a momentary mind's-eye vision of her (recognition doubtful) in a dress similar to one Miss Gleason was thinking of at the time. (2)

Dr. Holbrook has impression of Miss G.'s presence, with some coincidence. (3) Miss G. is wakened by feeling of presence and finds that a certain nurse had been in difficulties and wishing for her help at the time. Dates about 1885.[90] — JOURNAL OF SOCIETY FOR PSYCHICAL RESEARCH, UK, RECORDED 1889

PHANTOM ANNOUNCES UNEXPECTED ARRIVAL OF FRIEND
☞ Mrs. Seeley hears a voice saying the name of a friend of hers a short time before the friend in question calls on her unexpectedly. Date: November 10th, 1891.[91] — JOURNAL OF SOCIETY FOR PSYCHICAL RESEARCH, UK, RECORDED NOVEMBER 19TH, 1891

RELIGIOUS LAMP-CARRYING GHOST IN A CASTLE
☞ Received through the American Branch. Miss M. E. Williams, staying at Schloss Weierburg [Castle], in the Tyrol [Austria], sees a woman in a dark dress with a lamp in her hand, kneeling before the altar in the chapel, who goes away up some steps into the Castle. She finds that no one has been there, and hears later that an artist staying there had seen in the same place a similar figure, which went away up the steps. Undated.[92] — JOURNAL OF SOCIETY FOR PSYCHICAL RESEARCH, UK, RECORDED 1888

TENANTS DRIVEN OUT OF HOUSE HAUNTED BY UNHAPPY GHOST
☞ Through the American Branch. From Mr. P. In a house in Long Island [New York] in which he lived in 1864, mysterious noises were constantly heard by various members of household, one of whom saw several times figure of old woman with cane in hand moving about her room at night. Mr. P. left house on account of disturbances, which also drove away two succeeding sets of tenants. House supposed to be haunted by former owner, whose will had not been found.[93] — JOURNAL OF SOCIETY FOR PSYCHICAL RESEARCH, UK, RECORDED 1890

GIRL GHOST FRIGHTENS PEOPLE & DOGS
☞ Through Mr. W. A. Walker. Miss C. L. Greaves, staying at West Leake Rectory, Loughborough [England], heard rustling in her room at night and saw apparition of girl walking up and down; at same time felt a chill, which left her as the apparition vanished. She saw it three times afterwards, under the same circumstances.

Once a dog was present which showed signs of terror. She heard afterwards that the governess had seen it since in the same room. Undated.[94] — JOURNAL OF SOCIETY FOR PSYCHICAL RESEARCH, UK, RECORDED 1892

GHOST OF IRISH QUAKER WOMAN PRESAGES MARITAL ENGAGEMENT

☛ From Miss E. D. through Miss M. Benson. In the autumn of 1887 Miss D. saw in the afternoon an apparition of an old lady in Quaker dress (face not seen) in house in Ireland. Afterwards heard that such an old lady was supposed to appear when anything of importance was about to happen in the family, but that she had not been seen by anyone living. Soon afterwards Miss D. heard of the engagement of the son of the house to be married. There was a picture of the old lady in the house, which Miss D. must have seen.[95] — JOURNAL OF SOCIETY FOR PSYCHICAL RESEARCH, UK, RECORDED AUGUST 1890

MULTIPLE EYE-WITNESSES SEE GHOST IN DARK PASSAGE

☛ Ramsgate, England. Figure seen by Sister Maria (the matron) and several servants, generally in a dark (?) passage; once by three servants together—one having brought the others to look. Probably all knew of the haunt. Date, 1890.[96] — JOURNAL OF SOCIETY FOR PSYCHICAL RESEARCH, UK, RECORDED 1892

FRIGHTENING PARANORMAL OCCURRENCES ANNOUNCE FATHER'S DEATH

☛ From Mrs. Conrad Hall, of Winchcombe [England]. Daughter in Essex at the time of her father's death heard terrible shaking of window, as if a strong person shook it with all his might; and next morning heard her name called distinctly. A few minutes later she received telegram of her father's death. Date, October 1868.[97] — JOURNAL OF SOCIETY FOR PSYCHICAL RESEARCH, UK, RECORDED DECEMBER 1889

GHOST OF DECEASED WOMAN PROCLAIMS DEATH OF HER HUSBAND

☛ Mrs. N. heard the voice of a deceased friend say, "He's coming soon." Friend's husband died in Jamaica at the time the voice was heard.[98] — JOURNAL OF SOCIETY FOR PSYCHICAL RESEARCH, UK,

MAN'S GHOST WALKS & TALKS AT TIME OF DEATH
☛ Miss M. E. Godwin, when a child, was walking out with a friend when both of them saw a gentleman whom she knew well; she spoke to him, and he answered. Next day they heard that he had died from the effects of an accident exactly at the time she had seen him. Date, over 20 years ago. Further inquiries unanswered.[99] — JOURNAL OF SOCIETY FOR PSYCHICAL RESEARCH, UK, RECORDED 1891

AUDITORY & SENSE IMPRESSIONS HERALD DEATH & SAVE LIFE OF ANOTHER
☛ Through Maria, Lady Vincent. Experiences of Lady. (1) Borderland. She hears her name called twice, and 2 knocks at the door. At the same time a friend about whom she was anxious dies suddenly. Undated. (2) On a snowy afternoon she has impression that an old woman living 3 miles off is wanting her, goes to see, and finds that woman had fallen and been jammed in her staircase for 8 hours. Undated.[100] — JOURNAL OF SOCIETY FOR PSYCHICAL RESEARCH, UK, BOTH RECORDED 1890

SON'S GHOST APPEARS AT TIME OF DROWNING
☛ Mr. and Mrs. Cleverley hear footsteps, and Mrs. C., going out to investigate, sees apparition of her son in another room. He was drowned at the same time by the sinking of the ship *Eurydice*. Confirmed by Mr. C. Undated.[101] — JOURNAL OF SOCIETY FOR PSYCHICAL RESEARCH, UK

HUSBAND'S DECEASED WIFE RETURNS FROM THE SPIRIT WORLD TO OFFER WARNING
☛ The following is an accurate statement of a supernatural occurrence that took place at Gibraltar [Spain] in the year 1839, and which was carefully investigated by myself on the day after it took place, accompanied by the Rev. William Brown, now residing at Gravesend [England], and never afterwards discovered to have been anything but that which it professed to be.

In the month of September, 1839, the Rev. W. Brown called upon me for the purpose of making known that a story was current about the barracks of the 46th Regiment, to the effect that a ghost or spirit had been seen in one of the hospital wards occupied by that regiment, then quartered at the barracks on the Rock, called "The South," adding that he thought the case worth investigating, as two persons were said to have seen it at the same time.

I went with him to the hospital, and after hearing a version of the story from the hospital sergeant, desired that one of the two men (not the principal) who had seen the vision might be sent for.

A private of the 46th named Watson (and a patient in the ward) forthwith attended, and was cautioned by me to be truthful in his statement as I was about to take it down on paper for severe investigation. I then wrote down from his mouth the following:

> "Last night I was lying awake in bed some time after eleven o'clock, not being able to sleep as there was a rushlight at the far end of the ward where one of the patients was dying; also the ward had been disturbed for the previous two nights by the sound of footsteps slowly walking up and down the ward. Whilst turning round in my bed I saw someone sitting upon the foot of the bed of Corporal McQueen. At first I thought it was McQueen himself, but distinguished his head on the pillow. The person sitting remained so still that I thought it sufficiently singular to call out to McQueen, and I called to him, telling him 'there was someone sitting upon the foot of his bed.' He waked up and drew up his knees, and at the same time the person rose off the foot of the bed, and slowly went up to the head of it, rested one hand against the wall and stooped down as if to speak to Corporal McQueen. He drew back his head as if alarmed, and becoming alarmed myself, I don't know why, I buried my head under the sheets, and felt so faint that I did not look up again for perhaps half-an-hour, when I no longer saw anyone by McQueen, who was still sitting up and silent in his bed. I spoke to him, and he made answer for me to go to sleep and not talk."

I and Mr. Brown cross-examined Private Watson, and came fully to the conclusion that he was speaking truly according to his belief. He was not suffering at the time from any disorder affecting the brain. We dismissed him and called in Corporal McQueen. His disorder was simply an injury to the foot or ankle, and likewise not affecting the brain. I warned him as I had done Private Watson, and I then took down his statement in writing, as follows:

> "Last night about 12 o'clock I was awaked by Private Watson, who sleeps opposite to me. He told me that there was someone sitting upon the foot of my bed, and at the same time I saw a person just rising off it and coming towards me. There was enough light by means of a rushlight at the other end of the room to let me see it was not one of the patients, and I gradually distinguished the dress to be grave clothes—a long gown of flannel edged with black tape, and tied up about the wrists and neck with bows of the same; a kind of hood was swathed round the head and face. The figure leant down over me, and at first I felt much alarmed and shrank back. The figure said something, my name, I think, and added: 'I am the spirit of Mary Madden, and bespeak your attention.'
>
> "Mary Madden had been the wife of a comrade of that name, now

at the Depôt of the 46th in Ireland, and she had died just about this time last year. I was a great friend of hers, and was beside her when she died, and put her into her coffin. She was dressed precisely the same as the figure then before me."

"I then felt rather reassured, and asked her what she wanted. She replied that I must communicate with her late husband, Madden, and severely warn him as to a certain evil course he was pursuing; that he was to desist, and that, if he did not desist, his soul would be in immediate peril.' She then told me to warn him of some other matter, and finished by telling me, by way of proof that she was Mrs. Madden's spirit, a circumstance and conversation unknown to anyone in the world, that took place between us before her death, and this I must decline repeating. It was proof to me that Mary Madden's spirit was then beside me, and nothing on earth will convince me to the contrary. After exacting a promise from me that I would fulfil her wish, she said she would not again trouble the ward, and bid me farewell. She then went to the fireplace, and groped over it with her hands about the wall, then turned round and again came towards me, but gradually looked more and more indistinct until at last I lost sight of her altogether. I then became very faint and awe-struck, and remained awake until daylight.

"I have this morning written to her husband in Ireland, in compliance with her wish. There were about 18 men in the ward, but with the exception of the dying man in the corner and Private Watson, I think they were all asleep. This is all I can say of the matter."

Corporal McQueen about three months afterwards came to England with other invalids, and was with them placed under my command on board the *Basett*, Junior Transport. I reminded him of the above matter, and he steadily adhered to his story without the slightest variation. Mr. Brown and myself are fully of opinion that he was speaking the plain and unexaggerated truth.[102] — M. EMMETT, WEEDON BARRACKS, SEPTEMBER, 1854, CAPTAIN, ROYAL BUCKS MILITIA

SCREAMING PHANTOM ANNOUNCES SHIPWRECK

☛ In the autumn of 1859 we were expecting my youngest brother home from Australia, after an absence of eight years. He was a passenger on board the *Royal Charter*.

The night, or rather in the early dawn of the fatal morning of the wreck of that unhappy vessel, I suddenly started out of my sleep and found myself seizing hold of my husband's arm, horrified at the most awful wail of agony, which appeared to me to fill the house. Finding my husband still asleep—he was a medical man, and had been out the whole of the previous night, so was unusually tired—I slipped out of bed and went round to look at all the children and to the servants' room, but found all quietly sleeping, so thinking it must have been the wind only which so disturbed me, I lay down again, but could not sleep. I noticed that day was just breaking.

In the morning I asked different people if they had been disturbed by any unusual noise, but no one had heard it. The post brought a letter from a cousin in Liverpool, telling us the *Royal Charter* was telegraphed as having arrived at Queenstown [New Zealand], and we might expect to see Frank very shortly. We passed the day in most joyful anticipations of the meeting. My mother had his room prepared, a good fire burning, and his night-shirt and slippers laid out for use, and a nice supper ready.

Wheels were heard, but, instead of Frank, my cousin appeared. She, as soon as the awful news of the wreck reached Liverpool, started off herself to bring us the melancholy tidings. Even then I did not connect the fearful sounds I heard with the wreck, but when the newspapers came and I read the accounts of the eye witnesses of the wreck, and of the screams which rent the air as the ship broke her back and all on board were overwhelmed in the waves I could only shudder and exclaim, "*that* was what I heard."

This photograph of a mother (right background) and her daughter (left background) is overlaid by a psychic imprint of the mother's dead father, whose actual photo is shown at lower left.

It was months before I could forget the horror which thrilled my very soul at the remembrance of that awful night. A full month later my poor brother's body was recovered with several others, and was brought home to be laid in the dear little churchyard at Kinwarton. I never have had, at any other time than [this] one . . . a vivid dream of death, or an auditory hallucination of any kind.[103]

— FRANCES A. PURTON, FIELD HOUSE, ALCESTER, ENGLAND, 1884

LOVELY PALE BLUE LIGHT APPEARS TO GIRL AT TIME OF NEIGHBOR'S DEATH

☛ I was living at home with my parents at Eston-in-Cleveland [England]. There was a working man called Long living in the village, not far from our house, whose wife was taken ill. Dr. Fulton, who at that time was staying with us, came in one night between 9 and 10 o'clock and said Mrs. Long was dying. After that we sat talking over the fire a good while, and then my sister Isabella and I went off to bed.

We slept in a back bedroom, and after we got to this bedroom I said, "Oh, I've forgotten something in the large bedroom." To this latter I proceeded by myself, and, as I approached the door, something seemed to say to me, "You'll see something of Mrs. Long, living or dead!" But I thought no more of this, and entered the bedroom, which I had to cross to the opposite end for what I wanted.

When I had got the things in my hand, I noticed a lovely light hanging over my head. It was a round light—perfectly round. I had taken no light with me, but went for the things I wanted in the dark. I looked to see if there was any light coming in from the windows, but there was none in that direction there was total darkness. I grasped one hand with the other and stood looking at the strange light to be sure that I was not deceived and was not imagining it.

I walked across the room to the door, and all the way the light was hanging between my head and the ceiling. It was akin to the electric light: something of a cloud, though every part of it was beaming and running over with light. It left me at the bedroom door. On first seeing it a strange impression seized me, and after it left me I was so impressed that I could not speak of it to anyone for a day or two.

I wondered at the time whether it had anything to do with Mrs. Long, and on inquiry I found that she died just about the time when I saw the light. If there was any difference, I judged it would be a little before, but there would not be much in it. This would be about 11 p.m., and about four years ago. It left an impression on my mind which I have never forgotten, and never shall forget.

Mrs. Long was not ill many days—about two or three; she died rather suddenly. I was rather interested in her. I did not see her during her illness, but had often seen her and talked to her before. I was perfectly well at the time, and was in no trouble or anxiety. My age at the time was 23. I have had no experience of the kind before or since. I saw no figure, only a lovely light. Before telling my sister I made her promise she would not ridicule me nor call me superstitious. To the best of my recollection this is a correct statement.

P.S. The light which I saw was a palish blue. It emitted no rays, so that all the rest of the room was in darkness. It was wider in circumference than my head, so that as I walked I could see it above me without raising my head. As I left the room it remained, and when I looked again was gone. It was in a corner, where the darkness of the room was deepest and the least chance of illumination from the windows on the right and left, that I first saw it above my head. I had no fear, but a kind of sacred awe. The light was unlike any other that I ever saw, and I should say brighter than any other, or, at least, purer. Looking at it did not affect the eyes. It was midway between my head and the ceiling.[104] — MARY HELENA WILLIAMS, 11 CLEVELAND-TERRACE, COATHAM, REDCAR [ENGLAND], SEPTEMBER 23ᴿᴰ, 1889

THE SIGHING GHOST

☛ In the year 1890 we came to live at Firbeck House [UK], the family place, where Mr. Thompson's father and mother had lived, and where their two youngest children were born. We had been in the house about a month, and I and the three youngest children were sleeping in the room on the front landing hitherto occupied by Mr. Thompson's only sister, whose name is Margaret.

I had not gone to bed, but was sitting over the fire about 12 p.m., or later, when, hearing someone say "Margaret," I thought Mrs. Thompson (who slept on the same landing) was calling me, and I went out of the room expecting to find her in the passage. I stood a moment, seeing no one there, and heard a deep sigh close to me. I was so astonished at hearing this and seeing no one, as I had quite expected, that I felt I could not turn round, and I went backwards way into my room again and shut the door. It made me feel rather nervous.

The next morning I told the governess what I had heard, and said to her, "I will not tell Mrs. Thompson, as she is nervous in this house." This happened on the Saturday night.

On the following Monday, February 10ᵗʰ, Mrs. Thompson got a telegram in the afternoon to say Mr. Edward, her youngest brother-in-law, had just died quite suddenly of apoplexy at an hotel.

I was in my usual health; my age was nearly 37 years.

I had seen Mr. Edward about two months before, but we knew nothing of what he was doing at the time. Mr. and Mrs. Thompson have since been told that Mr. E. Thompson was ill on the Saturday night and Sunday morning, and that his thoughts were evidently dwelling much upon his sister, to whom all her brothers are much attached, and who was a good deal older than this brother. He was better on the Sunday afternoon, and his death on Monday was quite unexpected, and his family none of them knew that he was poorly till they heard of his death.

I told the governess next morning, and I told Mrs. Thompson after we heard of the death.[105] — MARGARET CLARKE, JANUARY 9TH, 1891

SPIRIT OF SICK FRIEND GRASP'S WOMAN'S ARM

☛ At Exeter, one afternoon in spring, March 1882, I had a distinct impression of feeling a hand grasp my arm, and felt a rough coat against my shoulder. I had a vague sort of impression that a friend of mine, who was then in South Africa, was appealing to me in some way, and was in distress. I wrote out to South Africa at once, and after some months discovered he was very ill, having fallen from the top of a house on that day.

I was writing a letter to a comparative stranger. I was in good health and spirits, and very busy. [My age was] 19.

I had not seen this friend for several years, but was much interested in him. I occasionally heard from him by letter. I was not thinking of him at the time, and was much startled by the sudden feeling.[106] — MISS A. T., NOVEMBER 14TH, 1889

DOCTOR'S GHOST APPEARS AT CHURCH

☛ On Saturday, July 1st, 1893, I was in L_____ for the purpose of looking over the old churches with a friend with whom I was staying. Among others we went to St. M_____'s. My friend had been telling me of a very dear old friend of the family who was buried in that church, and who had left a sum of money to have a window put in to his memory, and had even had the window prepared for the glass to be put in, but that the person who had inherited his fortune neglected his wish. (I don't know how many years he had been dead.)

After we had looked over the church, and among other things seen the brass over this gentleman's vault, we came to the window which ought to have been filled in. I remember that the neglect of his wish quite made me angry, and I said, looking at the window, "If I was Dr._____ I should come back and throw stones at it."

Just then I saw an old gentleman behind us, but thinking he was looking over the church took no notice. But my friend got very white and said "Come away, there is Dr._____!"

Not being a believer in apparitions, I simply for the moment thought she was crazy, though I knew they were a ghost-seeing family. But, when I moved, still looking at him, and the figure before my very eyes vanished, I had to give in. Then it dawned upon me that nobody could have been looking over the church but ourselves.

First, the church had been empty when we went in, and nobody could have come in without their footsteps being heard, and secondly, the part where we were standing ended in a *"cul de sac,"* and the person to get there would have been obliged to ask us to move, as we entirely blocked up the narrow aisle.

For the few moments he was visible I saw him distinctly; he was short and broad, and wore an old-fashioned tie, and a waistcoat cut low and showing a great deal of shirt-front. One hand was resting on a pew, and one down at his side holding his very tall hat. But the thing that struck me most was the sun shining on his white hair, and making it look like silver; even now I can see him distinctly in my mind's eye. It certainly surprised me to see what was apparently "too solid flesh" disappear before my very eyes, and when we got outside my friend told me that his was the figure which came to different members of their family so often, and, indeed, had been the cause of their leaving one house. One of her sisters had so been affected by it, that she will never sleep alone, or go upstairs alone. When we got home I easily recognised the Doctor by his photograph.[107] — MISS F. ATKINSON, 25 ALDERSHOT-ROAD, WILLESDEN-LANE, LONDON, ENGLAND, NOVEMBER 5TH, 1893

GHOST OF DECEASED SISTER IN SOUTH AMERICA & GHOST OF FRIEND IN INDIA MANIFEST IN LONDON

☛ A sister of mine went to South America, and married there. One morning I was in bed [in London, England] about 11 o'clock, when there was a knock at my door; thinking it was the house-maid with hot water, I said "Come in." No one came in. There was another knock; again I said "Come in," and turned towards the door. My sister was standing there. I, thinking she had returned unexpectedly, said "What, you, Elsie?" She then vanished.

When I went downstairs I told my husband, who said "Don't tell your mother, or she will think something has happened to her." We heard a month later that she had died, after a few hours' illness, about that time.

On December the 6th, 1892, I returned home about 11:30

P.M., after spending the evening with some friends. On going upstairs, I saw a tall man so close to me that I put out my hand to push him back, but my hand went into space. I again moved forward, when he was close in front of me, and, though I couldn't see his face, I recognised the figure of a great friend of mine in India. I went into my sitting-room, almost expecting to find him there.

A week later I got the news of his death at Bombay, on the evening of the 6th. He had always said that if anything happened to him, he would let me know. I may add I wrote to an old ship-mate of his, and told him of my experience, on the morning of the 7th.[108]
— MRS. SCOTT, THE ELMS, ACTON HILL, LONDON, ENGLAND, NOVEMBER, 25TH, 1893

UNSEEN SPIRIT COMMUNICATES WITH DAUGHTER
☛ Mrs. Tweedale one evening in January 1880, heard call, "Violet, come at once," repeated twice. Next day she received telegram from her sister at Nice [France], sent the evening before, summoning her to Nice, her mother having been taken ill there.[109]
— JOURNAL OF SOCIETY FOR PSYCHICAL RESEARCH, UK, RECORDED NOVEMBER 1892

DOG'S GHOST SEEN AT TIME OF NEAR-DEATH EXPERIENCE
☛ 2nd hand. Miss M. L. Pendered relates that a friend of hers and her mother saw a terrier who had gone out with the former's sister, curled up on the hearthrug. The sister came in half an hour later and told them that the terrier had been nearly drowned at the time they saw him. No date given.[110] — JOURNAL OF SOCIETY FOR PSYCHICAL RESEARCH, UK, RECORDED JANUARY 1891

VISION OF DYING WOMAN IN LONDON
☛ Some years since my brother paid a visit, one Saturday evening, to a family residing in one of the London suburbs. He was on the point of returning to town, when the lady of the house (who had been unusually vivacious during the evening) suddenly broke a blood-vessel in her head. A rupture had taken place once before in the same part, so a fatal termination was momentarily expected.

This impression was shared by my brother; but he does not seem to have felt it acutely until the following Sunday evening, when, under the gentle stimulus of an apparently tedious discourse, his thoughts reverted, for a short time, to the lady. Conversation, and a short walk with a friend, however, directed his attention

Our soul (which contains our mind and spiritual body) is connected to our physical body via an elastic-like "cord" that is attached to the region of the solar plexus, allowing out-of-body experiences, or OBEs, without actually dying—as illustrated here. This ethereal band, also known as the "life thread," is referred to in the Bible as the "silver cord," where it is noted that "the spirit shall return unto God" (i.e., death ensues) if and when the cord is severed (Ecclesiastes 12:6-14).

elsewhere; but after reading at his lodgings and partaking of a meal, he was attacked, precisely at 10 o'clock, by an extreme feeling of uneasiness. Again he thought of the sick lady, and discussed the subject of her illness with a younger brother, his anxiety now increasing. He retired to rest at 11 o'clock, and had scarcely laid down, when, being still wide awake, he thought he saw the lady in bed, with her servants and two men by her side. One of the men said: "She is dead"; but the other, whom he took for a physician, gave her some medicine. Hereupon the lady struggled, the vision vanished, and my brother felt impressed with the notion that she was perfectly well again.

A letter of inquiry having been sent the following Monday to his friends, my brother was informed that, as the local doctor feared the worst, a City physician was telegraphed for at 11 p.m., and that until midnight, when recovery took place, hope had been resigned. My brother had, therefore, been affected at first by only a simultaneous impulse; but he had anticipated the result of the crisis by three-quarters of an hour.[111] — EDMUND J. MILLS, D.SC., LONDON, ENGLAND (FROM THE *SPECTATOR*, MARCH 6TH, 1869)

BRILLIANT LIGHT & SHADOW PORTEND DEATH OF FRIEND

☛ The Rev. _____ L. on waking finds the room filled with a brilliant light, and sees the shadow of a woman on the blind. A friend of his dies the same night.[112] — JOURNAL OF SOCIETY FOR PSYCHICAL RESEARCH, UK, DATE 1885

DECEASED GREAT-AUNT APPEARS TO CHILD

☛ Mrs. R., when a child of 13 or 14, wakes one morning and sees her great-aunt standing by her grandmother's bed. The same day they heard of her death during the night.[113] — JOURNAL OF SOCIETY FOR PSYCHICAL RESEARCH, UK, UNDATED

PARENTS' GHOSTS RETURN TO HAUNT FAMILY
☛ My father [Rev. Henry O'Donnell, M.A., at one time Rector of Upton Modsbury, W. Worcester, and Chaplain to the late Lord Kingsdown], who was the direct descendant (pedigree in hands of my brother, Captain Henry O'Donnell, Royal Staff College) of Red Hugh [O'Donnell], left England at the commencement of 1873 in company with the Rev. X., an old friend of his. Their destination was to be Jerusalem, a visit long cherished by my father, but, unfortunately, he fell in with a man [here] designated by the name Colonel Y., afterwards proved to be a member of the Weymouth swindling gang. Persuaded by this individual to alter his course, he accompanied him to Massowah [Eritrea], leaving the Rev. X. to go on by himself.

On April 3rd my father went hunting, leaving the little village of Achiboin the company of several natives and—so we believe—his white comrade, Colonel Y. The exact manner of his death has never been ascertained, but it was suggested by various inhabitants of Massowah that he was murdered.

Now for the ghostly part of the narrative.

My father, shortly before leaving England, was heard by one Fanny Coldwell, then and now cook in our house, to say that if anything happened to him on his travels, he would let my mother know. My mother, being a nervous and superstitious lady, begged him not to say such things, whereupon he replied that he would not appear to her, but would make a horrible noise in the house; this he said laughingly.

From the time of his death to the end of the following May, every night at twelve o'clock, a terrible disturbance took place in the hall, sounds as if the furniture was being thrown about being distinctly heard, together with a tramping upstairs. Moreover, the reflection as of a lighted candle was seen under the crack of the nursery door, which, although bolted, was thrown violently open, and to the horrified inmates some one (whose voice they recognised as that of my father) was heard jabbering incoherently.

At the end of January 1881, my mother died. On the night of the burial, at about twelve o'clock, the servants distinctly heard some one (whose step they recognised as hers) walk round and round the middle landing, pausing outside each door, especially the one within which I lay coughing. Then they heard her open the room door where her body had lain, and which was locked, the key being departed elsewhere, and close it with a loud bang, relocking it.

A few days later the cook, upon running upstairs for something, saw my mother looking down at her from the landing above. Scared by the apparition, she turned and hurried back to the kitchen. These incidents I can vouchsafe as absolutely true, without the slightest blemish of exaggeration.[114] — ELLIOTT O'DONNELL, HENLEY HOUSE SCHOOL, MORTIMER-ROAD, KILBURN, N.W., LONDON, ENGLAND, JANUARY 13TH, 1899

The spirit image of this man's deceased wife appears on the right in this Victorian psychic photograph.

CHAPTER FIVE

STRANGE LOOKING GHOST TERRIFIES CHILD
☞ [From the same informant as above:] One evening, whilst I was in bed, it being about seven o'clock, and a candle still burning on the dressing table, I was amazed to see a strange looking man enter. Between the door and my bed was another bed, the valance of which was up. Being but a child, I was too curious to know who he was to be really frightened, for although he was ugly and covered with spots (a feature I distinctly remember), I merely regarded him in the light of a visitor who had come to amuse me.

For several moments he peeped at me from above and under the bed I have mentioned, accompanying each action with a grimace of increasing ferocity that at length frightened me so that I screamed and hid my face under the bedclothes, and when next I looked up he had gone; nor did I ever see him again.[115] — ELLIOTT O'DONNELL, 1899

GHOSTLY CYCLIST APPEARS & DISAPPEARS
☞ [From the same informant as above:] One afternoon in the spring of 1896, as I was riding along the main road from Wheedon to Daventry, I became aware of the presence of a cyclist in grey who rode slowly ahead of me. The curious part of it was that a second before I had looked round, and the road, a very long and level one, had been absolutely void of life. Now here was some one who had sprung suddenly and noiselessly to life.

For some distance we continued our course, until we came up to a large cart which was rattling along in the centre of the thoroughfare, the driver blissfully careless of any one else's welfare save his own. To my horror my mysterious companion ran with great force right into the back of the cart and disappeared. Not a vestige of either him or his machine was to be seen, and I rode on wondering whether I had been dreaming.[116] — ELLIOTT O'DONNELL, 1899

GHOST OF LIVING WOMAN SLAMS DOOR

☛ [From the same informant as above:] In August, 1885, I was staying with my relations at a lodging house in Newquay, Cornwall.

One afternoon I was standing on the staircase, when I saw a friend of ours, whom I will call Miss D., who was staying with us, come down the stairs followed by my two sisters. She disappeared into the sitting-room at the foot of the staircase, shutting the door with a bang. Each of us saw her, and all heard the door bang.

As a matter of fact, she had never entered that room nor been near it at the time, but subsequently appeared in a totally [different] part of the house. We feared this appearance was an augury of ill, but happily nothing followed to confirm our anticipations.[117] — ELLIOTT O'DONNELL & HELENA O'DONNELL, 1899

HORRIFIC FACE OF GHOSTLY MAN APPEARS TO CHILD

☛ It was in the morning of a day in the spring of 1873 that I saw the [spectre's] head, which was afterwards seen by another member of our family.

I had been sent out of the room for some one, and as I looked up to call them, I saw the most terrible head looking over the bannisters at me. It was the face of a man, but the hair was long like a woman's. The parchment-like skin was drawn closely over the face and gave a skull-like look to it. The mouth, full of great teeth, was twisted in a horrid leer; but what frightened me most was the expression of the eyes. They were so very light and full of the most wicked cruelty, as if they existed for the sole purpose of trying to terrify a little child like I was then.

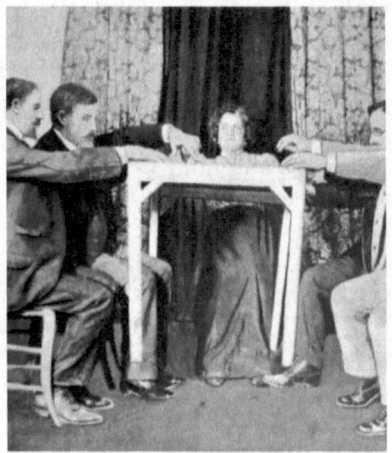

Victorian table levitation.

That was the impression the horrid thing gave me as I stood staring at it—that it knew it was frightening me nearly to death, and that it was hugging itself with joy at the thought; and, moreover, that that was why it was there, and that it was allowed to do this wicked deed for some purpose.

I had a great feeling of indignation in my heart, as I stood, for what seemed ages to me, looking at it, for I could not draw my eyes away. Then I went quietly back to the room I had come from, and, being proud and sensitive, never told any one a word about it for many years, when I found that my sister had seen it too, but some years after.

I said at the time that I thought some one was upstairs, and persuaded a servant to go and look, which she did. She thought I had heard a noise and been frightened by it: of course, she found no one there. [Note: There was a death in the family, though I did not hear of it till some time after.]¹¹⁸ — PETRONELLA O'DONNELL, 1899

WAILING DEATH-WRAITH BREAKS WINDOW

☛ During a night in the year 1812, or thereabouts, somewhere about 1 or 2 o'clock, as my mother lay half awake, after her first sleep, as it is termed, she was suddenly startled and alarmed by a terrible crash on the window of the bedroom, by which the whole glass was apparently shivered to pieces in a moment; and immediately thereafter, as if in the distance, a low, melancholy wail, though quite distinct, of "O Vale, Vale." My mother, in great trepidation, instantly awoke my father, and informed him that the whole window was smashed to pieces, so strongly was the circumstance impressed on her mind, begging him to procure a light instantly and ascertain what was wrong, for there was some one outside in terrible distress.

My father immediately proceeded to make the necessary investigation and found as perhaps he somewhat expected, the window quite intact, nor was there any storm, the night being comparatively calm, to account for the delusion under which my mother was labouring. She was, however, terribly agitated and insisted that inquiry should be made in the morning of the wife of the captain of a little vessel in which they were all interested, and who lived in the town about a mile distant.

Now, to understand properly the full bearing of all the circumstances attending the singular phenomenon, it will be necessary to relate some previous circumstances and arrangements entered into betwixt my father and certain other parties. My mother had a special school companion and friend of the name of "Vale" Fenwick (whatever contraction the Christian name may indicate) who married a young sailor who had been employed as a ship captain, but he had fallen out of employment after their marriage, and, in order to get him a more lucrative appointment, my mother, at her friend's instigation, induced my father to join him in purchasing a nice little brig for £900, of which each paid the one-half. The speculation turned out a very satisfactory one till the time that the curious little incident recorded above happened.

In the morning following the little episode related above, after a sleepless night, my mother's nervous agitation and anxiety for the safety of her early friend's husband, were little allayed, and a messenger was at once despatched to inquire of the captain's wife if she had had recent intelligence from her husband. She replied that she had had a letter from her husband a few days previously, from a port in the Moray Firth, and that they were all well.

Some little time afterwards, on communicating with the authorities at the port, from which the captain's last letter had been sent, my father was informed that the vessel had sailed thence, about eleven o'clock, at the flood-tide, without having shipped any ballast, having only a short distance to sail to another port, where she was to load a cargo, and this was ascertained to be on the very night on which my mother's singular illusion took place; and it was added that there was a rumour that a vessel of her size had been sighted by some boats setting out for the fishing early in the morning on her beam ends or bottom up, somewhere about 3 or 4 o'clock in the morning, and that she had settled down before they had lost sight of her, and this was the last that ever was heard of the ill-fated vessel or her crew.

When the melancholy facts were fairly brought home to the poor wife, she lost her reason for a time, and was ever after so nervous that she could never be trusted alone. There was no previous circumstance, whatever, that could form an association of ideas, or other connecting link, to account for the apparition, or rather, telepathic (?) influence. Of course, my evidence is, in a manner, second-hand, but as young people have always a hankering after the supernatural or ghost stories, we induced my mother to relate the circumstances to us over and over again, and all the minutia seemed quite indelible from her mind, as naturally the loss of the money was a serious consideration for the family, even without the vexation for an early friend, suddenly left in ruin and despair. As these narrations generally took place in my father's presence, we had his acquiescence in all the circumstances; and as to my mother's veracity, no one could possibly stand higher in the opinion of her family as a lover of the truth.[119] — MR. THOMAS HUME, 109, WARRENDER PARK ROAD, EDINBURGH, SCOTLAND, AUGUST 19TH, 1884

CADAVEROUS APPARITION TERRIFIES COLLEGE STUDENT

☛ In [Michaelmas term, 1897], I had gone to bed unusually late, about half-past one in the morning, and shortly after getting into bed I heard a noise in my sitting-room and called out "Who is there?" Receiving no answer, I got out of bed and went into my sitting-room. It was a moonlight night, the blind was up, and there was still a fire burning in the grate.

I saw a figure standing by the window with its back turned to me, which, as soon as I entered the sitting-room, turned round and walked towards me. It was about the middle height and loosely dressed, as I thought in grey. The face was a long clean shaven one, cadaverous and at the same time pitiful in expression, and I am perfectly confident when I say that I could see right through the figure and distinctly saw the bars on the window through it. I was naturally excessively frightened and for a second could do or say nothing.

Apparition of a girl spotted in an English churchyard.

Then I turned tail and bolted into my bedroom and locked the door and shortly afterwards I heard a shuffling noise as of some one leaving my room and passing along the passage. I then lit a candle and went into my sitting-room again and saw nothing. I was in a streaming perspiration and yet felt icy cold and my reflection in the glass showed my face as white as a sheet.

I have not been able to find any explanation of the apparition and did not see anything more of it, (though several other men in college had similar experiences of it) until Michaelmas term 1898. Then came my second experience.

I had been working till eleven and then went to bed. Some time in the night, I cannot say exactly when, I was awakened by a sound in my room (I should mention I had changed to different rooms on the same staircase, on the second instead of on the third floor) and I lit a candle and went into my sitting-room to see who was there;

for some moments I saw nobody and was going back to bed when I caught sight of a figure standing in a corner of my room.

It was exactly similar to the one I had seen before, [several] . . . terms previously; the face had the same pitiful and mournful-looking expression, and it advanced towards me holding out its hands as if it wanted something. I remember no more; I was terribly frightened and fainted right away. I was found by my scout the next morning, when he came to call me, lying in front of my fireplace with the extinguished candle on the floor.

I went to the Principal and told him the circumstances, but he was inclined to treat it as a joke. I can give no explanation of it and can only say that it was a ghastly experience.

I knew that a former undergraduate committed suicide on this staircase, about twenty years ago, but do not know if there be any connection between this and the apparition I saw. Other men have had similar visitations and one man had to go down three weeks before the end of term through being so much troubled by it.

I was genuinely and thoroughly frightened and am perfectly convinced it was a supernatural apparition that I saw. The idea of the ghost is looked upon far too seriously in the College for any one to play a practical joke, and I can only say that another such visitation would cause me to migrate elsewhere.[120] — MR. A., 1899

SPECTRAL FACE & DUELING SPIRITS APPEAR AT COLLEGE

☞ I am not quite sure about actual dates, etc., but my first experience was one night in the fifth week of the October term, 1897. I was a Freshman, and had the ground floor room on No. 3 staircase. I had been to sleep for sometime and woke up with a very uncomfortable feeling that something was wrong.

After sitting up and rubbing my eyes the feeling resolved itself into the conviction that some one was looking in [at] my bedroom window. I almost laughed at the idea, for though the window was just over the bed, the room being very small, there was a thick curtain drawn across it, and I put it down to imagination and tried to go to sleep again.

Failing to do so, I resolved to satisfy myself and, getting up, drew the curtain, and was very much startled to actually see a face gazing straight in. The face was really all I could see, and I think had that been the only time I saw it, that I could not have described it, for it appeared to vanish after I had looked at it for a very short time.

I lit a candle, and after thinking some time, came to the natural conclusion that it was somebody who had got into the churchyard immediately outside (though I afterwards found that this would be a very difficult matter). I looked at my watch, as I always do when I wake in the night, and found it was just after 2 o'clock a.m.

I said nothing about it to any one, and soon was quite satisfied in my mind that it was nothing mysterious.

However, two or three nights afterwards, I woke again with the same uncanny feeling (and to avoid repetition I might add that the appearances were always accompanied with this horrible or at least very uncomfortable feeling); and sitting up again saw the face, now at the end of my bed, gazing straight at me with a very sad expression. I noticed this particularly, as I was able to look at it fixedly for what seemed quite a long time, and this time I observed too that it was possessed by the figure of a man, which was too indefinite to describe accurately, but he had on what looked like a white front or ruffle. The face was rather thin, clean-shaved, and with clear-cut features. I also noticed that the hair was short and thin. Perhaps I did not notice all this on this occasion, but I find it difficult to detach from each appearance what I actually saw each time.

I reached for my matches and struck a light and when my eyes got accustomed to the light, there was nothing there. Now, nobody could pass out of my room without brushing past me, on account of the size of the room; neither, to my knowledge, is there any other exit.

After this the same thing happened two or three times, and I was able to see that the figure appeared to be dressed in knee-breeches and stockings of a dark texture, and each time all it did was to gaze sadly at me. I was never able to challenge it—I suppose on account of fright—and I maintained silence on the question until a more curious thing still happened, and this I think was one night in the seventh week of that term.

You will notice that up to this time it was nothing but a visual experience, unaccompanied by noise, and this was gradually tending to restore my nerve, and I slept for several nights without being aroused. The appearances were always at about the same time.

One night in the seventh week of term, I think, I was awakened in the same curious manner, and sitting up thought I heard a slight noise in my sitting-room. I listened, and it seemed to continue, as though a scuffle was going on, but I certainly felt the noise rather than heard it. What I mean by this is that the noise seemed to be more suggested to me than audible, but whatever it was I reached out of bed and pushed open the door, which I could not reach from the bed, and looked into the other room.

It was moonlight, and the light was coming in from the quad, although the blind was drawn. The noise was still going on in a dark corner of the room (granted it may have been rats!); but as I looked, two figures emerged from the dark into the patch of light which came through the window. They appeared to be fighting; I can only so describe it. It was just as though I was watching the enactment of a duel, for though I could see no weapons, yet the figures were apart, and one, for certain, had his hand towards the other!

There was no imagination about this! I had to watch it in spite of myself! And one figure was, I feel sure, the figure of my previous visitor.

I don't know how short or long the time was in which the "scuffle" lasted, but presently there was a slight thud, and then my sitting-room door shut audibly, as though some one had gone out. Then I jumped out of bed, and striking a match, inspected the room, but there was nothing to be seen.

Naturally I came to the conclusion that some of the men were playing a joke upon me, and in the morning I went to every one in turn to know if they had been to my room, as I had had enough of it. Every one emphatically disclaimed having done so, and a meeting was convened to consider the matter. I am sure from that time that nobody had part in it, and it was then that I was told of the supposed ghost.

I did not stay in my rooms at night after that. Two or three of us sat up for two nights, and on the second night, sitting up in the room overhead, we all heard the same sequence of noises, viz., the scuffle, the thud, and the door shutting, and this was at the usual time: five or six minutes past two. We kept watch on the window and the door of my rooms from the window upstairs; it was possible to do so; and nobody came out, and on immediately descending thither we could find nothing unusual. That day I came home with my nerves very much upset, and since then have occupied rooms on another staircase. Several different men have had experiences of a slighter nature, especially on No. 4 staircase. I have given my history of the case as nearly as possible, and hope there may yet be some explanation.[121] — MR. B., 1899

GHOST OF LONG-DECEASED WOMAN CLIMBS STAIRS

☛ My mother-in-law, Mrs. P., died in 1864. Mr. P., who died in 1882, lived at _____, Essex [England], and for some years before he died spent Christmas regularly with his daughter, my wife, at _____, where we now reside. I neither drink nor smoke; nevertheless, I always go to bed late and last.

At the top of the first flight of stairs a small side staircase leads to the room which Mr. P. always occupied when staying with us, and which he occupied on the night in question.

In the Christmas week of 1881, as I approached the top of this first flight of stairs to go to bed, I saw Mrs. P. walking up the side staircase. I stopped at the top of the first flight of stairs to let the candle burn steadier, and when Mrs. P. reached the last step of the side staircase she vanished at the door. There was no mistaking her figure and left side face as she walked in advance of me, and so natural was it that for a second I expected to hear her turn the door-handle. I had no thought of alarm and as the remembrance that she had died years ago came upon me, I mused as I reflected that Mr. P. was asleep within the room. Mr. P. died in the following July.[122] — OCTOBER 10TH, 1891

EXPERIENCES IN AN IRISH HAUNTED HOUSE

☛ In the year 1892 I was living in a house [near] the city of Londonderry [Northern Ireland]. It was early in January that the following incident happened.

I went to bed about 10:30 [P.M.] and shortly afterwards was sound asleep. During the night I heard loud talking in the room, but at first I did not open my eyes. As the talking continued, I looked up and distinctly saw an old lady standing at the foot of the bed, and gazing intently at me. To get a good view of her I sat up in bed and watched her for fully five minutes, she all the time looking quietly into my face. There was no light in the room at the time, but still I could see her quite distinctly, as there was a halo round her.

After watching her for some time I reached out my hand to the match-box to strike a light, but as soon as I moved my hand towards the matches I saw the face getting more indistinct. I therefore drew back my hand and watched the figure getting more and more dim till it suddenly vanished.

Then a curious thing happened.

Outside the house and within ten yards of the bedroom window I had two kennels, in which a bulldog and a fox terrier were chained. The moment the figure vanished these two dogs began to bark furiously and seemed terribly excited, as if they were trying to get at some one. I conclude that they must have seen the spirit after it left my room, for before it disappeared everything about the place was perfectly quiet. The dogs continued barking for a few minutes and then all was quiet again.

The following August I left this house and let it furnished. After [my tenant] had been in the house for about three months, I asked him one day if he ever saw or heard anything peculiar about the place. He laughed and said he did not believe in ghosts, but that their parlour-maid had seen something. I asked him what it was, and he told me that one night he and his wife were in the drawing-room and the servants had just gone upstairs to bed. A few minutes later the parlour-maid came into the room looking very frightened. She said that as she was passing the spare room (the one I was in the night I saw the spirit) an old lady suddenly walked out of the room, crossed the passage in front of her, and disappeared into the bedroom opposite. When I let the house I never mentioned to any one what I had seen, and the servants were entire strangers in the district, having come from Dublin.

I may add that a great deal of trouble came to us between the visit of the spirit to me and our leaving the house at the end of the following August. For one thing our only baby child died on the 1st of August, and on the night before the cook was too frightened, by hearing spirits around her, to go to her bedroom, but

Midnight attack: A fearsome spectre lunges at a terrified man in the moonlight.

preferred to sleep at the foot of the nurse's bed, where they both heard the strangest sounds, as did the nurse on the following night just before the child died.

After [my tenant] left, I put my gardener and his wife into the house to look after it, and although they had it rent free, nothing would persuade them to stay. They said they could not live in such a place, and detailed to us the strangest experiences.

The only other spiritual being I saw in the house (although I often heard them) was the day before we left, when about 6 P.M. I was standing under some trees about 100 yds. from the house. Then I saw a shadowy substance about 3 or 4 ft. high running quickly up the path beside me. I stepped out into the path to get a full view of it. It went very fast and I thought it was going to pass the house, but the moment it got opposite the hall door it suddenly bounded to the right through the doorway into the hall. The door was open and my wife came out a moment later, but had seen nothing.

After I had seen the first spirit of the woman, my wife asked a lady who had lived there previously if she had ever seen anything of the kind. She replied that their servant had on several occasions seen an old woman in spirit form, and from her account it was evidently the same as I had seen.[123] — MR. D., 1898

THE PHANTOM FACE IN THE WINDOW

☛ I may remark first of all I am considered by my friends as possessing iron nerves, am passionately fond of athletics, and certainly not given to letting imagination or fear run off with my senses. But although I can without boasting say I hardly know what fear is, I am peculiarly susceptible to mental impressions, that is, I can often tell what is passing in the minds of others (especially of my wife) when out walking with them, so much so that I have almost frightened one or two people by offering to tell them the subject on which they were thinking, and in some cases exactly what they were thinking about that subject.

However, I dare say that is common enough, but what I am particularly writing you on is to tell you two facts, one of which occurred 10 years ago, and the other seven years ago nearly. It seems along time ago to be produced, but to me the scenes are fresh as if they only happened yesterday.

The first was this. I was going from the house I lived at to a shop kept by my brother, and when about half-way it came on to rain very fast. I called in at the house of a lady friend and waited some time, but it did not clear, and as I was afraid my brother would be leaving, I said I must go. I rose to do so, and went into the hall and my friend rushed away upstairs to get an umbrella, leaving me in the dark.

In the higher part of the door was a glass window, and I all at once, in the darkness, saw a face looking through that window. The face was very well known to me, though for the instant I did not associate it with the original, as she was 300 miles away. I instantly opened the door, found nobody there, and then searched the ivy with which the porch and house are covered. Finding nothing, and knowing it was impossible anyone could have got away, I then for the first time inquired of myself whose was the face I had seen. I at once knew the face was that of a married sister-in-law of my wife's.

I told all our family of the circumstance directly I got home, and judge of our dismay when the next day we had a telegram to say she died at the very hour I saw her.[124] — T. W. GOODYEAR, FEBRUARY 9, 1884

A GHOSTLY HORSE & CARRIAGE

☛ To-day, December 27th, 1899, my mother, brothers, and sister had taken some small cousins and two other children to the pantomime [a popular particpatory theater event based around folk tales and music]. Some of the party, including my mother, went in a brougham [a four-wheeled, one-horse carriage]. During the performance the coachman seems to have taken more to drink than was expedient, for believing which there are reasons, though it cannot be proved that he was actually drunk.

On the way home the brougham collided with an omnibus [a horse-drawn vehicle that carried as many as 20 people], and suffered some injury, though no one in it was hurt.

The party started home from the theatre (the Lyceum) at about 5:10 or 5:15 p.m. At about 4:30 p.m. a maid saw the brougham waiting at the front door of this house. She saw the coachman's face, and says she could swear to its having been he. She also saw one of my cousins (who was not in the vehicle at the time of the accident) step out of the brougham and run up the steps toward the house. She heard no bell ring. A few minutes later she saw the brougham in the yard with the horse taken out and the coachman walking about in stable boots, as if cleaning the carriage. She told the housemaid what she had seen. She also told my grandmother.

My grandmother told me at about 4:55 p.m. that Howe (the maid) had seen the brougham. At about the time that the maid saw the brougham—I should say about 4:35 p.m.—I thought I heard a brougham draw up and some one get out and run up the steps. I heard no bell. I looked out of the window and saw a brougham drive out of the front garden. I assumed it to be ours, and watched it, wondering where it was off to; it did not take the direction I thought most probable. I then assumed it to have been the brougham of some visitor, but I subsequently found that the servants knew nothing of any one having called, nor did my grandmother.

When the latter told me that Howe had seen the brougham (i.e., our brougham) I said that it was a mistake and that it was some other brougham. When I came into the room where my grandmother was at about 5:30 p.m., I heard the maid saying something to her about going into the witness-box. My grandmother told me that the maid was positive she had seen our coachman. My mother and those with her arrived home about 6:30. Those of the party who came by train arrived about 6:15. The maid told me what she had seen at about 7:15 p.m.

When I cross-questioned her about it a little later, she said the time was about half-past four or a little later—about twenty-five minutes to five. When she found that the brougham had not returned she was in a great fright, and was afraid my mother must have been killed. Nothing of the kind had happened to her before, but she knew of a case that had happened in her village.

At about 10:30 p.m. I spoke to the housemaid, who told me that Howe had told her that she had seen the brougham and the coachman. It was about half-past four, or perhaps a little earlier, that she had told her this.

December 28th, 1899: All the servants deny that they saw or heard any brougham come yesterday. My grandmother heard a brougham come (she was with the maid Howe at the time, about 4:30) and saw the top of the brougham or the coachman's hat pass the window and then pass again as if driving away again. (This coincides with what I saw; a brougham would have to pass the window twice in turning round a flower-bed on the path before driving out again.) In the meanwhile Howe had left the room to tell the housemaid, and saw the brougham as described in the stable-yard.

I asked her to day whether she was very nervous when she found that the brougham had not really returned. She replied, "I was very frightened indeed." I then asked her whether she had prayed. She answered, "I committed Mrs. Milburn to God's care." It would take, I am told, three quarters of an hour to drive from here to the Lyceum. I have asked the coachman's wife whether he was here yesterday afternoon; she says no. Howe recognised the brougham and horse as well as the coachman, but she doubts whether my grandmother, who is very old and has a very uncertain recollection, either saw or heard anything. The brougham which I saw drive out went in the direction of Kingston; not towards London. The coachman, who has just returned from taking the brougham to be mended, denies that he was here yesterday afternoon, and declares that the horse was not put into the brougham again till 4:50.[125] — R. G. MILBURN, HOLLYWOOD HOUSE, WIMBLEDON COMMON, LONDON, ENGLAND, 1899

HAUNTED ROAD GHOST CONTINUES TO MANIFEST

☛ As I know you are interested in the movements of our ghost, I am writing to tell you another little anecdote about him.

A young lady, who is a governess in this neighbourhood, told me this afternoon of a meeting she had had with him this spring. She was returning home along the haunted road at about a quarter past four in the afternoon, when she was attracted by seeing in front of her a rather tall old man, dressed in a long black cloak, with one cape which came to a little below his shoulders; his hat, as on the occasions when my sisters and I saw him, was low-crowned, and the brim slouched over his eyes.

Ghosts often knock on doors late at night, much to the horror of the living occupants.

My informant was much interested in this peculiar-looking person, and did not take her eyes off him, whilst she watched him walk backward and forward between the turn of the road and a heap of stones about a hundred yards lower down; he repeated this six times, the last time stopping as if he were speaking to a man who was cutting the hedge at the time. What struck Miss Irvine as peculiar was that the man who was hedge-cutting did not look round, and seemed quite unconscious of the other's presence. Miss Irvine walked on, and was going to pass the old man, when, to her astonishment, he vanished when she was only about three yards from him.

I know that you will think it foolish of Miss Irvine not

questioning the hedger to whom the apparition looked as if he were speaking. I asked her why she had not, and she answered that she had not liked doing so, as the labourer would undoubtedly have thought her mad, as he clearly did not see any one.

I am sure you will think this story most interesting, knowing all our experiences in days gone by. The extraordinary part of this man is that he always frequents the same part of the road, and yet does not vanish twice on the same spot; when my sister and I saw him he became invisible on the left side of the road, and when Miss Irvine saw him he vanished on the right. Miss Irvine is most positive about all she told us, and says she will be delighted to send her account to Mr. Myers.

I do wish we could see "our man" again. I have passed along that road hundreds of times since he was first seen, and at all hours of the day. I think he cannot have liked the way I stared at him the last time. Another thing we think funny is the variety of coats which he seems to possess, and all of an antique cut. He has the long black cloak with the cape in which Miss Irvine saw him, and the clerical-looking cloak with the large deep pockets in which we met him; then on the other occasion, when the village girls saw him, he had round him the filmy-looking sheet. My sister has written to Sir George Douglas to ask him if he can tell her the exact spot on this road where an old man was murdered by gipsies coming from St. Boswell's fair many years ago. Sir George Douglas tells his story among a number of other old border tales, which no doubt you have read. I hope some day to be able to tell you more about the ghost. At present I am afraid he is underground. With kind regards, yours sincerely.[126] — MISS LOUISA SCOTT, LESSUDDEN HOUSE, ST. BOSWELL'S, SCOTLAND, AUGUST 14TH, 1894

MORE ON THE HAUNTED ROAD GHOST

☛ [From a sister of the above informant] . . . Our apparition is still seen. My latest experience was about a fortnight ago, when coming down the haunted road in the dusk I distinctly heard footsteps walking beside me, but could see nothing, though I am sure there must have been an unseen presence around from the state of nervous terror which generally makes itself felt on such occasions.

Last autumn, and again in the dusk, I was walking down the little wood adjacent to the road with my sister. We were both talking upon indifferent subjects and putting the ghost as far from our thoughts as possible, when suddenly I was carried spell-bound by distinctly seeing the apparition walking alongside of us on the other side of the hedge. My sister saw me gazing vacantly on space when I suddenly exclaimed "The man!"

When we came to the gate which divides the wood from the road there was no one to be seen either way, though "he" had walked within three feet of me the whole time; he was invisible to my sister.

It is a strange phenomenon altogether. He had the same countenance we have always seen, but I did not seem to have the power to look beyond his face. This ghost always appears when our thoughts are bound up in something else, but if the opposite, then we are sure not to see him, and many persons who have accompanied [us] up [and] down the road in hopes of seeing him have, like ourselves, failed to do so.[127] — MISS M. W. SCOTT, AUGUST 1898

MEETING THE GHASTLY APPARITION ON THE HAUNTED ROAD

☛ [From the same informant as above:] . . . Our experiences [of 1892 and 1893], after having become the talk of the town and a nine days' wonder, gradually subsided, and, personally, we had no further manifestations till the spring (April, I think) of 1897.

My sister and myself were paying an afternoon visit at a friend's house situated near the haunted road, and having rather overstayed our time, the dusk was just beginning to fall over the landscape around; it being then suggested that we should take a shorter cut home, we gladly availed ourselves of the permission to walk through the park and wood which open out of and enter the evil-reputed road.

Upon coming to the end of the park, there is a small gate and narrow pathway, separated from the road by a hedge and some trees; the space between being only a few yards, a pedestrian on the other side is distinctly visible. At the other end of the wood, again, there is another gate, which [leads to] the small incline and angle of the road, and, looking either way, the whole expanse is clearly defined. Just about this time we had nothing supernatural in our thoughts and were talking and laughing gaily together.

Suddenly by some magnetic influence our conversation seemed gradually to cease, for when we were quite half-way down the wood, I noticed a man's figure walking alongside of me between the hedge on the other side, which, either real or unreal, I was determined not to lose sight of. As though cast over by a spell my gaze became fixed, as in a moment I recognised the ghastly features of the apparition. I cannot tell how he was clothed, or if he wore a hat; my eyes seemed fixed only on the profile from just below the forehead. Instinctively I felt he moved beside me, but heard no sound or footsteps of any kind. My sister saw nothing, and not being equal to the occasion, I made no remark, until we had almost reached the end of the boundary, then exclaimed in French, "*L'homme!*" At that moment the ghost must have vanished, for when we opened the gate to pass through, not a living soul was there; had it been a person of either sex, we were perfectly certain to have met.

It was very strange my companion should perceive nothing unusual, though she remarked about me "staring into space." It is quite impossible to account for this phantom—it is no illusion formed by a disordered brain or based upon imagination or defective light; the sun had certainly set, the dusk slightly fallen, but giving quite sufficient power for mutual recognitions. The man had walked calmly on, looking straight in front of him, never appearing to notice anything, as though engaged in deep meditation.[128] — MISS M. W. SCOTT, DECEMBER 1899

WIFE'S WRAITH HERALDS HER DEATH

☛ The following occurrence took place about three years ago, but it has not been possible to fix the date with greater precision.

Mr. Phillips, the immediate percipient, has since died, but I have received the statement personally from Mrs. Phillips who, it will be clear from the circumstances attending the case, knew of the apparition at the time of its appearance and before there could have been any knowledge of the actual death.

Mrs. Robotham and her husband had lodged for four years with Mr. and Mrs. Phillips at their house, No. 4 Underhill Street, Camden Town [London, England], which they had occupied for more than forty years, and which is still tenanted by Mrs. Phillips. Mrs. Robotham was, consequently, particularly well known to Mr. and Mrs. P., who were the less likely to be mistaken in her identity. Some three years before her death, Mrs. Robotham and her husband left the house of Mr. and Mrs. P. and took rooms elsewhere, but the intimacy between the parties still continued, Mrs. Robotham frequently coming into the shop kept by her former landlord.

Finally, upon one occasion Mrs. Robotham called at the shop to say good-bye, her husband having obtained work in the country and wishing her to go to him. She was seen upon that occasion by Mrs. Phillips, who says she then looked very ill, and seemed quite unfit to travel.

About a fortnight later, Mr. Phillips was at work in his shop, being at the time alone, when, happening to look up, he distinctly saw the face of Mrs. Robotham, who seemed to be standing outside in the passage and looking round the edge of the door. The face disappeared almost immediately, but Mrs. Phillips says that her husband was absolutely convinced that Mrs. Robotham had actually been there. To put it as nearly as possible in her own words:

> "He (Mr. Phillips) came out and asked me whether Mrs. Robotham had come into the kitchen, as she had just looked into the shop and gone away again. I said I had not seen her, and that he must certainly be mistaken, as we knew she had gone away into the country. He was quite positive, however, that she had looked into the shop, and said he was certain he could not have been mistaken. So sure was he that he went to the street door and looked up and down the street in the full expectation of seeing her somewhere about. I asked him how she was dressed and he said, 'Like she always is in her black bonnet.' He had only seen the head and face. We waited several hours, expecting her to come back. When we found she did not do so, I said to Mr. Phillips that if he had really seen her it must have been her spirit and she must certainly be dead, as I knew she would never come to Camden Town without coming to see me. About a week afterwards Mr. Robotham came into the shop. I saw that he was in mourning, and at once said, 'You need not tell us. We knew a week ago that Mrs. Robotham was dead. We saw her spirit.' Mr. Robotham told us when his wife had died, and we reckoned that we had seen her on the same day or the day after."[129] — W. B. FOTHERINGHAM, JULY 20TH, 1900

FACES, FOOTSTEPS, & KNOCKINGS IN A HAUNTED HOUSE

☛ (1) I cannot describe the peculiar feeling that crept over me when one night about 12 o'clock I felt the touch of a hand, or as I thought that of the paw of my pet collie, who usually slept on my bed, but on putting out my hand to caress him I came in contact with an icy being instead of a lovely warm-coated creature. On looking up in astonishment, I saw at the foot of the bed a beautiful vision—a most ethereal face—oval in shape, with piercing violet eyes, and a mouth of speaking sympathy. I said, "What do you want?"

She replied, "I only come to tell you your son has just arrived safely at Perth." She vanished, but with the declaration she would come again. It was perfectly true that my son did arrive at Perth at the hour named. Once more did she appear to me at night to tell me of illness which the post only proved too true.

The curious noises about the house it is [possible] to understand on ordinary grounds (because rats and mice often cause bells to ring, and that occurred constantly), but the interesting part of the matter is as follows:

I. Footsteps on the stairs at early hours, from 1-4 or so.
ii. Footsteps overhead, when on searching the rooms no one was found.
iii. Knockings in a grate at 2 o'clock in the morning, like the hammering in of nails. These and other things give the house a strange interest.

(2) On going to bed one night about 10 I was startled by a lovely face gazing at me just beside the bedroom door; it seemed that of a young girl, and she wore a hood with a dark-coloured exterior, which covered her shoulders. I was so frightened that I screamed out and threw away both candlesticks and hat, etc., and fell down. Though there were several people in the house, no one seemed to hear me, on account of their talk and games, so I do not know how long I lay on the floor, only shall never forget the shock this apparition gave me.[130] — EMMA ELLIS, APRIL 26TH, 1899

COLLEGE POLTERGEISTS
☛I occupied two rooms at Cromwell Lodge, 4 Trumpington Street, Cambridge [England], during terms from October 1889 to June 1892. I most certainly heard many noises, the causes of which I have never been able to discover.

Often for a week or two bells would peal between 1 and 2 a.m., and until I became tired of doing so, and was convinced that no one outside pulled the street door bell, I frequently went downstairs and opened the front door (the bell ringing at intervals the while), or roamed about the passages. There were other noises of the nature of tapping or hammering, which I put down to rats or mice.

The most extraordinary occurrence, however, happened in the early summer of—I think—1895.

On that occasion an old college chum and I were staying at Cromwell Lodge for a night, and were sleeping on the same floor, but in different rooms. Before I was fully undressed I heard in the next (an unoccupied sitting) room a noise like the rattling of tea cups. When I had occupied the room in which I then was and the adjoining one regularly, I had kept my crockery in the cupboard under a bookcase. I therefore concluded that my friend had knocked to attract my attention, and so shaken the bookcase and crockery in it, for the bookcase had stood with its back to a wooden partition dividing the room in which it stood from one nearer the front of the house, in which my friend was (his bed-head backing on to the other side of the partition).

I shouted to my friend asking what he wanted. He assured me he had not knocked, and on opening my door, which led into my old sitting-room, I at once saw that there was no bookcase there. I had pictured the room as it was when I was in residence! I went into my friend's room, smoked a cigarette with him, and then went to bed. Half-an-hour afterwards the bells began.

I have never been able to account for these things, and merely state the facts. I may also add that my friend slept, or tried to sleep, on the floor in my room, declining to sleep apart from me, and vehemently declaring that he would never sleep in the house again.[131] — G. P. JOY, APRIL 26TH, 1899

HORRORS OF A HAUNTED LODGE

☛ [This report is connected to the previous entry.] This is the first time that I have attempted to put on record my experiences at Cromwell Lodge in January 1896. I will now do so in the plainest manner possible. The exact date I cannot fix accurately, though possibly I might with the aid of a calendar; it was, I think, on the 5th or 6th.

Victorian psychic photograph.

I reached Cambridge towards noon, and in the scepticism of my mental attitude and the courage bred of daylight I begged Mrs. [E. J.] Jephson to allow me to occupy the "haunted" room. Before I left, I had arrived at the conclusion that this term could be applied to every quarter of the house.

Mr. G. P. Joy, who also took part in the events of that night, arrived shortly afterwards. In the evening, after dinner, we visited the rooms of an undergraduate (of Pembroke), situated in the lane which runs by the side of the University Press, and subsequently joined a party of his friends who were playing poker. Between eleven and twelve o'clock we returned to Cromwell Lodge. I wish to lay stress on the manner in which we employed that evening, because many games of cards produce a reflex action on my mind and memory, so that when I have ceased playing I find my thoughts recurring to the incidents of the game, and I retire to rest with my mind abstracted from all matters except the details of the play. And it was so on that night.

After we had chatted for some thirty minutes with Mrs. Jephson and I had gone to my room, I put out my light and prepared to sleep, totally oblivious of my surroundings and of the character of the chamber I occupied, concerned only with the cards I had been holding, and with one hand in particular. It would be unreasonable, therefore, to ascribe the impressions I subsequently received to the supposition that I had, unconsciously perhaps, prepared myself to experience the uncanny, or was in a state of nervous tension favourable to its reception.

My room was on the first floor, Mr. Joy occupying one adjoining. The position will, perhaps, be made clearer by the following rough sketch [not reproduced here]. The space occupied by my bedroom and the drawing-room in this sketch had at one time formed one large room, but it was then divided by a partition which did not reach to the ceiling, draped on my side by dark curtains. These curtains faced the foot of my bed. On the other side of my bedroom, and behind the head of my bed, lay two rooms; one used as a study, and one that in which Mr. Joy was sleeping. From the head of the stairs to the doors of my room and the drawing-room ran the passage.

I had not been in bed ten minutes before I fell asleep, dreaming of the cards; within another twenty minutes I awoke with a start. There was nothing to disturb me, but I felt that something was wrong. I sat up and stared into the darkness. Then suddenly, from behind the partition at the foot of my bed, a sharp crashing noise resounded, continuing for the space of five seconds or more. It was as if one had dashed on the floor a heavy load of china or glass, which had broken as it fell. I sat still and listened. Within a few minutes it occurred again. Then through the wall I heard Mr. Joy shouting to me, asking what I was doing. I had no appetite for more, and fled to him without scruple, to find his astonishment on learning that I was not responsible for the noise no less than my alarm.

When I had thrown on a blanket we proceeded to the passage, and met Mrs. Jephson coming up the stairs with a light and her dog, a big collie. At that moment out on the silence broke the bells—bells of many varieties of tone and strength; it seemed as if every one in the house was ringing. No gentle tinkle, to which a rat crossing the wires might give cause, but a sharp staccato peal.

We rushed downstairs to the front door, opened it, and looked out. It was a clear night, but not a figure was to be seen; and the road runs straight and broad in either direction, affording no hiding for a considerable distance. Nor could a practical joker have pulled any but the front door bell. For some minutes we waited behind the door, and then returned upstairs, the dog following. We took up our stand outside the study, and so commanded the passage which led to the drawing-room.

A few minutes passed, and then, again from that quarter, and clearly in the hearing of us all, rose anew noise. It seemed the loud beating of a tray with a stick or something similar. The dog, and I remember this distinctly, crouched against the wall, cowering. It ceased; the bells, I think, pealed again, and all was still.

Polish medium Stanislawa Janina Tomczyk (center) with two friends.

We waited a while, and then, after bidding Mrs. Jephson a second good-night, I procured a light, and accompanied by Mr. Joy returned to my room. My object was to obtain the bedclothes, not to complete the night there; this was done on the floor of Mr. Joy's room, but we did not go to sleep for some two hours later, when at last the bells, which commenced pealing again, and continued to peal at intervals, shrilly, harshly, loudly, had ceased.

I have heard nothing like it before or since. It was impossible for any person in the house to have rung them all at the same time and with that force. The only two other occupants (besides those mentioned) were a young maid and Mrs. Jephson's old servant; they were safely in their room, together, I believe; and the latter was not given to such humour.

On the next morning the drawing-room whence the sounds proceeded remained intact, furniture and contents undisturbed. . . . I have to certify that the above is a plain, unexaggerated record of what transpired, and that the manner of its telling detracts from rather than adds to the horror of its nature.[132] — E. G. HADATH, 26 QUEEN'S ROAD, WEST DIDSBURY, MANCHESTER, ENGLAND

CHAPTER SIX

GHOST WALKS ACROSS SHIP DECK

☛ In the year 1849 I was serving in H.M.S. *Geyser*, on the east coast of Africa, and in company with H.M.S. *Brilliant*, anchored in Tamatave Roads, Madagascar. The following facts I can vouch for.

Some of our officers were dining on board the *Brilliant*. A boat's crew were ordered to be ready at six bells (11 p.m.) to fetch them on board. The lights were out on the lower deck and everything quiet. A messmate (T. Parker) and I, belonging to the boat, were sitting in the mess, abreast of the cook's galley, and opposite each other, he with his arms on the table, and face resting on them, and, as I thought, fast asleep, when all at once he jumped to his feet, declaring that he saw his mother cross the deck in front of the galley, and was very much excited. I pointed out to him that it was quite impossible, as his face was towards the table, at the same time laughing heartily at him for being so foolish. Our schoolmaster, Mr. T. Salsbury, was lying awake in his hammock, close by, and in the morning he made a note of the circumstances, putting down time and date.

On our arrival at the Isle of France, some time after, Parker received a letter from home stating that his mother died that very night. I am no believer in ghosts, but think this a very remarkable coincidence.[133] — "OLD TAR," MR. H. ATKINS, ROYAL MARINE OFFICE, 40 SPRING GARDENS, S.W., LONDON, ENGLAND, 1884

SON SHOCKS MOTHER WITH DIRE PREDICTION

☛ On Tuesday morning, the twenty-fourth of April, 1900, my son, Edward Howard Dunning, awakened me at about seven o'clock. He seemed much troubled and spoke in a very deliberate and serious manner. He said:

> "Mother, I'm afraid something terrible is going to happen; last night a spirit walked before me, and I know what it means. Something terrible is going to happen. You will have to bear it."

I felt myself quite dumb with amazement. I tried to argue with him and get a further explanation of what he had seen, or what he seemed to fancy that he had seen. He persisted in repeating his fears, adding with apparent pity for me, "You will have to bear it."

Further details finally given me by him elicited these facts—or what he claimed to be facts.

The previous evening while walking up and down the piazza of our home and about the grounds, smoking his usual after-dinner pipe, he saw, or said that he saw, a spirit moving just before him as he walked. He said that it remained just in front of him until he finally turned to enter the door, when it remained standing by one of the pillars of the piazza. I asked him if he recognised it, or I think I said, "Who was it?"

He answered, "I could not recognise it." He seemed to speak deliberately and with an evident desire to be accurate.

I asked again, "Was it a man or a woman?"

He once more answered, still with the same care, "I think it was a man." He then added, "I understood its message."

I asked, "Did it speak to you?"

For a moment he looked puzzled, then he slowly said, "Yes—but perhaps not as you mean 'speak.'"

I tried to jest about the matter, but his strange seriousness filled my heart with a nameless dread. His constant reply to all my jests and objections was, "Mother, I saw it."

This occurred first at about seven in the morning. Within several hours he complained of feeling ill, and our family physician was called in, but no serious symptoms developed until the afternoon. That evening it was decided that the case was a clearly defined one of appendicitis. My son declared several times during the next two days the truth of what he had told me just before the development of his illness.

An operation was performed on the second day. On the Sunday following, or on the 29th of April, 1900, he died at a half after

eleven o'clock in the evening. I have tried to exercise great care in recalling this occurrence, copying notes made not long after his death, and in no detail or statement have I exaggerated the facts.[134]
— KATHARINE M. C. MEREDITH, MAY 25TH, 1901

BABY INTERACTS WITH GHOST OF DECEASED FATHER

☛ [From the same informant as above:] When my daughter was about two years old her father, who was devoted to her, died. Two months after his death, the child was sitting on the bed in the room which had been his, playing with some toys. The nurse and I were packing his clothes away in some trunks.

Suddenly the child began talking and laughing with some one to us unseen. I asked her what she was doing, and she looked innocently surprised as she replied, "Talking to my papa."

I asked, "Where is papa?"

She replied, as if astonished, "Here."

I said, "Papa is not here."

She insisted that he was, and pointed at him, as she saw him at the bedside, with her finger. Then she said, "Now my papa's gone away!" Then added with burst of laughter, "My papa wore a funny dress—all white!"

She then went on playing with her toys as if nothing had happened. She knew nothing of her father's death, had been away from home at the time, and had merely been told that her father had "gone to heaven," which meant nothing to her, as she was too young to understand.

Of course, we thought it curious at the time, and spoke of it in our family merely as an occurrence which was difficult to explain. The nurse alone insisted that the child really saw what she claimed to see.

The dynamistograph, an early invention of two Dutch scientists, was said to allow communication with spirits. The machine could also scientifically analyze the astral body, or soul, which modern occultists assert weighs approximately 21 grams.

Now—after the [many other paranormal] experiences of the past year—I regard the matter from a different standpoint. Of course, as this occurred fourteen years ago, and no notes were made of it at the time by me, it is possible that I have not word for word used the exact language used at the time by the child. But it must have been very much as I have given it, and the main fact is absolutely true.[135] — KATHARINE M. C. MEREDITH, JULY 2ND, 1901

GHOST SIGHTINGS BY YOUNG BOY

☛ It was in July 1894, that I saw the figure. I was then about 14. I was getting ready for school at nine o'clock in the morning, and was about to walk through the box-room when I saw, as I thought, my brother coming through it towards me. He had remained in bed that morning, not being well, and I thought he must have dressed and be coming down after all. I spoke to him when I was still several yards from him, asking what was the matter, as I thought he looked very miserable, and as if he had been crying.

Without answering, the figure turned off through a door leading to a bedroom. I followed, still thinking it was my brother, and saw no one in the room. There is another door in this room by which my brother could have got back to his room, so I went there and found him still in bed. He told me he had not left his room. I had not then been told anything about the house being haunted.

When I went downstairs I told my parents what I had seen. I have never since seen anything of the kind in the house.

The figure looked about my brother's height, and he was then about 13. It had dark clothes and hair, and looked very pale. As far as I remember, it wore knickerbockers.

In March 1901, my grandfather being very ill, I was at his house one evening, and was standing talking to an aunt in a sitting room below his bedroom. My aunt had her eyes fixed on some work she was doing. I suddenly thought I saw some one standing near me, and, half turning round, thought my grandfather was standing looking at me. A second after I saw there was nothing there, but it startled me, as I saw my grandfather so plainly, fully dressed, and I even noticed a gold watch chain which he always wore. I said nothing to my aunt, as I knew she would be nervous. A short time after, my grandfather died.[136] — N. W., FEBRUARY 21ST, 1902

BROTHER RETURNS FROM THE DEAD TO FULFILL AN ERRAND

☛ The case we shall relate took place here in Petersburg [Russia], and has just occurred in the night of November 4th-5th. But let us begin in due order.

In the summer of the current year Mr. Sharoeff, an engineer and technical editor of the journal, *The Electrician*, ordered Alexander Semenoff, a peasant of the province of Tver, district of Novotorjok, and servant [*artelschik*] at the journal's office, to get the volumes of the "Proceedings" of the First Congress of Electricians, which took place, as is known, in December 1899, and gave him a receipt for 10 roubles, No. 153, signed by the Treasurer of the Congress. From [the appearance of] this receipt it was impossible to understand, without an external explanation, that it entitled one to receive the books in question, for it was a mere receipt for the payment of a "member's subscription" for taking part in the meetings of the late First Congress of Electricians, and contained no indication whatever of the address at which the "Proceedings" were edited; [besides, they began to be edited] when the Congress was already over.

The servant forgot to fulfil the errand, and M. Sharoeff forgot to remind him of it, as there was no more need of the books.

On September 30th [October 13th] of this year the servant, Alexander Semenoff, left on leave of absence for the country and died there, unexpectedly, on October 3rd [16th], his place being taken by his brother Ilya, whom the late *artelschik*, in consequence of his unexpected death, naturally could not have initiated in the affairs of the office—still less could have told anything about the unfulfilled errand. It must be observed that the late *artelschik* had been taken, as they say, "from the plough," taught, and set on foot by the chief editor of the journal, received 30 roubles wages [about 3 pounds] a month, and in consequence prized much his situation, and was punctual and careful in the affairs of the office.

On the evening of November 4th [17th] the new servant came back home and went to bed; after 11 o'clock he was already in bed and began to doze. He distinctly heard how the clock struck twelve.

Some more time passed, and then he suddenly sees his late brother, quite as if alive, approaching him, as always neatly dressed, in a black morning coat. Having appeared, the deceased spoke to his brother as follows:

"Ilyusha, I have come to tell you that, before dying, I forgot to fulfil one of master's errands. Go and search in my chest of drawers, among the papers, for a receipt, No. 153, in M. Sharoeff's name, from the Congress of Electricians. Go with this receipt to house No. 134 Catherine Canal. The offices of the journal *Electricity* are there. Show this receipt, and they will give you the volume of the 'Proceedings of the Congress.' When you have got them, bring them to master at once. By all means fulfil my errand, because I am much disturbed about my having forgotten to fulfil it then. Be sure to search well, Ilyusha, perhaps master wants those books. This tortures me much."

After these words the apparition vanished.

The new servant slept badly the rest of the night, and, having awakened in the morning, began to search for the receipt at once. There being in the chest of drawers of his late brother many papers of all kinds—bills, receipts, letters—he could not find at once what he wanted; but the idea of the necessity of fulfilling his late brother's errand pursued him unceasingly, and at last, after three days, when perusing a parcel of small papers, he found the receipt he wanted, No. 153.

Gladdened by this finding, the *artelschik* at once ran to the address given by his late brother, did actually receive, to his greatest amazement, the above-mentioned "Proceedings of the Congress of Electricians," and brought them to M. Sharoeff, who had long since forgotten to think about these books.[137] — "SOME ONE," FROM THE *PETERBURGSKAIA GAZETA* OF NOVEMBER 12TH [25TH], 1901

THE PSYCHOPOMP KNOWN AS THE "BLACK LADY"

☛ For some time I have been thinking it would be of interest to write an account of the "Haunting" of our old home, M_____ House.

The apparition was a woman, tall, slight, and always dressed in a black cloak with a hood over her head, except once when I saw her for two or three minutes in broad day-light of which more shortly. We nearly all saw her at one time or another, very often with no apparent cause; in fact, we got so accustomed to it that even my sisters were not at all nervous until some one belonging to us was ill, for we always saw her if any member of the family were going to die.

The first time I remember was in Jan. 1893. My mother had retired early, and two or three minutes after she had gone upstairs, I, wishing to speak to her, followed. When I got on to the landing I saw her room was in darkness and heard her walking in my brother's room, which faced hers. I stood still, and in a short time she (as I thought) came out, passed me and went into her room, I close on her heels. She crossed the room as if she was going to light the gas, by which time I was well within the door. As she did not do so, I thought she could not find the matches, and spoke to her.

I said "Mother," and at the same time my brother's door opened and she came out. It had not been she that I had followed. I made some remark, and went to my brother and told him what I had seen. He thought I had been mistaken, and said I must have fancied it. However, the next morning she was taken ill and died within three weeks.

I saw the "Lady," as we called her, some time after this, but, as I did not make a note at the time, I cannot give the exact date. I had stayed in bed with a slight cold, getting up about half-past eleven, and was nearly dressed, when I heard one of my sisters come upstairs and go into the store-room, which was up three stairs from the landing. I went to the foot of these stairs, and was just going up when I saw M_____ was not alone. Her companion was very tall and had yellow hair, but what struck me most was the way she was dressed, a long gown, the waist right under the arms and covered with small flowers.

My first thought was, "whoever has M_____ got with her?" then, "why does that girl always keep behind M_____?"

I did not go in, as I had my coat off, but stood for a minute or two wondering who it could be in such a remarkable "rig-out," when M_____ came out of the room and, making some remark, went downstairs. Then for the first time it flashed across my mind there was something strange about the person I had seen, and whom I had not lost sight of for a minute until M_____ had gone, when she had walked across the room beyond my view.

I went in and looked, but could find nothing that would in any way account for it. The room was only about nine feet by five, had a large window facing the door, and was lined with shelves all round, with absolutely nowhere in which anyone could hide. I told one of my other sisters about it, and she asked me not to mention it to M_____, as she had been feeling rather nervous for a day or two, but we would see if anything happened.

Nothing did.

The next time she was seen was when my father was dying. My eldest sister, who was sitting up with him on Jan. 21, 1900, came downstairs for something about half-past twelve a.m., and passed a figure in black on the front staircase. She was too much troubled to take much notice at the time, but thought again about it in the morning and told me of the occurrence. My father died at ten o'clock, which was about half-an-hour after she had told me what she had seen.

Another strange thing happened the night after he died.

My brother F_____ and I were sitting in the drawing-room

after all the others had gone to bed. We had been there for perhaps half-an-hour, when the piano began to play of its own accord; it started at mid C and went down in minor thirds. I heard it first, but made no remark, having often heard it before, and so had others members of the family. But at the second or third note F_____ jumped out of his chair, saying, "whatever is the matter with that piano?" He was as white as death.

"Don't touch it," I said, and going across took out the knee and front boards, during all of which time it went on with its weird runs. When it was all exposed, we saw that the wires were all vibrating, but the hammers were not moving. I had thought it might possibly be a mouse or rat, but, of course, when I had opened the piano I saw that was not the explanation. It still went on till we heard C_____ (another brother), who had come downstairs for some hot water, unbolting the door of the kitchen passage, and called for him to come into the drawing-room when it stopped and did not make itself heard again. So after a bit we went to bed feeling very mystified.

Nothing further was heard or seen until Feb. 18th, when I saw the apparition again.

This 19th-Century illustration is entitled "The Shadow of Death."

I had been sitting reading after the others had retired for the night, and it would be between twelve and one when I started to go up to bed. When I got to the top of the stairs I saw the door of my father's room was open, the gas full up, and standing before the dressing-table, resting her hands on it and gazing into the mirror, was the apparition. I stood still for a second, then moved to try to see past the figure into the mirror in order to get a view of her face. The first part of this was very easy, as the dressing-table was in the corner diagonally to the door, so that by moving a little to one side I could see very well into the glass, when what was my surprise to see there was no reflection. Just as I made this discovery she turned partly round, but not enough to enable me to see her face, and moved across the room beyond my vision. I rushed in, but there was nothing to be found, so [I] waited for a few minutes, and, as she did not return, I put out the gas and went to bed.

The next day my sister-in-law died, which made three, to put it at the least, strange coincidences.

She [the apparition] was seen once more before we left the house. That was on March 2nd.

I had remained at the works till ten o'clock, and was very tired when I got home. After supper and a smoke, on going upstairs about eleven, I saw the same figure standing on the landing. She went into my father's room as I got to the top of the stairs. As there were no lights at the time except the large glass lantern in the roof of the staircase, I thought it might possibly be an effect of light and shade, so walked backwards downstairs again, but could not reproduce the phenomenon. I said nothing about it in the morning, and almost forgot it till during the day, when I was seeing a friend off by train. I heard my name called from further down the train, and saw a cousin, who told me she had been telegraphed for to go to her father who was dying. (He died the same night.)

I said to my sister when I got home, "I saw the 'black lady' last night."

"Oh!" she remarked, "Uncle A_____ is worse." (He had been ill for some weeks, but we had no reason to expect his immediate death.)

"By Jove!" said I, "you have hit it. I saw N_____ at the station, and she told me she had been sent for."

We have here five appearances, four of which coincide with a death.

As I said before, it was seen many times by other members of the family, but, as there have been no careful notes kept by them, I can give no detailed account, nor do I enlarge on the noises of footsteps, the opening of doors, and similar phenomena; but will only mention one other circumstance which happened after we had left the house.

My brother F_____ was superintending the removal of a lot of old furniture which we were sending down to the auction rooms. One of the men who was doing the work had brought a large retriever dog, which F_____ was going to pat, when its owner told him not to, as it was so savage. They had got everything out, and the house locked up, when they discovered the dog was missing. The door being opened, they found him pressed against the wall, so paralysed with terror that his master had to fetch him out, as he dared not move. Such was the last we had to do with the "M_____ House Ghost."[138] — W. G. D., MARCH 3, 1902

CORROBORATING LETTER CONCERNING THE HAUNTED HOUSE IN PREVIOUS ENTRY

☛ . . . I fancy my earliest experiences at M_____ House must have been rather in the hearing than the seeing line. As of course you will remember I was a fearfully nervous and highly-strung child; nor must you forget the nightly horrors I underwent in the world of dreams.

To this day I recall most vividly lying in bed and listening to the sound of a heavy footfall on the stairs at the back of the house—Thump, thump! I call it a footfall, but it was rather a succession of loaded knocks appearing to mount the stairs. All that is more than twenty years ago, yet, to this day, I am puzzled to account for those noises.

The most terrible of all my experiences took place when I was about six or seven years of age. At that time, as you will remember, I was sleeping with you in the room which faced the top of the staircase. One night I awoke—as to the time I have little or no idea—but it was, to use a venerable term, "in the middle of the night." You were asleep. There was a sufficiently large gas [light] for one to see things plainly. Suddenly I was conscious of a strange noise in the passage outside as of someone slithering along in loose slippers. The door was slightly ajar; it now moved slowly and silently open, and there entered a shape and stood beside the bed. How can I describe that for which there are no words adapted? It was white, bulgy, and unutterably loathsome; that is all I can say. I remember I gave a piercing yell, and fled from the bed to the shelter of the next room, not however before the thing, whatever it was, had taken its departure. My first action had been to cover my head with a shield of bedclothes, and when I ventured to look again "Bogey" had gone. It was a credit to your powers of sleep that through all this you did not awake.

The only occasion on which I saw "the lady" must have been when I was about twelve years old. It was the night of your birthday, which I cannot remember, but either your eighth or ninth. You and F_____ were both in bed and asleep, but I remember the date because the Pater [father] had purchased some "animal books" for you that evening, and I wanted to have a look at them before I went to bed. I left the supper-table rather earlier than the others, leaving all the family downstairs except E_____. As I crossed the corridor upstairs I saw her (as I imagined) standing, with her back towards me, before the washing-stand in the Pater's dressing-room. I went into your bedroom; there was E_____ sitting reading by the bed.

"Why," said I in astonishment, were you not in father's dressing-room just now?"

"No," she answered. (Indeed, as she was talking to me she could not have been in the dressing-room at the other side of the house not thirty seconds before.) We went and made a search, but, of course, found nothing.

Regarding your curious experience with the Mater [mother], I am a little vague. I remember it, but not in detail. From the point of view of evidence, my memories on the subject are hardly worth putting down. I should be prepared to swear to the truth of the incident, because I have so often and for so many years heard you relate it without variation of a single detail, but I do not remember that you told me of it the night that it took place. You may well have done so, however, and I may well have forgotten it, as at the time I was entirely obsessed by the idea of the loss consequent on R.'s leaving England.

With regard to the piano episode I can be much more explicit. It was the night of the Pater's death; time about 11 o'clock, maybe a little later. I had gone upstairs to bed leaving you and F_____ in the drawing-room. Coming down for some hot water to the kitchen, I was in the act of unbolting the door leading thereto, when suddenly from the other end of the passage came your voice. I turned and saw you. You said: "C_____, come in here, the piano is playing." I remember saying "nonsense," or something of that kind, but came at once. The music, however, had stopped; the piano was in a more or less dismantled condition, and you both told me how you had been sitting by the fire, when suddenly F_____ said to you, "Why, the piano's playing!" You had heard it before he spoke, and now jumping up rushed to the instrument and took off the front. I remember the whole thing as vividly as if it had happened yesterday.[139] — C_____ D_____, FROM A LETTER TO HIS BROTHER (THE INFORMANT IN PREVIOUS ENTRY), MARCH 25, 1902

CORROBORATING LETTER CONCERNING THE HAUNTED HOUSE IN PREVIOUS ENTRY

☞ My brother has asked me to write an account of what I saw on the 21st of January 1900.

My father was ill of pleurisy, and I went downstairs out of his bedroom every hour, to fetch fresh hot bran-bags from the kitchen.

The kitchen was at the end of a long passage, into which all the downstairs rooms opened. The drawing-room and dining-room doors faced each other. I had left the gas lights in the passage and on the staircase partly up, and there was a kind of twilight, but quite sufficient to see anything by. As I came partly up the passage to go upstairs, I saw a figure in black standing between the two doors. I could not see the face, for it seemed to be covered all over with this black drapery, and when I looked again it was gone. I thought I was mistaken and there had been nothing there.

In the morning my father was better, and we thought the danger was over, but he died suddenly of heart disease about 10 a.m.

My brother told me twice within the following four weeks that he had seen some one, but each time it was upstairs in the room in which my father had died. In each case it was followed by death, my sister-in-law's on the 18th of February, and my uncle's on March 2nd. The figures he saw were of women, the one I saw was black, but so draped that I could not see whether man or woman.[140]

— K_____ D_____ (SISTER OF INFORMANT IN PREVIOUS ENTRY), MARCH 1902

CORROBORATING LETTER CONCERNING THE HAUNTED HOUSE IN PREVIOUS ENTRY

☞ In answer to your letter, I twice saw the lady who walks M_____ House.

The first time, in November 1882, I was going upstairs, and had just reached the landing by the green door, when, to my surprise, I saw her going up the four stairs leading to the back bedroom. I followed, for she looked very nice in a long satin dress and some lace like a scarf round her neck. She suddenly disappeared in the darkness. I am sure of the date, for it was just after my engagement was broken off. I told T_____, and said I wondered if it was a warning about R_____.

The next time was also in the winter. She was standing outside the front door, and I was coming downstairs; she looked so hard, and then disappeared. I went into the drawing-room, and mother said: "Come to the fire, child, you do look cold." I was frightened by the lady disappearing as she did. I must also say, being born on the stroke of twelve midnight, many people say it gives second sight.

R_____ S_____ [an old servant] was here last night, and told me what she saw. She seemed very frightened about the cellar, and says the figure beckoned her with its finger. This history is quite true in every word.[141] — MRS. M_____ C_____ P_____ (SISTER OF INFORMANT IN PREVIOUS ENTRY), MARCH 29, 1902

GHOST OF DYING MOTHER REACHES OUT TO DAUGHTER

☛ In my Northern-Irish home, I received a letter on the 7th November, 1865, from my brother in Warwickshire [England], saying that my mother was ill, and he wished I would go and see her. I started the same evening by Belfast [Northern Ireland] and Fleetwood [England]. I had been several hours in my berth, on the Irish Channel, and was half asleep, when I was startled by feeling a hand grasp my shoulder and a voice say, in a loud whisper, "Come quickly." I rose up and sat looking round the cabin, but could see no one. I called to the stewardess, but she was fast asleep, and so were all the other ladies.

I again lay down, but not to sleep, and in a very short time, not 20 minutes afterwards, the same pressure was put on my shoulder and the same words were distinctly uttered close to my ear, "Come quickly." I again called loudly to the stewardess and told her to light the lamp, for I was sure that some one must have been standing by me. She declared that no one had been in the cabin, and all around was so still and quiet.

I reached the station at half-past 12 at noon, when my brother met me. He said, "All is over, my mother passed away at 4 this morning." I ought to have stated that when I called to the stewardess and made her light the lamp, immediately after I heard the voice and felt the hand on my shoulder the second time, I then asked her to tell me what o'clock it was, and she said "Four o'clock." I looked at my own watch and it was the same.

I being an only daughter and my mother having been a widow the last five years of her life, she was much wrapped up in me and in my children, and the tie between us was of no ordinary kind. I have always looked upon this as a direct voice from herself, just as she was dying and passing into the spiritual world.[142] — MRS. HANCOCK, PENARTH LODGE, STOKE BISHOP, BRISTOL, ENGLAND, APRIL 14TH, 1884

LIVING SOLDIER'S GHOST APPEARS AS A CHILD TO WOMAN 600 MILES AWAY

☛ The following presents an unusual feature to me but possibly you can explain it.

My age is 34.

I was wounded in France July 24th, 1916, 3:30 p.m. [during World War I]. Between 1 and 2 a.m. July 26th, 1916, I appeared to Mrs. Jones (my wife's mother) at this address, waking her from sleep. The physical appearance corresponded with that of a photo taken when I was about 3 years old—the head was bandaged shewing only forehead, eyes, nose, mouth, and a little of the chin.

Except for the age and apparent height (only head was seen clearly) this was the condition I was in, and I was in hospital at Boulogne—to the best of my recollection asleep, and of course with 2 days' growth of beard.

The apparition was taken for [that is, believed to be that of] my son "in the flesh" at first and was asked what was the matter. Mrs. Jones then recognized me—I smiled and vanished.

The War Office telegram announcing the casualty was received at 9 p.m., July 26th. Mrs. Jones did not know me till I was about 19—at which time and ever since I have had a small moustache—and she always thinks of me as grown up—never as a child. In these circumstances, can you explain why I should appear as a child and not in my most easily recognizable form? That I appeared to Mrs. Jones I can understand as she is more psychic than my wife.[143] — G. E. W. BRIDGE, LT. DURH. L.I., ENFIELD, GATESHEAD, ENGLAND, NOVEMBER 2, 1916

UNACCOUNTABLY, WOMAN WITNESSES GHOST OF LIVING ADULT—BUT AS A CHILD

☛ [The individual writing this entry is the woman named "Mrs. Jones" in the previous entry.] During the early morning of Wed.,

July 26th, 1916, I woke from sleep, with the idea that someone was in my room. I opened my eyes to absolute darkness, but at the right side of my bed stood a misty figure, which I at first took for my little grandson, and I asked him why he was there. No answer came, but the face became more distinct, and I saw it resembled a photograph of my son-in-law, taken when he was about three years old. In the photograph one can see short curls, but in my vision the lower part of forehead, eyebrows, eyes, nose, mouth and part of chin were clearly visible, but hair, ears, lower part of chin and neck were hidden by white wrappings. As I looked and wondered, the mouth expanded into a smile, and the appearance vanished, the room being still in darkness.

My grandson had not been quite well the previous day, and my first thought was to go and see if he were worse, but as I knew his mother had settled to sleep in his room, I decided not to risk alarming her.

I did not mention the occurrence to anyone, as we only had servants in the house, and naturally I did not want to say anything to my daughter at once. I made up my mind to wait until she had had a letter from her husband of later date than July 26th, and then tell her how anxious I had felt.

The W.O. [War Office] wire came on the evening of July 26th, and in the rush and hurry of her departure I had no chance to tell her until she came home on Aug. 5th for a couple of nights, leaving her husband in hospital. When I described what I had seen, she told me that his head and neck were bandaged in that way. I could understand his appearing to me as he looks normally, as we have been great friends, and I have made my home with them for some years. The puzzle is why he should appear to me as a young child.[144]
— ELLEN M. JONES, ENFIELD, GATESHEAD, ENGLAND, NOVEMBER 5, 1916

THE TIMSBURY GHOSTS

☛ [Continuing from the previous entry:] The next instance that has occurred, since we occupied the house, is more remarkable still.

Mr. Sayce's two little boys slept together in the haunted room, when they stayed with us. On their return home their mother said, "You must have been very happy. Had you a pleasant visit?" They replied they were very happy all day, but "they did not think it was kind in Lily to dress up in white and come to their bed at night, and that they did not like it at all." These children had never heard of the Timsbury Ghosts, and never speak of what they saw there as anything but "Lily dressed up."

They told their nurse that "one night Lily went into their room, dressed up in white, to frighten them, but they were so sure it was Lily that they determined not to take any notice of her, as they were very tired."

Was not this most curious?

Frederick Holt, my brother-in-law, was all but frightened out of his senses, by an apparition which he saw in the haunted room. He had been lying awake for more than hour, one night, or rather very early one morning, when, from the corner whence it usually issues, where the dressing closet door opens into the bedroom, a figure appeared, and slowly passed the bed. Frederick felt his pulse and his heart, in order to ascertain whether he was any way excited or fevered, as he thought, at first, it must be an illusion, but his pulse was quite steady.

In about 10 minutes the figure returned, with its hands upraised, and with the most agonised expression of countenance that could be described.

Mrs. F. Holt was asleep by her husband one night when the apparition appeared to him. He says he did not awaken her at first for fear of frightening her, and that when the figure returned he felt completely paralysed. He had himself been awakened that night by what felt to be a hand pressed tightly over his face, and he then saw an elderly gentleman with a fine line of face passing from his bed. He was dressed in brown, in the old style, with a long rounded-off waistcoat, and a light neckcloth which was fastened with a brooch or pin. He passed from the dressing-closet, at one side of the room, to a kind of wardrobe-closet for hanging things in at the other.

Mr. Holt put his hand upon his own pulse to see if anything was the matter with him, and counted 80 beats, when the old gentleman came out of the hanging closet again, and again passed by his bed, but this time it stopped, raised up its arms, and, clasping its hands together, laid them down, pressing them on the bed in which Mr. and Mrs. Holt were lying. It then passed on again to the dressing-closet.

Mr. Holt then told his wife what he had seen. Mrs. Holt saw nothing, but they both of them heard loud whisperings and voices all about the room. Neither of them could understand what the voices said. They described the room as seeming all alive with voices.[145] — MISS LILY BOYD, CIRCA 1884

SOLDIER'S SPIRIT APPEARS TO HIS MOTHER THE NIGHT OF HIS DEATH

☞ My sister-in-law has asked me to write to you about an

impression I had of my son coming to me about the time of his death. I did not make any note of it at the time, but I know the date, because I spoke of my impression next day to a sister who came to visit me that day and to a servant who came home the same afternoon, March 28th.

When the German offensive began on March 21st [World War I], I was anxious about my son, because he was (2nd Lieut. in the 4th Bedfordshire), as I believed, somewhere in the neighbourhood of Arras [France]. On the night of the 27th March or in the early hours of the 28th (I don't know the time), I had what I can only describe as a waking dream. I mean that it did not seem just an ordinary dream to me.

When I got up on the Thursday morning it was so vivid that it haunted me, and I spoke of it, as I said, on that day. It seemed that I felt or heard footsteps along the verandah outside my bedroom window (I live in a bungalow), and that I rushed out knowing the steps were my boy's. (Bodily I did not leave my bed.) I seemed to see him with a "tin hat" and his pack with webbing equipment [a system of belts and straps], and my general feeling was great dismay that he should be in "Tommy's kit" [regulation British military uniform] and I exclaimed,

"Oh, David boy, you have never disgraced your officer's uniform and had to go back to Tommy's clothes."

(I am rather troubled at repeating this, because it almost seems to imply that I had doubts of my boy, which I certainly had not. He was a very dear son and brother, and had got on splendidly as Intelligence officer; he was a most happy and very keen soldier, and letters from his senior officers and men testify to his efficiency and courage, as well as to his thoroughly good and useful work.)

He passed as in a flash and I can't say that he looked at me, it was more a feeling of knowing he was there. From that time I expected bad news of him and I was not surprised to get a telegram from the W.O. [British War Office] on the 3rd April, to tell me that my son had been killed in action on March the 27th.

I think that the dream or impression, whichever it was, haunted me all the more, because on the last evening of my son's leave before he returned to France on Jan. 31, I was helping him to pack, and naturally there was one thought uppermost, though we were both quite cheerful. I said to him, "If what we can't help thinking about should happen, will you try to come to me?" He did not say anything, but he would always try to do anything he could that I asked him, and I believe if it were in his power that he would have willed to come to me at the time of his death.

On Friday, April 5th, two of my other sons came home. I was talking to them about my impression of their brother's coming to me and my trouble that he should be wearing Tommy's clothes. And they both said, "That is how he would have seemed to you."

I think that is all I can tell you, and it does not seem very much, but my sister-in-law asked me to write.[146] — MARIAN M. MACKLIN, WHITE WOOD CORNER, SANDY, ENGLAND, July 5, 1918

SON CALLS OUT TO HIS MOTHER AT TIME OF DEATH

☛ Dear Mr. Constable, in reply to your note this is as nearly as I remember what passed between Mrs. Ashley and myself on the day Arthur met with his accident.

I missed him at his usual dinner hour, but his mother then told me that he did not always come home at that time. After dinner I retired as usual to my little sitting-room and Mrs. Ashley to her duties at the back of the house. In about an hour's time I was surprised to hear her call out, "Is that you Arty?" and getting no reply she came into my room saying "Have you seen anything of Arthur?"

I said "No, I have not."

She then seemed very surprised, saying, "Well, I heard him call out 'Ma,' (a pet name for his mother) as plainly as I have ever heard him, and if that was not his voice I have never heard it."

I remarked that it was very curious, and she then added, I hope there's nothing the matter with him."

Seeing that she was much agitated I tried to soothe her and said, "Oh! he will be home all right presently."

Victorian psychic photograph.

This was all we said to each other and Mrs. Ashley then went away, but soon after I heard a knock at the door and some one said, "No answer," then I heard Mrs. Ashley cry out and on going to her to see what had happened she put a letter in my hand which she had just received from the works telling her of her son's accident [his arm had been crushed].

I think this is all you will want to know, and hope I have made it plain enough. I may add that I have been much impressed by such a clear premonition of the sad event.[147] — MISS C. A. DODD, PARSONAGE HOUSE, LIDDINGTON, NR. SWINDON, ENGLAND, OCT. 17TH, 1918

SPIRIT INDICATES LOCATION OF MISSING LETTER

☛ I had arrived in Boston [MA] expecting a very important letter to meet me there. It did not arrive. So, after two weeks waiting there, I prepared to leave for New York. I was living at the Vendome Hotel, where each room door contains a plate of ground glass. I was seated under a light near the door, when I saw what seemed to be the shadow of an arm and hand sweep by the glass on the outside. I opened the door, but the corridor was empty. Then I returned to my seat and took up my book.

Then a piece of furniture at my right, something like a chest of drawers, began to stir and creak, as do articles on a ship when the waves are high. Wondering what could cause such a demonstration, I rose and pushed the furniture aside to ascertain what was causing the disturbance. And there, on the floor, and until then completely hidden by that piece of furniture, was the missing letter! It had been pushed under the door by a bell-boy and pushed so hard that it had disappeared under the article of furniture. But for the moving and creaking of the furniture my attention would not have been called to it, and I would not have received the letter.

I have no explanation to offer; had not then, nor have I since, made any pretence of looking into "the Occult Sciences." I simply state the incident as it occurred.[148] — W. A. WHITECAR, NEW YORK, JAN. 26TH, 1918

HOLY SPIRIT GIFTS CREATOR OF "SHERLOCK HOLMES" WITH ACCURATE WORLD WAR I PROPHECY

☛ Dear madam, on the morning of April 4th, 1917, I woke up with a strong feeling that information of importance had been conveyed to me in my sleep. I had a feeling also that it was of a consoling nature. I could only remember one word, however, Piave. It rang in my head, Piave! Piave! It was as though it were some keyword, and if I could retain that, I should have the essence of the message.

No doubt in my reading I must have seen the word, and on my visit to the Italian front I had actually passed over the river, but I had retained the names of none of the many streams, save only the

Isonzo, upon which the war was at that time being waged. Thus Piave conveyed nothing to my mind. I was so impressed, however, that I went at once into my study and looked up the index of my Atlas. By this reference I discovered that the name was that of a river about fifty miles in the rear of the Italian front, which was at that time victoriously advancing. I could imagine few more unlikely things than that the war would be transferred to the Piave. Nonetheless I was so impressed by my dream that I drew up a paper at once, under the date April 4, 1917, in which I stated that I knew some great event of the war would centre on the Piave. This was witnessed that morning by two witnesses. In view of my feeling of elation on waking I took it that this event would be favourable, tho' how a favourable event could occur fifty miles in the rear was more than I could understand.

It is a matter of history how six months later the Italian army was driven from its positions. Whilst it was in retreat I sent a sealed envelope to the S.P.R. with an account of my dream. The army crossed several points, such as the Tagliamento, where a stand seemed probable, and halted eventually upon the line of the Piave, which had been said to be untenable, since it was commanded from the left rear. They were still there in February 1918, when I was writing my [book *The*] *New Revelation*.[149] In describing the incident I said,

> "If nothing more should occur the reference to the name has been fully justified, presuming that some friend in the beyond was forecasting the coming events of the war. I have still a hope, however, that more was meant, and that some crowning victory of the Allies at this spot may justify still further the strange way in which the name was conveyed to my mind."

This sentence appeared in print in April 1918.

It will be recalled that it was on June 17th, 1918, that the first battle of the Piave was fought. It was not a great victory, but it was a victory, and it is noteworthy that this date marked the whole turning point of the war. Up to then the Allies had in this year sustained three severe defeats, that of the second Somme battle, the battle of the Lys, and the second Aisne battle. On June 17th their prospects were very black. From the day of the Piave battle they never looked back again, and on every front they had an uninterrupted record of victory, culminating, in the case of the Italians, in the second Piave battle, which was the most decisive in the war. Thus in conveying the name "Piave" my comforter had given me the key name which would unlock the whole situation.

Now how could this be accounted for by coincidence? That is unthinkable. Even if my subconscious self had known there was a river called the Piave, that would not have shifted the Italian army back to it. Was it then telepathy? But no one in the world could have conjectured such a series of events. What then was it? I claim that the only possible explanation is that my friends on the other side, knowing how much I worried over the situation, were giving me comfort and knowledge. The ordinary spirit has, so far as my reading and experience teach me, only a very limited and uncertain gift of prophecy. Therefore I have some reason to hope that my information came from a high source. Why I should have been so privileged above others is the one point which is beyond my conjecture.[150] — [FAMED AUTHOR] ARTHUR CONAN DOYLE, WINDLESHAM, CROWBOROUGH, SUSSEX, ENGLAND, NOVEMBER 1918

UNSEEN SPIRIT ANNOUNCES RETURN OF SOLDIER
☛ On Tuesday, January 8, (at Grange-over-Sands, Lancs), Mr. Saunders (a retired gardener of ours) heard a message (Mr. Saunders has a grandson at the [war] front called Tom). The message is this, that Saunders heard "Tom is coming to-day." Saunders was wide awake (about 7:30 in the morning), and had been for sometime. He looked round to see who it was speaking; and there was no one to be seen. If the message had not been uttered loudly Saunders would not have heard, as he is extremely deaf.

When he went down to breakfast he told the incident to his family, they chaffed him and said he must have been dreaming. After breakfast (at 9 o'clock) when Saunders was washing up the breakfast things in walked the said Tom. On January 7th they received a printed card from Tom from France to say he was very well and a letter would follow. His leave was quite unexpected. The message Saunders received was on the following day, January 8th.[151] — MISS E. ARKWRIGHT, BOURNEMOUTH, ENGLAND, CIRCA 1918

British physician, author, and Spiritualist, Sir Arthur Conan Doyle.

CHAPTER SEVEN

MAN'S GHOST APPEARS TO HIS SISTER ON DAY OF HIS DEATH

☛ My step-mother Mrs. Bowyer-Bower asked me to write to you about the vision I had of my brother [Eldred Wolferstan Bowyer-Bower, Captain the East Surrey Regiment and R.F.C., son of Captain and Mrs. T. Bowyer-Bower, of 30, Bramham Gardens, S.W., [London, England], and of Ashanti, and grandson of the late Major-General Henry Bower. Twenty-two year old Eldred was a British pilot who died in action on March 19, 1917, in France during World War I. Editor's note, L.S.].

My brother appeared to me [as an apparition] on the 19th March, 1917. At the time I was either sewing or talking to my baby, I cannot remember quite what I was doing at that moment. The baby was on the bed. I had a very strong feeling I must turn round; on doing so, I saw my brother Eldred. Thinking he was alive and had been sent out to India, I was simply delighted to see him, and turned round quickly to put baby in a safe place on the bed, so that I could go on talking to my brother; then turned again and put my hand out to him, when I found he was not there.

I thought he is only joking, so I called him and looked everywhere I could think of looking. It was only when I could not find him I became very frightened and the awful fear that he might be dead. I felt very sick and giddy.

I think it was 2 o'clock the baby was christened, and in the church I felt he was there, but I could not see him.

Two weeks later I saw in the paper he was missing. Yet I could not bring myself to believe he had passed away. I did fancy once I saw my grandmother, but she seemed very misty, so it may have been fancy.

I did not tell any one of the vision I saw of my brother for quite 1 or 2 months after I heard of his death, as I was staying in the Grand Hotel, Calcutta, and did not know anyone there very well.

My husband was not with me and I did not write to him about it, because he did not believe in these sort of things. However, I finally told him before writing to Mrs. Bowyer-Bower. The only reason I did not mention it was, I felt nervous people would only say I had imagined it, so decided to keep quiet on the subject.[152] — DOROTHY C. SPEARMAN, JANUARY 12, 1919

GHOST MANIFESTS AS A YELLOW-BLUE RAY OF LIGHT

☛ [Concerning the same family and ghost in the previous entry:] During the night, either in the late part of Nov. or early part of Dec. 1917, I came over very hot indeed and turned down the eiderdown, etc. Some few moments later I became extraordinarily cold with a most unnatural coldness. I doubled the eiderdown over myself and tried to sleep and the feeling left me slightly, but came back again stronger than ever and far more intense.

While I wondered what I could do a yellow-blue ray came right across the room and I at once blamed the housemaid (to myself) for not drawing the "[Air] Raid" curtains together, thinking it was a light from the garage outside. I looked to make sure, but the curtains were all well together, and as I looked the ray moved right across the foot of my bed and then came round right across in front of where I lay.

I watched, not at all nervously, and something like a crumpled filmy piece of chiffon unfolded and the beautiful wavy top of Eldred's head appeared, a few seconds and his forehead and broad, beautiful brow appeared, still it waited and his lovely blue eyes came, but no mischievous twinkle, but a great intensity. It all shook and quivered, then his nose came. More waiting and quivering and then his tiny little moustache and mouth.

Curious "luminous bands" appear in many Victorian psychic photographs. I myself have captured similar phenomena while shooting photos.

At this point he turned his head very slightly and looked right into my face, and moistened his lips slightly with his tongue. I kept quite quiet, but it quivered and shook so much and no chin came, and in my anxiety I put out my hands and said: "Eldred, I see you," and it all flickered quite out, light and all.

It is possible it might have been a dream, one never can be certain at night, but in my own mind I am satisfied it was not.

The eiderdown was doubled over me in the morning when I was called, and it is not one of my habits to do things in my sleep. I certainly never slept after this, and I got slightly this cold feeling once or twice after and continued small rays several times during that night.[153] — F. M. B. B., JUNE 12, 1918

GHOST KNOCKS TWICE, APPEARS, THEN VANISHES
☛ [Concerning the same family and ghost in the previous entry:] I think I will tell you something that happened to me a short time ago. I certainly did not dream it, or imagine it, but of course it may be something to do with my brain. I was going to tell you before, only I thought you would think me mad.

I heard a number of raps when I was in bed and I began to talk to Eldred, and asked him to rap twice if he was ever going to show himself to me. Almost immediately two raps came; I waited a long time but saw nothing. Then I went to sleep. Afterwards I woke up and looked round and Eldred on the bed beside me, he was wearing his blue suit. I sat up and started talking to him, [Miss Highett records what she said, and that his lips started to move and made a reply "just above a whisper"]. I then tried to touch him, but my hand went through him, and like a fool I started to cry, and he disappeared . . . .[154] — MISS AETA HIGHETT (CAPTAIN BOWYER-BOWER'S FIANCÉE), THE LODGE, HYTHE, ENGLAND, JANUARY 4TH, 1918

DYING NEIGHBOR'S GHOST EMERGES NEAR HOUSE
☛ I went to see Mrs. B_____ in _____ Road, on October 4, 1918, [but] did not find her at home. As I came away from the house, I distinctly saw Mrs. S_____ who formerly lodged with Mrs. B_____ standing by the corner of the house. Just like a puff of cold air seemed to go over me. I saw exactly how she was dressed. I noticed she was wearing her black hat with a ribbon bow at the side. Her face was quite distinct. Having seen her so distinctly as I came round the corner of the house, the next moment she had disappeared. I felt quite a creepy feeling all over me.

At this time, I afterwards found Mrs. S_____ was dying at the Cuckfield Infirmary—Mrs. B_____ having gone to see her. She passed away at 2 a.m. the next morning. When I saw Mrs. B_____ a few days later she told me about Mrs. S_____ and how she had longed to go "home to die." She said this many times, but the doctor would not agree to her being removed. Before her death Mrs. S_____ told her daughter how much she wished to see me.[155]
— ADA ORR, NOVEMBER 6, 1918

GHOST OF BRITISH PILOT APPEARS TO FELLOW SOLDIER AT TIME OF HIS DEATH: THE FATHER'S INTRODUCTION

☛ Knowing your interest in psychical affairs, I take the liberty of giving you the particulars of the reported appearance of my son [David McConnel, Jr., a British military pilot during World War I] at the time of his death through an accident while flying. I enclose the copy of the written statement of Lieut. Jas. J. Larkin of Scampton Aerodrome, to whom the appearance was made.

I heard of the occurrence at my son's funeral on the 11th December (he was killed on the 7th December, 1918) and wrote as soon as I could to Lieut. Larkin, who replied on the 22nd December. The statement made to me on the 11th by Lieut. Hillman, who has attested the correctness of the account given, corresponds accurately with the account itself. Lieut. Hillman had not been back to Scampton, or seen Lieut. Larkin, between the time of the funeral and the writing of the account. Lieut. Hillman wrote his attestation on reading the account in my house. The event seems to have made a very vivid impression on the two or three of my son's friends who heard of it . . . .

One other matter of fact I may mention. My son was fully dressed for flying, with helmet, when he started. We happen to have a snapshot of him taken by a fellow-officer just before he climbed into the "camel" which he flew. [Note: The Sopwith Camel was a single-seat British fighter biplane, L.S.] The account states that he "appeared" with his naval cap on.

My son began his flying career in March last, entering through the R.N.A.S. [Royal Naval Air Service] before the amalgamation of the R.N.A.S. with the R.F.C. [Royal Flying Corps]. His elder brother had entered the R.N.A.S. and my son David was proud of his connection with the earlier service. Having a complete kit of the naval flying service, he always wore the naval flying uniform about the aerodrome, and was one of only three at the drome who had followed the same course in entering. His naval uniform was therefore well known. It would not be at all an unusual thing that he should have taken off his uncomfortable helmet on arriving back at the hangar, and exchanged it for his naval cap. Under the circumstances, however, it is to be remarked that he wore his helmet at the time of the accident; and in the [ghostly] appearance to Lieut. Larkin wore the naval cap. His mother informs me that he was dressed, as usual, in his naval uniform below his flying things, and that he had his naval cap with him in the fusilage to wear on reaching Tadcaster—the usual action. The O.C. states that my son left Scampton for Tadcaster at 11:35 a.m. December 7, 1918.

The circumstances of the flight were as follows. My son, with other officers, had been to a dance at Lincoln on the night of the 6th December. He got up rather late on the morning of the 7th, missed parade, and also had no breakfast. The formal completion of all his tests for "getting his wings" were to take place on the 7th.

As the account states, he was on his way to start for the Aerial Range to shoot off those final tests when he was asked by the O.C. to take one of two "camels" to Tadcaster. He went therefore unexpectedly, rather fatigued, and without food. I may say here that his O.C. [officer commanding] considered him a "born flyer," and that he was a very cautious and careful flyer, though not shirking necessary risks. By most unusual favour, he had been accepted for permanent service before he had won his "wings"—had been nominated for an instructorship in flying, and was to have left for the Camp of Instructors on the Monday following Saturday, 7th December.

The weather was fair when he left Scampton to fly to Tadcaster, a distance of 60 miles. He was accompanied by another "Avro" plane—a 2-seater—which was to have brought him back to Scampton after delivery of the "camel." You are probably aware that a "camel" scout plane is a notoriously difficult and sensitive one, and requires continued strain and effort to keep it down.

At Doncaster the two planes ran into fog. My son and his Avro companion descended, and my son described the situation to his flight commander and asked for instructions by telephone. The reply was "Use your own discretion." We suppose that my son's anxiety to finish his tests prompted him to continue. His companion states that neither of them lunched at Doncaster.

Between Doncaster and Tadcaster the fog became very thick. The Avro man had to come down, and made a forced landing, successfully. My son circled round him to see that he was all right and continued his flight to Tadcaster. Sixty miles is not a long flight. But the fog was very dense. In order to keep touch with the solid a flyer has to keep his plane under such circumstances about

150 ft. above the surface of the ground—a feat in a camel of considerable difficulty.

My son must have encountered difficulty, as he did not approach Tadcaster till nearly 3:30. Allowing for ½ or ¾ hour for the descent at Doncaster, he must have been flying for about 3¼ to 3½ hours on this occasion. I am told that it is as much as an ordinary flyer can do to fly a camel for 2 hours. The strain on the arms is intense. In fact, his mother, who saw his body on Monday the 9th at midday, observed that his hands were tightly clenched and his forearms swollen.

As he at last approached the Tadcaster Aerodrome, the machine was seen approaching by a man on the road about mile distant from the camp, who reported the fog to be extremely dense. During the evidence at the inquest a girl, or young woman, said she was watching the plane, and saw it apparently "side-slip," then right itself. It flew steadily for a minute or two, then mounted suddenly and immediately "nose-dived" and crashed. The engine was full on when the crash occurred. My son was thrown violently forward—his head striking the gun before him, which was not hooded. One arm was broken, one leg was torn.

The girl ran to the spot and "found the officer dead." The violence of contact seems to have stopped his watch, which registered 3:25 p.m. His cigarette case was almost doubled up.

These are the circumstances of the accident, so far as I am aware of them. I am informed by flying men that the reaction on reaching safety after a difficult flight is so "terrible," that fainting is not unknown. My son, it is thought, may have fainted; hence the crash, and his inability to save himself. Or there was possibly engine trouble. I am told also that when shot, or in danger, the immediate thought of the flyer is usually a quite trivial one, such as the sudden desire for a cup of cocoa, or to get undressed at camp, etc. I mention this because the appearance was not made at my son's home, or to his mother, who was there at the time, but in his own camp-room, and to a person who was a comparative stranger.

However, his mother did have a strange impression at the hour of his death, of which she is writing an account herewith enclosed.

My son had a happy, even joyous disposition. He had a brisk step and manner which would account for the "noise and clatter," which Lieut. Larkin remarked and reports in his account. My son was 18 on the 15th April, 1918, having left Bedales School, Hants, before military age, to enter the R.N.A.S. He had been headboy at Bedales during that winter term. He was the youngest headboy Bedales had had . . . . At Scampton, as at school, his conduct, character, and disposition made him as much loved as respected. His friends and his O.C. report that, though they are all accustomed to the sudden deaths which repeatedly occur, when the news of David's death reached camp, the camp was completely "broken up." I write these words to you that you may see what bearing his character may have had on the [ghostly] appearance, if indeed character has any influence in such things.[156] — DAVID R. MCCONNEL [SR.]

COPY OF THE WRITTEN STATEMENT OF LIEUT. JAS. J. LARKIN OF SCAMPTON AERODROME TO DAVID'S FATHER

[British military pilot] David McConnel [Jr.], in his flying clothes, about 11 a.m. went to the hangars intending to take a machine to the "Aerial Range" for machine gun practice. He came into the room again at 11:30 and told me that he did not go to the range, but that he was taking a "camel" to Tadcaster Aerodrome. He said, "I expect to get back in time for tea. Cheero." He walked out and half a minute later, knocked at the window and asked me to hand him out his map, which he had forgotten.

After I had lunch, I spent the afternoon writing letters and reading, sitting in front of the stove fire. What I am about to say now is extraordinary to say the least, but it happened so naturally that at the time I did not give it a second thought. I have heard and read of similar happenings and I must say that I always disbelieved them absolutely. My opinion had always been that the persons to whom these [ghostly] appearances were given were people of a nervous, highly strung, imaginative temperament, but I had always been among the incredulous ones and had been only too ready to pooh-pooh the idea.

I was certainly awake at the time, reading and smoking. I was sitting, as I have said, in front of the fire, the door of the room being about eight feet away at my back. I heard someone walking up the passage; the door opened with the usual noise and clatter which David always made; I heard his "Hello boy!" and I turned half round in my chair and saw him standing in the doorway, half in and half out of the room, holding the door knob in his hand. He was dressed in his full flying clothes but wearing his naval cap, there being nothing unusual in his appearance. His cap was pushed back on his head and he was smiling, as he always was when he came into the rooms and greeted us.

In reply to his "Hello boy!" I remarked, "Hello! back already?" He replied, "Yes. Got there all right, had a good trip."

I am not positively sure of the exact words he used, but he said, "Had a good trip," or "Had a fine trip," or words to that effect.

I was looking at him the whole time he was speaking. He said, "Well, cheero!", closed the door noisily and went out. I went on with my reading and thought he had gone to visit some friends in one of the other rooms, or perhaps had gone back to the hangars for some of his flying gear, helmet, goggles, etc., which he may have forgotten. I did not have a watch, so could not be sure of the time, but was certain it was between a quarter and half-past three, because shortly afterwards Lieut. Garner-Smith came into the room and it was a quarter to four.

Supernatural noises are a frequent occurrence in empty rooms.

He said, "I hope Mac (David) gets back early, we are going to Lincoln this evening."

I replied, "He is back, he was in the room a few minutes ago!"

He said, "Is he having tea?" and I replied that I did not think so, as he (Mac) had not changed his clothes, but that he was probably in some other room.

Garner-Smith said, "I'll try and find him!"

I then went into the mess, had tea, and afterwards dressed and went to Lincoln. In the smoking room of the Albion Hotel I heard a group of officers talking, and overheard their conversation and the words "crashed" "Tadcaster" and "McConnel."

I joined them and they told me that just before they had left Scampton, word had come through that McConnel had "crashed" and had been killed taking the Camel to Tadcaster. At that moment I did not believe it, that he had been killed on the Tadcaster journey. My impression was that he had gone up again after I had seen him, as I felt positive that I had at 3:30.

Naturally I was eager to hear something more definite, and later in the evening I heard that he had been killed on the Tadcaster journey.

Next morning, Garner-Smith and I had a long discussion about my experience. He tried to persuade me that I must have been mistaken, that I had not actually seen Mac on the previous afternoon about 3:30, but I insisted that I had seen him. As you can understand, Mr. McConnel, I was at a loss to solve the problem. There was no disputing the fact that he had been killed whilst flying to Tadcaster, presumably at 3:25, as we ascertained afterwards that his watch had stopped at that time. I tried to persuade myself that I had not seen him or spoken to him in this room, but I could not make myself believe otherwise, as I was undeniably awake and his appearance, voice, manner had all been so natural.

I am of such a sceptical nature regarding things of this kind that even now I wish to think otherwise, that I did not see him, but I am unable to do so.

The foregoing are just the plain facts of the case. Would you please give me your opinion? I have given you every detail and described easily and naturally just as it happened. I must thank you very much for David's photograph. I shall always treasure it. We had been very good friends though not intimate friends in the true sense of the word, as though I had known him for about four months, we had been room-mates for about six weeks only. We had lots of discussions, political, social, and educational, but not once did we discuss anything bordering on the occult or spiritual. Had we done so, I would perhaps have been able to account, in a measure, for his appearance in this room at the time of his death. As it is, I have no explanation whatever to offer.[157] — JAS. J. LARKIN, 2ND LT. R.A.F. [ROYAL AIR FORCE]

APPARITION CALLS PRIEST TO DYING WOMAN'S BEDSIDE

☞ One afternoon a short time back Father Brompton (to give the priest a fictitious name) was requested to visit a lady who was ill. When he arrived at her house he met the doctor who very urgently requested him not to administer the last rites at that particular moment, but to be satisfied with giving the patient a few cheering words. He very reluctantly consented but, when he saw the lady, greatly regretted his promise and the fact that the doctor should have made such a request, as he feared that the patient was very much worse than he had been made to understand. However, his promise had been given; so he arranged that he would come again in the morning and administer the Last Sacraments.

Before he left the house, however, he gave the nurse his telephone number and asked her to telephone should the patient become suddenly worse before the morning.

As usual, that night the telephone was switched on to one of the Father's rooms, as is the custom at the Oratory, with a view to any possible sick-calls. Fr. Brompton retired to bed at his usual hour after reciting his rosary, in which he did not forget to include his patient of the afternoon.

In the early morning he was startled out of a deep sleep by his bedroom door opening, and saw, by the light of the moon through his open, uncovered window, a medium-sized, dark-robed figure standing by it, and understood the person to say something about a sick-call. "For heaven's sake, man," he hastily answered, sitting up in bed and rubbing his eyes, not quite sure if it was the Father on duty or the lodge porter, "speak clearly."

"Be quick!" came the reply in clearer tones. "There is no time to lose. There is a telephone message."

"Right—right you are!" at once answered Fr. Brompton.

The word "telephone" brought back in a moment to his mind the sick-call of the previous afternoon, and it did not therefore occur to him to ask for the address. He sprang out of bed the door closed as he did so.

Turning on the light, he observed that it was just on the quarter to four. He quickly dressed, and went to the chapel for the Holy Oils and the Blessed Sacrament, remarking, by the way, on the forgetfulness of his caller to turn on the light for him. Making his way swiftly across the space between the house and the gates that shut it off from the main road, he found them locked as they should be, and had to knock up the lodge porter to let him out. Within a minute or two he was well on his way to the house he had visited the previous afternoon, and as he waited after his first ring at the bell and congratulated himself on his smart arrival, he looked at his watch and saw that it still wanted five minutes to four.

He rang again—and again. . . A clock in the vicinity chimed the hour. He rang and knocked. "Strange that there is no one ready to answer the door after telephoning," he thought.

In the stillness of the moonlight night he thought he was making enough noise to wake the dead. The dead! Could the worst have happened? His regret of yesterday came upon him with sudden force, so that he became alarmed. He banged at the door. The electric light was on in the hall and on the stairs, as he could see. He knew that there were only six people in the house—the sick lady in one room, her husband, given up as hopeless, in another, two day nurses (now evidently in a sound sleep), and the two night nurses in attendance on the patients. The children had all safely recovered from influenza and had been taken elsewhere. . .

A clock chimed the quarter past. At last, to the priest's great relief, the door opened.

"Come in, doctor," said a nurse; "I fear you have been kept waiting."

"I am not the doctor; I'm a priest."

"Oh, I suppose they telephoned for you? That's bad news. Will you go up?"

Fr. Brompton made his way up to the sick-room, and as he quietly entered he saw the nurse kneeling by the bedside and noticed that she was very startled as he entered. He also heard the sick person saying: "I do wish Fr. Brompton would come."

Afterwards he learned that for the space of about half an hour before his arrival the lady had been expressing a wish to see him. The nurse, not being a Catholic, and not realising that a priest would come outside the ordinary hours, suggested that she should recite some prayers from a Catholic prayer book. Fr. Brompton arrived while she was doing this.

He at once gave the lady the Last Sacraments, much to her relief and peace of mind. Within an hour or two she became unconscious. After reciting the prayers for the dying, the priest prepared to leave the house.

"Thank you so much for coming so opportunely," said the nurse, "but you quite startled me."

"On the contrary, thanks are due to you for telephoning."

"Oh, but I didn't!"

"Well, someone did. I expect it was Mrs. _____'s sister."

As the nurses were not Catholics, the priest took it that one of the lady's relations had telephoned in her anxiety about her sister. Fr. Brompton heard that she died a few hours later. She became a Catholic at the age of eighteen, and had been an excellent one up to her pious death at the age of thirty-two.

In the evening of the same day, Fr. Brompton had occasion to speak to the Father whose duty it had been to answer the telephone, and in the course of conversation said: "By the way, I'm sorry I spoke to you so sharply last night."

"Why, when do you mean?"

"When you came to call me."

"But I never called you last night!"

"My dear Father, you came to my room at a quarter to four this morning and told me there was a telephone sick-call."

"I never left my room last night. I had a sleepless night and happened to note that I was awake at that very time, as I had my light on. And what is more, there was no telephone call last night!"¹⁵⁸ — FROM THE *WESTMINSTER CATHEDRAL CHRONICLE* FOR MARCH, 1919

GHOST OF CLERGYMAN MANIFESTS AT HIS OLD CHURCH
☛ I am enclosing you a letter which with the story I shall relate will, I hope, interest you.

My cousin, Canon [Hopkinson] was Rector of L_____, about five miles from here. It is a family living and he was Rector for many years, but died suddenly in (I think) 1914, about a year after I came to W_____. His successor was a Mr. [Middleton], who went to live at the Rectory, and the enclosed is from Mrs. [Middleton].

I was at a neighbouring parish on November 26, and the wife of the Vicar told me that Canon [Hopkinson] had been seen since his death by Mrs. [Middleton] and the caretaker at the church; that the caretaker had seen him in his surplice by the altar rails and did

not know who it was till she got up to him, and that he turned and spoke to her and said: "I am glad to see you are still doing your old work."

I at once wrote to Mrs. [Middleton] whom I do not know personally . . . and the enclosed letter is her reply. You will note that she did not know the caretaker had seen anything, till I wrote. I have not seen the caretaker, but could easily do so. Would you care to come down one day and stay the night, and I would take you to interview her?¹⁵⁹ — J. STEVENSON, DECEMBER 9, 1919

(The letter enclosed from Mrs. Middleton was as follows:)

Dear [Mr. Stevenson]: I am sorry not to have answered your letter before, but we are moving here and are not yet into our Rectory, and so have been very busy. It is quite true that the woman who cleans L_____ Church and I have both seen Canon [Hopkinson], though there was an interval of three years between, and I never knew that she had seen him until I got your letter and went to ask her about it. Both times he was in a long white surplice and in the same place, she saw him at about 12:30 and I at about 4 p.m. I have never seen anybody before like that, and it seemed only natural to me that he should be in the Church that he was so fond of. Believe me, yours truly. — MRS. M. MIDDLETON, DECEMBER 5, 1919

GHOST OF DECEASED UNCLE APPEARS TO NEPHEW AT TIME OF DEATH

☛ Just before last Christmas I went over to Liverpool with one of my brothers and my sister. It was a very fine, clear day, and there was a great crowd of people shopping in the streets.

We were walking down Lord Street, one of the principal streets, when, passing me, I saw an old uncle of mine whom I knew very little, and had not seen for a very long time, although he lived near me. I saw three distinct shapes hobbling past (he was lame) one after the other in a line. It didn't seem to strike me at the moment as being in the least curious, not even there being three shapes in a line.

I said to my sister, "I have just seen Uncle E., and I am sure he is dead."

I said this as it were mechanically, and not feeling at all impressed. Of course my brother and sister laughed. We thought nothing more about it while in Liverpool.

The first thing my mother said to us on getting home was, "I have some news"; then she told us that this uncle had died very early that morning. I don't know the particular hour. I saw the three shapes at about 12 in the morning. I felt perfectly fit and well, and was not thinking of my uncle in the least, nor did I know he was ill. Both my brother and my sister heard me say that I had seen him, and believed he was dead, and they were equally astonished at hearing of his death on our return home. My uncle and I knew each other very little. In fact, he hardly knew me by sight, although he knew me well when I was a small child.[160] — MR. J. DOVE, NEW COLLEGE, OXFORD, ENGLAND, CIRCA 1892

GHOST OF CHILD APPEARS TO HIS YOUNG COUSIN AT TIME OF DEATH

☛ On the 25th of last month I was sitting in the nursery, and my little daughter Gwendoline was playing with her dolls, and she suddenly laughed so as to attract my attention, and I asked her what she was laughing at.

She said, "O mother, I thought I saw little Jack in that chair"—a vacant chair in the room—and indicating her little cousin. About five minutes after this the clerk telephoned from the office saying he had just received a telegram from Penzance announcing the death of little Jack.

It was about half-past nine in the morning when the incident occurred in the nursery at St. Helens. The death in Penzance took place at about half-past seven on the same morning.[161] — E. MICHELL, THE HOLLIES, ST. HELENS, LANCASTER, ENGLAND, MAY 8TH, 1894

GHOST CALLS OUT TO RELATIVE OF VICTIM OF LOST SHIP

☛ On the 1st November, 1892, soon after 11 a.m., while seated with Mr._____ in the office room of his house at _____, Poona [India], I distinctly heard a voice with which I was quite unacquainted call out in sharp clear tones, "Mrs. H_____! Mrs. H_____!" (my sister-in-law, who was lost in the [sinking of S.S.] *Roumania* [a British steamship] a few days previously) [October 27-28, 1892]. The voice seemed to be that of someone calling from above to my sister-in-law down stairs.

My age was 36, and at the time I was in good health, though in grief and anxiety about the loss of my sister-in-law; [I] was discussing an official report of mine, which Mr. S_____ who is the head of my Department, was reading out. Mr. S_____ distinctly heard the same voice, and we both started up and went outside into the verandah and all over the house, but there was no one about except the peons [unskilled laborers], who declared no one had called out. The ladies of the house were in one of the back bedrooms, but they had neither heard the voice, nor had they been calling out. I have never had an experience of this kind before.[162]
— MR. W., AUGUST 6TH, 1893

CORROBORATING STATEMENT FROM FELLOW EYEWITNESS TO ABOVE INCIDENT

☛ Mr. W_____'s statement is absolutely true. I heard the voice, clear and distinct, call out, "Mrs. H_____," twice. It was a voice not belonging to my household, and a strange voice, —the voice of a woman alarmed; and it sounded as if on board ship calling down a skylight.

I say this in perfect faith, as I began life as a sailor, and served seven years in the Indian Navy, and have had personal experience of the peculiar sound of voices calling down hatchways and skylights on board ship at sea. The voice was so real, and the name so distinctly uttered, that Mr. W_____ and I left the table at which we were seated and ran outside into the verandah of the bungalow in the endeavour, on the spur of the moment, and on natural impulse, to discover the owner of the voice; but there was no one at all near, within speaking or calling distance. Two peons, or native messengers, who were in the verandah, informed us that no European had been near, and these peons knew no English.[163] — MR. S., POONA, INDIA, AUGUST 6TH, 1893

EIGHT PEOPLE WITNESS GHOSTLY PHANTOM SKELETON
☛ Towards the end of year 1872, [I] saw [a] tall human skeleton enter [my] bedroom, dragging a coffin which it brought close to me. Over its right arm was a pall. Then pointing to the coffin, it threw the pall over me, causing a feeling of suffocation which left me very weak. Continued its visits almost every night about 10:30, for the space of about two years, then gradually disappeared.

Tried in many ways to dispel the illusion; did not believe in supernatural occurrences; have always been of lively disposition; excellent spirits which nothing seemed to affect; never saw a real skeleton; nor up to that time any representation of one; nor had any dread of death.

[When I saw it, I was] preparing to go to bed. As far as I was able to judge, was not out of health at the commencement of the visitations, nor in grief or anxiety. Aged 20.

I have wondered since whether I should have seen anyone had I looked in the coffin when the apparition pointed to it, the coffin giving me the impression that it was not a new one, nor the rope attached to it; but I had not the courage to look in. The room was lighted on every occasion; [I] never saw it in the dark.

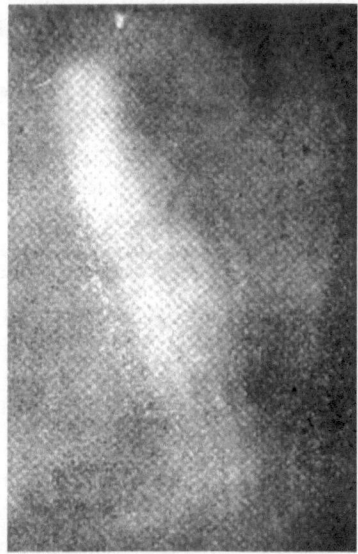
Victorian Spiritualists captured this photograph of a woman's "swaying" astral body during an experiment.

The phantom appeared again suddenly in August 1879, either the last week in August or first in September. This time there were eight persons present. Two persons saw the vision besides myself—a poor woman and an educated gentleman, the gentleman being thrown into a very nervous state for some time after and experiencing similar sensations to myself. Was out of health this time. Time 9:30 p.m.[164] — EMMA FOY, MARCH 16TH, 1892

SMOKEY GHOST OF INJURED LIVING MAN MANIFESTS TO FRIEND AT HOME

☛ On the evening of February 10th, 1894, I was sitting in my room expecting the return of two friends from a concert in the provinces where they had been performing. The friends in question had lived with me for some years, and we were more than usually attached to one another. I had no knowledge by what particular train they intended returning to town, but knew when the last train they could catch was due to arrive in London (9:5 p.m.) and how long to a few minutes they would take from the terminus to get home (about 10 p.m.).

Our profession entails a great deal of travelling; my friends have had plenty of experience in this direction, and there was no question of their being well able to look after themselves. I may just add that one of these friends has made this same journey weekly for the last eight or nine years, so that I knew quite well his usual time of arrival at Liverpool Street.

On the day mentioned they were performing at an afternoon concert, and I had every reason to believe they would be tired and get home as soon as possible. I allowed half-an-hour beyond the usual time (10:30 p.m.) of arrival to elapse before I got at all uneasy, speculating as people will under such circumstances as to what was keeping them, although arguing to myself all the time that there was not the slightest occasion for alarm.

I then took up a book in which I was much interested, sitting in an easy chair before the fire with a reading lamp close to my right side, and in such a position that only by deliberately turning round could I see the window on my left, before which heavy chenille curtains were drawn.

I had read some twenty minutes or so, was thoroughly absorbed in the book, my mind was perfectly quiet, and for the time being my friends were quite forgotten, when suddenly without a moment's warning my whole being seemed roused to the highest state of tension or aliveness, and I was aware, with an intenseness not easily imagined by those who have never experienced it, that another being or presence was not only in the room but close to me.

I put my book down, and although my excitement was great, I felt quite collected and not conscious of any sense of fear. Without changing my position, and looking straight at the fire, I knew somehow that my friend A. H. was standing at my left elbow, but so far behind me as to be hidden by the arm-chair in which I was leaning back. Moving my eyes round slightly without otherwise changing my position, the lower portion of one leg became visible, and I instantly recognised the grey-blue material of trousers he often wore, but the stuff appeared semi-transparent, reminding me of tobacco smoke in consistency. I could have touched it with my hand without moving more than my left arm.

With that curious instinctive wish not to see more of such a "figure," I did no more than glance once or twice at the apparition and then directed my gaze steadily at the fire in front of me. An appreciable space of time passed,—probably several seconds in all, but seeming in reality much longer,—when the most curious thing happened.

Standing upright between me and the window on my left, and at a distance of about four feet from me and almost immediately behind my chair, I saw perfectly distinctly the figure of my friend,—the face very pale, the head slightly thrown back, the eyes shut, and on one side of the throat, just under the jaw, a wound with blood on it. The figure remained motionless with the arms close to the sides, and for some time, how long I can't say, I looked steadily at it; then all at once roused myself, turned deliberately round, the figure vanished, and I realised instantly that I had seen the figure behind me without moving from my first position,—an impossible feat physically.

I am perfectly certain I never moved my position from the first appearance of the figure as seen physically, until it disappeared on my turning round.

I should like to state that for the last fifteen years I have been the witness of psychic phenomena of almost every kind, that in consequence I am not flurried or afraid at their appearance as one strange to them would be; but in all that time never once has anything of a psychical nature happened to me alone and unsought for; it was in fact a unique experience to me.

I was now of course thoroughly alarmed, and as rapidly as possible considered what was to be done. My first thought was to go to the railway terminus and see if anything had happened. I, however, carefully noted the time (10:50 p.m.) by the clock in front of me, and reflected that if the apparition meant an accident to my friend at anything like the time of its appearance, the last train had been due in London at least 1½ hours, so that it could not have happened on the journey home.

How I got through the next 40 minutes, with our housekeeper worrying about our missing friends, I don't know.

At the end of this time I heard a hansom [cab, a closed, two-wheeled, horse-drawn carriage] stop before the door (11:35 p.m.). My friends came in and apparently [did] not hurry themselves to come up and see me, from which fact I felt reassured that nothing very serious could have happened, or I should have been informed of it at once.

My friend B. then came up, saying, "Come and see A. H., what a state he is in."

I found him in the bathroom with his collar and shirt torn open, the front of the latter with blood upon it, and bathing a wound under his jaw which was bleeding. His face was very pale, and he was evidently suffering from a shock of some kind. As soon as I could, I got an account of what had happened.

They had arrived in London punctually, and feeling tired, although in good spirits, drove with a third gentleman, who had been performing with them, to a restaurant opposite King's Cross Station to have some supper. Before leaving the restaurant, my friend, A. H. (whose apparition I saw), complained of feeling faint from the heat of the place, went out into the street to get some fresh air, and had hardly got into the open when he felt his senses leave him, and he fell heavily forward, striking his jaw on the edge of the kerb, then rolling over on his back. On recovering consciousness, two policemen were standing over him, one of whom,—failing to unfasten his collar to give him air,—had cut both that and his tie. After informing the rest of the party of what had happened, a cab was called, and my two friends were driven home as quickly as possible.

This woman's dead husband's ghostly image was captured in this spirit photograph. Neither individual was known to the photographer.

The exact time that my friend, A. H., fainted was not of course noted by them; but judging by the average time a cab takes to do the distance, cut rather short on this occasion in the effort to get A. H. home quickly, it would correspond within three minutes to the time when the apparition appeared to me.

In conclusion it may be of interest to state that a curious mental sympathy seems to exist between A. H. and myself. In addition to the phenomenon of saying the same thing at the same time and being aware on special occasions of one another's thoughts, I have on many occasions distinctly felt his approach before seeing him, and generally when I have been walking in the street and he has overtaken me on the top of the bus. On one occasion I was making a purchase in a shop, and the man took his time wrapping up the article I wanted. Without any apparent reason, I began to get uneasy, and felt that unless he quickly handed me my parcel and let me go, I must leave it and go into the street. To his astonishment, I suddenly rushed out of the shop, saw my friend riding past on a bus, signed to him to come down, and we returned to the shop together. I don't know which of the three was most surprised.[165]
—PERCY KEARNE, JANUARY 9TH, 1895; ALFRED HOBDAY, JANUARY 9TH, 1895; ARTHUR BENT, JANUARY 9TH, 1895

A LIFETIME OF PARANORMAL EXPERIENCES
☛ Through American Branch. From Mrs. Y. Z. (1) Her husband is impelled to buy oysters, and finds on coming home that she had specially desired him to do so. (2) She has veridical impression as to her sister's illness. (3) She sees repeatedly—from age of about 5 upwards, and again when aged 20—an apparition of a little old woman. (4) Veridical impressions as to arrival of friends.[166] —JOURNAL OF SOCIETY FOR PSYCHICAL RESEARCH, UK, 1890

PSYCHIC CHILD
☛ Mrs. R. sees apparition of two girls in her bedroom. The same night a friend in another place sees similar apparition in her room; it happened about a 1891. (2) Mrs. R. when a child had impression that medicine just sent to her father was poison. Her mother took it back to the doctor and gathered that she was right about it.[167] —JOURNAL OF SOCIETY FOR PSYCHICAL RESEARCH, UK, 1895

GHOST ANNOUNCES DEATH OF CLERGYMAN BY PLAYING CHURCH ORGAN 4,000 MILES AWAY
☛ 3rd hand, as good as 2nd. Through Rev. J. Hartman Fisher. The Rev. H. Philpot, of Abaco, Bahamas, was in England seriously ill. Late one Sunday night a member of his church in the Bahamas heard the organ playing, and told Mr. Viner Bethel (who confirms) in the morning. We learn from the Rev. H. Philpot's brother that he died

early on the following Wednesday, having been speechless three days.[168] — JOURNAL OF SOCIETY FOR PSYCHICAL RESEARCH, UK, JULY 1891

GHOSTS VISIT NEIGHBORS PROPERTY AT TIME OF THEIR DEATHS
☛ On two occasions [1879 AND 1884] Mr. Viner Bethel's son announced that certain neighbours were on the premises. Search proved this to be a mistake, and it turned out that the persons died at about the time.[169] — JOURNAL OF SOCIETY FOR PSYCHICAL RESEARCH, UK, 1891

WOMAN SEES GHOSTS OF DECEASED AT TIME OF THEIR DEATHS
☛ Mrs. P.'s housekeeper, Mrs. S. (who has been interviewed by Mr. Myers), records that ever since childhood she has occasionally had correct impressions of events which were actually happening or which were about to happen—impressions being sometimes so vivid as to become actual visions. Sometimes she has seen distinct figures of persons who turned out to be dying at the time; and once of her dead brother.[170] — JOURNAL OF SOCIETY FOR PSYCHICAL RESEARCH, UK, DECEMBER 1889

SOUND OF GUNSHOT PRESAGES SUICIDE BY PISTOL
☛ Miss J. heard noise like pistol shot; not heard by two other ladies sitting in same room. For the succeeding 10 days she experienced acute depression and disquieting dreams about her brother in America, of whom she began to expect bad news, or that he would arrive ill. At last news came of his suicide by pistol shot, which occurred about the time of above impression.[171] — JOURNAL OF SOCIETY FOR PSYCHICAL RESEARCH, UK, AUGUST 1891

SPIRIT OF MAN APPEARS & SPEAKS TO RELATIVES AT TIME OF DEATH
☛ Mrs. Parker and her friend Miss Cooper see latter's brother on the stairs at the time he dies; they do not speak of the matter to each other until after the news arrives. The young man's mother, in another town, is also said to have heard his voice call her by name at the same time.[172] — JOURNAL OF SOCIETY FOR PSYCHICAL RESEARCH, UK, MAY 1891

DECEASED SCHOOL MATE APPEARS TO FRIEND AT TIME OF DEATH

☛ Borderland. Mrs. Shaw, during a period of ill health, saw old school friend, H. B., at foot of bed. She told her nurse, who saw nothing. When doctor called next day he announced illness of H. B., when Mrs. Shaw intimated that she knew her friend was dead—which was true.[173] — JOURNAL OF SOCIETY FOR PSYCHICAL RESEARCH, UK, DECEMBER 1890

NEPHEW'S GHOST ARISES AT GATE AT THE MOMENT OF HIS DEATH

☛ Mrs. Shaw has nephew at Mentone [Infirmary] for his health. No special anxiety on his account. One night (10 o'clock summer) she met his apparition at her mother's gate, and noted details of costume. Before she could speak figure vanished. Telegram announced death at that hour.[174] — JOURNAL OF SOCIETY FOR PSYCHICAL RESEARCH, UK, DECEMBER 1890

APPARITION OF DYING UNCLE MANIFESTS AT CONCERT

☛ After my marriage, I was sitting one evening in the Birmingham Town Hall with my husband at a concert, when there came over me the icy chill which usually accompanies these occurrences. Almost immediately I saw with perfect distinctness, between myself and the orchestra, my uncle, Mr. Ward, lying in bed with an appealing look on his face, like one dying. I had not heard anything of him for several months, and had no reason to think he was ill. The appearance was not transparent or filmy, but perfectly solid looking; and yet I could somehow see the orchestra, not through but behind it. I did not try turning my eyes to see whether the figure moved with them, but looked at it with a fascinated expression that made my husband ask if I was ill. I asked him not to speak to me for a minute or two; the vision gradually disappeared, and I told my husband, after the concert was over, what I had seen. A letter came shortly after, telling of my uncle's death. He died at exactly the time when I saw the vision.[175] — MRS. T., BIRMINGHAM, ENGLAND, 1884

England's Queen Victoria, who gave her name to the Victorian Period (1837 to 1901), was an ardent believer in the paranormal.

Chapter Eight

COUPLE'S SPIRITS APPEAR TO ONE ANOTHER

☞ On the 5th of July 1887, I left my home in Lakewood [New Jersey] to go to New York to spend a few days. My wife was not feeling well when I left, and after I had started I looked back and saw her standing in the door looking disconsolate and sad at my leaving. The picture haunted me all day, and at night, before I went to bed, I thought I would try to find out if possible her condition.

I had undressed, and was sitting on the edge of the bed, when I covered my face with my hands and willed myself in Lakewood at home to see if I could see her. After a little, I seemed to be standing in her room before the bed, and saw her lying there looking much better. I felt satisfied she was better, and so spent the week more comfortably regarding her condition.

On Saturday I went home. When she saw me, she remarked,

> "I don't know whether I am glad to see you or not, for I thought something had happened to you. I saw you standing in front of the bed the night (about 8:30 or before 9) you left, as plain as could be, and I have been worrying myself about you ever since. I sent to the office and to the depôt daily to get some message from you."

After explaining my effort to find out her condition, everything became plain to her. She had seen me when I was trying to see her and find out her condition. I thought at the time I was going to see her and make her see me.[176] — B. F. SINCLAIR, LAKEWOOD, NEW JERSEY, JUNE 12TH, 1894

WOMAN'S CRIES HEARD BY SISTER 200 MILES AWAY

☞ Dear Sir: At the request of Colonel Woodhull, I send you the following statement, which I hope may be of use to you.

When I was a child at my home in Rochester, N.Y., my elder sister had almost entire care of me. At night, after putting me in bed, she would sit beside me for a few moments until I fell asleep.

Frequently I would wake and finding myself alone and in the dark, of which I was much afraid, I would call out to her; she would come and soothe me to sleep again.

In 1875, I was living at Fort Hartsuff, Nebraska, a military post, the station of my husband. Our nearest railway station was Grand Island, on the Union Pacific Railroad, 75 miles away. My sister then lived at Omaha, about 300 miles east of Grand Island. Our mail reached us by buckboard from Grand Island every Wednesday and Saturday.

Victorian psychic photograph.

One night in November, I awoke from a dreamless sleep, wide awake, and yet to my own consciousness the little child of years ago, in my own room in the old home; the sister had gone, and I was alone in the darkness. I sat up in bed, and called with all my voice, "Jessie! Jessie!"—my sister's name. This aroused my husband, who spoke to me. I seemed to come gradually to [the] realisation of my surroundings, and with difficulty adjusted myself to the present. In that moment I seemed to live again in the childhood days and home. I cannot express too strongly the feeling of actuality I had.

For days after this the strange impression was with me, and I could recall many little incidents and scenes of child-life that I had entirely forgotten.

I wrote to my sister the next day, and told her of the strange experience of the night before. In a few days I received a letter from her, the date the same as mine, and having passed mine on the way, in which she said that such a strange thing had happened the night before; that she had been awakened by my voice calling her name twice; that the impression was so strong that her husband went to the door to see if it could possibly be I. No one else had called her; she had not been dreaming of me. She distinctly recognised my voice.[177] — MARY M. CLARKSON MANNING, 105 WINTER STREET, PORTLAND, MAINE, OCTOBER 28TH, 1894

SPIRIT RAPS ON HEADBOARD TO ANNOUNCE MOTHER'S DEATH 500 MILES DISTANCE

☛ Within [a] few days after receipt of your last communication, I had a quite remarkable experience, which is best told by submitting to you the letters relating thereto, which I enclose, with also the telegram announcing my mother's death.

I was visiting an old friend at Quitman, Mo., a friend of my girlhood days, and so far as I knew, my mother was in better health than a year before. I had not thought of her even, when my strange experience came.

We had talked over old times that evening. It was the second evening of my stay with family, and I had fallen asleep almost immediately after going to bed. I could not tell the exact time in the morning that the rap came upon headboard of bed, so it appeared to me, but that it was nearly morning I knew, because it was light and clear out-doors, and also because I did not sleep soundly after,—only passed into a half-sleeping condition again,—when apparently a large envelope was thrust before my face with mourning border around it, and death marked upon it.

I had left Quitman Friday morning—with still no indication what occurrence might mean,—until Saturday morning at Hamburg, Ia., the despatch came, telling me of my dear old mother's death. Even then there was a gap between time of occurrence and time of death which could not [be accounted] for, and which was only explained after my arrival in Northern Illinois, five hundred miles away from where I, in some way, heard her trying to call help to her bedside.

How did I hear, across three states, her call for help?

When that question is answered, who, or what, on that first evening, or night, of my mother's illness, knew she would die and gave me the death message, in the morning of the 23rd, that actually came the morning of the 25th?[178] — MATTIE P. KREKEL, KANSAS CITY, MO., JANUARY 17TH, 1894

INJURED SAILOR'S SPIRIT APPEARS TO HIS FATHER

☛ I had a son—a lad of sixteen—at sea in the capacity of an apprentice on board a British barque. One night, while in bed, I suddenly awoke, and saw with great distinctness an apparition of the upper half of my son stretched out on his back on a flat surface by the bedside. He appeared as if in his usual working dress, and I saw his features without the slightest obscurity. He was apparently writhing in pain, and yet unable to do more than move his head a little. Although I seemed to see him close to me, I yet felt that I was powerless to help, and this sense of inability caused me extreme mental distress.

After a while the vision faded, and a period elapsed that I cannot correctly estimate.

Then I again saw his form, prone as before, and with the features still indicating great pain; but this time it was at the opposite end of the room. The consciousness of inability to relieve still possessed me, till the vision faded and I fell asleep.

On awaking in the morning I had a clear recollection of the painful vision, and for weeks I could not shake off the impression that my son had sustained some serious injury. At last, to my great relief, a letter from him came to hand. In it was narrated rather briefly how he had fallen to the deck inconsequence of the breaking of a rotten rope on which he was hauling, and that in consequence he was totally helpless for more than a week. I had not recorded the exact date of the vision, but as nearly as I could make out at the time of reading the letter, the date corresponded with that of the accident.

On his return home, I eagerly asked my boy for the particulars of the occurrence, taking care not to put leading questions, and to keep him ignorant of my experience till he had told me all. I learned that he was stunned by the concussion, and that the first thing he was conscious of was that some persons were lifting him up. Finding him helpless, they laid him down again on the deck. The captain presently came and asked him if any bones were broken, to which he could only indistinctly reply. Then the captain told some one to draw him to one side of the deck, and said that he would come all right in a few hours.

The poor lad remained there without attention until some sympathetic member of the crew carefully lifted him from where he was lying and carried him to his bunk in the deckhouse, where he lay for eight days.

Making further inquiry, and taking the chronological difference into account, I found that the accident happened at an hour when I am usually in bed. Having thus stated the facts, I direct attention particularly to the coincidence (1st) in time of the accident and of my consciousness of it; (2nd) that my son lay for some time in two different places, and that the apparition was thus seen by me, and (3rd) that he felt most pain in his head and upper part of back, and this was evident to me at the time.[179] — W. H. SHRUBSOLE, SHEERNESS-ON-SEA, ENGLAND, EXCERPTED FROM *THE ENGLISH MECHANIC AND WORLD OF SCIENCE,* OCTOBER 7, 1887

SWEDISH MILITARY OFFICER'S GHOST MANIFESTS BEFORE FRIENDS IN RUSSIA AT TIME OF HIS DEATH

☛ On the 16th (28th) of February of this year (1895) between 9 and 10 o'clock in the evening, I, the undersigned, was sitting in our drawing-room—the small one—facing the large drawing-room which I could see in its entire length. My husband, his brother with his wife, and my mother were also sitting in the same room with me round a large round table. I was writing down my household accounts for the day, whilst the others were carrying on some gay conversation.

Having accidentally raised my head and looked into the large drawing-room, I noticed, with astonishment, that a large gray shadow had passed from the door of the dining-room to that of the antechamber; and it came into my head that the figure I had seen bore a striking resemblance in stature to [Swedish] Colonel Av-Meinander, an acquaintance of ours, who had lived in this very lodging for a long time.

At the first moment I wished to say at once that a ghost had just flashed before me, but stopped, as I was afraid of being laughed at by my husband's brother and his wife, and also of being scolded by my husband, who, in view of the excitement which I showed when such phenomena were taking place, tried to convince me that they were the fruit of my fancy. As I knew that Meinander was alive and well, and was commander of the "Malorossüsky" 40th regiment of dragoons, I did not say anything then; but when I was going to bed, I related to my mother what I had seen, and the next morning could not refrain from mentioning it to my husband.

Our astonishment was extreme when on the 18th of February (2nd of March) we learned that Nicholas Ottovitch Av-Meinander had actually died after a short illness on the 16th (28th) of February at 9 o'clock in the evening, in the town of Stashovo [government of Radom, Poland], where his regiment is stationed.[180] — ANNA NICOLAIEVNA BROUSSILOFF, ST. PETERSBURG, RUSSIA, APRIL 19TH, 1895

FEMALE DOG'S GHOST APPEARS TO OWNERS AT TIME OF HER DEATH

☛ I was at Menton [France] in the spring of 1883, having left at home with the gardener a very favourite black and tan terrier, "Judy." I was sitting at table d'hôte with my daughter and husband and suddenly saw Judy run across the room, and exclaimed, "Why, there's Judy!" There was no dog in the room or hotel, but I distinctly saw her, and when I went upstairs after table d'hôte, told my other daughter, Mrs. Wodehouse, what I had seen.

The next letter from home told me that Judy had gone out in the morning well, had apparently picked up some poison, as she was taken ill and died in half an hour; but I cannot say whether it was on the same day that I had seen her. She was almost a human dog, so wonderfully intelligent and understanding, and devoted to me.[181] — MRS. J. W. BAGOT, THE PALACE, HAMPTON COURT, ENGLAND, FEBRUARY 1896

LIVING MAN "WILLS" HIS SPIRIT TO VISIT FRIENDS

☛ I cannot remember the date; but one night two or three years ago, I came back from the theatre to my mother's flat at 6 S. Street [London, England]; and after I had been into her bedroom and told her all about it, I went to bed about 1 a.m.

I had not been asleep long when I started up frightened, fancying that I had heard some one walk down the passage towards my mother's room; but hearing nothing more went again to sleep. I started up alarmed in the same way three or four times before dawn.

In the morning, upon inquiry, my mother (who was ill at the time) only told me she had had a very disturbed night. Then I asked my brother, who told me that he had suffered in the same way as I had, starting up several times in a frightened manner. On hearing this, my mother then told me that she had seen an apparition of Mr. Rose.

Later in the day Mr. Rose came in, and my mother asked him casually if he had been doing anything last night; upon which he told us that he had gone to bed willing that he should visit and appear to us. We made him promise not to repeat the experiment.

A night or so just before, I remember the servant came into my mother's bedroom, alarmed, at 3 a.m.; she said she had heard the electric bell ring. The bell at that time of night is inaccessible to the casual passer-by, as the outer door is then closed. The servant, I believe, heard it more than once; she cried and fancied it was an omen of her mother's death.[182] — MRS. A., FEBRUARY 5TH, 1896

LIVING WOMAN'S GHOST APPEARS TO HER FIANCÉ DURING ILLNESS

☛ Before I was married, some 15 years ago, I was living in Rugby [England]. My present wife, to whom I was then engaged, and whose name was Jane Louisa Cox, was living in Oxford [England] as cook in the family of Mr. Arthur Sidgwick.

One Sunday night I was lying awake in bed, with no reason to believe that any harm was likely to happen to my fiancée, or that she was unwell. It must have been about 11 o'clock when I was startled to see her standing at the foot of my bed in her night dress and her hair down about her shoulders. She was looking at me in an attitude as if imploring help. The phantasm remained for about half a minute and then, slowly gliding towards the window on my left, disappeared. I am sure I was not asleep when the figure appeared. I was much impressed and slept little for the rest of the night.

It was Miss Cox's custom to write to me every Sunday afternoon, so that I got her letter by the first post on Monday. On the Monday after I saw the phantasm, I got no letter by the usual post. This made me feel uneasy, so I wrote off at once saying what I had seen and asking if anything was the matter.

My letter crossed one to me from Miss M., a fellow-servant of Jane Cox, telling me that she had been taken ill the night before and, not being able to write herself as usual, had got her to do so.[183]
— FREDERICK JOHN STAINES, ABBEY STREET, RUGBY, ENGLAND, FEBRUARY 15TH, 1896

APPARITIONS & CLAIRVOYANCE IN NEW YORK

☛ In June 1885 (the exact day is not remembered), I went to bed one evening about 9 o'clock. About an hour afterward, I was awakened from sleep by my wife, who said,

> "Charlie, granny has been here, and she spoke to me. She said to me 'Ellen, I am dead, but don't be afraid. When you come to the funeral, look at the left side of the back part of my head, and you will see the cause of my death.' Granny stood at the foot of the bed, with a night-cap on."

My wife said that when she had spoken to her she disappeared.

The next morning about 8 o'clock a.m., a telegram came, saying that the old lady was dead. My wife took the earliest possible train to the nearest railway station to where her grandmother had lived, which was Gansvoort (near Fort Edward, New York), and then rode some five miles into the country to the house where she had died. The old lady had not been put in her coffin yet, and lay in the front parlour with a night-cap still on her head. My wife said that she went and raised the night-cap and examined the head of the corpse, and found a large bump or bruise on the back of the head.

The place where the old lady died was about 50 miles from where we lived. She and my wife had mutually promised each other that the one who died first would come back and see the survivor, if possible.

The same summer, about a month later, my wife had another similar experience. She was sitting in a room sewing, and noticed a shadow at the door. On looking up, she saw my brother Matthew standing before her. She said, "Why, Mat, what are you doing here? I thought you were sick." She arose to get a chair, but when she turned toward him, he was gone. She looked up and down the street, but could find no trace of him. On my return in the evening, she told me what had happened, and expressed a fear that my brother was dead.

The next morning a telegram came, saying that my brother had died the previous day at about the hour in which she saw the vision. He died about ten miles distant.

During the fall of 1888, in the month of October, I was absent from my home in Albany. I was in Buffalo, New York, which is about 400 miles from my home. On returning, after an absence of about two months, my wife surprised me by informing me of where I had been and what I had done nearly every day while I was away. She was very correct in her information, which was derived wholly by some sort of clairvoyant power. She told me the hour at which I took trains for various places, and met me at the depôt on my return, although I had written her that I should be home several days later.[184] — CHARLES E. MARTRATT, ALBANY, NEW YORK, JULY 19TH, 1891

PARENTS' GHOSTS APPEAR TO DAUGHTER 200 MILES AWAY

☛ In July 1877 . . . Mrs. Jamieson knew that her mother was ill and dying. She, Mrs. J., was at Aldershot [England] with her husband, and was to go and see her mother in about a week.

One night she awoke feeling thirsty. She had not dreamt of her mother. Not caring to disturb her husband, she thought she would get water for herself. When about to get out of bed, she saw in the white dimity curtains at the foot of the bed the features of her mother, the whole figure standing upright, with her face bound up as if dead—like her mother, but not as though alive. Mrs. Jamieson is not certain whether there was a light in the room or not.

Mrs. Jamieson lay back in her bed and did not look for a minute or so, then looking up, saw it again and leant forward and shook the curtains. The figure disappeared; but at the same time she saw the shadow of her father just in the same form and appearance on the other curtain. She looked again and that was gone. She did not wake her husband at once, but did about a quarter of an hour after, as she felt faint, and later in the night told him what she had seen.

About eight o'clock the next morning, a telegram came, saying her mother had died at three o'clock. She is quite sure that her vision occurred on the same night, or rather morning, as the telegram was received.

Mrs. Jamieson's mother, Mrs. Griffith, died on July 13th, 1877, at Chester [England]. Her father did not die for many years after. When Mrs. Jamieson saw the vision, she felt sure her mother was dead. The face being bound up made her feel more convinced.[185]
— WRITTEN IN THE THIRD PERSON BY JANE ANNE JAMIESON, APRIL 13TH, 1896

CHILD SEES GHOST OF HER DYING MOTHER

☛ Philip [Spencer, of Holloway, Derbyshire, England] and his first wife, Martha, who was a cousin of mine, having no children of their own, adopted the little daughter of a young woman, who went to live at Derby. The child called them father and mother as soon as she could speak, not remembering her own parents, not even her mother.

The spirit image of this woman's deceased mother (upper left) was imprinted by a psychic in this Victorian ghost photograph.

While yet very young, she one day began to cry out that there was a young woman looking at her, and wanting to come to her, and according to her description of the person, it must have been her mother. As no one else saw the apparition, and the child continued for more than half an hour to be very excited, Philip took her out of the house to that of a neighbour; but the apparition kept them company, talking by the way. They then went to another house, where it accompanied them still, and seemed as though it wanted to embrace the child; but at last vanished in the direction of Derby—as the little girl, now a young woman, describes it—*in a flash of fire.*

Derby is about fourteen miles distant from Holloway, and as in that day there was neither railway nor telegraph, communication between them was much slower than at present. As soon, however, as it was possible for intelligence to come, the news arrived that the poor child's mother had been *burnt to death*; that it happened about the time when it saw her apparition; and, in short, that she was sorrowing and crying to be taken to the child during the whole of the time between being burnt and her expiration.

This is no "idle ghost story," but a simple matter of fact, to which not only Philip but all his old neighbours can testify; and the young woman has not only related it more than once to me, but she told it in the same artless and earnest manner to my friend, the late Dr. Samuel Brown, of Edinburgh, who once called at the cottage with me—repeating it still more clearly to Messrs. Fowler and Wells, on our recent visit.[186] — DR. SPENCER TIMOTHY HALL, 1863

THE GHOSTS OF AYECROFT HALL

☞ The ghost seen at Ayecroft Hall is the figure of a woman, sometimes black, and sometimes white. Only the back is generally seen—the face has never been seen. The figure has been seen in nearly all the rooms at different times. I have only seen it once myself, some years ago.

It was in broad daylight, about 11 a.m.; I was kneeling in a doorway, superintending its decoration for a party; I looked up and saw the figure—in black—which appeared to have walked over me, through the doorway. It went through a door on the left into the hall. Two people were in there. I followed quickly and questioned the people in the room. The figure was not there, nor had they seen anybody come in before me.

It has been seen in daylight since by a friend. I can give you his name and address: Theo. J. Bolland, Esq., Longreach, Keynsham, Somersetshire [England]. He says he will be glad to answer any questions you may ask him. Also Mr. Harrison; I will send you his statement.

My husband has seen the figure a great many times, and friends who have been staying with us, and servants have seen it. My husband has seen it at night. There is an archway from the hall (where we sit) into the entrance hall. There are two doors, one on right and one on left of entrance hall, one is the drawing-room and the other the library. My husband sitting in the hall, facing the entrance hall, has several times seen a figure cross from the drawing-room door to the library, and on following it at once, has found nobody there. There was no other door to library. My husband also saw it in daylight last summer in the same place.

There are strange noises heard about the house at times. We have frequently thought we heard a carriage drive up to the door in the evening, and have gone out and seen nothing; but we think this may be accounted for by trains passing. The appearance of the ghost has been followed by a death in either my husband's family or my own in every case. We know of no story in connection with the ghost, but my husband succeeded an old invalid lady, his cousin, and he had never seen her. She only lived at Ayecroft two months in the year.

I had a very vivid experience of a ghost, at Buxton [England], in an old house, some years ago. There was a story about that, and I described the man who appeared exactly, although I did not know anything about a ghost or any story, before seeing it.[187] — ALICE DAUNTESEY, AYECROFT HALL, MANCHESTER, ENGLAND, JUNE 15TH, 1896

POSTSCRIPT TO THE GHOSTS OF AYECROFT HALL

☛ Dear Sir: I am very glad to answer any questions you may wish to ask. I have never heard that any of the people who saw the ghost at Ayecroft had any of the symptoms you describe; they appeared to be startled only, and not even frightened.

My husband says that there was no gradual development from mist or shadow of the form he saw; it appeared as you describe it, full-blown, exactly as a living person would. As far as I know, this was the case when others saw it. My husband says he saw the apparition about six times, but in the two instances he mentioned to you the figure was very much more distinct than in the others. The appearances have spread over the 14½ years that we have been married. We never heard of anything being seen before then; but, as I told you, we were not likely to hear or know anything about the house.

My husband is of a very calm temperament, who looks the very last person one would connect with a ghost-story. He is absolutely "without nerves" as we say, and not in the least imaginative. I am of a very nervous temperament myself, and am very often wakeful at night, and yet I have only seen the ghost at Ayecroft once.

I hear that last week my head housemaid, a woman of over 30, had a fit of hysterics, caused by, as she says, a ghost walking along the passage outside her room. She is firmly convinced that it was no human footfall she heard. She was a new servant, as, strangely enough, all the others are, and my housekeeper assures me that nothing was known by any of them about the house being "haunted."

It is a strange thing, but everybody who has seen or heard a ghost at Ayecroft, seems to be absolutely certain that what they heard or saw was supernatural, and no amount of persuasion, of suggesting of other causes, will move them. I should prefer not to ask this woman to write her experience down, as it is important for me not to frighten the servants, and it would do so if I were to speak of it to them. I could, however, get you an account written by a former housemaid, who saw the ghost distinctly eleven years ago. She has been married some time, and would not be likely to be writing to any of the present servants.

With regard to the ghost I saw at Buxton, I can affirm that I had no idea that a ghost had ever been seen in those rooms, or that anybody had hanged himself over the banisters. I had heard some years before, but had entirely forgotten it, that in another part of the house, downstairs, "a little grey lady" passed through a swing door. I am sure this had no connection with the experience I had.

My ghost was an old gentleman dressed as I have described, and my mother-in-law told me some years after, and before I told her of my experience, that this old gentleman had been seen in the very doorway I mention. It had not been spoken of for many years, and my husband, who had lived there for many years of his early life, had entirely forgotten it. It certainly had never been mentioned to me. I had had an attack of faintness at the dinner table, and had gone up to my room to lie down, when I looked up and saw it. It was not quite dusk, but not broad daylight.

. . . [Back to] the ghost I saw at Buxton, the old gentleman I saw was dressed in a dark blue cloth coat, with brass buttons; the coat was cut away very much as an ordinary dress coat is now-a-days. He had a white necktie wound round and round his neck, of the kind described, I believe, as a "choker," with a tiny bow in front.

What I heard afterwards was this: that an old man who lived in the house a great many years ago, hanged himself over the banisters, and that 20 years previously to the time I saw the ghost, he had often appeared and had frightened the nursemaids. He had appeared exactly where I saw him. I feel quite certain that I had never heard the story until after I saw the figure, and it was two years after. My mother-in-law had left Wyelands for many years, and had gone back to it again to live, and that is the reason, I suppose, why the story had died out.[188] — ALICE DAUNTESEY, AYECROFT HALL, MANCHESTER, ENGLAND, JUNE 26TH, 1896

TESTIMONIES CONCERNING ONE OF DUBLIN, IRELAND'S MOST HAUNTED HOUSES

☛ *Testimony One:* At _____ Dublin, one evening, about 1878, in the twilight I was walking upstairs with a pair of shoes in my hand, when passing a landing on which there was a pedestal with a bust of William Shakespeare on it, I saw a tall lady dressed in grey suddenly appear before me and stand in front of the pedestal, which became hidden— which would prove it was not a "vapoury vision" I saw. I was so surprised and frightened at the extreme suddenness of the figure that I involuntarily threw my shoes at it, when the figure immediately vanished, my shoes striking the pedestal and seeming to pass through the impression.

I was unnerved a good deal. I was in the best of health at the time. About 15 years [old]. The face was not familiar [to me]. No [other persons were present]. I have since then frequently had the same impression of the same figure—always in grey. I now anticipate a certain amount of pleasure in the hope of seeing her, as the face was always kindly disposed.

We all call this figure the "Grey Lady," as several of us have seen her. I had occasion to let my stabling [animal accommodations] for some months last year, and the tenant informed me several times that there was another person in the place besides himself—a grey lady—but she seemed always pleased to see him, but would never speak, disappearing if spoken to. — MR. J. R., JULY 9TH, 1895

Testimony Two: I was standing one afternoon, some years ago, at the top landing of the house, Dublin, when I distinctly saw a tall lady, completely dressed in grey, walking up the top flight of stairs towards me. I was rather surprised, but not at all frightened, as she looked quite like an ordinary mortal. She turned to the left when she reached the top and smiling at me entered a room through a closed door. I immediately opened the door, but found no one there. (It was broad daylight at the time.)

I was talking to a nurse at the time. I was about 11 or 12 years old. I was in perfect health. The impression resembled nobody I ever saw before. When I asked [the nurse] did she see any one, she replied she saw a light passing by towards the door.

[Another time] I was sleeping in the room referred to, when one morning I saw a face looking round the door and smiling at me. This occurred some years before the first written impression, but I am certain it was the same face as the lady in grey had. I have frequently heard unaccountable noises in this room; others have also heard them. — MR. C. R., JULY 8TH, 1895

Testimony Three: I was sitting in the front drawing-room of _____ Dublin, some years ago, one Sunday evening, about 7:30, in summer, when I saw a tall woman, draped all in grey, standing in the archway dividing the rooms. The face was rather indistinct. I was startled and exclaimed, "Do you see that?" to a lady who was also in the room, (and whose house we were in) but as I spoke, the figure disappeared. I had been suffering from severe toothache all the evening; otherwise was in excellent health; was 17 or 18 [years old]. I had never seen any one at all resembling the figure, which looked something like a nun. One lady was in the room, but she saw nothing. — MISS A. R., JULY 8TH, 1885

Testimony Four: My sister has explained how and where our billiard room was situated. One evening—I think about September, 1883—my sister A., a nursery-maid, and myself were in the "workshop"; while there we heard footsteps overhead of people walking round the table, apparently playing billiards, as we heard the balls cannoning. On coming out of the "workshop" we saw the billiard room was lit up, so we crept upstairs, thinking we would surprise the players; the door had two panes of glass on top. When we got to the top of the stairs we saw light through them, but on opening the door the room was in utter darkness. We thought they had put out the light, but turned and fled into the house, and then discovered that no one had been out there. My sister and the maid both saw and heard exactly as I did.

Very nearly the same thing occurred once again when I was quite alone. I could not possibly say how often I have seen light in the billiard room from our back windows, when I knew no one was out there; and I may safely say a day never passed during the time we had the billiard table that the balls were not heard "clicking." I have heard it from the garden when with two or three other people, and have gone up to find the room empty and the table covered.

Noises coming from the mantle.

Since the stable has been let, not one of us has heard the sound of balls. Whether the "Grey Lady" played "dummy" billiards or not, I am not in a position to say.

I was a small child, and was coming upstairs to my nursery, which was on the top landing, when on the last flight of stairs and in view of the door of the room I saw a little old country woman (with a frilled cap under her bonnet and a shawl) standing in the doorway. At first I thought she was my nurse's mother, who was in the habit of coming to see us; but when I came nearer, I found she was some one I had never seen before. She smiled at me, and though I was not the least frightened, I turned and ran downstairs—I fancy because I was shy and did not like strangers. Afterwards I heard no stranger had been in the house. I never saw her again, and though many years ago, I should know the face if I ever did meet her.

One night in November 1894, when we had all gone up to our bedrooms, I wanted something out of the drawing-room. As all the lights were out, I brought down a candle. When I opened the drawing-room door, I saw "something," I really don't know what, but it was a sort of shadow leaning over a table in the window. However, it gave me such a fright that I dropped my candle and ran upstairs to my sister's room. She asked me what had frightened me so much; I then told her what I had seen. She offered to come down with me and see what it was; but I thought it better to go alone, so went down again without a light, and when I was in the room I struck a match and picked up my candle, etc., and looked all round, but there was nothing of any kind visible.[189] — MISS M. R., JULY 18TH, 1885; ALL FOUR TESTIMONIES SUBMITTED BY MRS. ST. GEORGE, OF 2 JERVIS PLACE, CLONMEL, IRELAND, JULY 10TH, 1895

"UNPLEASANT DRAPED FIGURE" EXTINGUISHES CANDLE
☛ In 1853 Dr. and Mrs. Gwynne were living in a house haunted by unaccountable noises—sighs and heavy breathing close to the side of the bed, for instance. One night they both awoke to see a draped figure passing along the foot of the bed towards the fireplace. "I had the impression," says Dr. Gwynne, "that the arm was raised, pointing with the hand towards the mantel-piece, on which a night-light was burning. Mrs. Gwynne at this moment seized my arm and the light was extinguished. The night-light in question was relit and placed in a toilette basin, and burned naturally. I tried to convince myself that it might have been a gust of wind down the chimney that put the light out."

Mrs. Gwynne says that her husband's statement accords with her recollection, "but I distinctly saw the hand of the phantom placed over the night-light, which was at once extinguished. Dr. Gwynne, on the appearance of the phantom, in order to calm my agitated state, tried to reason with me and to persuade me that it might have been the effects of the moonlight and clouds passing over the openings of the shutters, and possibly that a gust of wind might have extinguished the light, but I knew differently. When we had both been awakened at the same moment apparently, and together saw that unpleasant figure, tall and, as it were, draped like a nun, deliberately walk up to the mantel-piece and put out the light with the right hand, there could be no mistake about it."[190] — HENSLEIGH WEDGWOOD, 1887

GHOST HAND DISPLAYS DELIVERY OF LETTER

☛ [On] . . . February 4th, 1882, I had published an account of a night spent in a haunted house, and on the 17th, when I went downstairs about 8 o'clock to my study to dress, I found a letter on the hall-table, as usual, waiting for me, from a lady at Minehead [England], whose name I had never heard of, about [my published] narrative . . ., which had greatly interested her.

At that time my son Alfred and his wife were occupying different bedrooms, and when Alfred came down to breakfast at 9 he had not seen his wife, who was keeping her room. But soon after I had returned to my study Alfred burst eagerly in upon me, asking if I had received a letter that morning "all about ghosts," as his wife had seen such a letter coming for me the preceding night.

On going up to her I found that before going to sleep she had seen a hand coming from behind the screen at the foot of her bed, holding a letter in more sheets than one, and in a hand she did not know. The next morning at post-time she was looking out for the letter, and wondering who it could be from, when something said to her, "It is not for you; it is gone downstairs; it is all about ghosts."

When I showed her the letter she recognised it as the one she had seen, and remembered the post-mark, Minehead, a town whose name she had never heard of. The previous afternoon, when reading her book, she had seen the word Minehead written across the page, but she had not connected it with my letter until she saw the post-mark when I showed her the cover.[191] — HENSLEIGH WEDGWOOD

EVENTS IN A WELSH HAUNTED HOUSE

☛ One cold winter's night I awoke, and to my great surprise I found there was bright firelight in the room. I sat up in bed and noticed that the ordinary grate was not to be seen, but in its place appeared an old-fashioned open hearth upon which was blazing a splendid fire, the light of which filled the room and had woke me up. I saw a small strip of carpet laid down in front of the fire, but there was no fender. When we went to bed there had been a large fender, but no carpet and no fire.

As I looked with astonishment, I particularly remarked a bright pair of brass fire-dogs, with very curious and pretty twisted fire-irons resting upon them. By the side of the fire was a beautifully-carved oak arm-chair, made with a square seat, the point of which was in front, and a rounded back. It was such a chair as was used 200 years ago. In this chair was sitting an old man; he was resting his elbow on the arm of the chair, and with his hand supporting his head; he was looking directly towards me, with an intent, sad gaze. He was dressed in the style of the olden times—200 years ago—with knee breeches and stockings. I noticed, curiously, the flicker of the fire, as it was reflected in his bright knee and shoe buckles.

I woke my sister, who was sleeping with me, saying, "Do you not see that old man sitting by the fire? She sat up by my side, but saw nothing, and advised me to "Go to sleep," advice she acted upon herself, but I lay down and shut my eyes for a time, then sat up, and again saw the scene that I have described, and watched it for some little time, for I was not in the least frightened, not even at the sight of the old man, and I often wish I had spoken to him. At last I lay down and went to sleep.

On awaking in the morning, my sister asked me what I had been talking about in the night, fully admitting that when I awoke her I was myself most fully awake, and not in a dreaming condition. We had been living in the house about two months when this occurred, and we found that it was known throughout the town to be haunted. We lived there nearly two years, and during the whole time were annoyed by mysterious knockings and noises, but the "White Lady" did not show herself until just as we were leaving [i.e., moving out].

My father and mother had already returned home, sending me, with my younger sister and a young housemaid, to finish the packing up. On the Saturday evening my sister and I went out, leaving the servant to cord some boxes, and put the rooms in order; we did not return till past ten o'clock, when, to our surprise, we found the servant sitting in the hall with the front door open. She began to cry on seeing us, saying she had been much frightened. She told us that after we had gone out, and she had changed her dress, as she was coming out of her room, which opened on to the front staircase, she thought she saw me coming upstairs, only I had changed my dress, and had on a long white one; she exclaimed, "Oh! Miss A., you are never going out, just now, in your best white dress?"

By the time she had said this the figure was close up to her; then she saw it was a woman, dressed in a long trailing gown of some white material, but she could not distinguish any face. The figure stopped when quite close to her, and suddenly she thought what it really was—the ghost!—upon which, with a scream, she sprang over the flowing train, ran down into the hall, and had been sitting by the open door ever since. She had seen the figure walk into the drawing-room.

The girl was so much alarmed that I told her she could make up a bed for herself in the room that I, with my sister, was occupying. It was the bedroom where I had seen the old man by the fire.

That night passed quietly, but the next night a strange thing happened.

We were very late; it was past twelve before we all three retired to our room. You will understand that there was no one else in the house but our three selves. As the door would not latch securely, I placed before it, to keep it shut, a chair, with a heap of things upon it. The servant and my sister were in bed. I was standing by the dressing-table, when suddenly the door was pushed open so violently that the chair was thrown out into the middle of the room. I turned round sharply, and there saw, standing in the doorway, the tall figure of a woman in a long white dress, such as had been described by the servant. The sudden opening of the door had so terrified both the servant and my sister that I was compelled to give my attention to calming both of them down. I did not tell them what I had seen, as I would not frighten them more. I should add that when the figure went away, the door was drawn to again.

Some few minutes passed before I had quieted my sister. I then lighted a night-light, and put out the candle preparatory to getting into bed myself. To my surprise I saw, when the room was thus darkened, that there was a bright seam of light all round the door, which would not close tightly. I went and opened the door, and found the whole passage illuminated by this white light, as light as day, but I saw no more of the figure. This frightened me dreadfully, but I could only jump into bed and feel glad it was our last night in that house. I should say that for many years that room had been nailed up as unfit for occupation, on account of the haunting; it had not been very long unfastened when we went to stay there.[192] — MRS. MARY ETHEL MORRIS, PENTRABACH, TRECASTLE, BRECONSHIRE, WALES, 1878

AUDITORY PHENOMENA AT THE HAUNTED WELSH HOUSE

☛ [From the same informant as above:] During our stay of nearly two years' duration in the house before spoken of at L_____, we were constantly hearing odd noises, generally at night, or at evening.

A door leading to a cupboard in the drawing-room (which was directly under my bedroom) would sometimes bang loudly, although I and my sister, who shared my room, had carefully locked it before retiring for the night. This was of frequent occurrence. Also the sound of a heavy tread coming upstairs towards our room door, which sounded like the tread of a person coming slowly upstairs and wearing heavy boots, and always pausing when apparently close to the top. This sound was of a less frequent occurrence, and we sometimes thought might have been caused by rats. The house being old, rats abounded.

On one occasion, when sitting up with my father, both he and I and the servant, who had gone that instant to a bedroom opposite for a few hours' sleep, heard a most piercing and awful scream; so terrible was it that my father started up with the exclamation, "Good God! what's that?" I sprang from my chair, and Charlotte, the servant, came to the door in horror to know if I had "heard that." She had gone to my mother's room, who was quietly asleep; and on going from room to room we found every member of the family asleep. The scream lasted some seconds and seemed to fill the air of the whole house. It was beyond description.[193] — MRS. MARY ETHEL MORRIS, PENTRABACH, TRECASTLE, BRECONSHIRE, WALES, 1878

DECEASED MOTHER APPEARS TO DAUGHTER

☛ After two years since the death of my mother, when all sad recollections were gone, I was walking one day, at 10 a.m., downstairs by myself. All of a sudden I heard a kind of scuttle, and turned round to see what it was, and there saw distinctly my late mother coming out of her morning-room, dressed as usual, black silk dress, large white apron and collar, white stockings and black shoes. I watched for a moment or two, and saw her turn, to go up a pair of stairs to her late bedroom, when all of a sudden her head went off and the apparition disappeared. I related the fact at the time, and it was considered nonsense. I only saw it once, and hoped I should not again.[194] — MISS R. J., PLUCKLEY, KENT, ENGLAND, RECORDED CIRCA APRIL 1887

WOMAN'S SPIRIT MANIFESTS ON STAIRWAY

☞ [The ghost in the previous entry appeared two years later to a second relative in the same location, as recorded here:] On leaving the nursery, about eight o'clock in the evening, I saw the apparition of an old lady going slowly up a few stairs at the end of passage. There was no light where I was, but there was partial light on the stairs from the hall gaslight. I stood still, astonished, knowing there was no one in the house like her. The lady had her back to me, an elderly lady, rather small, a dark dress, a little shawl or something light about the shoulders, a cap. She vanished before reaching the top stair.

Some weeks after I mentioned the circumstance to a young lady, F. B., who was on a visit to us, and described the apparition. She said, "That is my grandmamma." (Died August 3rd, 1855.) I never saw the old lady in her lifetime. I did not keep a date of the occurrence, but, as far as I can remember, it was the winter of 1859.[195] — MRS. J. S. J., PLUCKLEY, KENT, ENGLAND, RECORDED CIRCA APRIL 1887

CLERGYMAN'S GHOST APPEARS TO OLD FRIEND

☞ When at Loweswater, I one day called upon a friend, who said, "You do not see many newspapers; take one of those lying there." I accordingly took up a newspaper, bound with a wrapper, put it into my pocket and walked home.

In the evening I was writing, and, wanting to refer to a book, went into another room where my books were. I placed the candle on a ledge of the bookcase, took down a book and found the passage I wanted, when, happening to look towards the window, which was opposite to the bookcase, I saw through the window the face of an old friend whom I had known well at Cambridge, but had not seen for 10 years or more, Canon Robinson, (of the Charity and School Commission). I was so sure I saw him that I went out to look for him, but could find no trace of him. I went back into the house and thought I would take a look at my newspaper. I tore off the wrapper, unfolded the paper, and the first piece of news that I saw was the death of Canon Robinson![196] — GEO. M. TANDY, VICAR OF WEST-WARD, CIRCA 1884

FUNERAL PROCESSION IN A DRAWING-ROOM
☞ Mrs. V., whose husband was in the Artillery in India, told me the following occurred to herself. The story is well known in her family. She has been dead some years, and it occurred when she was comparatively a young woman. I heard it from her 23 years ago last Christmas, at Southampton.

One evening, sitting in her drawing-room, she saw distinctly a military funeral procession pass at the further end of the room. The coffin borne on a gun-carriage. The men with arms reversed. Directly it passed away, she noted the circumstance, writing it down, and passed some months in greatest anxiety. It was before the days of overland route.

She heard of her husband's death, which had occurred that day, and allowing for the difference of time, the funeral had taken place at the moment she had seen the vision, death and burial following each other within a few hours in India.[197] — MRS. H. G. BLACK, 5 HAZLITT ROAD, WEST KENSINGSTON PARK, LONDON, ENGLAND, MARCH 14, 1884

Celebrated Victorian Scottish medium, Daniel Dunglas Home, noted for his many successful séances and amazing acts of bodily levitation. As with all those involved in paranormal mediumship, Home too was attacked and criticized by nonbelievers, who proposed numerous scientific theories in order to explain away his feats and discredit him. However, in the eyes of believers, hundreds of credible eyewitnesses to Home's powers have fully vindicated him.

CHAPTER NINE

EDITOR'S NOTE: I HAVE DEVOTED THIS ENTIRE CHAPTER TO ACCOUNTS CONCERNING A SINGLE HAUNTED HOUSE IN ENGLAND. L.S.

HAUNTED HOUSE IN AN ENGLISH COUNTRY VILLAGE

☞ [Shortly after purchasing it] the first thing that struck us as peculiar about our house was hearing footsteps in empty rooms.

January 8th, 1885: We had been in the house about six months. My mother and I were in the dining-room; there was one maid in the house and no one else. I was lying half asleep on the sofa. I heard someone walking up and down in the room overhead, which was then a spare bedroom (now a drawing-room). I was too sleepy at first to think it strange, though my mother more than once tried to call my attention to it. At last she roused me and said someone was in the house. The bells were ringing for Evensong, so it must have been between half-past four and five.

I got up and listened, and I then noticed the footsteps were heavy, like a man's, and that they went backwards and forwards as if he were going from the washhand-stand to the dressing-table and back again, not hurriedly, and not slowly; in fact, for the moment, it gave one the impression someone was dressing for dinner.

I called the maid and we all three heard the steps. We took our dog, a Skye terrier, knowing he would make a noise at a stranger, and went upstairs. I put the dog into the room first; he was quite quiet. I do not remember if he seemed frightened, but I think he ran out again. The room was quite empty. I was so certain someone must be there that I even looked in a large cupboard, but that, too, was empty.

Still, my mother was not contented, but sent for the gardener to come and see if anyone could be on the roof. He said no one could be there; the roof slants. As we went into the room my mother said she heard a sound like a crash of glass; there was no broken glass anywhere.

The next time, as nearly as I can remember, was on the 22nd of January; since then we have not kept much count.

Last winter a lady was staying with us. She called me into the dining-room to ask who was in the drawing-room. I heard the footsteps, but I was nearly certain no one could be in there, as I had put two boxes on the step leading to the drawing-room ready for the maid to take to the box-room. However, to make sure, I went and looked, and the boxes had not been moved.

At nights I have heard footsteps in the passage outside my bedroom (blue-room).

I was sleeping in the green bedroom, one night last winter, when I heard footsteps like a child, with bare feet, running across a piece of oilcloth that goes from one door to another.

I cannot say how often I have heard footsteps at one time and another in different parts of the house.

One afternoon I was quite alone in the house. Miss Blencowe had come to stay with me. I was obliged to leave her while I went into the village for a few minutes. She was sitting in the pink sitting-room. She afterwards told me she had heard someone walking about in the room overhead, which was the green-room.

The other day our German maid, who knows nothing about the ghost, came and told me someone had been walking about in my bedroom. I told her there was no one in the house to do so, but she persisted in what she said.[198]

One night, when I was sleeping in the green bedroom, I felt my bed, which is a very large, heavy one, shake, and then I heard something knocking on it.

Another time I was awoke just as the clock struck three by hearing a loud noise, as if some heavy substance were being struck by a piece of iron; there were about 25 blows. The next morning one of the maids told Emilie that she had not been able to sleep since three o'clock, as Miss Humble, who slept over her, had been knocking about her iron bedstead. Miss Humble, before I spoke, complained that she had been disturbed, and described the same kind of noise.

December 10th, 1887: My mother and Emilie were both with me in the blue bedroom; the other maid was in bed. We heard a door bang downstairs. A few minutes after, I went into the passage and heard some one crushing a piece of paper. I looked up and down, but could not see anyone.

Some nights ago there was so much noise downstairs, between 11 and 12, that I lit a candle and went down to see, but all was quiet.

January 24th, 1888: I was coming upstairs and heard something coming up after me. I thought it was one of the dogs, and kept looking first on one side and then on the other, but I could not see anything; I could only hear.

I was in the drawing-room (it was then my mother's bedroom), in the winter of 1885 or 1886, about eight o'clock one evening; the gas was lighted enough for me to see round the room, when I heard a gruff voice behind me. I could not distinguish the words, but thought it was the parrot mocking someone she had heard in the street. I turned quickly and there was no one. I then remembered the parrot was downstairs. I remained a few minutes, but heard nothing more.[199]

I was coming down the passage, one afternoon, about half-past four. I saw a fair-haired girl standing on the top of the stairs. It was dusk. I did not notice her face, but supposed it to be the maid; she was dressed in a greyish or mauve dress, such as would have been very common for servants some years ago. As we were in mourning at the time, I was surprised that the girl should have had on a coloured dress when she knew it would be against our wish. In a minute or two I went downstairs and found the maid, as usual in black; nor had she been upstairs.

In October, 1886, I was, one afternoon, quite alone in the house. My mother and the maids were out, but I sent for Miss Blencowe to come and stay with me. Before she came I had locked the doors (three) leading into the garden, leaving only the hall door unlocked. We were sitting in a little room out of the hall, when I thought I heard someone walk across the hall. Thinking it must be the gardener, who, unable to get in at the back door, had come through to unfasten one of the pantry doors, I went out to make sure, and, I suppose, to see what he wanted; but the hall was empty, and the pantry door leading into the garden locked. I went back and sat down a second, and a third time. I thought someone was in the house.

I said to my friend, "I must go upstairs and see if all be safe; I am afraid someone is in the house."

Miss Blencowe followed me. I went into the rooms, closing the doors and windows as I went. When I came out of my own room, I said to Miss Blencowe (without looking round), half in fun, "It must be the ghost." I then went down the back stairs, and so back to our room where we had been sitting.

When we got there Miss Blencowe said to me, "What do you mean by saying it is the ghost?"

I answered, still half in fun, "This house is haunted."

Miss Blencowe said, "Is it haunted by a woman dressed in mauve, and does she stand at the top of the stairs?"

Wondering what she meant, but never thinking for a moment she had seen anything, I said, "Yes, it is; but, why do you ask?"

She said, "I have seen such a figure."

She then went with me and showed me the place where I had seen the girl some time before.[200]

December 10th, 1887. Not feeling well, I was lying in bed about half past eight in the morning. Emilie came into my room in a hurry and asked what was the matter, as I was knocking about the furniture. I told her I was not doing anything of the kind; as I was in bed I could not be.

About 20 minutes passed and she came up again to know if I called, saying some one had called her three times. Soon after, my mother came in to speak to me; there was no one else in the house but the German maid, and she was downstairs. In a few minutes Emilie ran back into my room, looking frightened, and saying she had seen a figure standing on the top of the stairs, dressed in white, which she thought to be my mother till she heard her talking in my room.[201]

[One night my mother woke me up at 11:00 p.m., asking if I had called for her. I said "No."] A few seconds elapsed after I had asked [her] what o'clock it was; time enough for my mother to leave the room.

She then—or someone like her—a woman with dark hair, and wearing a red (what I believed to be a) dressing-jacket, bent over me. The figure held a candle in her hand, and said, "Won't you kiss me?"

I had been lying with my face to the wall, but I turned round, sat up, and kissed something which I quite believed to be my mother. Since then my mother has again and again been roused. Now she does not come unless she hears my bell.

Last New Year's eve, December 1887, my mother, Emilie, and I were in the drawing-room putting up some brackets. Suddenly, Emilie ran to the door saying someone was standing on the top of the stairs. I followed her, but no one was to be seen. It would have been quite impossible for any human being to have gone downstairs so quickly; we could see up the passage and down the stairs.²⁰²

January, Sunday, 22ⁿᵈ, 1888. I was in the drawing-room about 11 o'clock in the evening. The door was open; our German maid was in bed and my mother had gone into my bedroom. I heard Emilie come upstairs and pause outside the door, and then go down the passage to her own room. I did not look up. There was a screen between the door and myself; not a high screen. I was surprised Emilie did not come right into the room and see if I wanted anything.

Soon after, I went to bed, but, on looking out of my window, I saw the reflection of gas, so went into the passage and saw the light was left quite up; the one on the top of the stairs. I turned it out and went back to bed.

The next morning Emilie mentioned that she was coming into the drawing-room the previous evening, but that, as my mother had crossed the room and pushed the door to while she was there, she supposed we wanted to be alone, and so had turned out the gas on the top of the stairs and gone to bed. I told her my mother had not been in the room when she came upstairs, but she kept repeating that someone had pushed to the door while she was there; it did not seem to strike her for a moment that she had seen one of the ghosts.

I asked her what made her so certain it was my mother, and she said because she had on her light dressing-gown. My mother happened not to have on her light dressing-gown at all, but was in red; besides, as I said before, she was in my bedroom at the time. The dressing-gown is not unlike, in colour, the dress worn by the girl who stands on the top of the stairs, and might easily be mistaken for it. It is strange that Emilie turned out the gas and I found it [turned] up.²⁰³

My mother says On the 29ᵗʰ of December 1887, I was alone in

the house, except the German maid, who was downstairs. I was coming down the attic stairs; my little Yorkshire-terrier was in front of me. A girl with fair hair, in a lilac dress, passed me; she looked right into my face; she was very pale, and had something the matter with one of her eyes. The dog gave a howl, and dashed down to the dining-room. By the time I got into the passage she was gone. As I went down the stairs to the dining-room the German [maid] came to ask if I had rung, as the bell had been pulled violently.

I was coming down the passage some time ago. I saw a woman before me. I thought it was one of the maids; she went into the blue bedroom. I followed; but the room was empty. My little dog, a Skye-terrier, ran back into the sitting-room, and jumped up on to a chair, where he sat shivering.

About the end of December 1887, I was lying awake, when I saw a woman with brown hair hanging down her back. (My bedroom is a double one, with curtains between.) She was standing, holding back one of the curtains. She had on a slate-coloured silk dress and a red kind of opera cloak. She remained three or four minutes.[204]

January 31st. Last night was awoke by feeling my room shake. I roused myself and heard someone walk across the room twice. I looked about, but could not see anything; the steps seemed to be in the next room. I then listened and heard voices. At first I thought my mother must be ill, and it was one of the maids with her. I was going to get up and go in to her, when I heard someone crying. I then satisfied myself it was not my mother, but I thought it might be one of the ghosts.

When I heard the talking and walking about, and fancied something was the matter with my mother, it made me feel so ill that I could not go to sleep for some time; so there is not the least doubt but that I was wide awake; besides, when I went into my mother's room, this morning, the first thing she asked me was if I had been disturbed, as she had been roused by hearing a loud crash, as if a sack of coals were being emptied. She also told me that she had not been out of bed, nor had she spoken in the night.

Some time ago, about two years, I think, I was roused by a loud crash outside my door. A child was sleeping in a room over the drawing-room at the time, and my idea was that she must have been walking in her sleep, and fallen downstairs. For a minute I was afraid to open my door for fear I should find her lying there. As I came out of my room mother and Emilie came out of theirs. All was quite quiet. We went upstairs and found Winnie sitting up in bed. What had startled us, I suppose, had startled her.

Once or twice in the daytime we have been disturbed by hearing a crash, as if something had been broken. Constantly the doors shake as if someone had struck against them, or as if something heavy had fallen in some part of the house. The piano is heard at times.

February 14th, 1888. The house is locked up for the night and Emilie is with my mother and me. We have just been startled by a loud noise. I was at first afraid to go out of the room for fear someone had got into the house, for it seemed as if someone had come in at the hall door and banged it. The room we were in was shaken when the noise came. There have been two more noises.

March 28th, 1888. Both last night and to-night from eight to nine, I have been alone in the house, the others being at church. There has been one noise after another. Once or twice I thought someone had got into the house. To-night I was so frightened I felt I must go out into the garden. Though I know there is something supernatural about the place at the time, the noises are so like those made by living people, I cannot bring myself to believe it is not a living person making them. I am terrified of thieves breaking in. The ghosts might make as much noise as they liked, if I were certain at the time it was only the ghosts. Sometimes weeks and weeks have passed without one having noticed anything unusual.

Last Easter we were having some private theatricals. A great deal of the play depended on a ring I had to wear. Between the acts I went up to make some alteration in my dress. Miss Blencowe was with me. I took off the ring and laid it down. At the end of a few minutes, when I wanted it, it was gone. Miss Blencowe and I hunted high and low, but it could not be found, and I was obliged to wear another.

The next morning, the first thing almost that met my eyes was my ring lying on the dressing-table. I have lost that ring again and again.

The Christmas before last I had some money sent me for the church. I put it in two-shilling pieces in my purse. When I went to get it, one of the two-shilling pieces was gone. Of course, I replaced it with another, and sent it away. I then put the empty purse back in my pocket. After that day, the dress, which was an old velvet, was put away. The next day I had a new purse given to me, so forgot all about my old one. When we were going to have the theatricals at Easter, it struck me the dress might be made of use. Before altering it, Emilie turned out the pocket and brought me my old purse. I opened it, to see if there were any papers inside it, and I found a two-shilling piece.

Just before Christmas, this year, I have again lost a two-shilling piece, even more strangely. I had sent out for change for a sovereign. Both my mother and I counted the change. I laid the purse on the table beside me; in the evening I missed the two-shilling piece.

Once I had been out of the room for a few minutes, but there was no one in the house to steal it. I have at other times lost two-shilling pieces, but I have found them again. I have lost several things at different times, but they come back again.

February 13th, 1888. A book my mother bought for a Christmas box was lost on Christmas Eve, and since we have hunted high and low for it. This morning Emilie went into one of the bedrooms. No one sleeps there, but we are constantly in and out as we keep a number of things in the room that are in use. She found the book lying on the bed. At present there is no one in the house but my mother, Emilie, and myself, as our German maid has left; she has been gone some days.

Our little Skye-terrier has run in from the passage, shivering all over, and the other day the other little dog would not come through the green bedroom, though both doors were open; one of the maids had to go up for him.[205] — MISS F. S., ENGLAND, RECORDED 1888

PARANORMAL EXPERIENCES OF A SERVANT

☛ [Account by a female servant of the informant in the previous entry:] I was in the passage upstairs. There was no one else in the house but my mistress [Miss F. S.]. I heard the hall door open and close, and heavy footsteps. Thinking someone had got into the house I ran downstairs, but found the hall door locked. I went through the bottom of the house and found all the doors locked. It was impossible for any one to have got into the house. I then went and told my mistress.

In October 1887, I was sleeping in the green-room. A little girl was sleeping with me; there was no one else in the house. I was awoke by hearing someone walking about the room; the room shook with the footsteps; I started up thinking it was the child walking in her sleep. The gas was up enough for me to see around the room. There are two doors; I had locked them both before going to bed. I said, "Winnie, is that you?" I then saw the child was asleep. I heard the door leading into the bathroom creak, and saw it open and close again.

I have often, both day and night, heard footsteps in the hall,

A female medium during trance.

drawing-room, passage upstairs and green-room.

I was sitting in the pink-room last autumn, when both doors (it is a passage room) opened twice. I got up and closed them, and they opened again.

My sister, Polly Trays, and I were sitting in the same room. Both doors opened together. There was no wind. It was about half-past nine. The house was locked up for the night. There was no one in the house but my sister's baby. Polly said, "Who can that be walking about in the green-room?" I heard the footsteps, but knew no one could be in the house.

I was writing a letter, one evening; the candle was on the table, the doors and window were closed. There was no draught. The candle suddenly went out.[206]

About the spring, three years ago, I was sitting sewing in the room that is now a drawing-room. I heard some whispering behind my chair. I jumped up to see what it was. I said, "Is that you, ma'am?" thinking it must be my mistress, when I found I was alone. I felt nervous, so took my work downstairs.

I was sitting working in the pink bedroom when something shook my chair. Thinking it was the dog, I took no notice, and it happened again. I then got up and looked for the dog, and found the room quite empty and the door shut. I sat down again, and heard whispering and footsteps. I then called my sister to sit with me. I have heard noises as if the furniture were being knocked about, and my name, Emilie, has been called several times.[207]

I was in the hall, which is under the blue bedroom. I heard a knocking about, such as a chair banging on the floor. I went upstairs to see what was wanted. Twice more I heard the noises, but took no notice; then three times I heard some one call "Emilie." I went upstairs but no one had called.

Going up the back staircase, I went to my mistress's room. Not finding her there, [I] walked down the passage and, as I thought, saw her standing on the top of the stairs looking down. The figure was about my mistress's height (5 ft. 3in.), and dressed in light things. I did not notice her very closely, for when I heard voices in the blue bedroom I knew it was not my mistress I saw, and, I got frightened and ran back into the bedroom.[208]

I was in the drawing-room a little after six on New Year's eve, and I saw a figure dressed in light things (I thought it was the cook) standing on the top of the stairs, looking down. She had her hand up beckoning me. I ran to the door, but no one was to be seen. In that second no one could have got out of sight.[209]

I was standing in the garden one Sunday afternoon, and, looking up to the attic window, I saw a man, a dark, swarthy-looking man, with long black whiskers; his coat was buttoned up tightly, and he was dressed like a merchant sailor. I have often seen that man in the same place.

In September 1887, Miss Blencowe came in one evening after church; my sister Polly was in the pink bedroom. I heard the gate open and close with a bang. Polly came down and asked me to come to bed. After Miss Blencowe was gone I went upstairs. Polly said to me, "What a shame, Miss Blencowe's sister waiting outside at this time of night, and dressed in white."

I said, "What do you mean? Miss Blencowe's sister has not been outside."

Polly said, "I heard the gate open, and looking out of the window saw someone dressed in white, walking quickly up and down the garden; she then went out of the lower garden gate. I then closed the window, but wondering if she were gone, because then Miss Blencowe would be gone as well. I looked out again, and saw her walk from our gate to the gate of the house on the other side of the road, and there stand."

About five o'clock in the evening [very recently, but date is forgotten] I thought I saw Miss Flo standing with her head leaning against the dining-room door. The figure had on a light dress, and her hair down. As I came through the hall nearer to her, she vanished. The dining-room door was closed at the time.[210]

I was sitting working, one day; the dog was in a chair beside me; he suddenly jumped off and began to howl. I took him out of the room, and, after, he would not go back again, but remained shivering for some time.[211] — A SERVANT, EMILIE THORNE, ENGLAND, RECORDED CIRCA 1888

GHOST ENJOYS OPENING & CLOSING DOORS

☛ [Paranormal experiences in the same haunted house as the previous entry:] I was in the bathroom; one door was closed, the other open. I saw the closed door open, and heard footsteps pass through.

I was sitting in the dining-room. I was alone in the house; everyone had gone to church. I heard footsteps, and a child laugh and clap its hands just behind my chair.

I have seen the door leading from the green-room into the bathroom open and close. I have heard footsteps in the drawing-room, [and] green-room.[212] — MISS C. A. M. S., ENGLAND, RECORDED CIRCA 1888

A WALKING PHANTOM

☞ [Paranormal experiences in the same haunted house as the previous entry:] I was sitting in the dining- room one morning a few days ago talking to Emilie Thorne. The only other person in the house was Miss S., who was up in her room. I distinctly heard someone coming down the stairs (which are just outside the dining-room door). Whoever came down stopped outside the door for a second or two, then walked across the hall, and back again upstairs. Of course, I thought it was Miss S., until she came in a few minutes after, and told me she had only then come out of her room for the first time.

I have three or four times heard noises as of people walking up and down the drawing-room, when in the room underneath, knowing that there was nobody upstairs.[213]

One night just after the clock had struck 12 (I was occupying Miss S.'s room with her) we both heard the garden gate open and slam, and then a good deal of talking, which appeared to be in the next room to us, where Mrs. S. and Emilie

Thorne were. We both thought they had heard the noise and were looking out of their window to see what it was. The talking went on for some minutes.

In the morning they told us they had not talked at all. There was no one else in the house. We heard the gate slam again when the talking had ceased.

I have never seen anything supernatural, or heard anything either, until this month, when I have been staying with Mrs. S. While I was saying my prayers one night in the blue-room, which is the room next the drawing-room, where I heard the walking about, I heard someone breathing hard, almost like snoring.[214]— HELEN AUCHMUTZ, 12 MONTPELLIER GROVE, CHELTENHAM, ENGLAND, MARCH 1888

BANGING DOORS & THE GHOST GIRL

☛ [Paranormal experiences in the same haunted house as the previous entry:] October 1st, 1886, 6 p.m., I was spending the afternoon with Miss S., at _____. There were only ourselves in the house, Mrs. S. and the maid being from home for a few hours. We were startled by the banging of doors, so much so we thought we would go round the premises and fasten the doors, even going into cellars to satisfy ourselves that all was safe. We then returned to the kitchen and turned our attention to making some coffee, but not finding all the necessary things, Miss S. went up to her room to fetch the store-room keys.

Being quite dark, she lighted the gas, I having followed her, she left me in the room, going down by the back staircase to the kitchen. I called to her to know if I should turn the light out, and stood between the door and the passage while waiting for the reply. I saw the figure of a young girl, dressed in a lilac print dress, about 5ft. 3in. in height, standing on the top of the front stairs, looking in the direction of where I stood. The principal thing I noticed about her was the whiteness of the parting of her hair, and the peculiar colour of her gown. I looked at her till she gradually faded away, not feeling the least bit frightened, but only intensely cold and numb while she was visible.

After the disappearance of the figure, I went down and told Miss S. of the occurrence. She then said it was one of the ghosts I had seen.

My second experience was on the evening of February 19th, 1887, between the hours of eight and nine o'clock. On this occasion there were 12 people present, including myself. I was seated by the fireplace, Mrs. S. on the sofa directly opposite, facing the open door. A lady was sitting by her, and the dog Bruce was lying at his mistress's feet.

One of the company was playing at the time, when all at once the dog uttered a piercing shriek and rushed madly down the stairs into the hall. I, feeling the same coldness and numbness as before, turned my head, and saw the figure of the girl within a few feet of where I was sitting, looking straight at me. It remained for a second or so, then gradually disappeared. I went down and asked Mrs. S. and the lady who had been sitting by her, if they had seen anything, to which they replied in the negative.[215] — MISS BLENCOWE, 37 MONTPELLIER TERRACE, CHELTENHAM, ENGLAND, NOVEMBER 24TH, 1887

GHOST CALLS OUT FOR MOTHER

☛ [Paranormal experiences in the same haunted house as the previous entry:] One night I was awakened about 11 o'clock (I was then sleeping in room over dining-room) by a voice calling "Mother." Believing it to be my daughter's voice, I went to her room and listened outside her door. Hearing nothing I went to the maids' room, and found them both asleep. I returned to bed and was again roused by footsteps coming up the steps outside my room, and immediately after heard "Mother" repeated. I again got up and without a candle proceeded again to my daughter's room. I opened the door, keeping the handle in my hand, and asked "Did you call?"

She answered, "No; you have woke me, why have you come? What time is it?"

I answered "11," and then left her. During the few minutes in my daughter's room, I never left the handle of the door out of my hand.[216] — MRS. S., RECORDED CIRCA 1888

NIGHTLY GHOSTS & PIANO-PLAYING

☛ [Paranormal experiences in the same haunted house as the previous entry:] I send the account of what I saw at two separate times while we were with you [Miss F. S. above], but it is not very much I have to tell.

The first time I saw anything was one night (I think in February), somewhere between 11 and 12 when I had been fast asleep, and woke up suddenly broad awake as if I had been forced to do so. I noticed the fire still burning brightly, and was then attracted by the figure of a woman standing close to me, and leaning against the chimney-piece corner. I could hardly see the face, as it was turned from me, but she had hair reaching halfway down her back, and seemed to be dressed in a sort of loose Garibaldi body, and ordinary gathered skirt of a greyish tint.

I noticed all that at a glance, and even the burnish the firelight gave to the hair, which seemed of a light brown colour, and wavy. If I had not been afraid of waking mother, I think I should have spoken, for I did not feel afraid, but the figure vanished and did not reappear.

The next time was two days before we left, when I woke up suddenly, also to see, not a woman, but, at the corner of the fire-place furthest from me, a very evil-looking man dressed in what might be a white working suit. The eyes were dark and fixed on me, and I own I was frightened, their expression was so horrible, and I dared not look up again at once, and when I did he had gone. But I could not forget it for some days, and don't like to think of it now.

Those were the only times I ever saw anything, and I know for certain that I was awake, and not dreaming! Mother heard the heavy footsteps in the drawing-room when we knew nobody could be there, as the doorway was barred. And I also heard the piano being played that Sunday morning, as perhaps you may remember, when I thought it was Miss Blencowe practising a chant, and on inquiry afterwards found no one had been near the room at all. I heard it distinctly as I walked along the passage, and opened the door expecting to find someone at the piano, when to my surprise the room was empty. I also heard that strange noise which woke yourself and myself up one night, when it sounded like someone beating the iron curtain-rod in your room with a broom-handle, and you said the noise was dreadful, being so close to where you were.[217] — MISS HUMBLE, 15 THE TERRACE, GROSVENOR STREET, ST. HELIERS, JERSEY, ENGLAND, JANUARY 25TH, 1888

GHOSTS WHO INTERRUPT SLEEP & A FRIGHTENED DOG

☛ [Paranormal experiences in the same haunted house as the previous entry:] I will give an account of what I saw and heard in the house at _____ as near as I can.

It was in the year 1885. I was stopping there for July and August, but I cannot tell which month or what day of the month it was as I took no notice at the time. I only know that Miss S. and I had been sitting up rather late talking, and it must have been quite 12 o'clock when I went to bed. How long I had been asleep I don't know, but the first thing I remember was someone leaning over me and talking very softly. She (for it was a woman's voice) seemed to be pleading with me to do something for her, but I was too sleepy to know what it was. Then she asked me to kiss her. I answered, then, "No, I won't." She gave a sigh, then—such a sigh I shall never forget it.

I was wide awake then, and sprang up in bed and looked all round the room. I thought at first that some one had been playing me a trick, but I am quite sure no one went out of the room, for there was only one door leading out of it, and that was facing the foot of the bed, and the room was quite light. I never saw it, for when I looked up it was gone, nor did I have another visit from it while I was there.

The next time I was there, in February 1886, I slept in the same room I had before, but the house had been altered since I was there before, and this time there were two doors in my room, one exactly facing the other. The one I locked when I went to bed, the other was only shut.

I had been to sleep then, it seemed to me, some time, when I woke with a start. I felt as if someone had given me a good shake. It frightened me so I sprang straight up in bed, and standing quite close to me was—well, I don't know what it was—but [it had] the most horrible, devilish face. I could see nothing but the face and hands, which kept working as if they were trying to get at me and something kept them back. I was so frightened I did not dare to take my eyes off its face, and for a moment I did not know what to do. Then the thought came into my mind to make the sign of the cross and say some prayers. That had the effect, it vanished in a second. Of course, the whole thing only lasted a moment, but it seemed ages to me; but the look of baffled rage I never shall forget. I did not go to sleep again that night.

That is all I really saw or heard during my stay in the house. But there are two things I never could understand. One was the dog; he would stand and stare into a corner and shake all over, and once or twice I saw him go up the passage and then run back again, jump on a chair, and shake all over, and look quite frightened. The other was, that whether you were reading or working you must keep looking behind you as if you expected to see some one standing there.[218] — A FORMER SERVANT, MRS. SERPELL, OF 152 KING STREET, PLYMOUTH, ENGLAND, RECORDED CIRCA 1888

Victorian séance medium Henry Slade. Considered "controversial" by 19th-Century sceptics who could not fully disprove his impressive telekinetic and mediumistic feats, Slade remains an important figure in the annals of paranormal history.

CHAPTER TEN

GHOST WOMAN & WHITE MARBLE CROSS

☛ My son and I were staying in town, Bonchurch (Isle of Wight, England), last Easter vacation (1886). Our lodgings were quite close to the sea, and the garden of our house abutted on the beach, and there were no trees or bushes in it high enough to intercept our view. The evening of Easter Sunday was so fine that when Miss Jowett (the landlady's daughter) brought in the lamp, I begged her not to pull down the blinds, and lay on the sofa looking out at the sea, while my son was reading at the table. Owing to a letter I had just received from my sister at home, stating that one of the servants had again seen "the old lady," my thoughts had been directed towards ghosts and such things.

But I was not a little astonished when, on presently looking out of the window, I saw the figure of a woman standing at the edge of the verandah. She appeared to be a broad [heavyset] woman, and not tall (Mrs. A. is tall), and to wear an old-fashioned bonnet, and white gloves on her closed hands. As it was dark the figure was only outlined against the sky, and I could not distinguish any other details. It was, however, opaque, and not in any way transparent, just as if it had been a real person.

I looked at it for some time, and then looked away. When, after a time, I looked again, the woman's hands had disappeared behind what appeared to be a white marble cross, with a little bit of the top broken off, and with a railing on one side of the woman and the cross, such as one sometimes sees in graveyards.

After looking at this apparition, which remained motionless, for sometime, about 20 minutes, perhaps, I asked my son (then an undergraduate at B.N.C. [Brasenose College, Oxford]) to come and to look out of the window, and tell me what he saw. He exclaimed, "What an uncanny sight," and described the woman and the cross exactly as I saw it. I then rang the bell, and when Miss J. answered it, I asked her also to look out of the window and tell me what she saw, and she also described the woman and the cross, just as they appeared to my son and myself.

Some one suggested that it might be a reflection of some sort, and we all looked about the room to see whether there was anything in it that could cause such a reflection, but came to the conclusion that there was nothing to account for it. My son then went through the open side of the (low) window (we had seen the figure through the closed side) only a few feet distant from the figure, to see whether it was possible for a real woman to be there, but found nothing.

My impression is, that to us also the figure disappeared when my son went out, but as I was speaking to Miss J. at the time, I cannot be quite certain about this. Yet when he returned into the room the woman and the cross still appeared in the same place. We still continued to discuss what it could be, Miss J. having a strong idea that it portended death or misfortune to some one, and being very anxious that the apparition should not be in any way connected with herself and her family; and when we looked again all had disappeared. Altogether, from the time when I first saw it, the figure must have lasted for nearly an hour, from about 9 to 10 p.m., and nothing has occurred since that would throw any light upon the appearance. I have never had any similar experience.[219]— JANE S. ALDERSON, ENGLAND, VIA THE OXFORD PHASMATOLOGICAL SOCIETY, CIRCA 1888

FUNERAL PROCESSION IN A CHURCH

☛ Miss Campbell was at church in London with her mother. They remained to the Sacrament, and while standing in the chancel with her back to the church door, which was shut, Mrs. Campbell caught hold suddenly of her daughter's arm, and in a terrified manner pointed to the wall opposite, directly over the altar. Miss Campbell looked, but could see nothing, and could not get her mother to speak, and was much alarmed by the strange unearthly fear expressed on her countenance, and with her eyes, wide open, fixed on the wall. She got her quietly back to her seat, and her mother then told her that she had seen distinctly a funeral procession moving along the wall, but she could not tell who the people were.

Next day they heard that Miss Campbell's first cousin, a great friend of theirs, brother to Lady A., had dropped dead suddenly in his room at the exact hour when Mrs. Campbell saw the funeral pass before her eyes. He had no previous illness, but was a very strong man.[220] — A. BOLDERO, LONDON, ENGLAND, 1884

IRISH FUSILIER'S GHOST APPEARS AT TIME OF DEATH

☛ On the 1st of December, 1886, I was at lunch in the mess-room, Armagh Barracks, with Mr. R. E. W. Campbell and Mr. R. W. Leeper, of the 2nd Battalion Royal Irish Fusiliers, and Mr. A. B. R. Kaye, of the 3rd Battalion of the same regiment. We were talking about various things, when Mr. Campbell remarked that he had a very strange vision of a Major Hubbersty, who used to be in his regiment.

He thought he saw him on the night before, or early on the morning of that day, standing in his room, looking very pale and ghastly, and that he seemed to fall forward. He also described the clothes worn by the vision. As well as I remember, he said they were a sort of spotted cloth, with a red thread running through it. He then said he felt sure we should hear something about him very soon.

On the following Sunday, when I returned from church with Mr. Kaye, we found Mr. Campbell in the ante-room, and he read to us out of the *Times* newspaper the death of Major Hubbersty, late 2nd Battalion Royal Irish Fusiliers, the same man that had appeared to him in a vision a few nights before.[221] — T. E. SCOTT, LIEUTENANT 4TH BATTALION ROYAL IRISH FUSILIERS, RAVENSDALE PARSONAGE, CO. LOUTH, IRELAND, CIRCA 1887

OLD HAUNTED HOUSE IN FRANCE

☛ It was during the winter of 1845 that one evening I happened to be sitting by the side of a cheerful fire in my bedroom, busily engaged in caressing a favourite cat—the illustrious Lady Catherine, now, alas! no more. She lay in a pensive attitude and a winking state of drowsiness in my lap.

Although my room might be without candles it was perfectly illuminated by the light of the fire.

There were two doors—one behind me leading into an apartment which had been locked up for the winter, and another on the opposite side of the room, which communicated with the passage. Mamma had not left me many minutes, and the high-backed, old-fashioned armchair which she had occupied remained vacant at the opposite corner of the fire-place. Puss, who lay with her head upon my arm, became more and more sleepy, and I pondered on the propriety of preparing for bed.

Of a sudden I became aware that something had affected my pet's equanimity. The purring ceased, and she exhibited rapidly increasing symptoms of uneasiness. I bent down and endeavoured to coax her into quietness, but she instantly struggled to her feet in my lap, and spitting vehemently, with back arched and tail swollen, she assumed a mingled attitude of terror and defiance.

The change in her position obliged me to raise my head, and on looking up, to my inexpressible horror, I then perceived a little, hideous, wrinkled old hag occupied mamma's chair. Her hands were resting on her knees and her body was stooped forward so as to bring her face into close proximity with mine. Her eyes, piercingly fierce and shining with an overpowering lustre, were steadfastly fixed on me. It was as if a fiend were glaring at me through them.

Her dress and general appearance denoted her to belong to the French bourgeoisie; but those eyes, so wonderfully large, and in their expression so intensely wicked, entirely absorbed my senses and precluded any attention to detail. I should have screamed, but my breath was gone while that terrible gaze so horribly fascinated me. I could neither withdraw my eyes nor rise from my seat.

I had meanwhile been trying to keep a tight hold on the cat, but she seemed resolutely determined not to stay in such ugly neighbourhood, and after some most desperate efforts, at length succeeded in escaping from my grasp. Leaping over chairs and tables and all that came in her way, she repeatedly threw herself with frightful violence against the top panel of the door which communicated with the disused room. Then, returning in the same frantic manner, she furiously dashed against the door on the opposite side.

My terror was now divided, and I looked by turns, now at the old woman whose great staring eyes were constantly fixed on me, and now at the cat, who was becoming every instant more frantic. At last the dreadful idea that the animal had gone mad had the effect of restoring my breath, and I screamed loudly.

Mamma ran in immediately, and the cat, on the door opening, literally sprang over her head, and for upwards of half-an-hour ran up and downstairs as if pursued. I turned to point out the object of my terror; it was gone.

Under such circumstances the lapse of time is difficult to appreciate, but I should think that the apparition lasted about four or five minutes. Some time afterwards it transpired that a former proprietor of the house, a woman, had hanged herself in that very room.

The second apparition occurred at the time of the serious illness of one of the members of our family. I was leaving the patient's room for the last time that night when I met the old woman in the passage, but the sight caused no emotion. I was too anxious to be frightened.

I was, however, reminded of it next day by the sick nurse—a French nun—when she told us that not only she, but her patient also, had had a most disturbed night, owing to a succession of noises, such as rustling garments and footsteps in the room, and that her patient, usually quietly dozing, was constantly calling out to ask who was in the room. She declared she would not sit up alone another night.

This was the more remarkable that she had some time before expressed her determination to leave us if one of our party continued to sit up with her, as she wished to be allowed the sole control of the sick room, and in consequence she had been left alone till that night. She, however, saw nothing, only heard.

I have seen other apparitions, and am not aware of having had hallucinations.[222] — MISS H. K., BOULOGNE-SUR MER, FRANCE, 1845

DÖPPELGANGER PRESAGES SERVANT'S DEATH

☞ I was in my bedroom being undressed by my maid, Mrs. Gregory, who had been with me for 41 years, and she was unfastening my bracelet when I saw, just behind her about two feet off, her exact resemblance. She was then in perfect health. I said to her, "Why, Mrs. Gregory, I see your fetch." She smiled and said, "Really, ma'am," but was not in the least alarmed.

On the following Sunday, she was only poorly. I went for a doctor at once, who said she was a little out of sorts. On Wednesday evening she suddenly died. It was about the same time that her double had appeared to me just a week before. This was about 15 years ago.[223] — SOPHIE CHAPRONIERE, 2 HOTHAM-VILLAS, PUTNEY, ENGLAND, APRIL 14TH, 1888

GHOSTS SURPRISE A "FEARLESS" WITNESS

☞ Some time ago a friend of mine had the misfortune to lose her husband [on April 17th, 1884]. They had only been married about five years, and she expressed great grief at his loss, and asked me to go and reside with her. I went to her, and stayed six months.

One evening, towards the end of that summer, I remarked that I would go upstairs and have a bath. "Do," she replied, "but first I wish you would fetch me that little book I left on the drawing room table last night."

I started without a light (having been naturally fearless all my life, I am accustomed to go about in the dark), opened the drawing-room door, and stood for a minute, thinking where she had placed it, when I saw, to my amazement, her husband, sitting by the table; his elbow was resting on the table close to the book. My first thought was to pretend forgetfulness, my second to tell her what I had seen and return without the book. However, having boasted that I did not know the meaning of fear, I determined to get it, and advanced to the table.

He seemed to be smiling, as if he knew my thoughts. I picked up the book and took it to her without saying anything about it; then, going into the bathroom, I soon forgot it.

But after being there about 20 minutes I heard my friend go up and open the drawing-room door. I laughed, and listened to hear if he was still there, and very soon heard her run out of the room, and downstairs about four at a time, and ring the dining-room bell furiously. One of the maids came running up.

I dressed as quickly as possible and went down to her, and found her looking very white and trembling. "Whatever is the matter?" I said.

"I have seen my husband," she replied.

"What nonsense," I answered.

"Oh, but I have," she continued, "at least, I didn't actually see him, but he spoke twice to me; I ran out of the room, and he followed and put his cold hand on my shoulder."

Now this seems to me a very strange thing, because I had only seen the gentleman [when alive] about two or three times, therefore cannot understand his appearing to me, and I certainly was not thinking of him at the time.

The other apparition [I witnessed] was of an old lady whom I had never seen, and I only discovered for whom it was intended by describing her to someone who knew her. She appeared to me on several occasions . . . .

My father purchased the house [she was seen in] in June 1883, from Mrs. _____, whose aunt had died here—being found dead in bed one day, having died the night before, all alone. The lodger forced the door, fearing something was the matter; but I was not aware of this till a long time after.

This appearance occurred on a special *fête* day at the "Fisheries"—the proceeds of which were, I believe, intended to build a church. Some friends of mine were going, and had tried to persuade me to accompany them, but the house would have been left with no one in it if I had gone.

In an attempt to communicate with the Spirit World, Victorians experimented with numerous scientific and psychical methods, some of which are pictured here.

In the afternoon I had been sewing, and drawing my chair close to the window overlooking the garden at the back, I intended working as long as I could see. I sat for a few minutes looking out, and trying to imagine how the exhibition looked, and, upon turning, saw the old lady standing looking at me.

"Who can that be?" I thought (and looked out again) some one must have come here by mistake—possibly a neighbour. I looked at her again, long enough to take in all the details of her costume.

Again I turned to the window, wondering whether I had left any of the doors open, and how it was I had not heard her come in. Then thinking how stupid not to ask her, I got up to put the question—but she had gone, as noiselessly as she came. I looked all over the house—in cupboards, under bedsteads, etc., but not a trace of anyone or anything could be found.

The servant I had at that time had been a servant at the house before, I knew; so I resolved (of course without telling her why) to describe the old lady. I made several casual remarks about her, then I said, "I fancy I saw her one day, Phoebe, let me describe her. She was rather short, thin, had brown eyes, a long nose, and wore a black cap with a flower or red bow at the side, a black dress, black mittens, and a white neckerchief, edged with lace, folded cornerways and fastened with a brooch." Phoebe interrupted me several times by saying that was her, and ended by saying she always wore one of those kerchiefs.

About three weeks after, I happened to be again alone, and was hurrying out of the breakfast-room into the room where I had seen her, when, glancing up the staircase, I beheld my old lady coming down. This time she was attired in a lavender dress. I stood at the foot of the stairs, thinking as she passed I would take hold of her. We seemed to be looking at one another for 10 minutes, when she went backwards up the stairs like a human being. I now felt certain someone was playing me a trick (though I had heard no sound); I ran up quickly, but at the turn in the stairs, she vanished.

I searched the house as before, with the same result. When Phoebe returned, I said, "Did Miss S_____ ever wear a lavender-coloured dress?"

"Yes, miss, she did; she never wore the same twice running," said Phoebe.

I have never seen the old lady since. I was enjoying perfect health at the time.[224] — MISS LAURA A. LISTER, ENGLAND, MARCH 8TH and 13TH, 1888

APPEARANCE OF THREE SPIRITS FORESHADOWS THEIR DEATHS

☛ Our mother, Mrs. Cowpland, wife of the Rev. Robert Cowpland, late of Weeford Rectory, Staffordshire [England], on three occasions, and, we believe, on those three occasions only, saw a hallucinatory figure. On all three occasions the apparition coincided with the death of the person seen. On the first two occasions both of us heard of the apparition from our mother before the death was known; on the third occasion Mrs. Treloar alone so heard of it.

1. In 1857 our mother was bending over a chest of drawers in her bedroom, and on turning round saw, as she thought, her brother-in-law, the Rev. William Cowpland, rector of Acton

Beauchamp, Worcestershire [England], standing by her side. She exclaimed, "Ah, William! When did you arrive?" Next day a telegram came, saying he had been found dead in bed. The coincidence as to hour could not be traced. My mother mentioned the apparition to us both, at once, before the telegram came; and the matter was frequently spoken of afterwards.

 2. In 1860, or thereabouts, she heard a footstep, and went into the hall, and returned and told my father and us that she had seen William Dunn, a gardener at the house of some relatives of ours. We did not know that he was ill, but afterwards heard that he had died about the time that my mother saw him, and had expressed a wish to see her. We believe that the coincidence of hour was clearly made out.

 3. In 1862, my mother, being in bed, told me that she had seen a Mrs. F., a connection of ours, standing at the foot of her bed, and was sure she was dead, though we did not know that she was ill. This was in fact the case; and the hour in this case, too, was found to coincide. Mrs. F. had been mixed up in affairs with my mother, but there was no special affection.[225] — MRS. TRELOAR, DOVER, ENGLAND, APRIL 4TH, 1888

GHOST OF DYING MOTHER APPEARS TO SON

☞ In the year 1875, Captain A. B. MacGowan, 12th U.S. Infantry, was stationed at Camp Independence, California; having with him his wife. His two sons, Charles, aged 15, and George, aged 12, were at that time at school, at Napa College, California, and boarded in the house; and at the table of one of the instructors, Mr. George.

 Mrs. MacGowan was a lady of robust health, almost unacquainted with illness; and at this particular time was arranging to give an entertainment to their friends, military and civil. The station being not only far beyond the railroad, but out of the ordinary line of travel, guests would come to such a party with their own conveyance, and after several days' journey; and arrangements would be made to entertain them over-night and longer. Such a festivity would be quite an event for the outpost and for all those interested in it. There was no telegraphic communication with this camp; and the mails were slow, and the distance long. In fact, from Camp Independence, the school is nearly 600 miles. The boys knew what was going on at home by previous correspondence, and knew that, so far from there being any cause for uneasiness, the prospect was one of active enjoyment.

 On the morning of December 23rd, 1875, Charles, the elder of the boys at school, came to the breakfast-table with a disturbed countenance, but denied having any trouble when asked about it by the teacher. He was unable to eat any breakfast, although allowing himself to be helped; but when the teacher, at the meal, insisted on knowing the cause of his distress, fearing he might be ill, he burst into tears, and exclaimed, "My mother is dead." He then went onto say that, having gone to bed and to sleep as usual, and with no premonition of trouble, he was awakened in the night and saw his mother standing by his bedside; who said to him, "Charlie, be a good boy"; and then disappeared.

This occurred between 11 and 12 p.m. He had gone to sleep, not hearing 11 strike; but was awakened by this occurrence, and heard all the other hours strike, including 12 o'clock, till morning. The teacher endeavoured to make light of it; but the boy would not be comforted.

In a day or two a letter was received, saying his mother was indisposed, but not seriously; this was followed a few days later by the announcement that she had unexpectedly grown worse, and had suddenly died, at 11:20 p.m., of this same night (December 22nd, 1875), in which the apparition was seen. The teacher, Mr. George, made a note of the occurrence, and subsequently informed Captain MacGowan thereof.[226] — CAPTAIN A. B. MACGOWAN, CIRCA 1884

HAUNTED HORRORS OF THE "DRAB ROOM"

☛ About midway between Bath and Bristol is the village of Timsbury. The principal house in the place is one which was built during the reign of Henry VIII, and was known in the time of my boyhood as "The Court."

When I was 12 years of age my father moved to the neighbourhood of Bath, and was shortly afterwards requested by an old friend to ascertain whether there was a large house, with grounds attached, in the locality to be let furnished. Timsbury Court was the only one which could be heard of, and as it seemed exactly the kind of place that was wanted, Mr. B. agreed to take it. With his wife and daughter, and a staff of servants he brought with him, he accordingly took up his quarters in the house at the beginning of October. Neither he nor any of his household knew any of the inhabitants of the village, or were in any way acquainted with the neighbourhood.

The following December my brother (who was two years younger than myself) and I went on a visit to our friends at Timsbury. As we were the first guests they had received we were given what was considered the best bedroom in the house to sleep in. It was called the Drab Room, because the walls were hung with drab tapestry, and was approached by a corridor which branched off from the head of the stair. The nearest room to it was occupied by Miss B. [Miss Lily Boyd; see next case]. Opposite the door was a mullioned window. Between the door and the window was the entrance to a recess in the wall which was fitted up as a dressing room.

As my lungs were delicate, and the weather was cold, I was not allowed to leave the house during the week that I spent in it, and a fire was kept burning in the bedroom. On the Thursday afternoon I had been reading a book on mesmerism, a very undesirable one for a weakly boy to get hold of, and when it became too dark for me to read any longer without a light, I went upstairs to prepare for dinner.

While I was standing in the dusk before the looking-glass on the table in front of the window, brushing my hair, I happened to glance towards my right, and there distinctly saw the figure of a man standing at the entrance of the dressing-room, about a yard distant from me, with his eyes fixed upon myself. What he looked like I will state presently. The suddenness of the appearance startled me exceedingly, and I rushed downstairs into the drawing-room in an agony of terror, declaring that I had seen a "ghost." I was well laughed at for my folly, and told that I must not read any more books on mesmerism.

By the time dinner was over I had become reassured, and soon ceased to think any more about what I had seen.

The following Saturday night I chanced to awake when the fire, which had been blazing brightly when I went to sleep, now cast only a slight flickering light over the room, just sufficient to disclose the outlines of things but no more. I then saw distinctly a human figure come out of the dressing-room and walk by the side of the bed. My brother, who was sleeping on that side of the bed, happened to be awake also, and saw the figure as well as myself. I asked him who it was. "Only Lizzie" (that is Miss B.), he said, and satisfied with the answer I turned round and fell asleep again. My brother saw the figure pass to the foot of the bed and there lost sight of it.

In the morning I mentioned to Mrs. B. that her daughter had been in our room during the night, but no further notice was taken of it at the time.

I must not forget to add that on several occasions my brother and I were much disturbed by strange noises which we ascribed to the wind.

The following spring two young ladies who were on a visit to the house, slept in the Drab Room. Early on Sunday morning they awoke suddenly, and saw a figure come out of the dressing-room and walk to the foot of the bedstead, where it stood looking at them. They were greatly alarmed and covered their faces with the bed clothes, but the next morning determined to say nothing from fear of ridicule. In fact they did not mention what they had seen until some months afterwards.

In the course of the summer the room was occupied by Mrs. Hb., a lady of decidedly unimaginative character. On the Sunday morning after her arrival she appeared at breakfast looking pale and unwell, and, after breakfast, asked Mrs. B. if she might have her room changed. Mrs. B. of course assented, but pressed her visitor to tell her what was the matter with the room, as she fancied she might have been annoyed by rats or something similar. After a great deal of hesitation Mrs. Hb. confessed that though she knew her hostess would think her extremely foolish, she felt convinced that she had seen something supernatural that morning. She had been aroused from sleep, she said, by hearing the clock strike 4, and just afterwards saw a human figure come from the dressing-room and pass to the foot of the bed, where it stooped down, so as to be hidden from view. She thought someone was playing her a trick, and jumped out of bed to see who it was; she searched the room and found nothing. Mrs. B. naturally in her mind ascribed her guest's apparition to a nightmare, but nothing would persuade the latter that she had not actually seen it with waking eyes.

In the early part of September, Mr. B. received a visit from his son-in-law, Mr. H. and his wife, who like the five visitors before them, also occupied the Drab Room. I heard the following story from Mrs. H.'s own lips.

On the Thursday night after their arrival, she was sleeping on the side of the bed nearest the dressing-room, and was aroused from her sleep by feeling a cold clammy hand laid all across her face. It prevented her from opening her eyes, though she felt that if she could do so she would see something "uncanny." She kicked violently and awoke her husband, who told her she was suffering from nightmare, that was all. Mrs. H. was convinced that it was otherwise, and refused to sleep another night on that side of the bed.

The following night Mr. H. was prevented from getting any sleep by an attack of toothache, and in the morning again began to laugh at his wife, telling her that if "there were a ghost in the room he must have seen it as he had been awake all night." The toothache disappeared in the course of the morning, and the following (Saturday) night Mr. H. slept additionally soundly in consequence of his want of sleep the night before.

Suddenly he was startled from his slumbers by a cold clammy hand placed upon his forehead. He sprang up and saw a brown-looking figure, crouched up, hieing away from him into the dressing-room. He felt his pulse, which was beating normally, then he got out of bed, poured some water into the basin, and plunged both his face and his hands into it. Then he returned to bed, and sitting up in it looked at his watch, and found it was a little after 4 o'clock.

At ten minutes past 4 the figure came out of the dressing-room, and stood close to his pillow, so close indeed that he might have touched it had he chosen. This time the figure was erect, and he was able to measure its height against the window-frame, from which he discovered that it was not quite his own height. The figure was that of a man, dressed in a dark coat, which was fastened by gold buttons at the throat and wrist. The hair was dark and parted in the middle, the face pale and smooth, and the nose of the Greek type. In both face and dress the figure was precisely the same as that which I had seen. Mr. H. deliberated whether he should speak; while doing so he coughed, and immediately afterwards the figure melted before his eyes "like a mist." After this further sleep was out of the question, and Mr. H. agreed with his wife that they had better change their room.

As the next day, however, was Sunday, they thought they would pass one more night there. In the course of this Mrs. H. was awakened by "horrible shrieks, groans and sighs," that proceeded from some part of the room. Her husband was awake, and she asked him what it meant. He replied that he had been listening to those sounds for more than an hour. Then he sat up and said, "In the name of God I command you to be silent."

After this they heard no more.

The story soon became known in the village, and our friends then learned that the Drab Room had been held to be haunted from time immemorial, though they could hear of no legend to account for the supposed fact. In the time of their predecessors it had been closed inconsequence of the belief about it. So well-known in the village, indeed, was the belief, that some of the old people, as it turned out, refused to venture near the gates of the house itself after dark. Our friends remained there only a year or two after the discovery, as their servants became frightened and were accordingly disinclined to stay with them[227] — REV. PROFESSOR A. H. SAYCE, AS TOLD CIRCA 1884

SPIRITS OF LIVING SEND MESSAGES OF DISTRESS TO LOVED ONES

☛ In connection with . . . [the deaths recorded in the previous entry] . . . an event of another kind occurred to myself and a niece, Miss Maud Cowpland.

On August 26th, 1885, Mr. Treloar and I, then living at The Firs, Bromyard [England], dined with my brother, the Rev. W. Cowpland, who had succeeded my uncle in the rectory of Acton Beauchamp. Mr. Treloar's letter of March 3rd, 1888, will describe what happened:

> "My wife and I were dining with my brother-in-law, and there met my wife's sister, who lived a short distance from the rectory. It was a very lively party, and this lady was in the best of health and spirits. It was on a Wednesday, and as we left the house my wife promised to drive over to see her shortly, at her own house (Upper House, Bishop's Frome [England]), where she resided alone.
>
> On the Tuesday following, in the evening, about eight o'clock, my wife, who had been in the nursery during the half-hour the nurse was having her supper, went into our bedroom, where there was a lamp burning on the dressing-table; and as she passed the bed, in going round to the other end of the room, she saw, as she thought, a black dress on the other side of the bed, but on looking again, a figure slowly rose up from what appeared a bent position, and looked straight at her for the space of three or four seconds; and she then recognised her sister. Her face was very pale, and had a look of anguish on it.
>
> My wife came downstairs, and I noticed that she seemed troubled, and on asking her what had upset her, she told me. I, of course, thought it must have been a delusion.
>
> Next evening (Wednesday, September 2nd), just as we were sitting down to dinner, the groom of our doctor came to the house and said his master wished to see me. I went down and found him just about to start for my sister-in-law's residence, as he told me that she had sent for him, and from what he could learn she was in a most dangerous state from diphtheria. She died two days afterwards, and my wife never saw her, as it was, in the doctor's opinion, running too great a risk."

This account is correct, but does not state that just as I had told him of the apparition, my niece, Miss Maud Cowpland, who was staying with us, came rushing downstairs from her bedroom, whither she had gone a few minutes before—and simultaneously I began to tell her what I had seen, and she, scarcely heeding me, burst out, "I've seen Auntie Annie! I've seen Auntie Annie!" (Mr. Treloar confirms this.) I did not question her further then. . . . She left the house next day, I believe partly on account of the fright.

It is futile to attempt to *physically* defend yourself against a ghost.

I had never before seen, nor have I since seen, any apparition whatever, nor have I had any other experience at all resembling those which I here recount. After the first moment, I was not alarmed by the vision of my sister Anne. She was so remarkably vigorous and full of life that the idea of her death never occurred to me. In fact, what happened was this: there was diphtheria in the parish, and she most imprudently kissed a school-child suffering from that disease. On the Tuesday evening (when the figure was seen) she had retired early to her room, saying to her servants that she had a bad cold. They were young, and there was no one in her house to whom she would have spoken confidentially as to her state. All that can be known, then, of her condition at this moment is that she was alone in her room—whether asleep or awake we do not know—and that next day she sent for the doctor, and was fatally ill. There was a strong affection between her and myself.

I may add that the figure which I saw had a bonnet and veil on, the veil being tied back round her bonnet, as was my sister's wont. The lamp was bright, and so clearly did I see the figure that I observed the freckles on the nose. My sister had fine, expressive eyes, and their look in the apparition was full of anxiety and pain. The figure did not disappear instantaneously, but seemed to thin away into air. It is my belief that at many times of pain or crisis to one member of our family others have had impressions of distress, though at a distance.

I recall one incident of this.

In 1870 my brother (since deceased) broke his leg very badly when out hunting. The accident happened at about 4 p.m. He was taken to an inn and lay there all night in real danger. On that day Mrs. Gardiner, who was joining in a friendly gathering, felt a quite unique depression from 4 p.m. onwards. And that night, contrary to my habit, I could not sleep; and while lying awake was astonished to see my father come into my room and ask for some help and comfort, as he was sleepless and in distress. He was at that time in good health, and had never thus appealed to me before. I got up and gave him some brandy and water (which I had never done before), but all that night we both of us continued causelessly wretched.[228] — MRS. TRELOAR, DOVER, ENGLAND, APRIL 14TH, 1888

SPIRITS OF FATHER & BROTHER APPEAR TO ONE ANOTHER 10,000 MILES APART

☛ I hear from Mrs. R. Ellis that you wish to have the account from us of my father, who was dying in Kensington [England], seeing my brother Robert, who was at the time in Australia.

It was on Wednesday, December 29th, 1869, that my father, who was dangerously ill at the time, awoke from a sleep, and raising himself up in the bed pointed and looked most intently to one corner of the room and said to us (my sister Mary and me) "Look! don't you see? it is my poor boy Bob's head!" then turning to me he said, "Normanton [Australia], don't forget, Gulf of Carpentaria." He then sank back exhausted. This happened about 3 p.m.

We found, after his death, he had entered the address in red ink in his pocket book—my brother having left Bourke Town [Australia] and gone to Normanton—so that the next packet of letters were sent there. My father died on Thursday, December 30th, 1869.

When my brother returned home from Australia a few years after, he told us that one night, whilst camping out, he had gone to rest and had slept, and he awoke seeing my father's head distinctly in one part of his tent. It made such an impression on him that he went to his mate in the adjoining tent and said, "I have seen my father, you must come and stay with me."

By the next mail he received my letter telling him of my father's death. My brother said it must have been about 3 a.m. [in Australia] when he saw my father. Would not that correspond with our [English] 3 p.m.? I always think they must have seen each other at the same time.[229] — ALICE ELLIS AND MARY ELLIS, BRIGHTON, ENGLAND, JUNE 23RD, 1887

WIFE'S BROTHER'S GHOST APPEARS TO HER HUSBAND AT TIME OF DEATH

☛ In the autumn of the year 1875 my brother, John Phillips Clemes, a mining engineer, left England and went to Northern Mexico, in the employ of Señor Don Francisco Alsna, the proprietor of a silver mine in the Province of Sonora. He left England with the full intention expressed to me of remaining abroad but three years, although the position he filled was an extremely lucrative one.

Mr. Robert Ellis, to whom I was then engaged to be married, had made the acquaintance of my brother whilst he was in London, and entertained for him the warmest liking and respect. Indeed, the two men, though most dissimilar in character, had formed a sudden and warm friendship for each other.

It was in Christmas week—Tuesday, December 19th, 1876, and Mr. Ellis had called to see me, and spend the evening, as he generally did, twice a week. We were to have a small party of a few friends on Christmas Day, and on this evening I was discussing some of the small festive arrangements with him—the pudding especially as I remember, and laughing about it, and we were both unusually mirthful. The hour was between 6 and 7 p.m., and we were alone in the drawing-room after tea, Mr. Ellis being seated in a low occasional chair with his back to the door. I was standing beside him, and the room was brightly lit with gas.

I saw him suddenly look over his shoulder with a startled, almost terrified, look, two or three scared glances, and upon my asking him hurriedly what was the matter, he passed his hand over his eyes, and stammered that he had imagined he saw some one coming in at the door, which was standing slightly ajar. He refused to say any more, though I questioned him closely, and declared it must have been something the matter with his eyes.

Two months afterwards, when the sad truth was all known to me, Mr. Ellis told me what had occurred to startle him that evening was this. As he was sitting, a sensation came over him of some one standing at his back, and, looking over his shoulder, he distinctly saw, for the space of a few seconds, a tall, dark figure, a man's figure, draped in black, as it appeared. He could not distinguish features in the brief time, and in his own agitation.

In the month of January 1877, there came the news, by telegram, of my dear brother's sudden death by fever on Tuesday, the 19th of December. He expired after being quite unconscious for fourteen hours, at seven o'clock in the evening.[230] — MRS. ROBERT ELLIS, CIRCA 1888

SKEPTIC ATTENDS SEANCE & WITNESSES MATERIALIZATIONS

☞ The seance at which I was present was given by a well-known medium (Mr. Cecil Husk). Before the sitting took place I was courteously invited to examine the room, which I most carefully did in a good light, and can vouch for it being a plain ordinary room with no possibilities of trapdoors, pulleys, reflecting mirrors and such paraphernalia whereby the ordinary tricks of deception are practised. The walls and floor of the room were quite bare and there was only a single window and door, the sole furniture being a plain deal table and ordinary chairs. The only apparatus, if you can dignify them by the name, were a couple of cardboard slates, so prepared that they became luminous in the dark.

The sitting was conducted in darkness, and the circle consisted of about a dozen individuals holding hands in the usual way round the table, the medium being at the head of the table and forming part of the circle.

The first thing of interest to note was, that after a few minutes, in spite of the darkness, I became conscious there was present in the air a sort of phosphorescent vapour which had the appearance, as to form of that given by tobacco smoke when it curls upwards and spreads itself out in diaphanous draperies; but in addition to this I observed that it was dotted all over with countless numbers of minute points of bright light, like little glow lamps. The appearance was not unlike the phosphorescence of the sea seen at night in tropical waters. This luminosity is, I understand, in the phraseology of spiritists, called astral light, and is, I believe, considered by them to be luminous matter from which "spirit" forms take shape.

When the phantasms appeared, they were rendered visible by the luminous slates on the table rising automatically and thus casting a weird bluish light on their faces. Only the head and shoulders appeared in the centre of the table, in fact just that amount comprised in the area of the slates' luminosity. When they disappeared they did so gradually in a bluish scintillation of light through the centre of the table round which we were sitting. The faces I saw were perfectly clear and well defined, as real faces could be in ordinary objective vision, only the light they appeared in gave them a pale bluish and somewhat ghastly appearance.

I do not propose to give any opinion as to whether these were spirit faces of the departed, as they were alleged to be, or whether spirits generally are capable of rendering themselves thus visible, and communicating with those present.

I did not see or express a wish to see any of my departed relatives or friends. I saw the face, head and shoulders of one, who I was informed was called John King, whose "spirit" photograph, if I remember aright, is kept at the office of the London Spiritualist Alliance, and whose features I at once recognised from having previously seen it there. The head had as real and solid an appearance as that of any real person, and was draped together with the shoulders in a sort of white shawl; the face was very dark, with a long, flowing, black beard, and the features appeared of a somewhat oriental type. While the apparition lasted the lips were distinctly seen to move, and questions put to it by the sitters were answered in a deep stentorian voice.

Another face which I saw was that of a good-looking young girl; she was at once recognised by a lady present as that of a sister, who had died some years ago and to whom she was greatly attached. I had never seen the lady in life, but when her photograph was afterwards shown to me I at once recognised a striking resemblance between it and the phantasm presented at the seance.

Other phenomena took place, such as the floating about in the air of a heavy musical box, and also of a string instrument, which goes by the name of "fairy bells" and is somewhat like an aeolian harp; during the whole time this was taking place elaborate operatic music was being produced on it, at times very soft, whilst at others so loud that it seemed as if the strings must break with the violence with which they were being twanged.

I merely state what I actually saw and heard, with a mind quite cool, calm and free from prejudice. If I had any bias it was certainly rather that of the sceptic than otherwise, and I must say, in spite of this, that the appearances presented impressed me as being impossible of production by any coarse, ordinary trickery, and as being due to some form of psychic manifestation.[231] — DR. HENRY A. FOTHERBY, D.P.H. (CAMBRIDGE), L.R.C.P. LONDON, ENGLAND, 1906

SPIRIT OF DEAD AUNT APPEARS TO KIN FROM 500 MILES AWAY

☛ On the evening of September 27th, 1901, Mr. and Mrs. Smead had a sitting [seance], and the names of George Lowrey and George Smead were given, and an apparent attempt was made to "communicate" something. The George Lowrey mentioned was deceased, the fact being known to the Smeads. He was an uncle of Mrs. Smead. The possible and apparent significance of the name may be connected with the following experience, which followed closely upon the sitting to which I have just referred. The same night, September 27th, Mrs. Smead had a vision [saw an apparition]. I give her account of it.

> "I had been for a ride Friday afternoon and was very tired, so could not sleep very well during the first part of the night. About midnight I awoke with my right arm so painful that I could not move it from the wrist. I turned over to the left of the room and thought that it was very lonely without Cecil (the deceased son), and how much I would like to see him, if only for a few moments, when there was a loud rap in his room and another near me on the floor. I looked towards the spot where the rap came from, when I saw a vision [apparition] of an elderly lady. This vision was different from any that I had seen before. It looked very ghostly. It had snowy white hair and wore a white gown. The hands and face were very white, so much so that I looked very steadily at it to be sure that I was not mistaken. I thought that, perhaps, the lady we had seen that afternoon had died. This was not true. This person that I saw was very old and I was so much surprised at the difference in her appearance from those that I have seen before that when morning came I at once told my husband what I had seen. He told me to write it out at once. I said that I did not wish to do so, because it was so ghostly that I did not like to think of it."

James H. Hyslop.

Mr. Smead confirms the fact of having been told the narrative on the morning of the 28th, and the vision was soon afterwards written down as described. This was on September 30th. On the morning of September 30th they received a letter from a relative dated the same day, saying that an Aunt Sarah, aunt of Mrs. Smead, and living in Baltimore, some five hundred miles distant, had died.[232]
— JAMES HERVEY HYSLOP, 1906

CHAPTER ELEVEN

EXPERIMENTS IN BILOCATION

☛ The reality of the phenomena called "psychic" is now recognised by everyone who has studied the subject; and numerous very different theories have been suggested to explain these facts. The theory which at present seems to me nearest to the truth is that of the existence of the astral body; hence all experiments which tend to prove its existence and to define its properties are of considerable importance.

The phenomenon of bilocation is certainly one of those which is least open to other interpretations. Merely mentioning in passing that *numerous examples of this experience have been recorded in the lives of the saints* [my emphasis, L.S.], I will proceed to consider instances of its experimental production. The authors of *The Phantasms of the Living* quote seven completely attested cases with which all readers of the *Annals* must be acquainted. Here are four other cases which occurred a few years ago in the family of Mme. Agathe Hemmerlé, the learned friend of Baron Carldu Prel, whose principal works she translated into French. The incidents are related by her daughter Alma, at that time about eighteen years old, whose words I now quote—Albert de Rochas.

FIRST EXPERIMENT

This took place at Kherson (in Southern Russia) where my brother was completing his studies at the college. His class-mates frequently visited our house; and as my mother was studying psychic matters, in which we were all interested, we determined one evening to try an experiment.

We therefore arranged that, on the following night, two of these young men, M. Stankewitch and M. Serboff, should endeavour to send their doubles [astral bodies] to us; the former at 11 p.m., the latter at 11:30 p.m.

We timed our watches together and it was agreed that M.

Stankewitch should go to my brother in his bedroom, whilst M. Serboff should manifest in the drawing-room.

On the following evening my sister Irma sat in the dining-room, from whence she could see the open door which led into the drawing-room. My brother, as had been agreed, remained in his bedroom and stretched himself on his bed, in order the better to concentrate his attention on the phenomenon he expected. The bedroom adjoined the dining-room.

After having been with my sister for a few minutes, I entered my brother's room, and leaning my elbow on the rail at the foot of his bed, I asked him what o'clock it was. He pulled out his watch and said it was just 11 o'clock. The hanging lamp in the dining-room gave light enough to make it possible to distinguish objects in the bedroom. At the same moment I felt something push against my shoulder and I saw at my side, very distinctly, the form of M. Stankewitch; I could distinguish his dark uniform with the white metal buttons. At the same moment my brother said, "There he is, beside you," adding, almost immediately, "Did you see him?" for after the first remark the apparition had disappeared.

My sister, hearing us talking, came in, saying that she had just seen M. Stankewitch enter by the drawing-room door, pass near the table in the dining-room, and then disappear from her sight. She also had seen him in uniform, and was able to distinguish the white metal buttons.

We then immediately, all three of us, entered the drawing-room, which was lighted by the lamp in the dining-room, and awaited the apparition of M. Serboff. He did not appear until nearly midnight. This apparition seemed to us paler and less distinct than the preceding one. He entered the drawing-room by the ante-chamber, where he paused for a moment near the door, advancing now to the right towards one of the book-cases, then to the left towards the other one; then he suddenly disappeared. We kept silence for a while, thinking he might appear again, but he did not do so.

My brother then wrote out the results of our experiment, in detail, on two sheets of paper, enclosed them in envelopes and sealed them.

The following day at the college my brother asked his two friends whether they had not forgotten their promise. They at once described, in the presence of their comrades, details which corresponded exactly with all that my brother had written. He then put into their hands the sealed envelopes, which were opened, the contents being read aloud before the whole class. After having read the account of his own appearance, M. Serboff said that, at the moment when he entered the drawing-room, he was undecided which cupboard he would approach, because he had intended to open the bookcase and take out a book; but he had lost his power of concentration and returned to his normal self. He felt too fatigued to try again. M. Stankewitch added that he was surprised to feel a resistance on approaching the bed, for he had not expected me to be present. He thought the resistance was due to his having approached too near to the wall, since he only saw my brother.

We have lost sight of M. Stankewitch, but M. George Serboff is a barrister living at present in Kherson; my brother Alfred Hemmerlé lives at 14, Rue Chaterine, Odessa [Ukraine].

SECOND EXPERIMENT

My sister Irma went to spend a few days in the country with one of our friends, whilst I remained with my parents. It was the first time that I had been separated from my twin sister; and, as her absence was a great trial to me, I determined to go and see what she was doing.

It was 11 p.m. and I was in bed. Soon I saw myself in the room which she was sharing with our friend, and I saw my sister in her bed, a book in her hand, and reading by the light of a lamp, which had a green shade. She felt my presence, raised her eyes and saw me standing by the stove.

When I saw that she was looking at me I tried to hide myself behind the stove, being afraid that she would be frightened at the apparition, not being sure that she would recognise me.

On the following day I wrote her the details which I have just related, and I received a letter, dated the same day, telling me that she had seen me on the previous evening at 11 p.m., near the stove.

My sister and I have repeated this experiment several times, not always with success.

THIRD EXPERIMENT

One evening, when I was with four of my friends, sisters belonging to the family Spechnieff, the eldest, Mlle. Anna, said, with some anxiety, that her brother (who was an officer and who was to leave on the following day for Vladivostok [Russia]) had suddenly been seized with a bad attack of fever. Seeing that my friends were so anxious, I resolved, on returning home, to try and cure him by mental suggestion.

I saw myself transported into the room of the sick man, and I fixed my attention upon him with all my will, mentally making the suggestion to him of a complete cure.

When I went, on the following day, to see my friends and to ask after their brother, Mlle. Anna told me that he had started in good health, and that he had told her, on that very morning, that he had seen an apparition during the night: he had seen me at the further end of his room, and had felt my presence as a calming influence, and at the same moment the feverish condition had left him.

The other sisters also saw me on a day on which we had agreed that I should appear to them.

FOURTH EXPERIMENT

One of my cousins who was much interested in psychology has made numerous experiments in producing her own "double."

We were passing a few days in the country at the house of an aunt. One evening, wishing to know whether she would perceive my presence, I resolved to go and see her without previously informing her of my intention.

We were living in the right wing of the house, at the far end of the courtyard. Her room was on the ground floor and I wished to enter by the window that looked out on to the courtyard. I first tried to open the shutter, but did not succeed; I then determined to get in by a simple act of will. The noise I had made in attempting to open the shutter awakened my cousin, who jumped out of bed to see what the noise could be. She saw me in front of her, and guessing my object, she became calm.

The following day she told me of her astonishment at having observed that the astral body had the power of moving objects.[253]
— MISS ALMA HEMMERLÉ, CIRCA 1906

THE DOCTOR & THE GHOST CHILD

☛ One cold and blustery night he was sitting in his study when the door-bell rang. He answered the bell and at the door found a little girl some ten or twelve years of age, wearing a cloak with a red hood.

She asked if Dr. Mitchell was at home. When the doctor responded that he was Dr. Mitchell, the little girl said her mother was very sick, and would like to have the doctor visit her. He told the little girl that he was not engaged in the general practice of medicine, but told her that another physician, living across the street (pointing out the house) would visit her mother.

He returned to the library, and after a few moments the door-bell again rang, and upon going to the door, he found the same little girl there. Thinking that she had misunderstood him, he again had the same conversation with her and directed her to the residence of the other physician.

He again returned to the library, and in a little while the door-bell again rang, he again went to the door and found the little girl. He thereupon put on his overcoat and went with her.

After a walk of some distance they came to an apartment house. The little girl opened the door, he followed her in and then upstairs, and at the head of the stairs he heard a woman in distress in a room, the door of which was open. Without paying further attention to the little girl he went into the room and he found a woman very sick and apparently near to death. He gave her his attention and left for some medicine.

When he was about to leave the woman expressed her great gratitude at his coming and asked how it came that he had visited her. He said in answer that the little girl had come for him and had brought him. She replied that there was no little girl in the house; that her little daughter had died the day before and her body was lying in the next room.

Victorian spirit photograph showing ghostly woman on right. She was not visible at the time the photo was taken.

The doctor went into the next room and found the body of the dead little girl and the cloak with the red hood such as the little girl had worn who came for him, hanging upon the wall.

This is about the whole of the story. The doctor said he would undertake no explanation of it.[234] — TOLD BY CHARLES W. SMITH CONCERNING AN EXPERIENCE BY DR. S. WEIR MITCHELL OF PHILADELPHIA, PENN.

PROOF POSITIVE THAT GHOSTS ARE GENUINE

☛ There are many to whom the idea of a "ghost" or apparition as being in any sense a reality is simply absurd and a thing to be met with scoffs and jeers. Many who take this attitude pride themselves on their scientific tastes, inclinations, and way of thinking. Yet their attitude is utterly unscientific.

To deride and jeer at a class of phenomena because they do not understand them, and to deny the reality of the phenomena because they cannot comprehend them, is surely unworthy of a scientist. The fact that such eminent scientists as Professor Stokes and Sir Oliver Lodge, not to mention others, have been convinced as to the reality of these phenomena, at once puts to silence those who foolishly assert that no scientific man can possibly believe in such things.

Now, it has been argued that the fact that an apparition is seen in a certain garment shows at once that it has no reality, and the question is asked: Why is it necessary for the apparition to appear in a familiar guise? The reply is obvious. It is necessary for purposes of recognition primarily. If the spiritual being manifested itself in some unknown form or likeness, the object of its appearance would in most cases be frustrated.

Sometimes some marked characteristic in the appearance is apparently adopted for the sake of emphasis or to draw particular attention, either to the identity of the personality or to something connected with the death or earthly life of the departed one.

It is suggested that both the apparition and the clothes are constructed from some former memory by the mind of the observer. This is at once disposed of by the fact that there are very many well-authenticated instances of the apparitions showing wounds on the person, of which the observer had no previous knowledge, or appearing in garments not previously seen by the observer, both wounds and garments afterwards being minutely verified.

. . . There is abundant evidence now available to satisfy any reasonable man that the future life is a reality, and that death does not end a man's existence. The true attitude of mind must be one of patient investigation of such manifestations of what we term (for want of a better word) the supernatural, as come to us unbidden.

These events are of irregular but constant occurrence; probably not a week or even a day passes without some manifestation occurring. Personally I am in a disposition to add my own experience to the subject of the vesture of apparitions. I have carefully verified all the details, and hold written testimonies, which if necessary can be sworn to from two other persons. Briefly, my experience is as follows:

On the night of Friday, January 10, 1879, I retired to rest at an early hour. I awoke out of my first sleep to find the moon shining brightly into my room, the window of which faced due south. As I awoke my eyes were directed towards the panels of a cupboard let into the wall, and which was used as a wardrobe. As I lay I watched the moonlight, which brightly illuminated the east wall of the room, in which the cupboard or wardrobe was situated. As I gazed I suddenly saw a face form on the panels. Indistinct at first, it gradually became clearer, until perfectly plain, when I saw the face of my grandmother.

I gazed at it for a few seconds, when it gradually faded away into the moonlight. What particularly struck me and burnt itself into my recollection, was the fact that the face wore an old-fashioned frilled or goffered cap. I was not even startled, but arguing with myself that I was the victim of an illusion caused by the moonlight, I turned over and went to sleep again.

In the morning, at breakfast, I began to tell the experience of the night to my parents. I had got well into my story, when, to my surprise, my father sprang up hurriedly from the table, in great agitation, leaving his food almost untouched, and hastily left the room. As he walked towards the door I looked after him in amazement, saying to my mother, "What is the matter with father?" She held up her hand to enjoin silence. When the door closed I again repeated the question. She replied, "Well, Charles! It is the strangest thing I ever heard of, but when I awoke this morning, your father informed me that he had awakened in the night and saw his mother standing by the bedside, and that when he raised himself to speak to her she glided away."

This scene and conversation at the breakfast table took place about 8:30 a.m. on January 11. Before noon we received a telegram saying that my father's mother had died during the night. The affair did not end here, for my father was informed afterwards that his sister, who lived some twenty miles away, had seen the same appearance shortly after the death. Thus, three persons independently saw the apparition, at once disposing of any theory either of deception or illusion.

That this was the apparition of one who had passed through the change we call death is rendered certain by the time of the event. I have always been under the impression that my father noted the time and found it to be 2 a.m. I did not get up to see the time, but am able to ascertain it roughly in this way. The house, I find, faces due south, and the window of the apartment in which I slept also faces exactly south. Some weeks ago, when I set myself to verify the details, I asked Mr. Wesley, of the R.A.S. [Royal Astronomical Society], to give the time of the moon's southing on the night of January 10-11. The time obtained from the Nautical Almanac for that year is 14 hours, 19 minutes, G.M.T., i.e., 2:19 a.m. When on the meridian both walls of the room are equally illuminated by the moon. I was sleeping against the west wall, and know certainly that the east wall was illuminated, and also the north wall or back of the room. I am therefore certain that the moon was approximately on the meridian and the time close on 2 a.m., which confirms my father's time in a remarkable manner.

The evidence of my father's sister also places the time of the apparition to her as after the time of death, which took place at 12:15 a.m., conclusively proving that this apparition was no telepathic nor subjective manifestation, before or at the moment of death, but an actual objective and real apparition taking place a considerable time after the life had departed from the body, and therefore evidence that the departed one, though what we call dead, was sufficiently alive some hours after that event to manifest herself to relations separated by considerable distances.

To return, however, to the actual subject, "The Vesture of Apparitions": I merely described what I saw to my parents at the time, and did not make an attempt to verify the dress of the appearance I had seen. Some weeks ago, with a view to clearing the matter up, I wrote to my uncle (my aunt having passed from this life in 1900), asking him to give me particulars of the affair, and sending him a sketch from memory of what I saw. I may say that I have never previously communicated with him on this subject, nor had I seen my grandmother for some years previous to the apparition.

Here is an extract from his reply:

> "I can vouch for the truth of these details, as she died in my house on Saturday morning, January 11, 1879, at 12:15 a.m. She was dying all day on Friday, and passed away soon after midnight, according to the entry in my diary made at the time. I and my daughter well remember my wife relating this experience of the apparition to us. You ask me if the sketch you sent of the frilled cap is correct? It is remarkably so, and reproduces exactly the cap worn by your grandmother all the time she was ill in bed, and in which she died, so that your description of what you saw of her fully represents her appearance at the time she passed away. The above is a plain statement of the whole matter, and I can vouch for the truth of every particular and shall be ready, if required, to affirm the same on oath."

In this case it will be seen that the "vesture," i.e., the cap on the head, which I had not seen, was exactly verified. My father "joined the majority" in 1885; but my mother is alive, and remembers all the details clearly. Here is her letter confirming the same:

"I have carefully read my son's account of the strange apparition to him and to my late husband, Dr. Tweedale. I perfectly well remember the matter, my son telling us of what he had seen, and my husband telling me of the apparition to him; also the telegram informing us of the death during the night. I distinctly remember my husband being informed by his sister of the appearance to her."[235] — " REV. CHARLES L. TWEEDALE, F.R.A.S., WESTON VICARAGE, OLNEY, ENGLAND; EXCERPTED FROM *THE ENGLISH MECHANIC AND WORLD OF SCIENCE*, JULY 20TH, 1906

DECEASED SON'S SPIRIT APPEARS AT BEDSIDE OF DYING FATHER

☞ [What follows is my eyewitness account of an apparition of the dead appearing at the death-bed of a relative or friend.] It corroborates observations made abroad and those which I have myself collected in France, where doubtless many more might be got together by appealing to the memories of those who have been present at the death of those dear to them.

We lost one of our sons, from typhus fever, just as he had reached the age of manhood. I went to Paris to nurse him. Three days later I brought back his body.

I had left my husband very unwell, suffering from an affection of the stomach, to which he had been subject for many years. After our Paul's death every attack left my husband weaker, and he gradually declined, enduring much suffering with great courage and resignation. He could hardly take even a few teaspoonfuls of milk daily, and he only obtained a little sleep with the help of anesthetics. At last he was unable to leave his

Noted British Anglican clergyman Stainton Moses appears in this Victorian spirit photograph featuring an "unknown ghost."

bed, and I could not deceive myself as to his state. I summoned our children, trying to make ingenious pretexts for their arrival.

I succeeded —at least for a time.

He was calm, spoke little, but his mind was quite clear. He understood the situation and realised the sad motive which brought his children home:

"They have come—*sans secousse*" [that is, without difficulty], said he, as if speaking to himself.

He received the sacrament with full consciousness, and afterwards asked for some chrysanthemums which he had himself planted on the tomb of our son, in the little cemetery near by, where ground had been reserved for ourselves.

"If the plants are taken up carefully," said he, "and replanted again at once—they will root themselves again."

He placed these flowers about his bed and expressed a wish to keep them there. In the middle of the following night my daughter took my place at the bedside of her father. Towards 5 o'clock she called me. He was sinking rapidly but appeared happy to see me. I sat down by his bed and took his hand, which I pressed, holding it fast in both mine.

"You will remain, won't you?" he enquired, "until . . ." He hesitated to pronounce the fatal word.

"I will not leave you," I replied.

He murmured "Thank you!" and we remained in silence, surrounded by our remaining children.

I think he had already ceased to see us and did not feel the contact of my hand. To assure himself of my presence he said, with a sort of anxiety in his voice, "*caresse! caresse!*" I gently rubbed his poor hand, which was already cold, and brought back a little warmth into it, and his face regained the expression of calm.

Suddenly we saw him hold out the other hand, which was free, with the action of one who clasps another hand, saying: "Yes, my Paul, yes!"

"Do you then see Paul?" I asked.

"Yes, of course I see him," he replied, as if surprised at my question.

The same thought came to all of us, that Paul had come to fetch him and to assist him in the hour of death.

We were indeed thinking of that other death-bed, at which I had been present alone eighteen months before, but I do not think that any of us had the idea in our minds of a tangible intervention of our dear unseen one; this was not therefore due to a voluntary transmission of thought.

Several times my poor husband repeated the action of clasping the hand of a being invisible to us. Then, without a struggle or spasm, his soul breathed itself out in a faint sigh, and an expression of supreme serenity descended on his features.[236] — MME. E. LE NORMANT DES VARENNES, EXCERPTED FROM *REVUE DU MONDE INVISIBLE*, PARIS, FRANCE, JULY 1906

DECEASED HUSBAND'S WRAITH ANNOUNCES HIS DEMISE

☞ As an illustration of visual telepathy the following facts have been given me as the experience of a former patient of mine. Unfortunately I am unable at this distance of time to give full particulars of time and place, but I have every confidence in the veracity of my informer.

She told me that many years ago she was married to a man who ill-treated her and subsequently left her to go to America. For some time she lost all news of him, and did not know whether he was alive or dead.

One day when she was out walking she had a strong feeling that someone was, as it were, walking by her side. She happened at the time to be passing a church and as the service was proceeding she went in, and found that the hymn for those at sea was being sung.

That night, after she had gone to bed, she awoke and saw an apparition of her husband standing at her bedside with his clothes dripping wet. Subsequently she learnt that he had lost his life by drowning, but whether the time of his death corresponded actually with her visual impression I cannot now fully recollect, but in many such recorded cases this has also been noted.[237] — DR. HENRY A. FOTHERBY, D.P.H. (CAMBRIDGE), L.R.C.P. LONDON, ENGLAND, 1906

GHOST OF DYING WOMAN CALLS OUT TO BROTHER-IN-LAW

☞ My sister-in-law, Sarah Eustance, of Stretton [England], was lying sick unto death, and my wife had gone over there from Lawton Chapel [Church Lawton, England] (twelve or thirteen miles off) to see and tend her in her last moments.

One night before her death I was sleeping at home alone, and, awaking, I heard a voice distinctly call me. Thinking it was my niece Rosanna, the only other occupant of the house, I went to her room and found her awake and nervous. I asked her whether she had called me. She answered: "No; but something awoke me, when I heard someone calling."

On my wife returning home after her sister's death, she told me how anxious her sister had been to see me, craving for me to be sent for, and saying: "Oh, how I want to see him once more!" and soon after she became speechless. But the curious part was that, about the same time that she was "craving," I and my niece heard the call.[238] — ANONYMOUS, 1885

SUCCESSFUL ATTEMPTS AT BILOCATION

☞ One evening early last year (1878) I resolved to try to appear to Z. (Rev. Stainton Moses) at some miles distant. I did not inform him beforehand of my intended experiment, but retired to rest shortly before midnight with thoughts intently fixed on Z., with whose room and surroundings, however, I was quite unacquainted. I soon fell asleep, and woke up the next morning unconscious of anything having taken place.

On seeing Z. a few days afterwards I enquired, "Did anything happen at your rooms on Saturday night?"

"Yes," he replied, "a great deal happened. I had been sitting over the fire with M., smoking and chatting. About 12:30 he rose to leave, and I let him out myself. I returned to the fire to finish my pipe, when I saw you sitting in the chair just vacated by him. I looked intently at you, and then took up a newspaper to assure myself I was not dreaming, but on laying it down I saw you still there. While I gazed without speaking you faded away.

Though I imagined you must be fast asleep at that hour, yet you appeared dressed in your ordinary garments, such as you wear every day."

"Then my experiment seems to have succeeded," I said. "The next time I come, ask me what I want, as I had fixed in my mind certain questions to ask you, but I was probably waiting for an invitation to speak."

A few weeks later the experiment was repeated with equal success, I, as before, not informing Z. when it was made. On this occasion he not only questioned me upon the subject which was at that time under very warm discussion between us, but detained me by the exercise of his will, some time after I had intimated a desire to leave. As on the former occasion, no recollection remained of the event, or seeming event, of the preceding night.

Rev. Moses writes on September 27th, 1885, confirming this account. He also says that he has never on any other occasion seen the figure of a living person in a place where the person was not.[239]

— ANONYMOUS, 1878

VISION, HALLUCINATION, OR PHANTASMS?

☛ Two years ago I awoke, one night, with a curious sensation of being in a sick room, and of the presence of people who were anxiously watching by the bedside of some person, who was dangerously ill. It was not till some time after that we heard that one of my sisters, then living in Florida, had been very ill of a fever, and was at the time of the incident in a most critical state.

I have never had any other experience of an impression of sickness or death. The impression of sickness was not the continuation of a dream and hardly a distinct waking impression. I woke from a heavy sleep with a great sense of oppression, which gradually seemed to assume a distinct impression. It lasted about half an hour, that is, the actual impression, but I had a great feeling of uneasiness for several days. I have never had any hallucinations or dreams of death.[240] — MAGGIE E. PRITCHARD, TAN-Y-COED, BANGOR, WALES, JANUARY 30, 1884

GHOST OF LIVING MOTHER APPEARS AT DYING DAUGHTER'S BEDSIDE

☛ In October 1880, Lord and Lady Waldegrave came with their Scotch maid, Helen Alexander, to stay with us. (The account then describes how Helen was discovered to have caught typhoid fever.) She did not seem to be very ill in spite of it, and as there seemed no fear of danger, and Lord and Lady Waldegrave had to go a long journey the following day (Thursday), they decided to leave her, as they were advised to do, under their friends' care.

The illness ran its usual course, and she seemed to be going on perfectly well till the Sunday week following, when the doctor told me that the fever had left her, but the state of weakness which had supervened was such as to make him extremely anxious. I immediately engaged a regular nurse, greatly against the wish of Reddell, my maid, who had been her chief nurse all through the illness, and who was quite devoted to her. However, as the nurse could not conveniently come till the following day, I allowed Reddell to sit up with Helen again that night, to give her the medicine and food, which were to be taken constantly.

At about 4:30 that night, or rather Monday morning, Reddell looked at her watch, poured out the medicine, and was bending over the bed to give it to Helen, when the call-bell in the passage rang. She said to herself, "There's that tiresome bell with the wire caught again." (It seems it did occasionally ring of itself in this manner.)

At that moment, however, she heard the door open, and

looking round, saw a very stout old woman walk in. She was dressed in a night-gown and red flannel petticoat, and carried an old-fashioned brass candlestick in her hand. The petticoat had a hole rubbed in it. She walked into the room, and appeared to be going towards the dressing-table to put her candle down. She was a perfect stranger to Reddell, who, however, merely thought, "This is her mother come to see after her," and she felt quite glad it was so, accepting the idea without reasoning upon it, as one would in a dream. She thought the mother looked annoyed, possibly at not having been sent for before. She then gave Helen the medicine, and turning round, found that the apparition had disappeared, and that the door was shut.

A great change, meanwhile, had taken place in Helen, and Reddell fetched me, who sent off for the doctor, and meanwhile applied hot poultices, etc., but Helen died a little before the doctor came. She was quite conscious up to about half-an-hour before she died, when she seemed to be going to sleep.

During the early days of her illness Helen had written to a sister, mentioning her being unwell, but making nothing of it, and as she never mentioned any one but this sister, it was supposed by the household, to whom she was a perfect stranger, that she had no other relation alive. Reddell was always offering to write for her, but she always declined, saying there was no need, she would write herself in a day or two. No one at home, therefore, knew anything of her being so ill, and it is, therefore, remarkable that her mother, a far from nervous person, should have said that evening going up to bed, "I am sure Helen is very ill."

Reddell told me and my daughter of the apparition, about an hour after Helen's death, prefacing with, "I am not superstitious, or nervous, and I wasn't the least frightened, but her mother came last night," and she then told the story, giving a careful description of the figure she had seen.

The relations were asked to come to the funeral, and the father, mother, and sister came, and in the mother Reddell recognised the apparition, as I did also, for Reddell's description had been most accurate, even to the expression, which she had ascribed to annoyance, but which was due to deafness.

It was judged best not to speak about it to the mother, but Reddell told the sister, who said the description of the figure corresponded exactly with the probable appearance of her mother if roused in the night; that they had exactly such a candlestick at home, and that there was a hole in her mother's petticoat produced by the way she always wore it. It seems curious that neither Helen nor her mother appeared to be aware of the visit. Neither of them, at any rate, ever spoke of having seen the other, nor even of having dreamt of having done so.[241] — MRS. F. A. POLE-CAREW, ANTONY, TORPOINT, DEVONPORT (CORNWALL), ENGLAND, DECEMBER 31ST, 1883

HORSE-DRAWN GHOST HEARSE APPEARS TO CHILD

☛ There comes back to me the memory of an incident in my childhood which, analysed in the light of later experience, indicates from what sources we derive our gloomy, fearful views of death.

In an old white house, separated by a field from the home of my childhood, lived a venerable old gentleman. I remember him well, after the long lapse of years. He was, I think, fond of children, and whenever he met me on the road he had a cheery greeting and, on occasion, would conjure up a sweet from some mysterious recess of his coat-pocket. He died suddenly. I do not think his death caused me the least sorrow. I had a childish faith that all good people go to heaven, and a kind old gentleman who carried sweets in his pocket would certainly not be denied entrance to that happy land. I imagined him, as I had last seen him, with his large white hat, walking about the streets in Heaven giving sweets to small angels. He was dead; but he had gone to heaven, so what was the need of tears.

Four days after his death I was playing in the field which separated his house from ours, on a slope beside a hawthorn tree which still stands, when the sound of the muffled padding of lightly shod hoofs drew my attention from my play. Up the long avenue to the house there was coming a terrible apparition—a long, black coach, the top of which was surmounted by great black nodding plumes, drawn by two black horses with sweeping tails, and driven by a solemn-faced man from whose black hat a long streamer of crêpe fluttered in the wind. It was an old-fashioned funeral hearse. I had never seen one before, but the sight of it in some inexplicable way froze my heart, and it was as though a black cloud had passed across the face of the sun.

It was my first vision of the gloom of death, and I felt a strange desire to cry. I could no longer think of my old friend as happy in heaven. In some way this dreadful thing I had seen was associated with him, and death had ceased to be a safe transition from earth to heaven and had become a thing black, mysterious and awesome.

And so deeply do some of the memories of pain cut their impress upon the plastic heart of a child, that I never revisit that field and pass beneath the branches of the hawthorn tree without

recalling and revisualizing the whole scene. I can still hear the muffled beating of hoofs, and see the black and nodding plumes.[242]
— ROBERT WILLIAM MACKENNA, 1916

HIGHLY EVOLVED SPIRIT BEINGS REACH OUT TO WOMAN
☛ Very wonderful does it seem when for the first time one hears clearly the well-remembered voice of a friend who has passed into the Unseen World. This entirely unexpected experience came to me in August 1916, and since then the people and the conditions of the other life have become more and more perceptible to me without material apparatus of any kind. A friend, who had left the earth about five years before, at first gave me various convincing proofs of identity, and then went on to tell much that was interesting and illuminative about the next planes of existence.

Staged Victorian ghost photograph.

A few days later, a Heavenly Teacher also came to speak to me, through my unseen friend, and I could hear his voice even more clearly. Afterwards he visited us every Sunday evening, and as he spoke, word by word, sentence by sentence, in perfect sequence of thought, I said it aloud, and my husband took it down in shorthand.

　. . . I felt from the very first perfectly normal, not losing consciousness in any way, but I could not guess what the next word would be until I had heard it. "We just give you one word at a time, and then wait to see if you have grasped it," said my friend.

　The voice seemed to speak not to my outer ear but to my soul-ear, and I heard every intonation of it, suiting the nature of the thought, tender, grave, encouraging, hopeful, joyous: every human emotion that is true and beautiful seemed expressed in tones more musical than any outward voice can reach. The Teacher told me that before long I should also see him, without any effort on my part to develop clairvoyance. This promise was fulfilled a few months later. I was walking alone by the sea, when, in one sudden flash, I saw a tall figure beside me, clad in shining raiment that looked like moonlight, and with a face so wonderfully calm and beautiful that I could not forget it. I saw silver sandals upon the feet, and then the vision faded, but I again heard the now well-known voice.

After this, I often saw him, usually when not expecting to do so. Sometimes he would pace beside me for a few moments on some quiet road, speaking words of advice or caution, and answering my questions. I also saw him when he came to give us the Sunday talks.

It is not easy to describe the starry beauty of these radiant ones. The body looks like a rosy alabaster lamp through which the glory of the spirit shines forth, illumining even the raiment, and creating a surrounding atmosphere aura more or less dazzling according (I imagine) to the degree of spiritual development of the indwelling soul. Thus I see the aura of the Teacher like white flame, very dazzling, whereas that of our friend is softer, and looks more like candle-light.

I am conscious of the individual harmony and power of each of the spirits to an extraordinary degree, impressing me even more vividly than either sound or sight of them. Thus when the Teacher approaches, I feel deep calm, peace, tenderness, all dominated by a sense of power. The soul-atmosphere of our friend, on the other hand, brings gentleness, sympathy; and I feel also a soft breeze wafting the fragrance of flowers. These brief descriptions faintly suggest my impressions, which differ with each personality that comes.

As the months passed, I saw several other friends, and sometimes angels for a few wonderful seconds. The first of these experiences impressed me deeply, for the angel did not approach me on a level, as the friends or Teacher, but seemed to descend from a height, and I saw opalescent flame beneath the feet. The whole being looked more ethereal than that of even the Teacher, and the halo around the head framed the most exquisite of faces.[243]
— MARY BRUCE WALLACE, 1919

THE WRAITH OF CATHERINE THE GREAT

☛ In the exercise of his duties as one of the pages-in-waiting, [Comte de] Ribaupierre followed one day his August mistress into the throne-room of the palace. When the Empress, accompanied by the high officers of her court and the ladies of her household, came in sight of the chair of state which she was about to occupy, she suddenly stopped, and to the horror and astonished awe of her courtiers, she pointed to a visionary being seated on the imperial throne.

The occupant of the chair was an exact counterpart of herself. All saw it and trembled, but none dared to move towards the mysterious presentment of their sovereign.

After a moment of dead silence the great Catherine raised her voice and ordered her guard to advance and fire on the apparition. The order was obeyed, a mirror beside the throne was shattered, the vision had disappeared, and the Empress, with no sign of emotion, took the chair from which her semblance had passed away.[244] — ANDREW LANG, 1899 (FIRST RECORDED IN 1862)

THE PHENOMENON OF THE APPEARANCE OF LIVING SPIRITS

☛ There are [numerous] curious historical examples of . . . [ghost] appearances of the *living*. [For example, Johann Wolfgang von] Goethe declares that he once met himself at a certain place in a certain dress, and several years later found himself there in that costume. [Percy Bysshe] Shelley was seen by his friends at Lerici to pass along a balcony whence there was no exit. However, he could not be found there.[245] — ANDREW LANG, 1899

GHOST OF LIVING WOMAN APPEARS TO SOLDIER 5,000 MILES AWAY

☛ The determination [to live out my life unmarried] was the result of a very curious and strange incident that befell me during one of my marches to Hyderabad [India]. I have never forgotten it, and it returns to this day to my memory with a strangely vivid effect that I can neither repel nor explain. I purposely withhold the date of the year.

In my very early life I had been deeply and devotedly attached to one [woman] in England, and only relinquished the hope of one day winning her when the terrible order came out that no furlough to Europe would be granted.

One evening I was at the village of Dewas Kudea [India], after a very long afternoon and evening march from Muktul, and I lay down very weary; but the barking of village dogs, the baying of jackals and over-fatigue and heat prevented sleep, and I was wide awake and restless. Suddenly, for my tent door was wide open, I saw the face and figure [of my love] so familiar to me, but looking older, and with a sad and troubled expression; the dress was white and seemed covered with a profusion of lace and glistened in the bright moonlight. The arms were stretched out, and a low plaintive cry of "Do not let me go! Do not let me go!" reached me. I sprang forward, but the figure receded, growing fainter and fainter till I could see it no more, but the low plaintive tones still sounded. I had run barefooted across the open space where my tents were pitched, very much to the astonishment of the sentry on guard, but I returned to my tent without speaking to him.

I wrote to my father. I wished to know whether there were any hope for me. He wrote back to me these words: "Too late, my dear son—on the very day of the vision you describe to me, A. was married."[246] — COLONEL MEADOWS TAYLOR, 1878

ANIMALS & THE PARANORMAL

☛ [Besides humans] . . . animals may be equally affected [by ghosts], thus, if [one] seems alarmed, that may frighten his dog; or the alarm of a dog, caused by some noise or smell, heard or smelt by him, may frighten [others,], and make one or all of them see a ghost.

Popular opinion is strongly in favour of beasts seeing ghosts. The [early] people of St. Kilda [Scotland] . . . held that cows shared the visions of second-sighted milk-maids. Horses are said to shy on the scene of murders. Scott's horse ran away (home) when Sir Walter saw the bogle near Ashiestiel. In a case given later the dog shut up in a room full of unexplained noises, yelled and whined. The same dog (an intimate friend of my own) bristled up his hair and growled before his master saw the "Grey Lady."

The Rev. J. G. Wood gives a case of a cat which nearly went mad when his mistress saw an apparition. Jeremy Taylor tells of a dog which got quite used to a ghost that often appeared to his master, and used to follow it. [According to the story of] . . . "The Lady in Black," a dog would jump up and fawn on the ghost and then run away in a fright. Mr. Wesley's mastiff was much alarmed by the family ghost.

Not to multiply cases, dogs and other animals are easily affected by whatever it is that makes people think a ghost is present, or by the conduct of the human beings on these occasions. [There are also countless] . . . stories of the ghosts of animals.[247] — ANDREW LANG, 1899

SINGER'S GHOST APPEARS TO CHAPEL-MASTER

☛ Edwin Russell was on his way to sing bass in the church of St. Luke in San Francisco one Friday, when he fell in the street in an apoplectic fit. Three hours after his death the chapel master Reeves, who knew nothing of his death, was visited by the ghost of Russell, who held one hand pressed to his forehead and in the other he had a roll of music. It is evident that his last thought had been that he would not be able to get to the meeting, and that in this way he was notifying Reeves of the fact.[248] — CESARE LOMBROSO, 1909

GHOST OF PRINCESS APPEARS TO HER BABY

☛ Princess Schwartzenberg perished at Paris, at the great fire which took place at the Austrian Embassy. She had left her youngest children at Vienna. The Cardinal, being then a baby of six months old, was in his cradle one night, when suddenly his nurse, an old and very respectable, but by no means either a clever or imaginative woman, fell down on her knees and exclaimed, "Jesu, Maria, Joseph! there is the figure of the Princess, standing over the baby's cradle." Several nursery-maids, who were in the room, heard the exclamation, though they saw nothing, but to her dying day the nurse affirmed the truth of the vision, and, there being no telegraphs then, it was not for many days after that the news of the Princess Schwartzenberg's untimely fate reached Vienna.[249] — LADY GEORGIANA BLOOMFIELD, 1883

HAUNTED BEDROOM TERRIFIES TWO SISTERS

☛ [According to Miss Feilden] . . . during her youth her family removed to the Isle of Wight and rented St. Boniface House, between Bonchurch and Ventnor [England]. She was accustomed to sleep in a chamber on the first floor, while the French governess and the other sister, Charlotte, slept in the adjoining room. The English governess had a room on the floor above.

One night, while Miss Feilden and her sister were in bed, suddenly the door opened with a great noise and some one came into the chamber, producing a current of air. Then the bed-curtains were whisked up over their heads, and the bed-clothes dragged away.

The two sisters leaped out of bed, and at that moment the mattress also was pulled forcibly away. They ran out of the room, crying for help. The English governess came down in haste, and the servants, being called, found things all right in the chamber, the bed covers folded up and laid in three corners of the room, the mattress leaning against the wall, and the blanket by the fireplace.

They found out afterwards that similar things had happened to others there, and that the house had the reputation of being spooky. A lady had killed her babe in that room. Sometimes her ghost was visible, but usually she manifested her presence only by noise and movement of the furniture.[250] — CESARE LOMBROSO, 1909

Apparition of Victorian woman manifests in a church, startling worshippers.

Spiritualist Sir Arthur Conan Doyle (left) posing with publically proclaimed skeptic Harry Houdini (right) at the Auto Club, London, England, circa early 1920s.

CHAPTER TWELVE

MURDEROUS SPIRIT WANDERS LONELY SCOTTISH HOUSE
☛ Glenlee, in Scotland, is a very lonely country house. Some years ago it was occupied by a lady who poisoned her husband to marry a young officer with whom she was in love and with whom she went away to live.

He treated her so badly that she finally left him and returned to Glenlee, where she passed her time in sadly wandering through the halls of the house, until, grown old, she died.

It is her ghost that was seen there, but which, it is said, ceased to appear after a Catholic tenant of the property had had Mass said in the house.

At another time Mrs. Robert Gladstone was making a visit at the Maxwells', then owners of Glenlee. In the afternoon she went into the room assigned to her to rest, and presently it seemed to her that the space opposite to her was filling with mist. She thought it came from the chimney, but there was neither fire nor smoke there.

She looked to see if it could come from the window, but outside the sun was shining bright. Little by little the mist seemed to take shape, until it became the gray figure of a woman looking at the clock.

Mrs. Gladstone fainted away through terror. When she came to, the figure had disappeared. As soon as she learned that that was a haunted chamber she left the house.

Mrs. Stamford Raffles also went to visit at Glenlee. It was winter. She woke up in the night, and by the light of the fire that was burning in the fireplace she saw the same appearance of mist, which little by little condensed until it formed a human figure that stood looking at the clock. She felt at the same time an intense cold; then fainted from fright after having tried to waken her husband, who was sleeping by her side, but tried in vain, since her limbs and tongue seemed paralyzed. A little while after the

Maxwell family left Glenlee for good.

In this case the phantasm is certainly to be accounted for by the house and the sad events that had occurred there, and not to the presence of mediums. The visitors provoked the appearance of the apparition by entering the room and especially by sleeping there, and not by any mediumistic gifts they might have.[251] — CESARE LOMBROSO, 1909

THE POINTING GHOST

☛ . . . the celebrated Sir David Brewster once went with his daughter to pay a visit to the Stirling family at Kippenross in Scotland. In the night he took refuge in his daughter's chamber and asked her permission to remain there lying on a sofa till morning, so terrified had he been by the strange lamentations he had heard. Miss Brewster's maid had also heard strange noises that night and wanted to leave the house immediately.

Professor Cesare Lombroso.

In the afternoon Miss Brewster, while on the way to her room, saw at the head of the stairs a tall woman leaning against the banisters. She asked this woman to send to her her maid; but she only nodded her head thrice and pointed to a door in the hall, then descended the stairs. Miss Brewster spoke of the matter to Mrs. Stirling, who was deeply agitated by what the apparition presaged; for in the chamber to which it pointed were sleeping Major Wedderburn and his wife. Before the year ended both of them had been killed in the Sepoy Rebellion in India. The tradition in the house was that whoever was pointed out by the ghost died within the year.[252] — CESARE LOMBROSO, 1909

RICHLY DRESSED GHOST LADY AUGURS DEATH

☛ In the castle of Berry-Pomeroy [England] the wife of the major domo of the House of Pomeroy had been taken ill. Dr. Farquhar is called in, finds the disease of a very light character, and asks the husband as to the identity of the lady very richly dressed whom he had met in the ante-chamber. The husband is struck dumb with amazement and fear, knowing as he does that such a vision [apparition] has for a century and more always preceded the death of a member of the family. His wife died in the night.[253] — CESARE LOMBROSO, 1909

DISTURBING GHOST DRUM ANSWERS QUESTIONS WITH TAPS

☛ In a little house near Tedworth [England] Judge Mompreson and his family were annoyed every night as soon as they had gone to bed by the beating of an invisible drum, which sounded ominously in the interior of the house, accompanied by a reeling dance of all the pieces of furniture, which were whirled about by invisible hands. The dogs hid themselves, and the judge himself was compelled to flee the house. It is a curious fact that this drum replied to questions by taps corresponding to the succession of the letters of the alphabet, just as in séance experiments of the present day. And yet it was as far back as 1662.[254] — CESARE LOMBROSO, 1909

NORMAN CASTLE INFESTED BY HOBGOBLINS

☛ [Next we have] a case occurring in the castle of T., in Normandy. This castle had been in existence since 1835, and was restored and used again as a residence by M. de X.

In the month of October, 1867, extraordinary raps, or blows, began to be heard, with movement of tables, etc. They were renewed in 1875, and again more annoyingly in 1892. The castle was already notorious for having been in former days infested by maleficent hobgoblins.

In October, 1875, noises were heard as of steps upon the ground (at that time covered with snow), but no traces of footsteps could be seen. Armchairs and statues changed positions, large articles of furniture were dragged about, rapid steps were heard, and then came five loud raps on the staircase landing. On another day shrill cries, [and] the sound of the galloping of horses in the hall [were heard]. All this lasted from midnight up to three o'clock. Later the phenomena began to be noticed in the daytime as well.

One day the wife of X, wishing to enter a room where the noises were heard, reached out her right hand, and the key leaped out of the lock and struck her on the left hand. Under the influence of exorcisms the nuisance diminished a little, then ceased, but again appeared in 1891.[255] — CESARE LOMBROSO, 1909

BALL OF LIGHT ANNOUNCES SERVANT'S DEATH

☛ About the year 1841, I was in a room with my father in our house in the Isle of Wight, when he exclaimed, "Good God, what is that?" starting up as he spoke, and apparently looking at something. He then turned to me and said that he had seen a ball of light pass through the room, and added, "Depend upon it, Morse Simonds is dead." This was an old servant in London, to whom he had been sending money, in illness. In course of post came information that she passed away at the very time in question.[256] — REV. STEPHEN H. SAXBY, MOUNT ELTON, CLEVEDON, ENGLAND, 1884

TENANTS FLEE FROM HAUNTED HOUSE FILLED WITH TERRIFYING POLTERGEISTS

☛ Joseph Proctor communicated to the society [S.P.R.] a diary in which he had noted day by day the pranks and prodigies that took place in his father's house.

During the indwelling of the first tenant—a certain X—nothing singular was observed. But the house was abandoned by X's successor on account of the strange things that took place in it. No sooner had a certain nurse entered the house than she began to complain of roarings, stampings, clamorous cries, which were heard in the adjoining room. These noises were heard by all the other inmates of the house.

Two months afterward one of the members of the household saw one evening a white form at the window. On another evening the custodian, his wife, and his daughter saw in the same place a priest in white stole. This apparition lasted ten minutes. At intervals during six months the nursery-maids were repeatedly thrown out of bed. Later the servant-maid saw at the foot of her bed the ghost of an old man with his fingers interlocked.

In the month of June a friend who was staying over night as a guest fled from his bed terrified by the sight of phantasms and by frightful noises.

Two years passed, and then the inhabitants of the house heard their name pronounced here and there by invisible persons. Many and many a time there appeared before the children, while they were playing, the ghostly form of a nun, or the image of a pale head which vanished with a noise. After two years the tenants decided to abandon the house. The last night of their stay the noises and apparitions took place with redoubled frequency.

In their new home they heard no more noises and saw no more apparitions, as they had done in the ill-omened one they had left behind. On the other hand, those who succeeded them there were so rabidly persecuted by the poltergeists that they also had to give up the house. It was never rented again.[257] — CESARE LOMBROSO, 1909

HAUNTED RAMHURST MANOR HOUSE DISTURBED BY GHOSTS OF ORIGINAL OWNERS

☞ Mrs. R., who in October, 1857, and for many many months succeeding that, lived in the manor house of Ramhurst in Kent [England], was disturbed from the very first day of her occupancy by blows on the walls and by voices that could not be explained and which terrified every one.

A certain Miss S., who had been used, from infancy up, to the sight of apparitions (for she was at that time a medium), came to see Mrs. R., and scarcely had she entered the house when she saw at the entrance the forms of a couple of old people dressed in antique fashion, and they reappeared to her every day, surrounded by a kind of aura, or mist. The third time they spoke to her (in the mediumistic language) and said they had once been the proprietors of the house, that their name was "Children" (the old man said his name was Richard and that he had died in 1753), and that they were aggrieved that the castle, so dear to them, was now in the hands of strangers.

Mrs. R., to whom Miss S. repeated the communication, continued to perceive voices and noises, but not apparitions, except that a month after, when she was one day about to go down to dinner, she saw in her room (in bright light) the two figures, as her friend S. had described them, and glowing on the wall above the head of the old lady, in phosphoric light, the words *Dame Children*, and some other words indicating that she was "earth-bound."

After a good deal of research Mrs. R. learned from an old lady that many years before she had known an old man who had been assistant keeper of the hounds for certain "Children" who lived then in the manor house. Among them was a Richard who had died in 1753, that is, a century previous. Robert Dale Owen discovered, moreover, in the Hasted Papers in the British Museum [London, England] and in the History of Kent, that a Richard Children had settled at Ramhurst and died there in 1753 at the age of eighty-three; that the family had in the sequel emigrated elsewhere; and that after 1816 the house had become a kind of farmhouse.[258]
— CESARE LOMBROSO, 1909

FRENCH VILLA OCCUPIED BY REPENTANT SPIRIT

☞ Count Galateri relates that in 1852 his father, on retiring from the army in Annecy [France], acquired a villa, in which some years after certain strange events occurred: doors opened of themselves at night, pieces of furniture and boots struck one against another, etc., so that it was decided to sell the villa. During the last days of the stay there the countess, noticing that the noises increased in frequency and intensity in a small wine-cellar, and in fact always issued thence, tried the expedient of having excavations made there with a mattock, and presently the uproar ceased.

In 1864, four years afterward, the two Galateri men saw a newspaper fold itself up automatically and reopen on the table. It was half-past ten in the evening. At the very same hour, in another house, the mother of the Galateri family had been in a mediumistic séance at which her deceased daughter said to her, "I am going to run and give a surprise to papa and brother."

In another séance the mother with another medium affirmed that she saw at the door of the haunted villa of Annecy, of which I have just spoken, a soldier with a wooden leg, who confided to her how in a battle fought under Napoleon he was accustomed to despoil the dead, so that he grew rich, and that with his ill-acquired money he had bought that villa and in its wine cellar had hidden his little hoard. But now, having repented of what he had done, he had produced all those persistent noises to induce the countess to search for the treasure in order that she might distribute it to the poor.

Two years afterward, having returned to her old home (the Annecy villa), she learned that the then owners wanted to get rid of it at any cost, owing to the incessant clamor that occurred, notwithstanding the conjurations of the priest. She asked them to remain only two days more, dug in the cellar, and found a vessel containing several thousand francs in gold, which she distributed to the poor; and from that time forward the spiritistic phenomena ceased.[259] — CESARE LOMBROSO, 1909

"WHITE OBJECT" HERALDS DEATH OF IRISH AUNT

☛ Another case I give you, vouching for it on the veracity of a brother, long dead, whose word was never doubted by any who knew him, and upon whose statement I would rely as confidently as upon the evidence of my own senses. At the time of the occurrence he was a young man, about 23 years of age, in perfect health, of indomitable courage, and without a taint of superstition.

Riding home from hunting, with some friends, to Cheltenham, in the looming he saw, or believed he saw, an undefinable white object keeping pace with them by the side of the road; he drew the attention of his friends to the circumstance, but they could not see the object. They changed their pace, but whether walking, trotting, or cantering, to my brother's mind's eye the object remained with them until they reached the lights of the town. Thinking this very remarkable, my brother put the time down, and this agreed exactly with the hour of the demise of a much loved aunt in the south-west of Ireland.²⁶⁰ — MR. H. C. HURRY, C. E., 2 MALVERN TERRACE, SOUTH SEA, PORTSMOUTH, ENGLAND, JANUARY 4, 1884

ITALIAN HOUSE HAUNTED BY ANGRY RELIGIOUS GHOST
☛ [Count Cesar Baudi De Vesme relates the following account of a haunted house in Italy.] Crackings of whips, the overturning of articles of furniture, the turning inside out of women's garments, which were unexpectedly discovered to have been removed from boxes and wardrobes, then cut and placed on the window-sill—such are some of the hobgoblin performances that took place in the house of a certain Fer____ in Turin, Via Garibaldi, after the death of his sister, a lady of a very religious turn of mind. These pranks were repeated even out of the house, and wherever Signor Fer____ went.

They suddenly ceased after a typtological séance at which his sister confessed that she was the author of all those occurrences, she being irritated at her brother's living illegally with a certain woman. She said that, if he would marry her, every annoyance would cease. And so it proved. Now neither the woman nor Fer____ possessed mediumistic powers, and there was no one in the house who was gifted that way. Plainly the activity of the spirit of the departed is here shiningly conspicuous, nay, highly reasonable.²⁶¹ — CESARE LOMBROSO, 1909

VIOLENT RAPPINGS ANNOUNCE DEATH OF BROTHER
☛ In a case known to me, a girl was frightened into brain fever by violent rappings lasting nearly all night, and it turned out that her brother had been killed, a few minutes before the rappings began. It was before the war, and the young man was not in any specially dangerous employment, so there was no anxiety or expectation [of his death].²⁶² — JOHN ARTHUR HILL, 1917

GHOST OF CATHOLIC FRIAR APPEARS TO FRIEND AFTER DEATH
☛ When Friar James was dying, his friend Friar John "besought him dearly that he would return to him after his death and speak to him of his state; and Friar James promised this, if God so pleased." A certain day was fixed for the fulfilment of the compact, and, according to our modern notions of "suggestion," Friar John ought to have had a hallucination of his friend on that day, for he was expecting it. Certainly, if he had, we should have ruled it out as

non-evidential, because of his expectancy. But, as it happened, he saw no apparition of his friend on that day, though he saw Christ, with angels and certain saints.

On the day following, however, Friar James appeared, and Friar John asked: "Wherefore hast thou not returned to me the day that thou didst promise?"

Friar John replied: "Because I had need of some purgation."[263]
— JOHN ARTHUR HILL, 1917

GHOST OF MAN WALKS INTO COUNCIL MEETING PRESAGING HIS DEATH

☛ My wife's great-uncle was private secretary to Warren Hastings in India, and one day, when sitting in Council, they all saw a figure pass through the Council-room into an inner room, from which there was no other exit. One of the Council exclaimed, "Good God! that is my father." Search was made in the inner room, but nothing could be found, and Warren Hastings, turning to his secretary, said, "Cator, make a note of this, and put it with the minutes of to-day's Council."

Victorian psychic photograph of a spirit face above the head of Major R. E. E. Spencer.

As a small incident in the story, it was noticed that the figure had one of our modern pot hats. Some months after, a ship arrived bringing the news of the old gentleman's death and the first pot hats that had been seen in India.

I simply tell it you as I heard it from a Mr. Sparkes, who is now dead, and who, as well as my wife, was a great-nephew to—and probably heard it from—the old Mr. Cator who was present at the Council. I never heard him say whether he heard it direct from Mr. Cator, but I think it likely, as he was rather nearly related, and from his age must have known him.[264] — MR. W. C. MORLAND, OF LAMBERHURST COURT LODGE, KENT, ENGLAND, AUGUST 11TH, 1883

SPIRIT OF MURDERED MAN APPEARS TO HIS SISTER

☛ My mother's family name, Tantum, is an uncommon one, which I do not recollect to have met with, except in a story of Miss Leslie's. My mother had two brothers, Francis and Richard. The younger, Richard, I knew well, for he lived to an old age. The elder, Francis, was at the time of the occurrence I am about to report, a gay [i.e., cheerful] young man, about twenty, unmarried, handsome, frank, affectionate, and extremely beloved by all classes throughout that part of the country. He is described, in that age of powder and pigtails, as wearing his auburn hair flowing in ringlets on his shoulders, like another Absalom, and was much admired, as well for his personal grace as for the life and gaiety of his manners.

One fine calm afternoon, my mother, shortly after a confinement, but perfectly convalescent, was lying in bed, enjoying, from her window, the sense of summer beauty and repose: a bright sky above, and the quiet village before her. In this state she was gladdened by hearing footsteps which she took to be those of her brother Frank, as he was familiarly called, approaching the chamber-door. The visitor knocked and entered.

The foot of the bed was towards the door, and the curtains at the foot, notwithstanding the season, were drawn, to prevent any draught. Her brother parted them, and looked in upon her. His gaze was earnest, and destitute of its usual cheerfulness, and he spoke not a word.

"My dear Frank," said my mother, "how glad I am to see you. Come round to the bedside; I wish to have some talk with you."

He closed the curtains, as complying; but instead of doing so, my mother, to her astonishment, heard him leave the room, close the door behind him, and begin to descend the stairs.

Greatly amazed, she hastily rang, and when her maid appeared she bade her call her brother back. The girl replied that she had not seen him enter the house. But my mother insisted, saying, "He was here but this instant. Run! quick! call him back! I must see him."

The girl hurried away, but, after a time, returned, saying that she could learn nothing of him anywhere; nor had anyone in or about the house seen him either enter or depart.

Now, my father's house stood at the bottom of the village, and close to the high-road, which was quite straight; so that anyone passing along it must have been seen for a much longer period than had elapsed. The girl said she had looked up and down the road, then searched the garden—a large, old-fashioned one, with shady walks. But neither in the garden nor on the road was he to be seen. She had inquired at the nearest cottages in the village; but no one had noticed him pass.

My mother, though a very pious woman, was far from superstitious; yet the strangeness of this circumstance struck her forcibly. While she lay pondering upon it, there was heard a sudden running and excited talking in the village street.

Briefly, the cause of the disturbance was that Mr. Francis Tantum had just been killed. He had been dining at Shipley Hall, about a mile off, and was riding home after the early country dinner of that day—somewhat elated, it may be, with wine. He stopped at the door of an ale-house at Heanor, where he offended the young man who served him, by striking him with his whip. The youth ran into the house, seized a carving-knife, darted back, and stabbed him.[265] — MRS. HOWITT WATTS, HEANOR, DERBYSHIRE, ENGLAND, RECORDED CIRCA 1886

SPIRIT OF DECEASED FATHER APPEARS ON SHIP DECK

☛ Some time ago my son told me that a friend of his, a rough and simpleminded fellow, had returned from Shields, and told him a curious tale. The man is a sailor, and had served with his father ever since he was a boy in a collier which trades between this port and the North.

The youth, having become very proficient in his calling, went on his voyages, leaving his father, now an elderly man, at home. During a stormy voyage, and not far off the Humber [River], the young sailor saw his father, whom he had left in excellent health, pacing the deck, and calling out several times, as he was wont to do: "Mind your helm, Joe!" The young man wished to speak to his father, but could not; some occult power prevented him.

At the end of the voyage a letter awaited the young sailor, announcing the death of the father at the precise time when he appeared to his son; but please to remark (a matter of some importance, I think) that the apparition remained on deck some three hours, until the vessel got to Grimsby. I disbelieved my son's story, and requested him to ask his friend to come and take tea with me, that I might hear the account from his own mouth.

He came. The simplicity of his manner, his plain, open-hearted account, and I may even say his stupidity, manifested in his peculiar diction, imparted an impress to his tale.

At our request Mr. Lyons interrogated Edward Sings more formally the next time that the latter visited Folkestone. The following is the *procès-verbal* [written record] of the examination:

"What is your name?"

"Edward Sings."
"When did you leave your father last?"
"About six years ago, on a Good Friday."
"Was he in good health when you left him?"
"Yes."
"What happened on your voyage?"
"We was in a gale of wind, and we was running in the Humber; we carried the main gaff away; I was at the wheel steering her in. He come to me three or four times, tapped me on the shoulder, and told me to mind the helm, and I told the captain my father was drowned, or something happened to him. After we got in, when it was my watch, he was walking to and fro with me, and I went down below and told my mate I could not stop up, and I did not like to. My mate took my watch. I never could speak to my father, for something kept me from doing so. I heard of my father's death a week afterwards. No one else saw my father's spirit. My father stopped on deck with me an hour, and as I could not stand it any longer I went below, and my mate took my place. We cast both anchors, and were towed into Grimsby. My mother and sister were at my father's death-bed, and they told me that my father asked several times whether I was in the harbour. I certify this to be a true account. Folkestone, 29th December, 1882, Edward Sings."[266] — MR. LOUIS LYONS, OF 3 BOUVERIE SQUARE, FOLKESTONE, ENGLAND, 1884

GHOST OF DROWNED STUDENT APPEARS IN BEDROOM

☛ A Cambridge [England] student, my informant, had arranged, some years ago, with a fellow student that they should meet together in Cambridge at a certain time for the purpose of reading. A short time before going up to keep his appointment, my informant was in the South of England.

Waking in the night, he saw, as he imagined, his friend sitting at the foot of his bed. He was surprised at the sight, the more so as his friend was dripping with water. He spoke, but the apparition (for so it seems to have been) only shook its head and disappeared. This appearance of the absent friend occurred twice during the night.

Information was soon received that shortly before the time of the apparition being seen by the young student, his friend had been drowned whilst bathing.[267] — BISHOP OF CARLISLE, ENGLAND, JANUARY 1884

SPIRIT OF ACCIDENT VICTIM MANIFESTS IN BEDROOM OF COUSIN

☛ On the night of January ___, 1871, I awoke up with the idea that someone was moving by the bedside. I was a little frightened, and I saw the curtain at the side of the bed slightly pulled aside, and a hand, with the back turned towards me, appearing round the curtain. I recognised the ring on the hand as that of my cousin and dear friend (Captain C. M.).

I told my sister in the morning that I had seen a hand, wearing a ring, but did not tell her that I had recognised the ring, as I did not care to make too much of the incident. On that day, as we learnt from a letter received a few days afterwards, my cousin died in Canada, from the effect of an accident.[268] — MISS L. BARR, CIRCA 1884

MILITARY OFFICER'S GHOST GLIDES THROUGH FRIEND'S BEDROOM

☛ An attack of rheumatism and nervous prostration left me far from well for some weeks last spring, and one night I had a strange unaccountable vision which has left a vivid impression upon my memory.

I had gone to bed early and was lying awake alone, with a night-light burning in order in some degree to dispel the gloom. Suddenly across the lower end of the room passed Major G.'s figure, dressed in his usual everyday costume, neither his features nor his figure any whit altered. It was no dream, nor was I in the least delirious or wandering, therefore a conviction seized me that something must have occurred; in consequence I particularly marked the hour, when the clock struck 11 shortly afterwards.

The next morning I was not the least surprised when my sister handed me a note from Miss G. announcing her brother's death, and was fully prepared before reading it to find that he had passed away before 11 the previous evening—which presentiment, strange to say, was fully verified; Major G. having died at a quarter to 11.

Major G. had returned in a bad state of health from Egypt, where he had been serving in the campaign of 1883. For some time he appeared to recover and was able to go about and enter into society during the winter, but during the last month the old symptoms had returned, and gradually he grew worse and worse, until no hopes of his recovery were entertained. Though not personally intimate with him, we were well acquainted with his family, and naturally his case formed a topic of conversation among us.

We had also received bad accounts a few days before and were aware that he was in a critical condition; nevertheless at the time of his death he had been quite out of my thoughts and mind. I had never before had any apparition of any description whatsoever, nor has this one been followed by any other.[269] — "C. P.", CIRCA 1884

SOLDIER'S GHOST KISSES SISTER IN MIDDLE OF NIGHT

☛ I have a very vivid recollection that, towards dawn on the morning of August 3rd, 1867, I was roused from my sleep to find my brother, an officer in the 16th Lancers, then quartered in Madras [India], standing by the bed. My impression is that he bent over me, kissed me, and passed quietly from the room, making signs to me not to speak, and that I was full of joy, thinking he had returned home unexpectedly, and lay awake till the maid called me, when my first words to her were that my brother had come home and I had seen him.

I remember my bitter disappointment when at last made to believe that this was not so, and that it was quite impossible I could have seen him; also that I was scolded and silenced for holding to my story.

I cannot remember how much time elapsed before the news came by telegram that my brother died suddenly of jungle fever on August 2nd; full particulars did not reach us for weeks later, and it was not till long afterwards that I put two and two together, as the saying is, and, found that, as I then and now firmly believe, my favourite brother came to me at the hour of his death.

The date I fixed by reference to a childish diary I then kept, long since destroyed, but I cannot give you the exact hours. I know by letters that my brother died soon after 10 o'clock p.m. on August 2nd, and I know that my room was not quite dark when I saw him, and that I did not fall asleep again before morning on August 3rd.[270] — MRS. M. A. BROOKE, WOODLANDS, KENFORD, EXETER, ENGLAND, JUNE 29TH, 1884

THE GHOST STORY OF TWO SISTERS

☛ On the 4th of July, 1868, my sister Lizzie and myself left Detroit and went to Saginaw [Michigan], for the purpose of making a short visit with friends there. Our train was due in Saginaw about 7 p.m., but through detention did not arrive there until between 10 and 11. Owing to the lateness of the hour of arrival, we did not go to the residence of our friends, but to the Bancroft House, then the principal hotel in that city.

The weather was very warm, our ride had been very dusty, and we were very tired. We had supper, and soon after retired. My sister and I occupied the same room and bed. It was nearly or quite 12 o'clock when we retired. As I now recollect, I went immediately to sleep.

I was awakened by feeling what seemed to be a hand on my shoulder. I saw my brother Stewart standing by the bedside, and I had an impression at the same time that my brother-in-law Phillip Howard was also in the room.

My brother said to me: "Kate, mother wants you! get up and go home."

I at once became very much excited and awakened my sister, and told her that I had seen Stewart and what he had said, and that I felt sure that mother was sick or in trouble, or that something unusual had happened to her. We got up, and immediately after heard the clock strike one. There was bright moonlight that night, and all objects in the room and outside the windows were plainly visible. There had been a menagerie in town that day, and it was yet in the neighbourhood, and we could hear the noises of the animals, and talked about them. My sister did not share in my alarm or anxiety, and ridiculed what she called my "Ghost Story," and we soon retired again.

My mind was somewhat troubled with what had occurred, and I did not go to sleep quite so soon as my sister did, but I did go to sleep again, and the air being somewhat cooler, before going to sleep I had pulled the sheet up over my neck.

While asleep I was again awakened by feeling the sheet pulled down off me, and I again saw my brother Stewart, and he repeated the same language as on the first occasion. At this time his appearance was very much more persistent than before, but his face seemed to retire and gradually fade away. He looked pale and ill, but at that time my concern and anxiety was on account of my mother. I supposed that she was threatened with some serious illness, and that the appearance had relation to that.

I again aroused my sister and told her what had occurred, and we both got up and dressed, and did not retire again that night. I am not sure that I mentioned the circumstance to any of our friends that day. If I did, I am not in a position now to obtain the verification of it.

We returned home on the afternoon of Monday, the 6th of July, arriving there between 6 and 7 o'clock. We found our father and mother very much disturbed in consequence of a telegram which they had received to the effect that Stewart was dying. When my mother communicated the news to us, I answered "He is dead"; for then the significance of what had occurred at Saginaw first flashed upon me.

It was but a very short time after this, the same evening, that we received another telegram giving the tidings of his death. My sister Lizzie had received a letter from him but a day or two before we went to Saginaw, in which he promised to make us a visit in the following October, and there was nothing to afford any ground for anxiety on his account in the letter. As I have been since informed, he died about a quarter before 1 o'clock on the morning of the 5th of July, about the time of his first appearance to me, as near as I can ascertain.

I have a letter from my sister Lucy, the wife of Phillip Howard, at whose house he died, giving full particulars of his death, from which it seems that he was taken suddenly and violently ill on the 3rd or 4th of July, of what was supposed to be yellow fever.

During his illness he talked a great deal about our mother, and seemed in his delirium to be watching for her and to think that she was coming to see him. He died, as stated, that Sunday morning, and was buried by order of the authorities on the afternoon of the same day.

You inquire if I have ever had any previous hallucination of that kind. I have never had but one; that occurred when I was 7 years old. At that time a young girl, a relative and playmate of mine, was ill with some form of fever. I had not been allowed to see her for two or three days. On waking one morning, I saw or dreamed she came and kissed me and bade me good-bye. This was before I had arisen. My mother soon afterwards came into the room, and I told her that _____ had come and kissed me and bid me good-bye. Within a few minutes after this some one of the family came from the house where the little girl resided, and said that she was dying. My mother immediately went over to the house, which was not far off, and when she arrived there the little girl was already dead.

These are the only cases of what you call "hallucination" that have occurred in my experience.

The occurrences at Saginaw were real, and I have never had a doubt about my brother, in some way or form, appearing to and communicating with me.[271] — MRS. KATE SHERMAN, MUSKEGON, MICHIGAN, NOVEMBER 18TH, 1885

GRANDFATHER'S SPIRIT BIDS FINAL FAREWELL TO GRANDDAUGHTER

☛ In the early autumn of 1860, when I was between 19 and 20, I was staying with friends who lived near Rugby [England]. I had gone to bed and fallen asleep, and was awakened by a consciousness of some one being in the room. I saw, as I imagined, my grandfather standing at the foot of the bed. He was then, as far as I knew, at his own house a few miles out of Liverpool. Immediately the figure moved to the side of the bed, the curtains of which had not been drawn. The figure did not, so far as I remember, touch either the bed or the curtains. The only remark he made was "Good-night, Miss Nellie, Ma'am"—he was always in the habit of calling me "Nellie" and sometimes in fun, "Miss Nellie, Ma'am," quoting the way in which Irish servants used to address my grandmother, after whom I was christened. He was the only person who ever called me "Miss Nellie" or "Nellie," my father having a great objection to all pet names.

I soon fell asleep again, and next day mentioned the circumstance to my friends, and the day after received from my father the news of my grandfather's sudden death, about the time when he had appeared to me. So little did I anticipate such news that before I broke the black seal on my father's letter I exclaimed, "Dear me, I fear poor Edward has gone," alluding to my youngest brother who had been ailing for some time.[272] — ELLEN BIBBY, CHACELEY LODGE, TEWKESBURY, ENGLAND, 1883

GIRL'S GHOST VISITS EMPLOYER FROM THE SPIRIT WORLD

☛ An Italian girl named Rosa was in my employ for some time, but was finally obliged to return home to her sister on account of confirmed ill-health. When I took my customary exercise on horseback I frequently called to see her.

On one of these occasions I called about 6 o'clock p.m., and found her brighter than I had seen her for some time past. I had long relinquished hopes of her recovery, but there was nothing in her appearance that gave me the impression of immediate danger. I left her with the expectation of calling to see her again many times. She expressed a wish to have a bottle of a certain kind of wine, which I promised to bring her myself next morning.

During the remainder of the evening I do not recollect that Rosa was in my thoughts after I parted from her. I retired to rest in good health and in a quiet frame of mind. But I woke from a sound sleep with an oppressive feeling that someone was in the room. I reflected that no one could get in except my maid, who had the key of one of the two doors of my room—both of which doors were locked. I was able dimly to distinguish the furniture in the room. My bed was in the middle of the room with a screen round the foot of it. Thinking someone might be behind the screen I said, "Who's there?" but got no answer.

Just then the clock in the adjoining room struck 5; and at that moment I saw the figure of Rosa standing by my bedside; and in some way, though I could not venture to say it was through the medium of speech, the impression was conveyed to me from her of these words: "*Adesso son felice, son contenta* ["Now I am happy and content"]. And with that the figure vanished.

At the breakfast table I said to the friend who shared the apartment with me, "Rosa is dead."

"What do you mean by that?" she inquired; "You told me she seemed better than common when you called to see her yesterday."

I related the occurrence of the morning, and told her I had a strong impression Rosa was dead. She laughed, and said I had dreamed it all. I assured her I was thoroughly awake. She continued to jest on the subject, and slightly annoyed me by her persistence in believing it a dream, when I was perfectly sure of having been wide awake.

To settle the question I summoned a messenger, and sent him to inquire how Rosa did. He returned with the answer that she died that morning at 5 o'clock. I was living in the Via Babuino [Rome, Italy] at the time.[273] — HARRIET GOODHUE HOSMER, SCULPTOR, RECORDED JULY 15TH, 1885

GHOST OF SERVANT APPEARS TO HER EMPLOYER AT THE HOUR OF HER DEATH

☙ I had in my service a charwoman, of about 60 years of age, who had served me faithfully for more than 20 years. Her husband had been one of my husband's coastguardmen, and on his death the poor woman had to work to support herself and four children, two of whom turned out badly. I had helped her as much as I could besides employing her, and found her very valuable in being trustworthy. She regarded me with great affection, and used to say to my daughters that there was no one to her like "the mistress," as she always called me.

In October of last year I had agreed to visit my sister, who resides in Edinburgh [Scotland], and having fixed the day, a Wednesday, had arranged for Mrs. Halahan to come as usual. My son, who was going with me, persuaded me to set out on the day previous. Mrs. H. arrived, expecting to see me. Strange to say, she was very much taken aback and moved, and exclaimed, "The mistress gone without seeing me!" She went to my house as usual during my absence (about a month).

One day, while working at my married daughter's house, she was taken suddenly ill, about 6 o'clock in the evening—was conveyed home in a cab, and died next morning.

Meanwhile my daughters did not mention to me the death of my dear servant, but only that she was ill, knowing it would grieve me; but just at the time of her death (10 days before I returned home) I was sleeping in the room with my sister in Edinburgh, when, in the dusk of the morning, I was awakened by a loud knock, and saw the figure of a woman in a loose dress, standing at the side of the bed, looking towards me. I sat up, and said emphatically, "Who are you, and what do you want?"

I repeated the question twice, which awoke my sister, who asked who I was speaking to?

This Victorian psychic photograph is entitled: "Abnormal Portrait of a Lady."

I replied, "To the woman standing there." Immediately the figure melted away like a shadow.

I was so impressed with what I had seen that I went up to the room on several successive evenings, wondering whether that shadow-like form would again appear, but it never came.

On returning home, the first question I asked my daughter was about my old servant, as, thinking she was ill, I wished to go to see her. I was astonished and grieved at the news of her death. All at once the truth flashed across my mind, and I exclaimed, "Why, I saw her myself," and then related to my son and daughter the above facts. My description was so clear and vivid that they were equally impressed as to its truth, and feel as sure as I do of the occurrence being a fact.

I never saw anything of the sort before, nor have I or my family ever believed in ghosts; but they implicitly believe this, knowing that I am in no way fanciful. I feel sure that my dear servant (who was, I find, speechless for some hours before her death) had me on her mind. I can only think that the dusk of the morning and the darkness of the room (between 5 and 6 in the morning, the hour at which she died) prevented my recognising the features, but I can truly vouch for the above facts.[274] — ELEANOR E. WOODHAM, 5 ROYAL NAVAL COTTAGES, PENGE (LONDON), ENGLAND, JUNE 26TH, 1884

DEATH PACT KEPT BETWEEN MOTHER & SON
☛ My father was a Baptist minister at Soham, Cambridgeshire [England]. In the year 1849, being one of a large family, I went from home to begin the battle of life. There was great love between my mother and me. When I had been away about a year, I was sent for in a hurry to see my dear mother, who was thought to be dying.

I got leave of absence for a week and went home, and the last day before returning to business, while sitting by my mother's side, I said, "Mother, if it is possible, when you pass away will you come and tell me?" She said, "I will if I possibly can."

On the morning of October 7th, 1850, I awoke and felt like a soft hand touch me, and heard the well-known voice say, "I am gone," and something seemed to glide away from my side. I awoke the young man who was sleeping with me, and said, "My mother is gone. She has just been here and told me so;" and just as I said it the clock standing on the stairs struck 3. The news came to hand that my mother had died at five minutes to 3.[275] — TIMOTHY COOPER, 21 CADOGAN TERRACE, VICTORIA PARK, E. (LONDON), ENGLAND, JANUARY 1882

SPIRIT OF LIVING FELLOW BARRISTER VISITS FRIEND IN THE NIGHT
☛ In October, 1885, I was stopping for the night at the Swan Hotel at B., on circuit. My bedroom was No. 17. My friend K., a brother barrister, occupied No. 16. Between No. 17 (my room) and No. 18 there was a communicating door, and before retiring to rest I was under the impression that the door was between my room and my friend K.'s. I had told my friend K. so, when bidding him good-night, and he had jokingly remarked that he would come in and frighten me during the night. I discovered before going to bed that our rooms did not communicate.

I must have been asleep some hours, when I woke up with a sensation that someone was close to my bed, and feeling about the other side of the chintz curtain at the head of the bed. I could hear the rustling and crackling of the curtain close to my face. I felt perfectly unable to move, or protect myself—not through any fear, but from a want of power of movement.

After a few seconds this powerlessness went off, and I sprang out of bed, and saw the figure of my friend K. retreating towards the foot of the bed. He kept his face averted, his head a little bent, but I could see the wire and one of the glasses of his spectacles as he turned from me; he was dressed in his night-shirt. And what made me believe in the reality of the appearance was the "solidity" of the white nightdress, and the light on the spectacles. The room was in dim light, owing to gas lamps in street, and a fanlight over door admitting light from gas in passage.

I grasped at my friend with both hands and supposed I had missed him as my hands met in the grasp. I attempted again to grasp him, when he disappeared as if through the floor under the washing-stand. I then realised, with some interest, that it was a hallucination [apparition], and I sat on the bed, wide awake, interested in thinking it over.

I told K. of it next morning. I am uncertain whether there was a fan-light over the door, but such was my impression at the time; anyway, the room was light.[276] — MR. T. H. L., ENGLAND, DECEMBER 21ST, 1885

WIFE HEARS HUSBAND COME HOME BEFORE HE ACTUALLY ARRIVES

☛ I was expecting my husband home, and shortly after the time he ought to have arrived (about 10 p.m.) I heard a cab drive up to the door, the bell ring, my husband's voice talking with the cabman, the front door open, and his step come up the stairs.

I went to the drawing-room, opened it, and to my astonishment saw no one. I could hardly believe he was not there, the whole thing was so vivid, and the street was particularly quiet at the time.

About 20 minutes or so after this my husband really arrived, though nothing sounded to me more real than it did the first time. The train was late, and he had been thinking I might be anxious.

To me the whole thing was very noisy and real, but no one else can have heard anything, for the bell I heard ring was not answered. It was a quiet street in town, and there was no vehicle of any kind passing at the time; and on finding no one on the landing as I expected, I went at once to the window, and there was nothing to be seen, and no sound to be heard, which would have been the case had the cab been driven off.[277] — AMY C. POWYS, ENGLAND, JULY 1882

CHAPTER THIRTEEN

LIVING FRIEND'S GHOST APPEARS & DISAPPEARS
☞ While a resident of the city of Philadelphia [Pennsylvania], I made an appointment to meet a personal friend. At the appointed hour I was at the designated place. My friend was tardy in his appearing. After a while, however, I saw him approaching (or thought I did). So assured was I of his advance that I advanced to meet him, when presently he disappeared entirely.

The locality where I thought I saw his approach was open, and unobstructed by any object behind which he could have disappeared. Only by leaping a high brick wall (an enclosure of a burying-ground) could he have secreted himself. The hallucination [apparition] was complete—so distinct as to lead me to advance to meet him without a thought of optical illusion.

I immediately went to the office of my friend, and there learned from him that he had not been away from his desk for several hours. The appointment was forgotten by my friend, as he stated in his apology when I entered his office.[278] — REV. F. R. HARBAUGH (PASTOR OF THE PRESBYTERIAN CHURCH), RED BANK, MONMOUTH CO., NEW JERSEY, U.S.A., FEBRUARY 7TH, 1884

LIVING HUSBAND'S DOUBLE APPEARS TO WIFE BEFORE ARRIVING HOME
☞ My father and mother lived, when young, near St. Albans [England], in a house separated by three fields from the high road. My father had been staying in Warwickshire, and was returning by the night mail coach. My mother had risen early to be ready for his return, and after seeing that breakfast and a bright fire were ready for his reception, she took her work to the window and sat there awaiting my father's return.

She presently looked up and saw him approaching; she watched him until close to the house, when she went to the house door intending to meet him, but he had vanished. Half an hour after-wards he really arrived.

My mother was a Quakeress of exceeding truthfulness, and possessing to the full the perfect self-command and self-repression inculcated by her sect. I have often heard her say that she never had seen my father more distinctly than on that occasion.[279] — MRS. SMITH, OF 9 MORDEN ROAD, BLACKHEATH, ENGLAND, CIRCA 1880S

GHOST OF DECEASED WOMAN HIDES HER DISFIGURED FACE

☛ In the month of April 1871, about 2 o'clock in the afternoon, I was sitting in the drawing-room of my father's house, in Pall Mall [London, England]. The window of the room fronted south; and the sun was shining brightly in at the window. I was sitting between the fire-place and the window, with my back to the light; my niece was sitting on the opposite side of the fire-place; and opposite me, at the further corner of the room, was a door partly open, leading directly to the staircase.

I saw what I supposed at the first moment to be dirty soapy water running in at the door; and I was in the act of jumping up to scold the housemaid for upsetting the water, when I saw that the supposed water was the tail or train of a lady's dress. The lady glided in backwards, as if she had been slid in on a slide, each part of her dress keeping its place without disturbance. She glided in till I could see the whole of her, except the tip of her nose, her lips, and the tip of her chin, which were hidden by the edge of the door. Her head was slightly turned over her shoulder, and her eye also turned, so that it appeared fixed upon me. She held her arm, which was a very fine one, in a peculiar way, as if she were proud of it. She was dressed in a pale blue evening dress, worked with white lace.

Victorian psychic photograph showing multiple spirits.

I instantly recognised the figure as a lady whom I had known some 25 years or more before; and with whom I had frequently danced. She was a bright, dashing girl, a good dancer, and we were good friends, but nothing more. She had afterwards married, and I had occasionally heard of her, but do not think I had seen her for certainly more than 20 or 25 years. She looked much as I used to see her—with long curls and bright eyes, but perhaps something stouter and more matronly. I said to myself, "This is one of those strange apparitions I have often heard of. I will watch it as carefully as I can."

My niece, who did not see the figure, in the course of a minute or two exclaimed, Uncle A., what is the matter with you? you look as if you saw a ghost!"

I motioned her to be quiet, as I wished to observe the thing carefully; and an impression came upon me that if I moved, the thing would disappear. I tried to find out whether there was anything in the ornaments on the walls, or anything else which could suggest the figure: but I found that all the lines close to her cut the outline of her figure at all sorts of angles, and none of these coincided with the outline of her figure, and the colour of everything around her strongly contrasted with her colour.

In the course of a few minutes, I heard the door-bell ring, and I heard my brother's voice in the hall. He came upstairs, and walked right through the figure into the room. The figure then began to fade away rather quickly, at first losing the colours and then the form; and though I tried, I could in no way recall it.

I frequently told the story in society, treating it always as something internal rather than external, and supposing that the lady was still alive; and rather making a joke of it than otherwise. Some years afterwards I was staying with some friends in Suffolk [County, England] and told the story at the dinner table, saying that it was no ghost, as the lady was still alive.

The lady of the house said, "She is not alive as you suppose, but she has been dead some years."

We looked at the peerage, and we found she had died in 1871. (I afterwards found out that she had died in November, whereas the apparition was in April.)

The conversation continued about her, and I said, "Poor thing, I am sorry she is dead. I have had many a merry dance with her. What did she die of?"

The lady of the house said, "Poor thing, indeed, she died a wretched death; she died of cancer in the face." She never showed me the front of her face; it was always concealed by the edge of the door.[280] — MR. W. A. S., ENGLAND, JANUARY 14TH, 1883

GHOST OF IRISH GRANDFATHER MANIFESTS ON DARK ROAD

☛ As well as I can remember, it was in the year 1862. I know it was in the early part of my courting days, so that it must have been 1862 or 1863. I was walking home one night about 10 p.m.—the night was not dark, I could see clearly for many yards ahead—when I met face to face a man in the bye-road which leads from the high road to my father's house. I felt that sort of start one does when you feel you are coming against something in the dark, without actually striking against it. Then the thought came, "Confound his impudence, why does he not move out of my way?" and I stepped straight forward, intending to walk bang into him, but as I stepped right up to him, with my chest up to him, he was gone, and the instant as he vanished I thought, "Oh, Lord, that is my Grandfather Gibson." I felt rather queer, I can tell you, but I looked well round, and there was no one near.

I carefully went to that place night after night again, and watched the spot often other nights over our wall, and I could never either see or think I saw anything again. My grandfather was dead about 11 years at the time, and was never much in my thoughts, as I had never been much with him; and at the time I was thinking only of the events of the evening, as I suppose most young men madly in love, as I was, would have been. I was about as happy and as full of health and life as I suppose any fellow could possibly be.

It was quite a puzzle to me for many years what it could have been for; but I think I know now [as, at that time, I was becoming involved in an affair that turned out badly.][281] — MR. R. GIBSON, OF MULGRAVE COTTAGE, LIMERICK, IRELAND, FEBRUARY 25TH, 1884

DRAPED FEMALE GHOST APPEARS IN MOONLIGHT

☛ [When a boy, I awoke one night to find the moon brightly illuminating the side of the room facing my bed.] While gazing, I distinctly saw—rising in the moonlit space between the curtains at the foot of the bed—what appeared to be vapour or cloud, and as this grew higher, it gradually assumed the shape of a draped female figure, holding towards me in one hand a lamp and in the other a basin, from which steam seemed to rise. The form vanished slowly, and I afterwards fell asleep without experiencing either fear or horror.[282] — MR. ROBERT COLLINGS, OF 118 EARL'S COURT ROAD, S.W. [LONDON, ENGLAND], CIRCA 1880S

WOMAN'S GHOST SPEAKS TO SISTER AT TIME OF DEATH
☛ On the night of the 10th of November, 1861 (I do not know the exact hour), I was up in my bed watching, because there was a person not quite well in the next room. I heard a voice, which I recognised at once as familiar to me, and at first thought of my sister. It said, in the brightest and most cheerful tone, "I am here with you."

I answered, looking and seeing nothing, "Who are you?"

The voice said, "You mustn't know yet." I heard nothing more, and saw nothing, and am certain that the door was not opened or shut.

I was not in the least frightened, and felt convinced that it was Lucy's (Miss Lucy Gambier Parry's) voice. I have never doubted it from that moment. I had not heard of her being worse; the last account had been good, and I was expecting to hear that she was at Torquay [England].

In the course of the next day (the 11th), mother told me that she had died on the morning of the 10th, rather more than 12 hours before I heard her voice.[283] — SISTER BERTHA, SUPERIOR OF THE HOUSE OF MERCY AT BOVEY TRACY, NEWTON ABBOT, ENGLAND, DECEMBER 29TH, 1885

APPARITION OF INJURED MAN APPEARS TO FRIEND
☛ Years ago, a friend and myself made the time-worn arrangement that whichever died first would endeavour to return to visit the other. Some years after, I asked this man's sister to remember me to him and say, did he remember his promise, and having received for answer "Perfectly, and I hope I shall appear to and not she to me," the whole matter passed out of my mind.

My friend was in New Zealand, his sister I don't know where. One night I awoke with a feeling someone was in the room. I must tell you that I always have a bright light burning on a table, not far from my bed. I looked about, and presently saw something behind the little table; felt myself grow perfectly cold; was not in the least frightened, rubbed my eyes to be sure I was quite awake, and looked at it steadfastly.

Gradually a man's head and shoulders were perfectly formed, but in a sort of misty material, if I may use such a word. The head and features were distinct, but the whole appearance was not substantial and plain; in fact it was like a cloud, formed as a man's head and shoulders. At first I gazed and thought, who is it, someone must be here, but who? Then the formation of the head and forehead (which are most marked in my friend) made me exclaim to myself "Captain W_____." The appearance faded away.

I got up and put the date down; and waited until news from New Zealand was possible. I made inquiries about my friend, never doubting but that he was dead. The answer always came "No news." At last this also, "We are so anxious; it is so long since we have heard. We shall again wait another mail, and write to so-and-so."

And then came the news, a mere scrap, "Have had a severe fall off the coach; can't write; head all wrong still."

That was all, and pretty much the exact words as far as I can remember. In due time we heard more. He had fallen off the coach, and was insensible for some time, and then, as he had said, his head was not clear for a while. I have never had the slightest doubt but that, while insensible, his spirit came here. The appearance to me was coincident with the time of his insensibility. I have never had but this one experience of an apparition.[284] — MISS E. W. R., DECEMBER 17TH, 1883

SCOTTISH AUNT'S GHOST APPEARS ON DAY OF HER DEATH

☛ Early in October, 1872, whilst at H. M. Embassy, at Constantinople [Istanbul, Turkey], to which I belonged, when crossing a garden (which separated the secretary's house, where I lived, from the Ambassador's palace), on my way to dine there, about 8 o'clock in the evening (it was about dusk), I felt some irresistible, magnetic sort of influence compel me to turn round and look behind me.

I saw an indistinct white form, about the height of a human being, gazing at me, as if it were trying to attract my attention. It was only a very few yards off. I at once walked towards it, and spoke, but it vanished. So convinced was I that something had got within the precincts of the Embassy walls and gates (all being well secured and watched), that I returned to my own quarters, examined the closed gate, and questioned the guard on duty as to whether any stranger could have entered. "Impossible," he said; and our sporting dogs, none of which were white, were sleeping peacefully on the doorsteps.

I then returned, through the same garden, to the Embassy Palace, to dinner, and back again at night. I saw nothing. Again I made inquiry whether any intruder had entered the gates, but it was proved to me to be materially impossible; nor could any one have scaled the high wall, or disappeared as quickly as did the white figure when I advanced towards it.

Very soon after, I learnt that a married aunt of mine, to whom my family and myself were much attached, had died in my father's house, in the North of Scotland, during the afternoon of the same day on which I saw the figure.[285] — J. G. F. RUSSELL, 32 UPPER BROOK STREET, W., ADEN, ABERDEENSHIRE, SCOTLAND, JANUARY 3RD, 1886

GHOST OF AMERICAN INDIAN APPEARS TO ENGLISH AUTHORESS

☛ On the day [in the American Rocky Mountains] in which I parted with [my Native-American friend] Mountain Jim [Nugent], he was much moved and much excited. I had a long conversation with him about mortal life and immortality, and closed it with some words from the Bible. He was greatly impressed, but very excited, and exclaimed, "I may not see you again in this life, but I shall when I die." I rebuked him gently for his vehemence, but he repeated it with still greater energy, adding, "And these words you have said to me, I shall never forget, and dying I swear that I will see you again."

We parted then, and for a time I heard that he was doing better, then that he had relapsed into wild ways, then that he was very ill after being wounded in a wild quarrel, then lastly that he was well, and planning revenge. The last news I got when I was at the Hotel Interlaken, Interlaken, Switzerland, with Miss Clayton and the Kers.

Shortly after getting it, in September 1874, I was lying on my bed about 6 a.m., writing to my sister, when, looking up, I saw Mountain Jim standing with his eyes fixed on me, and when I looked at him he very slowly but very distinctly said, "I have come, as I promised"; then waved his hands towards me, and said, "Farewell."

When Miss Bessie Ker came into the room with my breakfast, we recorded the event, with the date and hour of its occurrence. In due time news arrived of his death, and its date, allowing for the difference of longitude, coincided with that of his appearance to me.[286] — ISABELLA BIRD, WELL-KNOWN ENGLISH TRAVELLER & AUTHORESS, CIRCA 1870S

BOY'S SPIRIT VISITS FRIEND ON NIGHT OF HIS DEATH

☛ When I was about 15, I was staying on a visit to Dr. J. G., of Twyford, Hampshire County [England], and I formed a friendship with my host's cousin, a boy of 17 [named Bertie]. We became inseparable, boating and riding together and sharing all our fun, just like brother and sister. He was very delicate, and I took care of him, and looked after him, until we never passed an hour away from each other. I tell you this to show there was not a particle of morbid sentiment between us; we were like two boys together.

One night Mr. G. was sent for to see his cousin [Bertie], who had been taken suddenly very ill with inflammation of the lungs, and the poor boy died the next night. They did not tell me how ill he was, so I was quite unaware of his danger, and therefore not anxious in any way. The night he died, Mr. G. and his sister went round to their aunt's house, leaving me alone in the drawing-room. There was a bright fire, and like many girls I delighted to sit by the fender, reading by firelight. Not knowing of my friend's danger I was not uneasy, only vexed that he could not come and spend the evening with me, so I felt lonely.

Examining ghost photos after being developed.

I was reading quietly when the door opened, and Bertie (my friend) walked in. I jumped up to get him an arm-chair near the fire, as he looked cold, and he had no greatcoat on, and as it was snowing, I began to scold him for coming out without his wraps. He did not speak but put up his hand to his chest and shook his head, which I mistook to mean his cold was on his chest, and that he had lost his voice, to which he was subject. So I reproached him again for his imprudence. While speaking, Mr. G. came in and asked me to whom I was speaking. I said, "There's that tiresome boy without his coat, and such a bad cold he can't speak; lend him a coat and send him home."

I shall never forget the horror and amazement on the good doctor's face, as he knew (what I did not) that the poor boy had died half-an-hour ago, and he was coming to break the news to me. His first impression was that I had already heard it, and that I had lost my senses. I could not understand either why he made me leave the room, and spoke to me as if I were a small child. For a few moments we were at cross purposes, and then he explained to me that I had had an optical illusion; he did not deny that I had seen Bertie with my eyes, but explained it all most scientifically, as he was anxious not to frighten me or leave a distressing impression.

I have never spoken of it to anyone before now, partly as it is a most distressing remembrance, and partly in the fear of being thought fanciful and being disbelieved. My mother said I was dreaming, and forbad me ever to mention it. I was not dreaming, but reading a book called *Mr. Verdant Green*, not at all a book to send one to sleep, and I well remember at the time the door opened I was laughing heartily over some of its absurdities.[287] — MRS. I. STELLA, CHIERI, ITALY, JANUARY 14TH, 1884

FEMALE GHOST GLIDES ACROSS BEDROOM
☞ Mr. B. is a gentleman whom I have known for more than 15 years. He is practical, shrewd, and very trustworthy. I am indebted to him for the following narration: One morning, a few months ago, at 5 o'clock, he was awakened by a noise outside his room, but near his room door. Opening the door he saw no person. He returned to bed, and had scarcely composed himself when he was very disconcerted by seeing the form of a lady friend of his glide or flit across the room. He there upon woke Mrs. B. and informed her of the fact. This was Saturday, and at the end of the next week Mr. B. called at the house of his friend, the subject of his vision, and was informed that the lady had thrown herself out of the window the previous Saturday at about 5 o'clock in the morning, and was instantaneously killed.[288] — MR. D. H. WILSON, ROSEMONT, HYÈRES, FRANCE, OCTOBER 24TH, 1883

YOUNG MAN PROJECTS HIS SPIRIT DOUBLE 10,000 MILES
☞ My younger brother was in Australia, and had not written to his family for some four or five months, from which my mother had concluded he must be dead. I was sitting with her and my sister in our dining-room one morning, about 11 o'clock, engaged with my sister in writing a German exercise. Being at a loss for the right declension, I looked up, repeating the declension, when I saw my brother standing on the lawn in front of the window apparently looking at us.

I jumped up, saying to my mother, "Don't be frightened, mother, but there is T. come back all right." (My mother had heart disease, and I feared the sudden shock.)

"Where?" said my mother and sister, "I don't see him."

"He is there," I answered, "for I saw him; he is gone to the front door," and we all ran to the door.

My father, who was in his library, heard the commotion, and opened his door to ask the cause. I had by this time opened the front door, and not seeing my brother, I thought he was hiding for fun among the shrubs, so I called out, "Come, T., come in, do not play the fool or you will kill dear mother."

No one answered, and then my mother exclaimed, "Oh, you did not see him really, he is dead, I know he is dead."

I was mystified, but it did not seem to me the right solution of the mystery. I could not think he was dead, he looked so honestly alive. To tell the truth, I believed for some time that he was in the garden. However, he was not, nor was he dead.

About a year afterwards he returned home, and when recounting his troubles, he told us that he had been very ill, and that while he was delirious he had constantly requested his comrades to lay him under the great cedar tree on his father's lawn, and turning to my father he went on, "Yes, father, and do you know I seemed to see the dear old place as plain as I do now."

"When was that?" said my father.

He gave the date, and my mother, who had written it down, looked and said, "Why, that was the very time when your sister declared she saw you on the lawn."

"Yes," said my father, and your mother at once killed you," and there was a good laugh at my expense.

I have often thought over it, but have never been able to account for it. This brother was not a particular favourite. Had it been my sister, I could have supposed that, as she was rarely absent from my mind, I might have conjured up her form in my imagination. Then I would have bitten my tongue out rather than have startled my mother. But I never doubted for a moment that my brother was there. I was about 25 years of age, and had no theory as to ghosts or spirits in general. I was at that time far too much occupied with the cares and anxieties of the family to have time to dwell on such fancies, and was also too matter-of-fact to think much about such phenomena.

I remember at the time, that I saw my brother dressed as he usually was when he came home from London, not as he was when he left home, nor as he could be in Australia, nor as I had ever seen hint when walking in the garden. He had on a tall hat and a black cloth suit, neither of which he had taken with him. Of course, at the moment none of these thoughts occurred to me, but when, in consequence of the jokes and ridicule at my expense, I tried to follow up the ideas that had been floating through my mind, to see whether they had any connection with my absent brother, I could make nothing of it.[289] — MISS A. CRESSY, RIVERHEAD, ENGLAND, DECEMBER 18TH, 1883

SERVANT'S GHOST APPEARS TO FORMER EMPLOYER
☛ About March 1875, the circumstances hereafter detailed happened to me at Gibraltar. I wrote an account of them from memory in 1878. It was published in *All the Year Round*, of August, I think, that year, but I have not since seen it, so I can only give the story as far as I remember it now.

I was lying down in my drawing-room on a bright sunshiny afternoon, reading a chapter on Chalk Streams in *Kingsley's Miscellanies*, when I suddenly felt that some one was waiting to speak to me. I looked up from my book and saw a man standing beside an arm-chair, which was about 6 feet from me. He was looking most intently at me, with an extraordinary earnest expression in his eyes, but as I walked forward to speak to him, he disappeared.

Victorian spirit photograph.

The room was about 18 feet long, and at the further end of it I saw our servant (Pearson), holding open the door as if he had admitted a visitor. Thinking that perhaps he too was but a delusion, I spoke to him, asking if anyone had called. To which he replied, "No one, ma'am," and walked away.

I then tested myself as to whether I had been sleeping, seeing that it was 10 minutes since I lay down. I said to myself what I thought I had read, began my chapter again, and in 10 minutes had reached the same point.

I then thought it over again. I knew the face quite well, but could not say whose it was, but the suit of clothes impressed me strongly as being exactly like one which my husband had given to a servant named Ramsay the previous year. This man was a discharged soldier whom I had found in a dying state in Inverness, and who had been taken into our service after leaving the infirmary. He turned out badly and I had to send him away before we went to Gibraltar (in February 1875), but he was taken on as waiter at the Inverness Club, and I had no cause to be anxious about him, as I thought he was well and doing well, and would probably profit by his past experience and keep that situation.

I told my husband when he came in what I had seen, and also told his colonel's wife (now Lady Laffan), but did not put down the date. But almost as soon, I believe, as a letter could have come from Inverness, my husband received one from his late sergeant, to say that Ramsay was dead, but giving no particulars. To this my husband wrote that he was sorry, and would like to hear "any particulars of his illness and death." This was the answer: "Ramsay died in hospital, raving, and calling incessantly for Mrs. Bolland."

I will only add that I believe the face of the man I saw was that of Ramsay as I had known him at first, when I visited him as a dying man in the infirmary. But seeing him every day as my servant, and in health, it had passed from my mind, or rather did not connect itself with this man in my memory.

I may add that I had been in ill-health for some years, but at that time was stronger than I ever was in my life, the warm climate suiting me so well that I felt a strength and enjoyment of life for its own sake, which was a delight to me.[290] — MRS. KATE E. BOLLAND, 7 CRANBURY TERRACE, SOUTHAMPTON, ENGLAND, JULY 1884

GHOST CARRIAGE & PASSENGERS DRIVE DOWN COUNTRY LANE

☛ In August 1881, I had been ordered by my doctor to take absolute rest, not even to read at all, and to do no work whatever. I therefore took lodgings in a cottage near London for a few weeks. During the last 6 or 7 years, I had been rather intimate with a lady (Mrs. A.), whose daughter I had instructed during that period. This lady had gone to the sea-side with her family during the summer holidays, but had sent me a message, before she left town, that the suddenness of her departure had prevented her from coming to see me, but that she would certainly do so on her return. In the meantime I had heard, through mutual friends, that she and her family were in good health, and would probably return about the middle of September.

About 3 weeks after Mrs. A.'s departure, I was expecting a friend to come and see me, and had ordered a carriage, to take her

[on] a drive. The morning proved wet, and she did not come, and after waiting some time, I went out alone, in an open landau, at about 3:30 or perhaps as late as 4 p.m.

I had not left the house more than 20 minutes, when, in an open lane, I saw coming towards me Mrs. A. with one of her younger children. She was sitting in her own victoria [a stately horse-drawn carriage], which I knew well. As she sat I saw only the three-quarter face; but I recognised the bonnet, and also the sealskin jacket, which she was wearing, as one that she generally wore in winter. I remember them particularly, because it struck me, as the carriage approached, that it was very odd of her to be wearing a sealskin jacket in August.

Just as the carriage came up to me, and was passing me, so near that if I had put out my arm I could have touched it, I sat up, and called out, "Oh, Mrs. A."

She did not move or turn her form towards me, but seemed to be half-turned towards the child, who sat on the further side of me. I was very much astonished at this, and then I turned round to look after the victoria, and, as far as my recollection serves me, I saw it slowly drive away. I am perfectly sure that I could not have been mistaken; I was never more certain of anything in my life than that I had actually seen my friend and her little child.

For the next 10 minutes or so, I was puzzling to think what could have brought her back to London, and was very vexed with myself for not having at once told the coachman to turn and drive after the carriage. I did, however, as soon as I could collect my senses, tell him to drive home as quickly as possible; and as soon as I reached the cottage I said to my landlady, "There is a lady and a little girl waiting for me upstairs, I suppose?" When she assured me that there was not, I at once sent the servant over to my sister's house, about 10 minutes' walk off, to see if Mrs. A. had perhaps gone there. When the servant came back with no tidings of her, I was very much astonished, and couldn't help wondering over it for the rest of the evening.

"Two or three days afterwards, I asked the landlady to get me a daily paper, feeling a longing to read something; and, at my landlady's urgent entreaty not to tire myself, I said that I would only look at the births, deaths and marriages. There I saw the announcement of the death of Mrs. A. at the sea-side, on the very day when, as I thought, I had passed her in her carriage, near London.

I afterwards learned from her relations that she had died after a very short illness, at 6 p.m. on that day, and that she had lain in a state of unconsciousness for some hours before her death. It could not have been much less than two hours before her death—that is during the time when she lay unconscious—that I saw her.[291] — MISS E. L. S., ENGLAND, MARCH 11TH, 1884

DYING MOTHER'S GHOST APPEARS IN DAUGHTER'S SCHOOLROOM

☞ I have not the least objection to giving an account of the apparition I had of my mother, which appeared to me at the time of her death, although it is a subject I have very rarely mentioned, partly that it is an occurrence I hold very sacred, and partly that I do not care to have my story doubted or laughed at.

I went to school in Alsace [France] in October 1852, when I was 17, leaving my mother in England in delicate health. About Christmas, 1853, 14 months after I left home, I heard that my mother's health was worse, but I had no idea that she was in any danger.

It was the last Sunday in February 1854, between 1 and 2 o'clock, I was seated in a large schoolroom reading, when suddenly the figure of my mother appeared to me at the far end of the room. She was reclining as if in bed, in her night-dress. Her face was turned towards me with a sweet smile, and one hand was raised and pointing upwards. Gently the figure moved across the room, ascending as it went until it disappeared. Both the face and figure were wasted as if by sickness, as I never had seen her in life, and deadly pale.

From the moment I saw the apparition I felt convinced my mother was dead. So impressed was I that I was unable to attend to my studies; and it was positive pain to me to see my younger sister playing and amusing herself with her companions.

Two or three days after, my governess, after prayers, called me to her private room. As soon as we entered I said, "You need not tell me. I know my mother is dead!" She asked me how I could possibly know. I gave no explanation, but told her I had known it for three days. I afterwards heard my mother died on that Sunday, at the time I had seen her, and that she had passed away in an unconscious state, having been unconscious for some day or two before her death.

I am by no means an imaginative, sensitive woman, and never before or since have I experienced anything similar.[292] — ISABEL ALLOM, 18 BATOUM GARDENS, WEST KENSINGTON PARK, W., LONDON, ENGLAND, JUNE 28TH, 1885

GHOST OF CLERGYMAN APPEARS IN "DAZZLING WHITE" CLOTHING

☞ In March 1869, while we were at Malvern Wells [England], an event occurred, which the reader will, of course, take for what he thinks it is worth, but which I cannot see my way to explain as a coincidence. Lady Chatterton had a great regard for Father Hewitt, O.S.B.; and he had always shown a very marked sympathy for her in her difficulties.

One afternoon she said, "I am sure that dear Father Hewitt is dead. I saw him just now, when I went upstairs, as clearly as possible, dressed in the Benedictine habit, only it was of dazzling whiteness. He seemed high above me in the air, and he looked at me. I knew then that he was dead." It was about 2 o'clock in the afternoon.

The next morning's post brought us the news that he died at the time when she saw him.[293] — EDWARD H. DERING, FROM *MEMOIRS OF GEORGIANA, LADY CHATTERTON*, 1878

THOUSANDS OF ANGELS ANNOUNCE DEATH OF LOVED ONE

☞ When I was about 18 or 19, I went to stay in Guernsey [British Isles]. This would be about 30 years ago. About 10 a.m., one day, I was sitting in the kitchen, blowing up the fire with the bellows. I heard some very beautiful music, and stopped to listen, at the same time looking up. I saw above me thousands of angels, as tight as they could be packed, seeming to rise far above and beyond me. They were only visible as far as the head and shoulders. In front of them all I saw was my friend, Anne Cox. As I looked and listened, the music seemed to die away in the distance, and at the same time, the angels seemed to pass away into the distance, and vanish like smoke.

I ran up to Miss White, the young lady staying in the house, and told her what I had seen. She said, "You may be sure your friend, Anne Cox, has gone to Heaven."

I wrote home at once, to Lyme Regis, and found that Anne Cox had died that very day.

Anne Cox and I had been very close friends. She was just my own age, and was almost like a sister to me.[294] — MRS. M. A. LARCOMBE, 8 RUNTON STREET, HORNSEY RISE, N., LONDON, ENGLAND, JULY 17TH, 1882

DEATH-PACT KEPT AS PROMISED

☞ In the biography of William Smellie is the history of a compact he made with his friend William Greenlaw, whereby it was mutually agreed that whoever died first should return and give the other an account of his condition after death.

Shortly after the anniversary of his death, the ghost of Greenlaw is reported to have appeared to Smellie, and in a solemn tone informed him that he had experienced great difficulties in procuring permission to return to this earth, according to their agreement; that he was now in a much better world than the one he had left, but added that the hopes and wishes of its inhabitants were by no means satisfied, as, like those of the lower world, they still looked forward in the hope of eventually reaching a still happier state of existence.[295] — THOMAS FIRMINGER THISELTON DYER, 1898

TWO CASES OF THE IRISH BANSHEE

☛ Among some of the recorded instances of the Banshee's appearance may be mentioned one related by Miss Lefrau, the niece of Sheridan, in the Memoirs of her grandmother, Mrs. Frances Sheridan. From this account we gather that Miss Elizabeth Sheridan was a firm believer in the Banshee, and firmly maintained that the one attached to the Sheridan family was distinctly heard lamenting beneath the windows of the family residence before the news arrived from France of Mrs. Frances Sheridan's death at Blois [France]. She added that a niece of Miss Sheridan's made her very angry by observing that as Mrs. Frances Sheridan was by birth a Chamberlaine, a family of English extraction, she had no right to the guardianship of an Irish fairy, and that therefore the Banshee must have made a mistake.

Then there is the well-known case related by Lady Fanshawe, who tells us how, when on a visit in Ireland, she was awakened at midnight by a supernatural scream outside her window. On looking out she saw a young and rather handsome woman, with dishevelled hair, who eventually vanished with two shrieks similar to that which had at first attracted her attention. On communicating the circumstance in the morning, her host replied, "A near relation of mine died last night in the castle, and before such an event happens, the female spectre whom you have seen is always visible."[296] — THOMAS FIRMINGER THISELTON DYER, 1898

THREE STORIES OF PHANTOM GHOST-LIGHTS

☛ Stories of mysterious lights suddenly illuminating the nocturnal darkness of unfrequented spots have long been current throughout the world. . . . Although science has years ago explained many such phosphoric appearances as governed by certain atmospheric laws, superstitious fancy has not only attributed to them supernatural causes, but associated them with all kinds of weird and romantic tales. According to one popular notion, strange lights of this kind are the spirits of persons who, for some reason, cannot remain quiet. Thus a spectre known as the "Lady and the Lantern," has long been said to haunt the beach at St. Ives, Cornwall, in stormy weather. The story goes that a lady and her child had been saved from a wreck, but the child was swept away and drowned, and she is supposed to be hunting for its body.

Similar tales are told elsewhere, but the object of [the] search is not always the same. A light, for instance, hovers about a stone on the Cornish coast, locally designated "Madge Figg's Chair," which is supposed to be the ghost of a wrecked lady whom Madge stripped of her jewels. In Scotland the appearance of a spectral "lady of the golden casket" was attended by a phantom light, and it is also related how the ghost of a murdered woman is seen by her lover at sea, approaching in the shape of a bright light, which assumes the human form as it draws nearer. She finally calls him, and he springs into her arms, and disappears in a flash of fire.[297] — THOMAS FIRMINGER THISELTON DYER, 1898

THE "RADIANT BOY"

☛ There is the popular legend of the "Radiant Boy"—a strange boy with a shining face, who has been seen in certain Lincolnshire houses and elsewhere. This ghost was described to Mr. [Sabine] Baring-Gould by a Yorkshire farmer, who, as he was riding one night to Thirsk [England], suddenly saw pass by him a "radiant boy" on a white horse. To quote his own words, "there was no sound of footfall as the boy drew nigh."

He was first aware of the approach of the mysterious rider by seeing the shadow of himself and his horse flung before him on the high road. Thinking there might be a carriage with lamps, he was not alarmed till, by the shortening of the shadow, he knew that the light must be near him, and then he was surprised to hear no sound. He thereupon turned in his saddle, and at the same moment the "radiant boy" passed him. He was a child of about eleven, with a fresh bright face.

"Had he any clothes on? and if so, what were they like?" I asked.

But the old man could not tell. His astonishment was so great he took no notice of particulars. The boy rode on till he came to a gate which led into a field; he stooped as if to open the gate, rode through, and all was instantly dark.[298] — THOMAS FIRMINGER

THISELTON DYER, 1898

AN ACCOUNT OF "SILKY" THE FEMALE APPARITION

☞ At the commencement of the present century [1800s] the little village of Black Heddon, near Stamfordham, in Northumberland, was greatly disturbed by an apparition known as "Silky," from the nature of her dress. She suddenly appeared to benighted travellers, breaking forth upon them in dazzling splendour, in the darkest and most lonely parts of the road. This spirit exercised a marvellous power over the brute creation, and once, it is said, waylaid a waggon bringing coals to a farm near Black Heddon, and fixed the team upon a bridge, since called, after her, "Silky's Brig." Do what he could, the driver could not make the horses move a step, and there they would have stayed all night had not another farm servant come up with some mountain ash about him. It was generally supposed that Silky, who suddenly disappeared, was the troubled phantom of some person who had died miserable because she owned treasure, and was overtaken by death before she had disclosed its hiding-place.[299] — THOMAS FIRMINGER THISELTON DYER, 1898

TERRIFYING ACCOUNTS OF IRELAND'S "WEE FOLK"

☞ A striking trait in the Irish fairy tales is the number of observances caused by the presence of fairies, rules of ordinary living, so to speak. For instance, nothing is more pleasing to fairies than a well-swept kitchen and clean water. A dirty kitchen and foul water bring their resentment.

The ghosts or night-walking dead, as they belong to the other world, seem to have at least in some cases the same likes and dislikes as the fairies. In . . . [one tale, for example,] Michael Derrihy, the dead man brought from the tomb by Kate, kills the three brothers because the people in the house did not throw out dirty water and brought in none that was clean, and he is determined that they shall stay killed, for he tries to do away with the only cure that can bring them to life again.

Various acts of personal uncleanliness involve punishment from the fairies. In one tale they carry off from a mother an infant which she fails to wash properly; in another a careless, untidy girl, who rises in the night and commits offensive acts in the kitchen, is punished in a signal manner. There is present a whole party of fairies, men and women, though unseen by the girl. One of the women, who is making tea, takes a saucer and hurls it at her as she is returning to bed. The saucer is broken; one half flies over the bed to the wall beyond, the other is buried in the girl's hip. She screams and wakes the whole house. No one can help her. She is in bed for three years after that in great suffering. No relief for her till her mother, who had just earned the gratitude of the fairies by acts of service, prays to have her daughter cured.

The fairy woman tells how the daughter offended and how she was punished, says that if the mother will go to the wall she will find one half of the saucer there; if she applies that to the affected part of the daughter's body it will cure her. The mother does as directed. One half of the saucer comes out of the hip to join the other, and the girl is cured straightway.

When the fairies are maltreated or despised they take ample vengeance; they punish severely. They are generous in a like degree for services or acts of kindness. So far as fairy methods of action are revealed to us in tales and popular beliefs, they constitute a system of rewards and punishments regulating the intercourse between this world and another. They are parts of an early religion in which material services are rewarded by material benefits, and in which conduct bordering upon morality is inculcated. The ghosts, mainly malignant and nearly all women, are represented as partly under fairy rules and partly under Church punishment. Their position is not fixed so definitely.[300] — JEREMIAH CURTIN, 1895

THE GHOST WITH THE BROWN BROCADE

☛ The haunting at Rainham, Norfolk, the seat of the Townsend family, has been mentioned in one or two Spiritual publications, but in a passing manner, without any details. I think that many may be interested by an account of it which I received from an eye-witness. All the names are given. The time was about 1835-40. I am unable to fix the date more exactly.

A large party had assembled at Rainham for Christmas. Lord and Lady Charles Townsend were the host and hostess. Among the guests were Colonel and Mrs. Loftus and Miss Page, a cousin of hers. Colonel Loftus was a brother of Lady Charles, and cousin to Lord Charles, consequently a Townsend on his mother's side.

There was a family tradition that at special times the apparition of a lady dressed in brown brocade had been seen, but nothing had occurred for a long time, and the stories were well-nigh forgotten. One night Colonel Loftus and a gentleman named Hawkins sat up rather late over a game of chess; they went upstairs, and were bidding each other "good night," when Mr. Hawkins exclaimed, "Loftus, who is that standing at your sister's door? How strangely she is dressed." Colonel Loftus, who was near-sighted, put up his glass and followed the figure, which went on for some little distance, when he lost sight of it.

A second night she appeared to him, and this time, to prevent her escape, he went up a staircase which would bring him face to face with her. There, in a full light, she stood, a stately lady in her rich brocade, a sort of coif on her head, the features clearly defined, but where there should have been eyes, dark hollows.

These were the two appearances he described to me, and he sketched her afterwards. I saw the sketch just after his return from Rainham.

A Victorian séance.

The lady was seen by several others, and I have heard the stories, but not from their own lips, so I forbear to give them, but perhaps I should mention that the cousin of Mrs. Loftus, Miss Page, whom I knew very intimately, asked Lord Charles if he too believed in the apparition. He replied: "I cannot but believe, for she ushered me into my room last night."

The servants were frightened and gave warning, and Lord Charles, thinking after all that it might be a trick, made alterations in the house in the way of bolts and locks, and had down from London some of the police, whom he put in his own livery, but they discovered nothing during their stay. After some time the hauntings ceased.[301] — SHUTE HAYE, WALDITCH, BRIDPORT, ENGLAND, 1878

CHAPTER FOURTEEN

STRANGE GHOSTLY ENCOUNTER WITH BROTHER-IN-LAW

☞ At the time of this event, 1855, I was nineteen years old, without any knowledge of Spiritualism, the name of which I had never heard. I was brought up very strictly in the Greek Catholic religion; superstitious fears, as well as any tendency to enthusiasm or mysticism, were foreign to my nature, and I was of a calm and happy disposition.

In May 1855, we were living at Romanoff-Borrisogliebsk, capital of the province of Jaroslav [Russia]. My sister-in-law, then the wife of Dr. A. F. Sengireef, now a widow after a second marriage with Colonel Tichonof, and living in Moscow, was at that time residing at Ranneuburg, capital of the province of Rjäsan, where her husband held a post under Government; we were, therefore, about one hundred miles distant from one another. In consequence of the overflow of the rivers in the spring, all communication was attended with delay, so that though we had been for a long time without news from my sister-in-law, we felt no sort of anxiety, as we ascribed it to the above cause.

On the evening of May 12th I had said my prayers as usual, and had taken a last look at my baby-girl, then six months old, whose cradle stood in my room, so that I could see her from my bed. After lying down, I began to read a book, but presently hearing the great clock in the dining room strike twelve, I laid my book on the table beside the bed, and raised myself on my left elbow, to put out the light. At that moment I distinctly heard the door of the antechamber open, and a man's footstep come across the dining-room. I regretted that I had just extinguished the light, as I believed it could be none other than my husband's manservant Nicholas, who had probably come to announce that my husband had been sent for by a patient, as very often happened. Only one thing surprised me, which was, that the man-servant, and not my own maid, as was usual, should be the bearer of the message.

    Raising myself upon my left arm, I listened to the approach of the footsteps, and when they appeared to be in the drawing-room, which adjoined my bed-room, and the door of which stood open at night, I called out, "Nicholas, what do you want?" There was no answer; the footsteps came nearer and nearer, and I could hear them at last close behind the screen at the head of my bed; then, with a sudden, indescribable feeling, I fell back on my pillow.

    Before my eyes, in a corner of the room, stood a crucifix, before which a night-lamp always burned, whose light was sufficient for the nurse in the care of the child. (The nurse also slept in my room, behind the screen, which stood against my head.) By the light of this lamp I could now distinctly see the person who had entered, and who was now standing on the left side of my bed, was my brother-in-law Sengireef, in a costume quite strange to me—a long, black, monastic looking garment, with long black hair hanging down on his shoulders, and a large round beard, such as I had never seen him wear. I tried to shut my eyes, but could not, and I felt my body become completely rigid, and incapable of the slightest movement; even my voice failed me, that I could not call for help; at the same time my hearing, sight, and the power to understand all that was happening remained so fully under my control that I was able on the following day to recall precisely at what hour the nurse had got up to quiet the baby, and other details. I remained in this state from twelve o'clock till three in the morning of the 13th of May, at which hour the following took place:

    The apparition came close to my bedside, placed himself at my left hand, and turning his face on mine, laid his left, deathly-cold hand on my mouth and said aloud, "Kiss my hand." Being physically unable to liberate myself, I resisted this command in thought with my whole willpower. As if guessing my meaning, he pressed his hand more firmly against my lips, and repeated in a louder and more peremptory tone, "Kiss this hand." I again resisted with still greater energy of thought. He then repeated for the third time with still greater emphasis the same movement and the same words, and I thought I must have been stifled under the weight and coldness of the hand pressing upon my mouth, but I neither could nor would give way.

    At this moment the nurse got up for the first time, and I hoped that she would, for some reason or other, come near to me and would see what was taking place. My expectation, however, was disappointed; she only rocked the child a little, without taking it out of the cradle, returned to her couch, and went to sleep again.

Victorian psychic photograph.

Seeing that there was no help for me, and believing, without knowing why, that my death was inevitably at hand, I suddenly thought of repeating the Lord's Prayer. Scarcely had this idea entered my mind than the figure withdrew his hand from my lips, and said quite loudly, "So you will not kiss my hand? Well, then, this is what awaits you." Saying these words, he laid with his right hand on the table at my side a roll of parchment of the length of an ordinary sheet of writing paper, and as he withdrew his hand, I heard distinctly the sound of the parchment rolling together, and could see sideways with my left eye a part of the sheet, which then remained in this half-rolled up state. Then the standing figure turned himself away from me, went forward a few steps, placed himself in front of the crucifix, hiding the light from me by his body, and began to repeat loudly and clearly the words of the prayer I had thought of, from beginning to end, slowly bowing from time to time; each time he bowed the light became visible to me, and was again obscured when he stood upright.

After he had finished the said prayer with another bow, he stood motionless, as if waiting for something; my condition had not altered in the least, and when I again wished in thought to address a prayer to the Holy Mother of God, he began again to repeat this just as loudly and clearly, and so on with a third prayer desired by me. Between the two last prayers there was a pause, during which the nurse got up, attended to the child, and went to sleep again. During the repetition of the prayers I heard distinctly the striking of the clock, and, as already remarked, every movement of the nurse, and of the child, whom I ardently longed to have near me, that I might take leave of it and bless it before my expected death; no other wish was uppermost in my mind, but it was not to be fulfilled.

The clock struck three.

Then I remembered suddenly that the six weeks after the holy festival of Easter were not yet over, and that "Christ is Risen" would still be sung in all the churches, and I felt a strong desire to hear it. As if in answer to this there resounded all at once from a distance the divine tones of the sacred hymn, sung by a numerous choir at an immeasurable height. The sound came nearer and nearer, became fuller and clearer, and I heard such heavenly harmonies that I felt breathless with pure delight; the fear of death fled away, and I was consoled with the hope that these sounds would quite encompass and absorb me, and carry me with them into endless space.

In the song of the choir I could distinguish the words of the hymn, which were also repeated by the standing figure. Suddenly the whole room was flooded with a strange light, which was so powerful and dazzling that I could no longer distinguish the flame of the night-lamp, nor the walls of the room, nor the apparition. This light remained a few seconds, during which the sounds swelled higher till they became overpowering. Then the brightness diminished, and I could again see the figure standing before me, not in its full extent, but only from the head to the waist; and, curiously enough, the form became less and less distinct, till it dissolved in the light, in proportion as this grew darker, and at last quite vanished; the parchment lying at my side disappeared in like manner.

As the light diminished, the tones faded away, just as gradually as they had formerly increased. I felt that I was losing consciousness, and was soon in a deep swoon, accompanied by convulsions of the whole body. This attack roused those in the house, and lasted, in spite of all remedies, until nine o'clock in the morning, when they succeeded in subduing the symptoms, and restoring me to consciousness. The three following days I lay motionless with exhaustion, in consequence of an attack of blood-spitting.

The day after this terrible event we received the news of the illness of my brother-in-law Sengireef, and about a fortnight later, tidings of his death, which took place in that night of the 12th-13th of May, about five o'clock in the morning.

The following is noteworthy: When my sister-in-law, a few weeks after the death of her husband, came to live with us at Romanoff-Borissogliebsk, she mentioned incidentally to a lady in my presence, that her husband had been buried with long hair hanging down to his shoulders, and with a large curious-looking beard, which had grown during his illness. She also mentioned, as something unusual, that the body had been laid out for burial in a

long garment of black cloth, nothing fitter being at hand.³⁰² —
SOPHIE AKSAKOF, CIRCA 1878

SCHOOL FRIEND'S GHOST MANIFESTS FROM 600 MILES AWAY
☞ I had an old schoolfellow, who was afterwards a college friend, with whom I had lived in the closest intimacy. Years, however, passed away without our seeing each other.

One morning I had just got out of bed, and was dressing myself, when suddenly my old friend entered the room. I greeted him warmly: told him to call for a cup of tea in the verandah, and promised to be with him immediately. I dressed myself in haste, and went out into the verandah, but found no one there. I could not believe my eyes. I called to the sentry, who was posted at the front of the house, but he had seen no strange gentleman. A fortnight afterwards news arrived that he had died, six hundred miles off, about the very time I saw him at Maulmain [Burma].³⁰³
— LIEUT.-GENERAL ALBERT FYTCHE, PYRGA PARK, HAVERING-ATTE-BOWER, LONDON, ENGLAND, 1878

WRAITH OF DECEASED WOMAN APPEARS ON SHEEP FARM
☞ [One of my employees, James Sutherland,] while in charge of a sheep-station for me, went to an out-station with two men to count the sheep looked after by a man and his wife. The party arrived in the evening and found the woman very ill, so they camped out some little distance from the hut. At daylight, one of the men asked Mr. Sutherland if he would go and see how the woman was. He answered, "She is dead, I have just seen her wraith." The man went to the hut, and found that the woman had just expired.³⁰⁴ — MR. JOHN CARSON, BRUNSWICK HOUSE, CLAPHAM COMMON, LONDON, ENGLAND, JANUARY 23ᴿᴰ, 1879

SAILOR WITNESSES HIS FATHER'S SPIRIT ON SHIP
☞ In the year 1857 I sailed as apprentice in the ship *Tinto*, of Bridgewater, from Hull [England] to Bombay [India]. Our second mate [Henry Morgan] (to whom what I narrate occurred) was a grave, and, for a sailor, unusually consistently serious and religious young fellow, of some twenty-four years—one who in several voyages with him, I never knew to even distort the truth or utter an oath. We were great chums, and I knew him well. His parents lived at Patrington, near Hull.

One night—it was the 18ᵗʰ August 1857—we were off the

Malabar coast, distant from Bombay about two hundred miles, slowly proceeding before a light breeze. The second mate and I were on watch together, having the first watch, viz., from 8 P.M. to midnight. At the relief of the watch, the second mate went down to our berth (we shared one cabin between us), while I remained on deck for a moment to answer some questions asked me by the chief mate, who had relieved us.

When I went into the berth my friend was, to my great surprise, leaning against the door, looking as white as a sheet, and apparently hardly saved from falling by holding on to the bunk. He appeared unable to reply to my queries at first, but on my fetching him a drop of spirits from the saloon he rallied, and then told me, that immediately on entering his cabin, he saw his father as plainly as he saw me, dressed as usual, standing in the middle of the floor.

"I knew in a moment," said he, "that it could not be himself, but was his spirit—and I know he is dead."

"How long did he remain?" asked I.

"For about a minute," he replied; "in fact, until I heard you coming, and then he seemed to melt away suddenly. I was thinking of nothing less than him when I came in, for I thought of nothing but that ugly bank of clouds" (a cloud bank on our port-beam that portended a squall all our watch). We took the exact time in writing when he saw the appearance; it was, by the ship's chronometer, 8 minutes past 12 midnight, the 18th August (or rather 19th properly) 1857.

Soon after reaching Bombay, a letter from home informed him that (computing for the difference of longitude) at that very day, hour, and minute, his father had died in his house at Patrington, passionately longing with his last breath that he might be allowed to see his son.[305] — MR. W. T. DREWRY, 38 CRAWSHAY ROAD, NORTH BRIXTON, LONDON, ENGLAND, FEBRUARY 1879

GHOST CONVERTS ANOTHER SKEPTIC

☛ [The story goes that] . . . in 1836, Lord Chedworth was then a man who suffered deeply from doubts of the existence of the soul in another world; and that he had a friend, very dear to him, as sceptical as himself.

Whilst one morning relating to his niece, Miss Wright, at breakfast that his [sceptical] friend appeared to him the night before, exactly as he appeared in life, and told him he died that night at eight o'clock, and that there was another world, and a righteous God who judgeth all; and whilst Miss Wright was ridiculing the idea of the apparition, a groom rode up the avenue, bringing a letter announcing the fact of his friend's sudden death, at the time stated by the spirit. [The writer adds:] "The effect it had upon the mind of Lord Chedworth was as happy as it was permanent: all his doubts were removed, and for ever.[306] — MRS. CRAWFORD, CIRCA 1880S

GRANDFATHER'S SPIRIT APPEARS AT HOUR OF DEATH

☛ A person well known to me, told me that she was staying in the house of an aunt, with her two cousins. One of them one morning was low-spirited and moody. At last, going up to her aunt she burst into tears, and said, "I saw grandfather last night."

"Nonsense, child, you know he is not here; don't be fanciful."

"But I did see him."

"Then you were dreaming."

"Aunt, I was quite awake, and he came in at the window and stood at the foot of my bed he looked just as he always looks, but I was frightened, and covered my head over with the blanket. When I looked up again he was still there, but the third time he was gone."

The grandfather died, as they heard afterwards, just at that very hour when she saw him. The poor girl fasted and wept the whole of that day.[307] — REV. JAMES S. POLLOCK, M.A., INCUMBENT, ST. ALBANS, BIRMINGHAM, ENGLAND, 1874

WRAITH OF DROWNED MAN APPEARS TO SISTER

☛ Mrs. Paquet on the morning of October 24th, 1889, after her husband had gone to work and the children to school, feeling gloomy, was making some tea for herself, when she saw a vision of her brother, Edmund Dunn, standing only a few feet away; and her report continues:

"The apparition stood with back toward me, or rather, partially so, and was in the act of falling forward—away from me—seemingly impelled by two ropes or a loop of rope

drawing against his legs. The vision lasted but a moment, disappearing over a low railing or bulwark, but was very distinct. I dropped the tea, clasped my hands to my face, and exclaimed, 'My God! Ed is drowned.' At about half-past ten a.m. my husband received a telegram from Chicago [Illinois] announcing the drowning of my brother. When he arrived home, he said to me, "Ed is sick in hospital at Chicago; I have just received a telegram," to which I replied 'Ed is drowned; I saw him go overboard.' I then gave him a minute description of what I had seen. I stated that my brother, as I saw him, was bareheaded, had on a heavy, blue sailor's shirt, no coat, and that he went over the rail or bulwark. I noticed that his pants' legs were rolled up enough to show the white lining inside. I also described the appearance of the boat at the point where my brother went overboard. I am not nervous, and neither before nor since have I had any experience in the least degree similar to that above related. My brother was not subject to fainting or vertigo."[308] — AGNES PAQUET, CIRCA 1890S

GHOST OF SUICIDE VICTIM MANIFESTS TO GODCHILD

☛ A gentleman of some note shot himself in London in the spring of 1907. There can be little doubt that his mind was unhinged at the time by the receipt that morning of a letter from a lady that blighted his hopes; before taking his life he scribbled a memorandum leaving an annuity to a young lady, who was his godchild and to whom he was much attached.

Three days afterwards (on the day of his funeral) he appeared to this godchild, who was being educated in a convent school on the Continent, informing her of the fact of his sudden death, of its manner, and of the cause which had led him to take his life, and asking her to pray for him.

The mother, anxious to conceal from her daughter the distressing circumstances of her godfather's death, waited to write until a few days after the funeral, and then only stated that her uncle (as he was called) had died suddenly.

Subsequently, upon meeting her daughter on her return from the Continent, the mother was amazed to hear not only of the apparition, but that it had communicated to her daughter all the circumstances which she had never intended her daughter to know. Careful inquiry shows that it was impossible for the information to have reached her daughter through normal means.[309] — NAME WITHHELD, CIRCA 1890S

UNCLE'S GHOST APPEARS AT EXACT HOUR OF DEATH
☛ My mother who lived in Burgundy [France], heard one Tuesday, between nine and ten o'clock, the door of the bedroom open and close violently. At the same time, she heard herself called twice: "Lucie, Lucie!" The following Tuesday, she heard that her uncle Clementin, who had always had a great affection for her, had died that Tuesday morning, precisely between nine and ten o'clock.[310]
— P. D., CIRCA 1900

SPIRIT OF BROTHER REVEALS HIS CAUSE OF DEATH
☛ Two years ago my brother, who was a designer, undertook a journey of exploration in Africa, accompanying the mission of M. Bouchamps. I had had no news from him for a long time, when one night, suddenly awakening, I saw my brother pierced by the spear of a savage.

This made so deep an impression on me that I did not go to sleep again that night, and I was haunted for several weeks by the vision.

Some weeks later I received news of the death of my brother in Abyssinia, killed by a spear-thrust by an Abyssinian. The fact coincided with my vision, but unhappily I had omitted to set down the exact date. However, I am certain that the vision came to me in November.[311] — A. NYFFELEY- POTTER, CIRCA 1890S

EMACIATED GHOST APPEARS AT FOOT OF BED
☛ In January 1868, I took a house close to Hastings [England]. . . . One night there was a heavy storm, the weather was bitterly cold, and a fire was burning in my bedroom when I went to bed at 10:30. I tried to go to sleep, but it was no use; the noise of the wind and the rain kept me awake.

I must have been lying like this for a couple of hours when I became conscious of what seemed like a light in the room. . . . I thought the fire must have re-kindled itself, and crawled along on my knees on the bed to look at the fire over the high wooden foot, to see how this might be. I had no thought of anything but the fire, and was not nervous in the slightest degree. As I raised myself on my knees and looked over the foot of the bed, I found myself face to face, at a distance of about three feet, with the semblance of a man. I never for a moment thought he was a man, but was struck with the feeling that this was one from the dead.

The light seemed to emanate from round this figure, but the only portions which I saw clearly were the head and shoulders. The face I shall never forget; it was pale, emaciated, with a thin, high-bridged nose, and eyes deeply sunk and glowing in the sockets with a sort of glare. A long beard was seemingly rolled in under a white comforter, and on the head was a slouched felt hat. I had a nervous shock, and felt a dead person was looking upon me—a living one, but had no sensation of being actually frightened, until the figure moved slowly as if interposing between me and the door, then horror overcame me and I fell back in a dead faint.

How long I remained unconscious I know not, but I came to myself cold and cramped; the room was quite dark and nothing was visible. Thoroughly tired out, I got into bed, and slept soundly until morning.[312] — MRS. LEWIN, CIRCA 1880S

GHOST OF SLAIN WOMAN EMERGES AT CRIME SCENE

☛ In the year 1856, I was staying with my wife and children, at a favorite watering place. In order to attend to some affairs of my own, I determined to leave my family there for three or four days. Accordingly, on the 8th of August, I took the railway, and arrived that evening an unexpected guest at the Hall—the residence of a gentleman whose acquaintance I had recently made, and with whom my sister was then staying.

I arrived late, soon afterwards went to bed, and before long fell asleep. Awaking after three or four hours, I was not surprised to find that I could sleep no more—for I never rest well in a strange bed. After trying, therefore, in vain to induce sleep, I began to arrange my plans for the day.

I had been engaged some little time in this way, when I became suddenly sensitive to the fact that there was a light in the room. Turning round, I distinctly perceived a female figure; and what attracted my special attention was that the light by which I saw it emanated from itself. I watched the figure attentively. The features were not perceptible. After moving a little distance, it disappeared as suddenly as it had appeared.

My first thoughts were that there was some trick.

I immediately got out of bed, struck a light, and found my bedroom door still locked. I then carefully examined the walls, to ascertain if there was any other concealed means of entrance or exit, but none could I find. I drew the curtains and opened the shutters, but all outside was silent and dark, there being no moonlight. After examining the room in every part, I went back to bed, and began thinking calmly over the whole matter.

What had I seen? And why did it appear?

In the morning, as soon as I was up and dressed, I told my sister what I had seen. She then informed me that the house had the reputation of being "haunted"; and that a murder had been committed in it; but not in the room in which I had slept. Later in the day I left after making my sister promise to do all she could to unravel the mystery.

On the following Wednesday morning, I received a letter from my sister, in which she informed me that, since I left, she had made inquiries and had ascertained that the murder was committed in the very room in which I slept! She added that she proposed visiting us the next day, and that she would like me to write out an account of what I had seen—together with a plan of the room, and that on that plan she wished me to mark the place of the appearance and disappearance of the figure.

This I immediately did; and the next day when my sister arrived, she asked me if I had complied with her request? I replied, pointing to the drawing room table: "Yes, there is the account and the plan."

As she rose to examine it, I prevented her, saying: "Do not look at it until you have told me all you have to say, because you might unintentionally color your story by what you may read there."

Thereupon she informed me that she had had the carpet taken up in the room I had occupied, and that the marks of blood from the murdered person were there, plainly visible, on a particular part of the floor. At my request she also then drew a plan of the room, and marked upon it the spots which still bore traces of blood. The two plans—my sister's and mine—were now compared; and we verified the most remarkable fact that the place she had marked as the beginning and ending of the traces of blood coincided exactly with the spots marked on my plan as those on which the female figure had appeared and disappeared![313] — NAME WITHHELD, CHAPLAIN TO THE BRITISH LEGATION IN FLORENCE, CIRCA 1880S

GHOST HORSEMAN SAVES LIFE OF TRAVELER

☛ One summer day, at the commencement of the present century, I was travelling from Bala, in Merionethshire, to Machynlleth, in the neighbouring county of Montgomery [Wales] in order to attend a religious meeting. I left Bala about 2 p.m., and travelled on horseback and alone. My journey lay through a wild, desolate part of the country, and one which at that time was almost uninhabited.

When I had performed about half my journey, as I was emerging from a wood situated at the commencement of a long, steep decline, I observed coming towards me a man on foot. By his appearance, judging from the sickle which he carried sheathed in

The wraith of Mabel Warren appeared in this spirit photo of Honorable Moses A. Dow (of Boston, MA).

straw over his shoulder, he was doubtless a reaper in search of employment. As he drew near, I recognised a man whom I had seen at the door of the village inn of Llanwhellyn, where I had stopped to bait my horse. On our meeting he touched his hat and asked if I could tell him the time of day. I pulled out my watch for the purpose, noticing at the same time the peculiar look which the man cast at its heavy silver case. Nothing else, however, occurred to excite any suspicion on my part, so, wishing him a "good afternoon," I continued my journey.

When I had ridden about half-way down the hill, I noticed something moving, and in the same direction as myself, on the other side of a large hedge, which ran nearly parallel with the road, and ultimately terminated at a gate through which I had to pass. At first I thought it an animal of some kind or other, but soon discovered by certain depressions in the hedge that it was a man running in a stooping position. I continued for a short time to watch his progress with some curiosity, but my curiosity soon changed to fear when I recognized the reaper with whom I had conversed a few minutes before, engaged in tearing off the straw band which sheathed his sickle.

He hurried on until he reached the gate, and then concealed himself behind the hedge within a few yards of the road. I did not then doubt for a moment but that he had resolved to attack—perhaps murder—me for the sake of my watch and whatever money I might have about me. I looked around in all directions, but not a single human being was to be seen, so reigning in my horse, I asked myself in much alarm what I could do. Should I turn back? No; my business was of the utmost importance to the cause for which I was journeying, and as long as there existed the faintest possibility of getting there, I could not think of returning. Should I trust to the speed of my horse, and endeavour to dash by the man at full speed? No; for the gate through which I had to pass was not open. Could I leave the road and make my way through the fields? I could not; for I was hemmed in by rocky banks or high hedges on both sides. The idea of risking a personal encounter could not be entertained for a moment, for what chance could I—weak and unarmed—have against a powerful man with a dangerous weapon in his hand? What course then should I pursue? I could not tell; and at length, in despair rather than in a spirit of humble trust and confidence, I bowed my head and offered up a silent prayer.

This had a soothing effect upon my mind, so that, refreshed and invigorated, I proceeded anew to consider the difficulties of my position.

At this juncture my horse, growing impatient at the delay, started off: I clutched the reins, which I had let fall on his neck, for the purpose of checking him, when happening to turn my eyes, I saw to my utter astonishment that I was no longer alone. There, by my side, I beheld a horseman in a dark dress, mounted on a white steed. In intense amazement I gazed upon him; where could he have come from?

He appeared as suddenly as if he had sprung from the earth. He must have been riding behind and have overtaken me. And yet I had not heard the slightest sound: it was mysterious, inexplicable. But the joy of being released from my perilous position soon overcame my feelings of wonder, and I began at once to address my companion. I asked him if he had seen any one, and then described to him what had taken place, and how relieved I felt by his sudden appearance, which now removed all cause of fear. He made no reply, and on looking at his face, he seemed paying but slight attention to my words, but continued intently gazing in the direction of the gate, now about a quarter of a mile ahead.

I followed his gaze, and saw the reaper emerge from his concealment and cut across a field to our left, resheathing his sickle as he hurried along. He had evidently seen that I was no longer alone, and had relinquished his intended attempt. All cause for alarm being gone, I once more sought to enter into conversation with my deliverer, but again without the slightest success. Not a word did he deign to give me in reply.

I continued talking, however, as we rode on our way towards the gate, though I confess feeling both surprised and hurt at my companion's mysterious silence. Once, however, and only once did I hear his voice. Having watched the figure of the reaper disappear over the brow of a neighbouring hill, I turned to my companion and said, "Can it for a moment be doubted that my prayer was heard, and that you were sent for my deliverance by the Lord?"

Then it was that I thought I heard the horseman speak, and that he uttered the single word, "Amen." Not another word did he give utterance to, though I tried to elicit from him replies to my questions, both in English and Welsh.

We were now approaching the gate, which I hastened to open, and having done so with my stick, I waited at the side of the road for him to pass through; but he came not; I turned my head to look—the mysterious horseman was gone! I was dumbfounded; I looked back in the direction from which we had just been riding, but though I could command a view of the road for a considerable distance, he was not to be seen. He had disappeared as mysteriously as he had come.

What could have become of him? He could not have gone through the gate, nor have made his horse leap the high hedges which on both sides shut in the road. Where was he? Had I been dreaming? Was it an apparition, a spectre which had been riding by my side for the last ten minutes?

Could it be possible that I had seen no man or horse at all, and that the vision was but a creature of my imagination? I tried hard to convince myself that this was the case, but in vain; for, unless some one had been with me, why had the reaper resheathed his murderous looking sickle and fled? Surely no; this mysterious horseman was no creation of my brain. I had seen him; who could he have been?

I asked myself this question again and again; and then a feeling of profound awe began to creep over my soul. I remembered the singular way of his first appearance—his long silence—and then again the single word to which he had given utterance; I called to mind that this reply had been elicited from him by my mentioning the name of the Lord, and that this was the single occasion on which I had done so. What could I then believe?—but one thing, and that was, that my prayer had indeed been heard, and that help had been given from on high at a time of great danger.

Full of this thought, I dismounted, and throwing myself on my knees, I offered up a prayer of thankfulness to Him who had heard my cry, and found help for me in time of need. I then mounted my horse and continued my journey. But through the long years that have elapsed since that memorable summer's day, I have never for a moment wavered in my belief that in the mysterious horseman I had a special interference of Providence, by which means I was delivered from a position of extreme danger.[314] — REV. JOHN JONES, HOLIWELL, FLINTSHIRE, WALES, 1853

IRISH WRAITH AUGURS DEATH OF WIFE
☛ There was living, in the summer of the year 1802, in the south of Ireland, a clergyman of the Established Church, the Rev. Mr. _____, afterwards Archdeacon of _____, now deceased. His first wife, a woman of great beauty, sister of the Governor of _____, was then alive. She had been recently confined, and her recovery was very slow. Their residence—an old-fashioned mansion, situated in a spacious garden—adjoined on one side the park of the Bishop of _____. It was separated from it by a wall, in which there was a private door.

Mr. _____ had been invited by the bishop to dinner; and as his wife, though confined to bed, did not seem worse than usual, he had accepted the invitation. Returning from the bishop's palace about ten o'clock, he entered, by the private door already mentioned, his own premises. It was bright moonlight.

On issuing from a small belt of shrubbery into a garden-walk, he perceived, as he thought, in another walk, parallel to that in which he was, and not more than ten or twelve feet from him, the figure of his wife, in her usual dress. Exceedingly astonished, he crossed over and confronted her. It was his wife. At least, he distinguished her features, in the clear moonlight, as plainly as he had ever done in his life.

"What are you doing here?" he asked.

She did not reply, but receded from him, turning to the right, towards a kitchen-garden that lay on one side of the house. In it there were several rows of peas, staked and well-grown, so as to shelter any person passing behind them. The figure passed round one end of these.

Mr. _____ followed quickly, in increased astonishment, mingled with alarm, but when he reached the open space beyond the peas the figure was nowhere to be seen. As there was no spot where, in so short a time, it could have sought concealment, the husband concluded that it was an apparition, and not his wife, that he had seen.

He returned to the front door, and, instead of availing himself of his pass-key as usual, he rang the bell. While on the steps, before the bell was answered, looking round, he saw the same figure at the corner of the house. When the servant opened the door, he asked him how his mistress was.

"I am sorry to say, sir," answered the man, "she is not so well. Dr. Osborne has been sent for." Mr. _____ hurried up-stairs, found his wife in bed and much worse, attended by the nurse, who had not left her all the evening. From that time she gradually sank, and within twelve hours thereafter expired.[315] — MR. _____, CANADA, CIRCA 1850S

GHOSTS OF TWO LIVING PERSONS APPEAR IN THE SAME HOUSE ON THE SAME DAY

☛ I resided for several years in a spacious old stone house, two stories high, agreeably situated, amid fruit-trees and shrubbery, on the banks of the Ohio River, in Switzerland County, Indiana. Two verandahs, above and below, without side stairs leading up to them, ran the entire length of the house on the side next the river. These, especially the upper one with its charming prospect, were a common resort of the family.

On the 15th of September, 1845, my younger sister, J_____, was married, and came with her husband, Mr. H_____ M_____ to pass a portion of the honey-moon in our pleasant retreat.

On the 18th of the same month, we all went, by invitation, to spend the day at a friend's house about a mile distant. As twilight came on, finding my two little ones growing restless, we decided to return home. After waiting some time for my sister's husband, who had gone off to pay a visit in a neighbouring village, saying he would soon return, we set out without him. Arrived at home, my sister, who occupied an upper room, telling me she would go and change her walking dress, proceeded up-stairs, while I remained below to see my drowsy babes safe in bed. The moon, I remember, was shining brightly at the time.

Suddenly, after a minute or two, my sister burst into the room, wringing her hands in despair, and weeping bitterly. "Oh, sister, sister!" she exclaimed; "I shall lose him! I know I shall! Hugh is going to die."

In the greatest astonishment, I inquired what was the matter; and then, between sobs, she related to me the cause of her alarm, as follows:

As she ran up-stairs to their room she saw her husband seated at the extremity of the upper verandah, his hat on, a cigar in his mouth, and his feet on the railing, apparently enjoying the cool river breeze. Supposing, of course, that he had returned before we did, she approached him, saying, "Why, Hugh, when did you get here? Why did you not return and come home with us?"

As he made no reply, she went up to him, and, bride-like, was about to put her arms round his neck, when, to her horror, the figure was gone and the chair empty. She had barely strength left (so great was the shock) to come down-stairs and relate to me what her excited fears construed into a certain presage of death.

It was not till more than two hours afterwards, when my brother-in-law actually returned, that she resumed her tranquillity. We rallied and laughed at her then, and, after a time, the incident passed from our minds.

Previously to this, however,—namely, about an hour before Hugh's return,—while we were sitting in the parlour, on the lower floor, I saw a boy, some sixteen years of age, look in at the door of the room. It was a lad whom my husband employed to work in the garden and about the house, and who, in his leisure hours, used to take great delight in amusing my little son Frank, of whom he was very fond. He was dressed, as was his wont, in a suit of blue summer-cloth, with an old palm-leaf hat without a band, and he advanced in his usual bashful way, a step or two into the room, then stopped, and looked round, apparently in search of something. Supposing that he was looking for the children, I said to him, "Frank is in bed, Silas, and asleep long ago."

He did not reply, but, turning with a quiet smile that was common to him, left the room, and I noticed, from the window, that he lingered near the outside door, walking backwards and forwards before it once or twice. If I had afterwards been required to depose on oath, before a court of justice, that I had seen the boy enter and leave the room, and also that I had noticed him pass and repass before the parlour window, I should have sworn to these circumstances without a moment's hesitation. Yet it would seem that such a deposition would have conveyed a false impression.

For, shortly after, my husband, coming in, said, "I wonder where Silas is?" (that was the boy's name).

"He must be somewhere about," I replied: "he was here a few minutes since, and I spoke to him."

Thereupon Mr. D_____ went out and called him, but no one answered. He sought him all over the premises, then in his room, but in vain. No Silas was to be found; nor did he show himself that night; nor was he in the house the next morning when we arose.

At breakfast he first made his appearance. "Where have you been, Silas?" said Mr. D_____. The boy replied that he had been up to the island fishing.

"But," I said, "you were here last night."

"Oh, no," he replied, with the simple accent of truth. "Mr. D_____ gave me leave to go fishing yesterday; and I understood I need not return till this morning: so I stayed away all night. I have not been near here since yesterday morning."

I could not doubt the lad's word. He had no motive for deceiving us. The island of which he spoke was two miles distant from our house; and, under all the circumstances, I settled down to the conclusion that, as in my sister's case, her husband had appeared where he was not, so in the case of the boy also, it was the appearance only, not the real person, that I had seen that evening. It was remarkable enough that both the incidents should have occurred in the same house and on the same day.

It is proper I should add that my sister's impression that the apparition of her husband foreboded death did not prove true. He outlived her; and no misfortune which they could in any way connect with the appearance happened in the family. Nor did Silas die; nor, so far as I know, did anything unusual happen to him.[316]

— MRS. D_____, WASHINGTON, D.C., CIRCA 1850S

YOUNG MAN'S GHOST NEARLY SENDS HIM TO PRISON

☛ In the latter part of the last century, in the city of Glasgow, Scotland, a servant-girl, known to have had illicit connexion with a certain surgeon's apprentice, suddenly disappeared. There being no circumstances leading to suspicion of foul play, no special inquiry was made about her.

In those days, in Scottish towns, no one was allowed to show himself in street or public ground during the hours of church service; and this interdiction was enforced by the appointment of inspectors authorized to take down the names of delinquents.

A female medium psychically imprinted this Victorian photograph with the spirit image of the woman's deceased uncle (upper left). His actual photo (upper right) is included for comparison. The photographer "developed the plate alone in his dark room."

Two of these [inspectors], making their rounds, came to a wall, the lower boundary of "The Green," as the chief public park of the city is called. There, lying on the grass, they saw a young man, whom they recognised as the surgeon's assistant. They asked him why he was not at church, and proceeded to register his name; but, instead of attempting an excuse, he merely rose, saying, "I am a miserable man; look in the water!" then crossed a style and struck into a path leading to the Rutherglen road. The inspectors, astonished, did proceed to the river, where they found the body of a young woman, which they caused to be conveyed to town.

While they were accompanying it through the streets, they passed one of the principal churches, whence, at the moment, the congregation were issuing; and among them they perceived the apprentice. But this did not much surprise them, thinking he might have had time to go round and enter the church towards the close of the service.

The body proved to be that of the missing servant-girl. She was found pregnant, and had evidently been murdered by means of a surgeon's instrument, which had remained entangled in her clothes. The apprentice, who proved to have been the last person seen in her company before she disappeared, was arrested, and would, on the evidence of the inspectors, have been found guilty, had he not, on his trial, established an incontrovertible alibi; showing, beyond possible doubt, that he had been in church during the entire service. The young man was acquitted. The greatest excitement prevailed in the public mind at the time; but all efforts to obtain a natural explanation failed.[317] — ROBERT DALE OWEN, 1860

LIVING MAN'S SPIRIT APPEARS IN PUBLIC, FORESHADOWING HIS DEATH SOON AFTER

☛ In the month of May, and in the year 1840, Dr. D_____, a noted physician of Washington [D.C.], was residing with his wife and his daughter Sarah (now Mrs. B_____) at their countryseat near Piney Point, in Virginia, a fashionable pleasure resort during the summer months.

One afternoon, about five o'clock, the two ladies were walking out in a copse-wood not far from their residence; when, at a distance on the road, coming towards them, they saw a gentleman.

"Sally," said Mrs. D_____, "there comes your father to meet us."

"I think not," the daughter replied: "that cannot be papa: it is not so tall as he."

As he neared them, the daughter's opinion was confirmed. They perceived that it was not Dr. D_____, but a Mr. Thompson, a gentleman with whom they were well acquainted, and who was at that time, though they then knew it not, a patient of Dr. D_____'s. They observed also, as he came nearer, that he was dressed in a blue frock-coat, black satin waistcoat, and black pantaloons and hat. Also, on comparing notes afterwards, both ladies, it appeared, had noticed that his linen was particularly fine, and that his whole apparel seemed to have been very carefully adjusted.

He came up so close that they were on the very point of addressing him; but at that moment he stepped aside, as if to let them pass; and then, *even while the eyes of both the ladies were upon him*, he suddenly and entirely disappeared.

The astonishment of Mrs. D_____ and her daughter may be imagined. They could scarcely believe the evidence of their own eyes. They lingered, for a time, on the spot, as if expecting to see him re-appear; then, with that strange feeling which comes over us when we have just witnessed something unexampled and incredible, they hastened home.

They afterwards ascertained, through Dr. D_____, that his patient Mr. Thompson, being seriously indisposed, was confined to his bed; and that *he had not quitted his room, nor indeed his bed, throughout the entire day.*

It may properly be added, that, though Mr. Thompson was familiarly known to the ladies, and much respected by them as an estimable man, there were no reasons existing why they should take any more interest in him, or he in them, than in the case of any other friend or acquaintance. He died just six weeks from the day of this appearance.[318] — ROBERT DALE OWEN, 1860

GHOSTS CANNOT BE FOOLED

☛ In November of the year 1843, Miss H_____, a young lady then between thirteen and fourteen years of age, was on a visit to a family of her acquaintance (Mr. and Mrs. E_____), residing at their country-seat in Cambridgeshire, England. Mrs. E_____ was taken ill; and, her disease assuming a serious form, she was recommended to go to London for medical advice. She did so; her husband accompanied her; and they left their guest and their two children, the youngest only ten weeks old, at home.

The journey, however, proved unavailing the disease increased, and that so rapidly that, after a brief sojourn in the metropolis, the patient could not bear removal.

In the meantime the youngest child, little Fannie, sickened, and, after a brief illness, died. They wrote immediately to the father, then attending on what he felt to be the death-bed of his wife; and he posted down at once. It was on a Monday that the infant died; on Tuesday Mr. E_____ arrived, made arrangements

Psychic photograph of a baby, obtained without a camera.

for the funeral, and left on Wednesday to return to his wife, from whom, however, he concealed the death of her infant.

On Thursday, Miss H_____ received from him a letter, in which he begged her to go into his study and take from his desk there certain papers which were pressingly wanted. It was in this study that the body of the infant lay in its coffin; and, as the young lady proceeded thither to execute the commission, one of the servants said to her, "Oh, miss, are you not afraid?" She replied that there was nothing to be afraid of, and entered the study, where she found the papers required. As she turned, before leaving the room, to look at the babe, she saw, reclining on a sofa near to it, the figure of a lady whom she recognised as the mother. Having from infancy been accustomed to the occasional sight of apparitions, she was not alarmed, but approached the sofa to satisfy herself that it was the appearance of her friend. Standing within three or four feet of the figure for several minutes she assured herself of its identity. It did not speak, but, raising one arm, it first pointed to the body of the infant, and then signed upwards. Soon afterwards, and before it disappeared, the young lady left the room.

This was a few minutes after four o'clock in the afternoon. Miss H_____ particularly noticed the time, as she heard the clock strike the hour a little before she entered the study.

The next day she received from Mr. E_____ a letter, informing her that his wife had died the preceding day (Thursday) at half-past four. And when, a few days later, that gentleman himself arrived, he stated that Mrs. E_____'s mind had evidently wandered before her death; for, but a little time previous to that event, seeming to revive as from a swoon, she had asked her husband "why he had not told her that her baby was in Heaven." When he replied evasively, still wishing to conceal from her the fact of her child's death, lest the shock might hasten her own, she said to him, "It is useless to deny it, Samuel; *for I have just been home, and have seen her in her little coffin.* Except for your sake, I am glad she is gone to a better world; for I shall soon be there to meet her myself." Very shortly after this she expired.[319] — ROBERT DALE OWEN, JANUARY 1859

English poetess and Spiritualist, Elizabeth Barrett Browning, participated in séances and table-tipping experiments, among other psychical phenomena.

CHAPTER FIFTEEN

ODD APPEARANCE OF LIVING SISTERS' GHOSTS PORTENDS THEIR DEATHS ONE YEAR LATER

☞ In the month of October 1833, Mr. C_____, a gentleman, several members of whose family have since become well and favourably known in the literary world, was residing in a country house, in Hamilton County, Ohio. He had just completed a new residence, about seventy or eighty yards from that in which he was then living, intending to move into it in a few days. The new house was in plain sight of the old, no tree or shrub intervening; but they were separated, about half way, by a small, somewhat abrupt ravine. A garden stretched from the old house to the hither edge of this ravine, and the further extremity of this garden was about forty yards from the newly erected building. Both buildings fronted west, towards a public road, the south side of the old dwelling being directly opposite to the north side of the new. Attached to the rear of the new dwelling was a spacious kitchen, of which a door opened to the north.

The family, at that time, consisted of father, mother, uncle, and nine children. One of the elder daughters, then between fifteen and sixteen years old, was named Rhoda; and another, the youngest but one, Lucy, was between three and four years of age.

One afternoon in that month of October, after a heavy rain, the weather had cleared up; and between four and five o'clock, the sun shone out. About five o'clock, Mrs. C_____ stepped out into a yard on the south side of the dwelling they were occupying, whence, in the evening sun, the new house, including the kitchen already referred to, was distinctly visible. Suddenly she called a daughter, A_____, saying to her, "What can Rhoda possibly be doing there, with the child in her arms? She ought to know better, this damp weather." A_____, looking in the direction in which her mother pointed, saw, plainly and unmistakably, seated in a rocking-chair just within the kitchen-door of the new residence,

A Victorian experiment in intentional astral projection, in which the woman (lower right) visits a distant friend (upper left) in her astral body, or "phantasmal form."

Rhoda, with Lucy in her arms.

"What a strange thing!" she exclaimed; "it is but a few minutes since I left them up-stairs."

And, with that, going in search of them, she found both in one of the upper rooms, and brought them down. Mr. C_____ and other members of the family soon joined them. Their amazement, that of Rhoda especially, may be imagined. The figures seated at the hall-door, and the two children now actually in their midst, were absolutely identical in appearance, even to each minute particular of dress.

Five minutes more elapsed, in breathless expectation, and there still sat the figures; that of Rhoda appearing to rock with the motion of the chair on which it seemed seated. All the family congregated, and every member of it—therefore twelve persons in all—saw the figures, noticed the rocking motion; and became convinced, past all possible doubt, that it was the appearance of Rhoda and Lucy.

Then the father, Mr. C_____, resolved to cross over and endeavour to obtain some solution of the mystery; but, having lost sight of the figures in descending the ravine, when he ascended the opposite bank, they were gone.

Meanwhile the daughter A_____ had walked down to the lower end of the garden, so as to get a closer view; and the rest remained gazing from the spot whence they had first witnessed this unaccountable phenomenon.

Soon after Mr. C_____ had left the house, they all saw the appearance of Rhoda rise from the chair with the child in its arms; then lie down across the threshold of the kitchen door; and after it had remained in that recumbent position for a minute or two, still embracing the child, the figures were seen gradually to sink down, out of sight.

When Mr. C_____ reached the entrance, there was not a trace nor appearance of a human being. The rocking-chair, which had been conveyed across to the kitchen some time before, still stood there, just inside the door, but it was empty. He searched the house carefully, from garret to cellar; but nothing whatever was to be seen. He inspected the clay, soft from the rain, at the rear exit of the kitchen, and all around the house, but not a footstep could he discover. There was not a tree or bush anywhere near, behind which any one could secrete himself, the dwelling being erected on a bare hill-side.

The father returned from his fruitless search, to learn, with a shudder, what the family, meanwhile, had witnessed. The circumstance, as may be supposed, made upon them a profound impression; stamping itself, in indelible characters, on the minds of all. But any mention of it was usually avoided, as something too serious to form the topic of ordinary conversation.

I received it directly from two of the witnesses, Miss A_____ and her sister, Miss P_____. They both stated to me, that their recollections of it were as vivid as if it had occurred but a few weeks since.

No clue or explanation of any kind was ever obtained; unless we are to accept as such the fact, that Rhoda, a very beautiful and cultivated girl, at the time in blooming health, died very unexpectedly, on the 11th of the November of the year following, and that Lucy, then also perfectly well, followed her sister on the 10th of December, the same year: both deaths occurring, it will be observed, within a little more than a year of that day on which the family saw the apparition of the sisters.[320] — ROBERT DALE OWEN, 1860

GHOST OF DECEASED MAN ARRIVES FOR TEA

☛ When the celebrated [British novelist and poet] Miss Anna Maria Porter was residing at Esher, in Surrey, an aged gentleman of her acquaintance, who lived in the same village, was in the habit of frequenting her house, usually making his appearance every evening, reading the newspaper, and taking his cup of tea.

One evening Miss Porter saw him enter as usual, and seat himself at the table, but without speaking. She addressed some remark to him, to which he made no reply; and, after a few seconds, she saw him rise, and leave the room without uttering a word.

Astonished, and fearing that he might have been suddenly taken ill, she instantly sent her servant to his house to make inquiries. The reply was, that the old gentleman had died suddenly about an hour before.[321] — ROBERT DALE OWEN, 1860

NONBELIEVER UNCONVINCED BY THE APPEARANCE OF HIS FRIEND'S WRAITH

☞ In the year 1814, I became acquainted with Colonel Nathan Wilson, a man of strong intellectual powers, who had served many years in India under Sir Arthur Wellesley, afterwards Duke of Wellington. I was introduced to him by Sir Charles Forbes, at a shooting-lodge at Strathdon, and there we had an opportunity of becoming intimate. I had, from his own lips, the narrative I am about to relate to you, and which I may preface by a few words touching the opinions of the narrator.

Colonel Wilson made no secret of his atheism. In India especially, as I have myself observed, the tendency of many minds, influenced by considering the great diversities of religious belief around them, is toward scepticism. Colonel Wilson, fortified by the perusal of [Comte de] Volney, [Baron] D'Holbach, [Claude Adrien] Helvetius, [M. de] Voltaire, and others of similar stamp, rejected, as untenable, the doctrine of a future state of existence, and even received with some impatience any arguments on a subject as to which, he seemed to think, no one could any further enlighten him.

In the year 1811, being then in command of the 19th regiment of dragoons, stationed at Tellicherry [India], and delighting in French literature, he formed an intimacy with Monsieur Dubois, a Roman Catholic missionary priest, an ardent and zealous propagandist and an accomplished man. Notwithstanding the great difference in their creeds, so earnest and yet liberal-minded was the Frenchman, so varied his store of information, and so agreeable and winning his manner, that the missionary and the soldier associated much together, and finally formed a strong attachment to each other. The former did not fail to avail himself of this intimacy by endeavouring to bring about the conversion of his friend. They conversed often and freely on religious subjects; but Colonel Wilson's scepticism remained unshaken.

In July 1811, the priest fell ill, much to the regret of the little circle at Tellicherry, where he was greatly beloved. At the same time, a mutiny having broken out at Vellore [India], Colonel Wilson was summoned thither, and, proceeding by forced marches, encamped on an extensive plain before the town.

The night was sultry; and Colonel Wilson, arrayed as is common in that climate, in shirt and long light calico drawers with feet, sought repose on a couch within his tent; but in vain. Unable to sleep, his attention was suddenly attracted to the entrance of his tent: he saw the purdah raised and the priest Dubois present himself. The pale face and earnest demeanour of his friend, who stood silent and motionless, riveted his attention. He called him by name, but without reply: the purdah fell, and the figure disappeared.

The colonel sprang up, and, hastily donning his slippers, rushed from the tent. The appearance [apparition] was still in sight, gliding through the camp, and making for the plain beyond. Colonel Wilson hastened after it, and at so rapid a pace that when his brother officers, roused by the sentries, went in pursuit of him, it was with difficulty he was overtaken. The apparition having been seen by Captain Wilson only, his comrades concluded that it was the effect of slight delirium produced by fatigue. But when the surgeon of the regiment felt the colonel's pulse, he declared that it beat steadily, without acceleration.

Colonel Wilson felt assured that he had received an intimation of the death of his friend the missionary, who had repeatedly promised, in case he died first, to appear to him as a spirit. He requested his brother officers to note the time. They did so; and when subsequent letters from Tellicherry announced the decease of Dubois, it was found that he had died at the very hour when his likeness appeared to his friend.

Desirous to ascertain what effect this apparition had produced on Colonel Wilson's opinions touching a future state, I put the question directly to him. "I think it a very curious phenomenon," he replied, "not to be accounted for in the present state of our knowledge, and requiring investigation. But it is not sufficient to alter my convictions. Some energetic projection from Dubois's brain, at the moment of approaching annihilation, might perhaps suffice to account for the appearance which I undoubtedly witnessed.[322] — DR. ASHBURNER, LONDON, ENGLAND, CIRCA 1860

WRAITH OF A SPANISH PRINCESS

☛ At Kiel (Cill Challum Chille), in Morvern [Scotland], the body of the Spanish Princess said to have been on board one of the Armada blown up in Tobermory Bay [Scotland] was buried. Two young men of the district made a paction, that whoever died first the other would watch the churchyard for him. The survivor, when keeping the promised watch, had the sight of his dead friend as well as his own. He saw both the material world and spirits. Each night he saw ghosts leaving the churchyard and returning before morning. He observed that one of the ghosts was always behind the rest when returning. He spoke to it, and ascertained it to be the ghost of the Spanish Princess. Her body had been removed to Spain, but one of her little fingers had been left behind, and she had to come back to where it was.[323] — JOHN GREGORSON CAMPBELL, SCOTLAND, 1900

CORPSE-CANDLE FORETELLS DEATH OF CHILD
☛ A minister, newly inducted in his curé, was standing one evening leaning over the wall of the churchyard which adjoined the manse, when he observed a light hovering over a particular spot.

Supposing it to be somebody with a lantern, he opened the wicket and went forward to ascertain who it might be; but before he reached the spot, the light moved onward; and he followed, but could see nobody. It did not rise far from the ground, but advanced rapidly across the road, entered a wood, and ascended a hill, till it at length disappeared at the door of a farmhouse.

Unable to comprehend of what nature this light could be, the minister was deliberating whether to make inquiries at the house or return, when it appeared again, seeming to come out of the house, accompanied by another, passed him, and, going over the same ground, they both disappeared on the spot where he had first observed the phenomenon.

He left a mark on the grave by which he might recognise it, and the next day inquired of the sexton whose it was. The man said it belonged to a family that lived up the hill (indicating the house the light [known as a corpse-candle] had stopped at), named McD_____, but that it was a considerable time since any one had been buried there.

The minister was extremely surprised to learn, in the course of the day, that a child of that family had died of scarlet fever on the preceding evening.[324] — CATHERINE CROWE, ENGLAND, 1850

DÖPPELGANGER PORTENDS DEATH OF BOTH ITS LIVING DOUBLE & THE OBSERVER

☞ Mr. H_____ was one day walking along the street, apparently in perfect health, when he saw, or supposed he saw, his acquaintance, Mr. C_____ walking before him. He called to him aloud; but he did not seem to hear him, and continued moving on. Mr. H_____ then quickened his pace for the purpose of overtaking him; but the other increased his, also, as if to keep ahead of his pursuer, and proceeded at such a rate that Mr. H_____ found it impossible to make up to him.

This continued for some time, till, on Mr. C_____'s reaching a gate, he opened it and passed in, slamming it violently in Mr. H_____'s face. Confounded at such treatment from a friend, the latter instantly opened the gate, and looked down the long lane into which it led, where, to his astonishment, no one was to be seen.

Determined to unravel the mystery, he then went to Mr. C_____'s house, and his surprise was great to hear that he was confined to his bed, and had been so for several days.

A week or two afterward, these gentlemen met at the house of a common friend, when Mr. H_____ related the circumstance, jocularly telling Mr. C_____ that, as he had seen his wraith, he of course could not live long. The person addressed laughed heartily, as did the rest of the party; but, in a few days, Mr. C_____ was attacked with putrid sore throat and died; and within a short period of his death, Mr. H_____ was also in the grave.[325] — CATHERINE CROWE, ENGLAND, 1850

FIANCÉ'S GHOST WARNS OF HIS IMPENDING DEATH

☞ A respectable young woman was awaked, one night, by hearing somebody in her room, and on looking up she saw the young man to whom she was engaged. Extremely offended by such an intrusion, she bade him instantly depart, if he wished her ever to speak to him again. Whereupon he bade her not be frightened, but said he was come to tell her that he was to die that day [in] six weeks,—and then disappeared.

Having ascertained that the young man himself could not possibly have been in her room, she was naturally much alarmed, and, her evident depression leading to some inquiries, she communicated what had occurred to the family with whom she lived—I think as dairy-maid; but I quote from memory. They attached little importance to what seemed so improbable, more especially as the young man continued in perfectly good health, and entirely ignorant of this prediction, which his mistress had the prudence to conceal from him.

When the fatal day arrived, these ladies saw the girl looking very cheerful, as they were going for their morning's ride, and observed to each other that the prophecy did not seem likely to be fulfilled; but when they returned, they saw her running up the avenue toward the house in great agitation, and learned that her lover was either dead or dying, from an accident.[326] — CATHERINE CROWE, ENGLAND, 1850

HUSBAND'S DOUBLE MANIFESTS THREE DAYS BEFORE HIS DEATH

☛ A lady, an entire disbeliever in these spiritual phenomena, was one day walking in her own garden with her husband, who was indisposed, leaning on her arm, when seeing a man with his back toward them, and a spade in his hand, digging, she exclaimed, "Look there! who's that?"

"Where?" said her companion; and at that moment the figure leaning on the spade turned round and looked at her, sadly shaking its head, and she saw it was her husband.

She avoided an explanation, by pretending she had made a mistake. Three days afterward the gentleman died,—leaving her entirely converted to a belief she had previously scoffed at.[327] — CATHERINE CROWE, ENGLAND, 1850

CLERGYMAN TRANSFORMED BY SEEING HIS DÖPPELGANGER

☛ A canon of a catholic cathedral, of somewhat dissipated habits, on coming home one evening, saw a light in his bedroom. When the maid opened the door, she started back with surprise, while he inquired why she had left a candle burning up stairs; upon which she declared that he had come home just before, and gone to his room, and she had been wondering at his unusual silence.

On ascending to his chamber, he saw himself sitting in the arm-chair. The figure rose, passed him, and went out at the room-door. He was extremely alarmed, expecting his death was at hand. He, however, lived many years afterward, but the influence on his moral character was very beneficial.[328] — CATHERINE CROWE, ENGLAND, 1850

AN EXAMPLE OF THE DOCTRINE OF PROTECTING SPIRITS

☛ [A college theology professor in Berlin, Germany, related the following personal experience to his students.] As he was going home the last evening, he had seen his own imago, or double, on the other side of the street. He looked away, and tried to avoid it, but, finding it still accompanied him, he took a short cut home, in hopes of getting rid of it, wherein he succeeded, till he came opposite his own house, when he saw it at the door.

It rang, the maid opened, it entered, she handed it a candle, and, as the professor stood in amazement, on the other side of the street, he saw the light passing the windows, as it wound its way up to his own chamber. He then crossed over and rang; the servant was naturally dreadfully alarmed on seeing him, but, without waiting to explain, he ascended the stairs.

Just as he reached his own chamber, he heard a loud crash, and, on opening the door, they found no one there, but the ceiling had fallen in, and his life was thus saved.

The servant corroborated this statement to the students; and a minister, now attached to one of the Scotch churches, was present when the professor told his tale. [What we have here is an example of the doctrine of protecting spirits.][329] — CATHERINE CROWE, ENGLAND, 1850

AN UNSEEN ANGEL SAVES CHILDREN FROM CERTAIN DEATH

☞ A very interesting case of an apparent friendly [spirit] intervention occurred to the celebrated Dr. A_____ T_____, of Edinburgh, Scotland. He was sitting up late one night, reading in his study, when he heard a foot in the passage, and knowing the family were, or ought to be, all in bed, he rose and looked out to ascertain who it was, but, seeing nobody, he sat down again.

Presently, the sound recurred, and he was sure there was somebody, though he could not see him. The foot, however, evidently ascended the stairs, and he followed it, till it led him to the nursery-door, which he opened, and found the furniture was on fire; and thus, but for this kind office of his good angel, his children would have been burned in their beds.[330] — CATHERINE CROWE, ENGLAND, 1850

CHILD SEES GHOST OF HIS FATHER BEFORE HIS DEATH

☞ A lady with her child embarked on board a vessel at Jamaica, for the purpose of visiting her friends in England, leaving her husband behind her quite well. It was a sailing packet; and they had been some time at sea, when one evening, while the child was kneeling before her saying his prayers previous to going to rest, he suddenly said: "Mamma, papa!"

"Nonsense, my dear!" the mother answered, "you know your

papa is not here!"

"He is indeed, mamma," returned the child, "he is looking at us now."

Nor could she convince him to the contrary.

When she went on deck, she mentioned the circumstance to the captain, who thought it so strange, that he said he would note down the date of the occurrence. The lady begged him not to do so, saying it was attaching a significance to it which would make her miserable.

He did it, however; and, shortly after her arrival in England, she learned that her husband had died exactly at that period.[331] — CATHERINE CROWE, ENGLAND, 1850

APPEARANCE OF SAILOR'S WRAITH PRECEDES HIS DEATH

☛ A maid-servant in one of the midland counties of England, being up early one morning, heard her name called in a voice that seemed to be her brother's, a sailor then at sea; and running up, she found him standing in the hall; he said he was come from afar, and was going again, and mentioned some other things; when her

mistress, hearing voices, called to know who she was talking to: she said it was her brother from sea.

After speaking to her for some time, she suddenly lost sight of him, and found herself alone.

Amazed and puzzled, she told her mistress what had happened, who being led thus to suspect the kind of visitor it was, looked out of the window to ascertain if there were any marks of footsteps, the ground being covered with snow. There were, however, none,—and it was therefore clear that nobody could have entered the house. Intelligence afterward arrived of the young man's death.[332] — CATHERINE CROWE, ENGLAND, 1850

LIFE IN A HAUNTED HOUSE

☛ I have heard of several [haunted] houses, even in populous cities, to which some strange circumstance . . . is attached—in London even, and some in this city and neighborhood; and, what is more, unaccountable things actually do happen to those who inhabit them. Doors are strangely opened and shut, a rustling of silk, and sometimes a whispering, and frequently footsteps, are heard.

There is a house in Ayrshire [Scotland] to which this sort of thing has been attached for years, insomuch that it was finally abandoned to an old man and woman, who said that they were so used to it that they did not mind it. A distinguished authoress told me that some time ago she passed a night at the house of an acquaintance, in one of the midland counties of England. She and her sister occupied the same room, and in the night they heard some one ascending the stairs. The foot came distinctly to the door, then turned away, ascended the next flight, and they heard it overhead.

In the morning, on being asked if they had slept well, they mentioned this circumstance. "That is what everybody hears who sleeps in that room," said the lady of the house. "Many a time I have, when sleeping there, drawn up the night-bolt, persuaded that the nurse was bringing the baby to me; but there was nobody to be seen. We have taken every pains to ascertain what it is, but in vain; and are now so used to it, that we have ceased to care about the matter."[333] — CATHERINE CROWE, ENGLAND, 1850

APPARITION BENDS OVER SLEEPING MAN
☛ A respectable citizen of Edinburgh [Scotland], not long ago, went to America to visit his son, who had married and settled there. The morning after his arrival, he declared his determination to return immediately to Philadelphia [Pennsylvania], from which the house was at a considerable distance; and, on being interrogated as to the cause of this sudden departure, he said that in the previous night he had heard a man walking about his room, who had approached the bed, drawn back the curtains, and bent over him. Thinking it was somebody who had concealed himself there with ill intentions, he had struck out violently at the figure, when, to his horror, his arm passed unimpeded through it.[334] — CATHERINE CROWE, ENGLAND, 1850

THE CASE OF "SPINNING JENNY"
☛ There is a Scotch family of distinction, who, I am told, are accompanied by an unseen attendant, whom they call "Spinning Jenny." She is heard spinning in their house in the country, and when they come into town she spins here; servants and all hear the

sound of her wheel. I believe she accompanies them no further than to their own residences, not to those of other people. Jenny is supposed to be a former housemaid of the family, who was a great spinner, and they are so accustomed to her presence as to feel it no annoyance.[335] — CATHERINE CROWE, ENGLAND, 1850

THE GHOST IN THE KILMARNOCK NIGHTCAP

☛ Two young ladies were passing the night in a house in the north, when the youngest, then a child, awoke and saw an old man, in a Kilmarnock nightcap [a Scottish knitted woolen hat], walking about their bedroom. She said, when telling the story in after-life [i.e., in later years], that she was not the least frightened—she was only surprised! but she found that her sister, who was several years older than herself, was in a state of great terror. He continued some time moving about, and at last went to a chest of drawers, where there lay a parcel of buttons, belonging to a travelling tailor who had been at work in the house. Whether the old man threw them down or not, she could not say; but, just then, they all fell rattling off the drawers to the floor, whereupon he disappeared.

"Spirit photograph obtained by a lady on October 21, 1893."

The next morning, when they mentioned the circumstance, she observed that the family looked at each other in a significant manner; but it was not till she was older she learned that the house was said to be haunted by this old man. "It never occurred to me," she said, "that it was a ghost. Who could have thought of a ghost in a Kilmarnock nightcap!"[336] — CATHERINE CROWE, ENGLAND, 1850

A HAUNTED HOUSE IN WILLINGTON, ENGLAND

☛ We have of late years settled it as an established fact that ghosts and haunted houses were the empty creation of ignorant times. We have comfortably persuaded ourselves that such fancies only hovered in the twilight of superstition, and that in these enlightened days they had vanished for ever. How often has it been triumphantly referred to, as a proof that all such things were the offspring of ignorance, that nothing of the kind is heard of now? What shall we say, then, to the following facts?

Here we have ghosts and a haunted house still. We have them in the face of our vaunted noonday light—in the midst of a busy and a populous neighborhood—in the neighborhood of a large and most intelligent town—and in a family neither ignorant nor in any other respect superstitious. For years have these ghosts and hauntings disturbed the quiet of a highly respectable family, and continue to haunt and disturb, spite of the incredulity of the wise, the investigations of the curious, and the anxious vigilance of the suffering family itself.

Between the railway running from Newcastle-on-Tyne to North Shields, and the river Tyne [in England], there lie in a hollow some few cottages, a parsonage, a mill, and a miller's house: these constitute the hamlet of Willington. Just above these the railway is carried across the valley on lofty arches, and from it you look down on the mill and cottages, lying at a considerable depth below. The mill is a large steam flour-mill, like a factory, and the miller's house stands near it, but not adjoining it. None of the cottages which lie between these premises and the railway, either, are in contact with them. The house stands on a sort of little promontory, round which runs the channel of a water-course, which appears to fill and empty with the tides.

On one side of the mill and house, slopes away upward a field to a considerable distance, where it is terminated by other enclosures; on the other stands a considerable extent of ballast hill—i.e., one of the numerous hills on the banks of the Tyne made by the deposit of ballast from the vessels trading thither. At a distance, the top of the mill seems about level with the country around it. The place lies about half-way between Newcastle and North Shields.

This mill is, I believe, the property of, and is worked by, Messrs. Unthank and Procter. Mr. Joseph Procter resides on the spot in the house just by the mill, as already stated. He is a member of the society of friends [Quakers]—a gentleman in the very prime of life—and his wife, an intelligent lady, is of a family of friends in Carlisle [England]. They have several young children. This very respectable and well-informed family, belonging to a sect which of all others is most accustomed to control, to regulate, and to put down even the imagination—the last people in the world, as it would appear, in fact, to be affected by any mere imaginary terrors or impressions—have for years been persecuted by the most extraordinary noises and apparitions.

The house is not an old house, as will appear; it was built about the year 1800. It has no particularly spectral look about it. Seeing it in passing, or within, ignorant of its real character, one should by no means say that it was a place likely to have the reputation of being haunted. Yet looking down from the railway, and seeing it and the mill lying in a deep hole, one might imagine various strange noises likely to be heard in such a place in the night, from vessels on the river—from winds sweeping and howling down the gulley in which it stands from engines in the neighborhood connected with coal-mines, one of which, I could not tell where, was making at the time I was there a wild sighing noise, as I stood on the hill above. There is not any passage, however, known of under the house, by which subterranean noises could be heard; nor are they merely noises that are heard,—distinct apparitions are declared to be seen.

The hazy ghost lady in this Victorian psychic photograph, captured in 1892, appeared in the spirit images of other photographers as well.

Spite of the unwillingness of Mr. Procter, that these mysterious circumstances should become quite public, and averse as he is to make known himself these strange visitations, they were of such a nature that they soon became rumored over the whole neighborhood.

... The following ... case of an apparition seen in the window of the [haunted Willington] house from the outside, by four credible witnesses, who had the opportunity of scrutinizing it for more than ten minutes, is given on most unquestionable authority.

One of these witnesses is a young lady, a near connection of the family, who, for obvious reasons, did not sleep in the house; another, a respectable man, who has been many years employed in, and is foreman of, the manufactory; his daughter, aged about seventeen; and his wife, who first saw the object and called out the others to view it. The appearance presented was that of a bareheaded man, in a flowing robe like a surplice, who glided backward and forward about three feet from the floor, or level with the bottom of the second story window, seeming to enter the wall on each side, and thus present a side view in passing. It then stood still in the window, and a part of the body came through both the blind, which was closed down, and the window, as its luminous body intercepted the view of the framework of the window. It was semi-transparent, and as bright as a star, diffusing a radiance all around. As it grew more dim, it assumed a blue tinge, and gradually faded away from the head downward.

The foreman passed twice close to the house under the window, and also went to inform the family, but found the house locked up. There was no moonlight, nor a ray of light visible anywhere about, and no person near. Had any magic lantern been used, it could not possibly have escaped detection; and it is obvious nothing of that kind could have been employed on the inside, as in that case the light could only have been thrown upon the blind, and not so as to intercept the view both of the blind and of the window from without. The owner of the house slept in that room, and must have entered it shortly after this figure had disappeared.[337] — WILLIAM HOWITT, ENGLAND, CIRCA MID 1800S

CORPSE-LIGHT AUGURS SERVANT'S DEATH
☛ With regard to the perplexing subject of corpse-lights, there would be little difficulty attending it if they always remained stationary over the graves; but it seems very well established that that is not the case. There are numerous stories, proceeding from very respectable quarters, proving the contrary; and I have heard two from a dignitary of the church, born in Wales, which I will relate:

A female relation of his had occasion to go to Aberystwith [Wales], which was about twenty miles from her home, on horseback; and she started at a very early hour for that purpose, with her father's servant. When they had nearly reached the half-way, fearing the man might be wanted at home, she bade him return, as she was approaching the spot where the servant of the lady she was going to visit was to meet her, in order to escort her the other half.

The man [servant] had not long left her, when she saw a light coming toward her, the nature of which she suspected. It moved, according to her description, steadily on, about three feet from the ground. Somewhat awestruck, she turned her horse out of the bridle-road, along which it was coming, intending to wait till it had passed; but, to her dismay, just as it came opposite to her, it stopped, and there remained perfectly fixed for nearly half an hour, at the end of which period it moved on as before.

The servant presently came up, and she proceeded to the house of her friend, where she related what she had seen.

A few days afterward, the very servant who came to meet her was taken ill and died: his body was carried along that road; and, at the very spot where the light had paused, an accident occurred, which caused a delay of half an hour.[338] — CATHERINE CROWE, ENGLAND, 1850

BRILLIANT LIGHT HERALDS DEATH OF FAMILY MEMBER

☛ [Continued from the previous entry.] The other story was as follows:

A servant in the family of Lady Davis, my informant's aunt, had occasion to start early for market. Being in the kitchen, about three o'clock in the morning, taking his breakfast alone, when everybody else was in bed, he was surprised at hearing a sound of heavy feet on the stairs above; and, opening the door to see who it could be, he was struck with alarm at perceiving a great light, much brighter than could have been shed by a candle, at the same time that he heard a violent thump, as if some very heavy body had hit the clock, which stood on the landing. Aware of the nature of the light, the man did not await its further descent, but rushed out of the house—whence he presently saw it issue from the front door, and proceed on its way to the churchyard.

As his mistress, Lady Davis, was at that period in her bed, ill, he made no doubt that her death impended; and when he returned from the market at night, his first question was, whether she was yet alive: and though he was informed she was better, he declared his conviction that she would die, alleging as his reason what he had seen in the morning—a narration which led everybody else to the same conclusion.

The lady, however, recovered; but, within a fortnight, another member of the family died: and as his coffin was brought down the stairs, the bearers ran it violently against the clock upon which the man instantly exclaimed, "That is the very noise I heard!"[339] — CATHERINE CROWE, ENGLAND, 1850

GHOST GIVES AGE HE WOULD HAVE BEEN IF STILL ALIVE

☛ A gentleman of fortune and station, in Ireland, was one day walking along the road, when he met a very old man, apparently a peasant, though well dressed, and looking as if he had on his Sunday habiliments. His great age attracted the gentleman's attention the more, that he could not help wondering at the alertness of his movements, and the ease with which he was ascending the hill.

He consequently accosted him, inquiring his name and residence; and was answered that his name was Kirkpatrick, and that he lived at a cottage, which he pointed out. Whereupon the gentleman expressed his surprise that he should be unknown to him, since he fancied he had been acquainted with every man on his estate.

The ghost images of this woman's dead husband and dead father imprinted on this psychic photograph. The photographer and sitter were unknown to one another.

"It is odd you have never seen me before," returned the old man, "for I walk here every day."

"How old are you?" asked the gentleman.

"I am one hundred and five," answered the other; "and have been here all my life."

After a few more words, they parted; and the gentleman, proceeding toward some laborers in a neighboring field, inquired if they knew an old man of the name of Kirkpatrick. They did not; but on addressing the question to some older tenants, they said, "Oh, yes;" they had known him, and had been at his funeral; he had lived at the cottage on the hill, but had been dead twenty years.

"How old was he when he died?" inquired the gentleman, much amazed.

"He was eighty-five," said they so that the old man gave the age that he would have reached had he survived to the period of this rencontre.

This curious incident is furnished by the gentleman himself and all he can say is, that it certainly occurred, and that he is quite unable to explain it. He was in perfect health at the time, and had never heard of this man in his life, who had been dead several years before the estate came into his possession.[340] — CATHERINE CROWE, ENGLAND, 1850

GHOST CHATS WITH LIVING FRIEND FOR TWO HOURS
☞ Mr. Grose went to see Mr. Shaw on the 2nd of August last. As they sat talking in the evening, says Mr. Shaw: "On the 21st of the last month, as I was smoking a pipe, and reading in my study, between eleven and twelve at night, in comes Mr. Naylor (formerly fellow of St. John's college, but had been dead full four years). When I saw him, I was not much affrighted, and I asked him to sit down, which accordingly he did for about two hours, and we talked together. I asked him how it fared with him. He said, "Very well."

"Were any of our old acquaintances with him?"

"No!" (at which I was much alarmed), "but Mr. Orchard will be with me soon, and yourself not long after."

As he was going away, I asked him if he would not stay a little longer, but he refused. I asked him if he would call again.

"No;" he had but three days' leave of absence, and he had other business.

N. B.—Mr. Orchard died soon after. Mr. Shaw is now dead: he was formerly fellow of St. John's college—an ingenious, good man. I knew him there; but at his death he had a college-living in Oxfordshire, and here he saw the apparition.[341] — CATHERINE CROWE, ENGLAND, 1850

REMEMBER THE BLACK DOG!
☞ A young lady of the name of P_____, not long since was sitting at work, well and cheerful, when she saw, to her great surprise, a large black dog close to her. As both door and window were closed, she could not understand how he had got in; but when she started up to put him out, she could no longer see him.

Quite puzzled, and thinking it must be some strange illusion, she sat down again and went on with her work, when, presently, he was there again. Much alarmed, she now ran out and told her mother, who said she must have fancied it, or be ill. She declared neither was the case; and, to oblige her, the mother agreed to wait outside the door, and if she saw it again, she was to call her.

Miss P_____ re-entered the room, and presently there was the dog again; but when she called her mother, he disappeared.

Immediately afterward, the mother was taken ill and died. Before she expired, she said to her daughter, "Remember the black dog!"³⁴² — CATHERINE CROWE, ENGLAND, 1850

RED-HAIRED BANSHEE HERALDS FAMILY MEMBER'S DEATH
☛ While paying a visit to Lady Honor O'Brien, Lady Fanshawe was awakened the first night she slept there by a voice, and, on drawing back the curtain, she saw a female figure standing in the recess of the window, attired in white, with red hair and a pale and ghastly aspect.

> "She looked out of the window," says Lady Fanshawe, "and cried in a loud voice, such as I never before heard, 'A horse!—a horse!—a horse!' and then with a sigh, which rather resembled the wind than the voice of a human being, she disappeared. Her body appeared to me rather like a thick cloud than a real solid substance. I was so frightened," she continues, "that my hair stood on end, and my night-cap fell off. I pushed and shook my husband, who had slept all the time, and who was very much surprised to find me in such a fright, and still more so when I told him the cause of it, and showed him the open window. Neither of us slept any more that night, but he talked to me about it, and told me how much more frequent such apparitions were in that country than in England."

This was, however, what is called a banshee: for in the morning Lady Honor came to them, to say that one of the family had died in the night, expressing a hope that they had not been disturbed: "for," said she, "whenever any of the O'Briens is on his death-bed, it is usual for a woman to appear at one of the windows every night till he expires; but when I put you into this room, I did not think of it." This apparition was connected with some sad tale of seduction and murder.³⁴³ — CATHERINE CROWE, ENGLAND, 1850

FLOCK OF GHOST SHEEP STARTLE TOWNSPEOPLE
☛ During the seven years' war in Germany, a drover lost his life in a drunken squabble on the high road. For some time there was a sort of rude tombstone, with a cross on it, to mark the spot where his body was interred; but this has long fallen, and a milestone now fills its place. Nevertheless, it continues commonly asserted by the country people, and also by various travellers, that they have been deluded in that spot by seeing, as they imagine, herds of beasts, which, on investigation, prove to be merely visionary.

Of course, many people look upon this as a superstition; but a very singular confirmation of the story occurred in the year 1826, when two gentlemen and two ladies were passing the spot in a post-carriage. One of these was a clergyman, and none of them had ever heard of the phenomenon said to be attached to the place. They had been discussing the prospects of the minister, who was on his way to a vicarage, to which he had just been appointed, when they saw a large flock of sheep, which stretched quite across the road, and was accompanied by a shepherd and a long-haired black dog.

As to meet cattle on that road was nothing uncommon, and indeed they had met several droves in the course of the day, no remark was made at the moment, till, suddenly, each looked at the other and said, "What is become of the sheep?" Quite perplexed at their sudden disappearance, they called to the postillion to stop, and all got out in order to mount a little elevation and look around; but still unable to discover them, they now bethought themselves of asking the postillion where they were, when, to their infinite surprise, they learned that he had not seen them.

Upon this, they bade him quicken his pace, that they might overtake a carriage that had passed them shortly before, and inquire if that party had seen the sheep; but they had not.

Four years later, a postmaster, named J_____, was on the same road, driving a carriage, in which were a clergyman and his wife, when he saw a large flock of sheep near the same spot. Seeing they were very fine wethers, and supposing them to have been bought at a sheep-fair that was then taking place a few miles off, J_____ drew up his reins and stopped his horse, turning at the same time to the clergyman to say, that he wanted to inquire the price of the sheep, as he intended going next day to the fair himself. While the minister was asking him what sheep he meant, J_____ got down and found himself in the midst of the animals, the size and beauty of which astonished him.

They passed him at an unusual rate, while he made his way through them to find the shepherd, when, on getting to the end of the flock, they suddenly disappeared. He then first learned that his fellow-travellers had not seen them at all.[344] — CATHERINE CROWE, ENGLAND, 1850

GIRL WITNESSES GHOST SCENE OF UNCLE'S DROWNING

☛ A medical friend of mine, who practised some time at Deptford [London, England], was once sent for to a girl who had been taken suddenly ill. He found her with inflammation of the brain, and the only account the mother could give of it was, that shortly before, she had run into the room, crying, "Oh, mother, I have seen Uncle John drowned in his boat under the fifth arch of Rochesterbridge!"

The girl died a few hours afterward; and, on the following night, the uncle's boat ran foul of the bridge, and he was drowned, exactly as she had foretold.³⁴⁵ — CATHERINE CROWE, ENGLAND, 1850

MAN SEES INJURED GHOST OF FUTURE SELF

☞ Mrs. A_____, an English lady, and the wife of a clergyman, relates that, previous to her marriage, she with her father and mother being at the seaside, had arranged to make a few days' excursion to some races that were about to take place; and that the night before they started, the father having been left alone, while the ladies were engaged in their preparations, they found him, on descending to the drawing-room, in a state of considerable agitation—which, he said, had arisen from his having seen a dreadful face at one corner of the room.

Victorian psychic photograph.

He described it as a bruised, battered, crushed, discolored face, with the two eyes protruding frightfully from their sockets; but the features were too disfigured to ascertain if it were the face of any one he knew.

On the following day, on their way to the races, an accident occurred; and he was brought home with his own face exactly in the condition he had described. He had never exhibited any other instance of this extraordinary faculty, and the impression made by the circumstance lasted the remainder of his life, which was unhappily shortened by the injuries he had received.³⁴⁶ — CATHERINE CROWE, ENGLAND, 1850

GHOST OF DROWNED BOAT CREW ASCENDS CLIFF

☞ Not long ago, a servant girl on the estate of D_____, of S_____, saw with amazement five figures ascending a perpendicular cliff, quite inaccessible to human feet; one was a boy wearing a cap with red binding. She watched them with great curiosity till they reached the top, where they all stretched themselves on the earth, with countenances expressive of great dejection. While she was looking at them they disappeared, and she immediately related her vision.

Shortly afterward, a foreign ship, in distress, was seen to put off a boat with four men and a boy: the boat was dashed to pieces in the surf, and the five bodies, exactly answering the description she had given, were thrown on shore at the foot of the cliff, which they had perhaps climbed in the spirit![347] — CATHERINE CROWE, ENGLAND, 1850

GIRL WITNESSES FATHER'S GHOST PRIOR TO HIS DEATH

☛ A maid-servant residing in a family in Northumberland [England], one day last winter was heard to utter a violent scream immediately after she had left the kitchen. On following her to inquire what had happened, she said that she had just seen her father in his night-clothes, with a most horrible countenance, and she was sure something dreadful had happened to him.

Two days afterward there arrived a letter, saying he had been seized with delirium tremens, and was at the point of death; which accordingly ensued.[348] — CATHERINE CROWE, ENGLAND, 1850

APPENDIX

SIX PROOFS THAT GHOSTS ARE REAL
by Hereward Carrington, 1919

1. The fact that several people may see the figure at one time. These are the so-called "collective cases," of which there are a number on record.

2. The fact that these appearances have occasionally been photographed. Apart from the ordinary cases of fraudulent "spirit-photography," respective scientific evidence exists in favour of the view that an ethereal body of some sort has been photographed in such cases.

3. The fact that animals often behave queerly when a ghost is seen, or even felt. Aside from mere legend, this has been observed at first hand on a number of occasions.

4. The fact that these phantasmal forms sometimes move material objects, close the door, snuff the light, etc. A hallucination, no matter how vivid, cannot do this! It rather points to the existence, in space, of a semisolid body.

5. The fact that such figures have often given information unknown to any person present, but afterward found to be correct.

6. The fact that the person seeing the phantasmal figure may afterward recognize the face on a photograph shown him—he never having known the person in life. In so-called "haunted houses" this has often been observed.[349]

Swedish scientist and Christian mystic, Emanuel Swedenborg, had numerous encounters with supernatural beings.

NOTES

ALL FOOTNOTES, ENDNOTES, & NOTES IN GENERAL ARE MINE, UNLESS OTHERWISE INDICATED. L.S.
(ALL BIBLE CITATIONS ARE FROM THE KJV.)

1. *Journal of the Society for Psychical Research*, Vol. 1, 1884-1885, pp. 19-20. (The title of this entry is mine. L.S.)
2. *Journal of the Society for Psychical Research*, Vol. 1, 1884-1885, p. 27.
3. *Journal of the Society for Psychical Research*, Vol. 1, 1884-1885, p. 75. (The title of this entry is mine. L.S.)
4. *Journal of the Society for Psychical Research*, Vol. 1, 1884-1885, pp. 240-241. (The title of this entry is mine. L.S.)
5. *Journal of the American Society for Psychical Research*, Vol. 13, 1919, pp. 32-34. (The title of this entry is mine. L.S.)
6. Seabrook, *Your Soul Lives Forever*, pp. 190-191. (The title of this entry is mine. L.S.)
7. *Journal of the American Society for Psychical Research*, Vol. 13, 1919, pp. 261-267. (The title of this entry is mine. L.S.)
8. *Journal of the American Society for Psychical Research*, Vol. 13, 1919, pp. 272-273. (The title of this entry is mine. L.S.)
9. *Journal of the American Society for Psychical Research*, Vol. 13, 1919, pp. 273-274. (The title of this entry is mine. L.S.)
10. *Journal of the American Society for Psychical Research*, Vol. 13, 1919, pp. 372-376. (The title of this entry is mine. L.S.)
11. Seabrook, *Your Soul Lives Forever*, pp. 191-192. (The title of this entry is mine. L.S.)
12. Seabrook, *Your Soul Lives Forever*, pp. 56-57. (The title of this entry is mine. L.S.)
13. *Journal of the American Society for Psychical Research*, Vol. 13, 1919, pp. 378-382. (The title of this entry is mine. L.S.)
14. *Journal of the American Society for Psychical Research*, Vol. 13, 1919, p. 426. (The title of this entry is mine. L.S.)
15. *Journal of the American Society for Psychical Research*, Vol. 13, 1919, pp. 426-427. (The title of this entry is mine. L.S.)
16. Seabrook, *Your Soul Lives Forever*, pp. 58-60. (The title of this entry is mine. L.S.)
17. *Journal of the American Society for Psychical Research*, Vol. 13, 1919, p. 434. (The title of this entry is mine. L.S.)
18. *Journal of the American Society for Psychical Research*, Vol. 13, 1919, p. 435. (The title of this entry is mine. L.S.)
19. *Journal of the American Society for Psychical Research*, Vol. 13, 1919, p. 435. (The title of this entry is mine. L.S.)
20. *Journal of the American Society for Psychical Research*, Vol. 13, 1919, pp. 435-436. (The title of this entry is mine. L.S.)
21. *Journal of the American Society for Psychical Research*, Vol. 13, 1919, pp. 442-443. (The title of this entry is mine. L.S.)
22. *Journal of the American Society for Psychical Research*, Vol. 13, 1919, pp. 444-445. (The title of this entry is mine. L.S.)
23. *Journal of the American Society for Psychical Research*, Vol. 13, 1919, pp. 580-582. (The title of this entry is mine. L.S.)
24. *Journal of the American Society for Psychical Research*, Vol. 13, 1919, pp. 592-593. (The title of this entry is mine. L.S.)
25. *Journal of the American Society for Psychical Research*, Vol. 13, 1919, pp. 595-597. (The title of this entry is mine. L.S.)

26. *Journal of the American Society for Psychical Research*, Vol. 13, 1919, pp. 656-657. (The title of this entry is mine. L.S.)
27. Seabrook, *Your Soul Lives Forever*, pp. 49-50. (The title of this entry is mine. L.S.)
28. *Journal of the Society for Psychical Research*, Vol. 6, 1893-1894, see pp. 9-11. (The title of this entry is mine. L.S.)
29. *Journal of the Society for Psychical Research*, Vol. 6, 1893-1894, pp. 13-14. (The title of this entry is mine. L.S.)
30. *Journal of the Society for Psychical Research*, Vol. 6, 1893-1894, p. 14. (The title of this entry is mine. L.S.)
31. *Journal of the Society for Psychical Research*, Vol. 6, 1893-1894, p. 14. (The title of this entry is mine. L.S.)
32. *Journal of the Society for Psychical Research*, Vol. 6, 1893-1894, pp. 14-15. (The title of this entry is mine. L.S.)
33. *Journal of the Society for Psychical Research*, Vol. 6, 1893-1894, p. 15. (The title of this entry is mine. L.S.)
34. *Journal of the Society for Psychical Research*, Vol. 6, 1893-1894, p. 15. (The title of this entry is mine. L.S.)
35. Seabrook, *Your Soul Lives Forever*, pp. 263-265. (The title of this entry is mine. L.S.)
36. *Journal of the Society for Psychical Research*, Vol. 6, 1893-1894, p. 15. (The title of this entry is mine. L.S.)
37. *Journal of the Society for Psychical Research*, Vol. 6, 1893-1894, p. 15. (The title of this entry is mine. L.S.)
38. *Journal of the Society for Psychical Research*, Vol. 6, 1893-1894, p. 15. (The title of this entry is mine. L.S.)
39. *Journal of the Society for Psychical Research*, Vol. 6, 1893-1894, p. 15. (The title of this entry is mine. L.S.)
40. *Journal of the Society for Psychical Research*, Vol. 6, 1893-1894, pp. 15-16. (The title of this entry is mine. L.S.)
41. *Journal of the Society for Psychical Research*, Vol. 6, 1893-1894, p. 16. (The title of this entry is mine. L.S.)
42. *Journal of the Society for Psychical Research*, Vol. 6, 1893-1894, p. 16. (The title of this entry is mine. L.S.)
43. Seabrook, *Your Soul Lives Forever*, p. 169. (The title of this entry is mine. L.S.)
44. *Journal of the Society for Psychical Research*, Vol. 6, 1893-1894, p. 16. (The title of this entry is mine. L.S.)
45. *Journal of the Society for Psychical Research*, Vol. 6, 1893-1894, p. 16. (The title of this entry is mine. L.S.)
46. *Journal of the Society for Psychical Research*, Vol. 6, 1893-1894, pp. 22-23. (The title of this entry is mine. L.S.)
47. *Journal of the Society for Psychical Research*, Vol. 6, 1893-1894, p. 25. (The title of this entry is mine. L.S.)
48. *Journal of the Society for Psychical Research*, Vol. 6, 1893-1894, p. 27. (The title of this entry is mine. L.S.)
49. *Journal of the Society for Psychical Research*, Vol. 6, 1893-1894, pp. 28-29. (The title of this entry is mine. L.S.)
50. *Journal of the Society for Psychical Research*, Vol. 6, 1893-1894, pp. 29-30. (The title of this entry is mine. L.S.)
51. *Journal of the Society for Psychical Research*, Vol. 6, 1893-1894, pp. 74-75. (The title of this entry is mine. L.S.)
52. *Journal of the Society for Psychical Research*, Vol. 6, 1893-1894, p. 75. (The title of this entry is mine. L.S.)
53. *Journal of the Society for Psychical Research*, Vol. 6, 1893-1894, p. 75. (The title of this entry is mine. L.S.)
54. *Journal of the Society for Psychical Research*, Vol. 6, 1893-1894, p. 75. (The title of this entry is mine. L.S.)
55. *Journal of the Society for Psychical Research*, Vol. 6, 1893-1894, pp. 75-76. (The title of this entry is mine. L.S.)
56. *Journal of the Society for Psychical Research*, Vol. 6, 1893-1894, p. 76. (The title of this entry is mine. L.S.)
57. *Journal of the Society for Psychical Research*, Vol. 6, 1893-1894, p. 76. (The title of this entry is mine. L.S.)
58. *Journal of the Society for Psychical Research*, Vol. 6, 1893-1894, p. 76. (The title of this entry is mine. L.S.)
59. *Journal of the Society for Psychical Research*, Vol. 6, 1893-1894, p. 76. (The title of this entry is mine. L.S.)
60. *Journal of the Society for Psychical Research*, Vol. 6, 1893-1894, p. 76. (The title of this entry is mine. L.S.)
61. *Journal of the Society for Psychical Research*, Vol. 6, 1893-1894, p. 108. (The title of this entry is mine. L.S.)
62. Seabrook, *Your Soul Lives Forever*, pp. 266-267. (The title of this entry is mine. L.S.)
63. *Journal of the Society for Psychical Research*, Vol. 6, 1893-1894, p. 108. (The title of this entry is mine. L.S.)
64. *Journal of the Society for Psychical Research*, Vol. 6, 1893-1894, p. 108. (The title of this entry is mine. L.S.)
65. *Journal of the Society for Psychical Research*, Vol. 6, 1893-1894, p. 108. (The title of this entry is mine. L.S.)
66. *Journal of the Society for Psychical Research*, Vol. 6, 1893-1894, p. 108. (The title of this entry is mine. L.S.)
67. *Journal of the Society for Psychical Research*, Vol. 6, 1893-1894, p. 108. (The title of this entry is mine. L.S.)
68. *Journal of the Society for Psychical Research*, Vol. 6, 1893-1894, p. 108. (The title of this entry is mine. L.S.)
69. *Journal of the Society for Psychical Research*, Vol. 6, 1893-1894, p. 129. (The title of this entry is mine. L.S.)

70. Seabrook, *Your Soul Lives Forever*, p. 50. (The title of this entry is mine. L.S.)
71. *Journal of the Society for Psychical Research*, Vol. 6, 1893-1894, p. 131. (The title of this entry is mine. L.S.)
72. *Journal of the Society for Psychical Research*, Vol. 6, 1893-1894, p. 134. (The title of this entry is mine. L.S.)
73. *Journal of the Society for Psychical Research*, Vol. 6, 1893-1894, pp. 135. (The title of this entry is mine. L.S.)
74. *Journal of the Society for Psychical Research*, Vol. 6, 1893-1894, pp. 137-138. (The title of this entry is mine. L.S.)
75. *Journal of the Society for Psychical Research*, Vol. 6, 1893-1894, p. 139. (The title of this entry is mine. L.S.)
76. *Journal of the Society for Psychical Research*, Vol. 6, 1893-1894, p. 140. (The title of this entry is mine. L.S.)
77. *Journal of the Society for Psychical Research*, Vol. 6, 1893-1894, p. 140. (The title of this entry is mine. L.S.)
78. *Journal of the Society for Psychical Research*, Vol. 6, 1893-1894, p. 140. (The title of this entry is mine. L.S.)
79. *Journal of the Society for Psychical Research*, Vol. 6, 1893-1894, p. 140. (The title of this entry is mine. L.S.)
80. *Journal of the Society for Psychical Research*, Vol. 6, 1893-1894, p. 140. (The title of this entry is mine. L.S.)
81. *Journal of the Society for Psychical Research*, Vol. 6, 1893-1894, p. 140. (The title of this entry is mine. L.S.)
82. *Journal of the Society for Psychical Research*, Vol. 6, 1893-1894, p. 140. (The title of this entry is mine. L.S.)
83. *Journal of the Society for Psychical Research*, Vol. 6, 1893-1894, pp. 145-146. (The title of this entry is mine. L.S.)
84. Seabrook, *Your Soul Lives Forever*, p. 267. (The title of this entry is mine. L.S.)
85. *Journal of the Society for Psychical Research*, Vol. 6, 1893-1894, pp. 146-148. (The title of this entry is mine. L.S.)
86. *Journal of the Society for Psychical Research*, Vol. 6, 1893-1894, pp. 149-150. (The title of this entry is mine. L.S.)
87. Seabrook, *Your Soul Lives Forever*, pp. 301-302. (The title of this entry is mine. L.S.)
88. *Journal of the Society for Psychical Research*, Vol. 6, 1893-1894, p. 207. (The title of this entry is mine. L.S.)
89. *Journal of the Society for Psychical Research*, Vol. 6, 1893-1894, p. 207. (The title of this entry is mine. L.S.)
90. *Journal of the Society for Psychical Research*, Vol. 6, 1893-1894, p. 207. (The title of this entry is mine. L.S.)
91. *Journal of the Society for Psychical Research*, Vol. 6, 1893-1894, p. 207. (The title of this entry is mine. L.S.)
92. *Journal of the Society for Psychical Research*, Vol. 6, 1893-1894, p. 171. (The title of this entry is mine. L.S.)
93. *Journal of the Society for Psychical Research*, Vol. 6, 1893-1894, p. 172. (The title of this entry is mine. L.S.)
94. *Journal of the Society for Psychical Research*, Vol. 6, 1893-1894, p. 172. (The title of this entry is mine. L.S.)
95. *Journal of the Society for Psychical Research*, Vol. 6, 1893-1894, p. 172. (The title of this entry is mine. L.S.)
96. *Journal of the Society for Psychical Research*, Vol. 6, 1893-1894, p. 172. (The title of this entry is mine. L.S.)
97. *Journal of the Society for Psychical Research*, Vol. 6, 1893-1894, p. 172. (The title of this entry is mine. L.S.)
98. *Journal of the Society for Psychical Research*, Vol. 6, 1893-1894, p. 172. (The title of this entry is mine. L.S.)
99. *Journal of the Society for Psychical Research*, Vol. 6, 1893-1894, p. 172. (The title of this entry is mine. L.S.)
100. *Journal of the Society for Psychical Research*, Vol. 6, 1893-1894, p. 172. (The title of this entry is mine. L.S.)
101. *Journal of the Society for Psychical Research*, Vol. 6, 1893-1894, p. 172. (The title of this entry is mine. L.S.)
102. *Journal of the Society for Psychical Research*, Vol. 6, 1893-1894, pp. 179-181. (The title of this entry is mine. L.S.)
103. Seabrook, *Your Soul Lives Forever*, pp. 267-268. (The title of this entry is mine. L.S.)
104. *Journal of the Society for Psychical Research*, Vol. 6, 1893-1894, pp. 181-182. (The title of this entry is mine. L.S.)
105. *Journal of the Society for Psychical Research*, Vol. 6, 1893-1894, p. 183. (The title of this entry is mine. L.S.)
106. *Journal of the Society for Psychical Research*, Vol. 6, 1893-1894, p. 184. (The title of this entry is mine. L.S.)
107. *Journal of the Society for Psychical Research*, Vol. 6, 1893-1894, pp. 230-231. (The title of this entry is mine. L.S.)
108. *Journal of the Society for Psychical Research*, Vol. 6, 1893-1894, p. 280. (The title of this entry is mine. L.S.)
109. *Journal of the Society for Psychical Research*, Vol. 6, 1893-1894, p. 375. (The title of this entry is mine. L.S.)

110. *Journal of the Society for Psychical Research*, Vol. 6, 1893-1894, p. 375. (The title of this entry is mine. L.S.)
111. Seabrook, *Your Soul Lives Forever*, pp. 169-170. (The title of this entry is mine. L.S.)
112. *Journal of the Society for Psychical Research*, Vol. 6, 1893-1894, p. 375. (The title of this entry is mine. L.S.)
113. *Journal of the Society for Psychical Research*, Vol. 6, 1893-1894, p. 375. (The title of this entry is mine. L.S.)
114. *Journal of the Society for Psychical Research*, Vol. 9, 1899-1902, p. 123. (The title of this entry is mine. L.S.)
115. *Journal of the Society for Psychical Research*, Vol. 9, 1899-1902, p. 124. (The title of this entry is mine. L.S.)
116. *Journal of the Society for Psychical Research*, Vol. 9, 1899-1902, p. 125. (The title of this entry is mine. L.S.)
117. *Journal of the Society for Psychical Research*, Vol. 9, 1899-1902, p. 125. (The title of this entry is mine. L.S.)
118. *Journal of the Society for Psychical Research*, Vol. 9, 1899-1902, pp. 126-127. (The title of this entry is mine. L.S.)
119. Seabrook, *Your Soul Lives Forever*, pp. 268-270. (The title of this entry is mine. L.S.)
120. *Journal of the Society for Psychical Research*, Vol. 9, 1899-1902, pp. 154-155. (The title of this entry is mine. L.S.)
121. *Journal of the Society for Psychical Research*, Vol. 9, 1899-1902, pp. 155-157. (The title of this entry is mine. L.S.)
122. *Journal of the Society for Psychical Research*, Vol. 9, 1899-1902, p. 241. (The title of this entry is mine. L.S.)
123. *Journal of the Society for Psychical Research*, Vol. 9, 1899-1902, pp. 245-246. (The title of this entry is mine. L.S.)
124. Seabrook, *Your Soul Lives Forever*, pp. 50-51. (The title of this entry is mine. L.S.)
125. *Journal of the Society for Psychical Research*, Vol. 9, 1899-1902, pp. 247-248. (The title of this entry is mine. L.S.)-1902
126. *Journal of the Society for Psychical Research*, Vol. 9, 1899-1902, pp. 299-300. (The title of this entry is mine. L.S.)
127. *Journal of the Society for Psychical Research*, Vol. 9, 1899-1902, pp. 300-301. (The title of this entry is mine. L.S.)
128. *Journal of the Society for Psychical Research*, Vol. 9, 1899-1902, pp. 302-303. (The title of this entry is mine. L.S.)
129. *Journal of the Society for Psychical Research*, Vol. 9, 1899-1902, pp. 307-308. (The title of this entry is mine. L.S.)
130. *Journal of the Society for Psychical Research*, Vol. 9, March 1901, pp. 43-44. (The title of this entry is mine. L.S.)
131. *Journal of the Society for Psychical Research*, Vol. 9, March 1901, p. 44. (The title of this entry is mine. L.S.)
132. *Journal of the Society for Psychical Research*, Vol. 9, March 1901, pp. 45-46. (The title of this entry is mine. L.S.)
133. Seabrook, *Your Soul Lives Forever*, pp. 51-52. (The title of this entry is mine. L.S.)
134. *Journal of the Society for Psychical Research*, Vol. 9, November 1901, pp. 136-137. (The title of this entry is mine. L.S.)
135. *Journal of the Society for Psychical Research*, Vol. 9, November 1901, pp. 139-140. (The title of this entry is mine. L.S.)
136. *Journal of the Society for Psychical Research*, Vol. 9, July 1902, pp. 265-266. (The title of this entry is mine. L.S.)
137. *Journal of the Society for Psychical Research*, Vol. 9, October 1902, pp. 275-276. (The title of this entry is mine. L.S.)
138. *Journal of the Society for Psychical Research*, Vol. 9, December 1902, pp. 308-310. (The title of this entry is mine. L.S.)

139. *Journal of the Society for Psychical Research*, Vol. 9, December 1902, pp. 311-312. (The title of this entry is mine. L.S.)

140. *Journal of the Society for Psychical Research*, Vol. 9, December 1902, p. 313. (The title of this entry is mine. L.S.)

141. *Journal of the Society for Psychical Research*, Vol. 9, December 1902, pp. 313-314. (The title of this entry is mine. L.S.)

142. Seabrook, *Your Soul Lives Forever*, p. 349. (The title of this entry is mine. L.S.)

143. *Journal of the Society for Psychical Research*, Vol. 18, 1917-1918, pp. 19-20. (The title of this entry is mine. L.S.)

144. *Journal of the Society for Psychical Research*, Vol. 18, 1917-1918, p. 21. (The title of this entry is mine. L.S.)

145. Seabrook, *Your Soul Lives Forever*, pp. 64-65. (The title of this entry is mine. L.S.)

146. *Journal of the Society for Psychical Research*, Vol. 19, 1919-1920, pp. 4-5. (The title of this entry is mine. L.S.)

147. *Journal of the Society for Psychical Research*, Vol. 19, 1919-1920, p. 8. (The title of this entry is mine. L.S.)

148. *Journal of the Society for Psychical Research*, Vol. 19, 1919-1920, pp. 9-10. (The title of this entry is mine. L.S.)

149. Conan Doyle, the brilliant Victorian author, was an ardent spiritualist and keen student of the paranormal, which has led some to doubt that he was actually the creator of the ultra-objective, atheistically inclined, scientifically minded fictional detective Sherlock Holmes—a fascinating conspiracy theory if there ever was one. Note: I have created, edited, and published an edition of Conan Doyle's splendid book, *The New Revelation* (Sea Raven Press, 2021).

150. *Journal of the Society for Psychical Research*, Vol. 19, 1919-1920, pp. 10-12. (The title of this entry is mine. L.S.)

151. *Journal of the Society for Psychical Research*, Vol. 19, February-March 1919, p. 30. (The title of this entry is mine. L.S.)

152. *Journal of the Society for Psychical Research*, Vol. 19, April 1919, pp. 41-42. (The title of this entry is mine. L.S.)

153. *Journal of the Society for Psychical Research*, Vol. 19, April 1919, pp. 45-46. (The title of this entry is mine. L.S.)

154. *Journal of the Society for Psychical Research*, Vol. 19, April 1919, p. 46. (The title of this entry is mine. L.S.)

155. *Journal of the Society for Psychical Research*, Vol. 19, April 1919, p. 47. (The title of this entry is mine. L.S.)

156. *Journal of the Society for Psychical Research*, Vol. 19, July 1919, pp. 77-80. (The title of this entry is mine. L.S.)

157. *Journal of the Society for Psychical Research*, Vol. 19, July 1919, pp. 80-82. (The title of this entry is mine. L.S.)

158. *Journal of the Society for Psychical Research*, Vol. 19, July 1919, pp. 84-86. (The title of this entry is mine. L.S.)

159. *Journal of the Society for Psychical Research*, Vol. 19, November 1920, p. 262. (The title of this entry is mine. L.S.)

160. *Journal of the Society for Psychical Research*, Vol. 7, 1895-1896, pp. 7-8. (The title of this entry is mine. L.S.)

161. *Journal of the Society for Psychical Research*, Vol. 7, 1895-1896, pp. 8-9. (The title of this entry is mine. L.S.)

162. *Journal of the Society for Psychical Research*, Vol. 7, January 1895, p. 9. (The title of this entry is mine. L.S.)

163. *Journal of the Society for Psychical Research*, Vol. 7, January 1895, pp. 9-10. (The title of this entry is mine. L.S.)

164. *Journal of the Society for Psychical Research*, Vol. 7, January 1895, p. 10. (The title of this entry is mine. L.S.)

165. *Journal of the Society for Psychical Research*, Vol. 7, February 1895, pp. 26-28. (The title of this entry is mine. L.S.)

166. *Journal of the Society for Psychical Research*, Vol. 7, March-April 1895, p. 79. (The title of this entry is mine. L.S.)
167. *Journal of the Society for Psychical Research*, Vol. 7, March-April 1895, p. 79. (The title of this entry is mine. L.S.)
168. *Journal of the Society for Psychical Research*, Vol. 7, March-April 1895, p. 80. (The title of this entry is mine. L.S.)
169. *Journal of the Society for Psychical Research*, Vol. 7, March-April 1895, p. 80. (The title of this entry is mine. L.S.)
170. *Journal of the Society for Psychical Research*, Vol. 7, March-April 1895, p. 80. (The title of this entry is mine. L.S.)
171. *Journal of the Society for Psychical Research*, Vol. 7, March-April 1895, p. 80. (The title of this entry is mine. L.S.)
172. *Journal of the Society for Psychical Research*, Vol. 7, March-April 1895, p. 80. (The title of this entry is mine. L.S.)
173. *Journal of the Society for Psychical Research*, Vol. 7, March-April 1895, p. 80. (The title of this entry is mine. L.S.)
174. *Journal of the Society for Psychical Research*, Vol. 7, March-April 1895, p. 80. (The title of this entry is mine. L.S.)
175. Seabrook, *Your Soul Lives Forever*, p. 52. (The title of this entry is mine. L.S.)
176. *Journal of the Society for Psychical Research*, Vol. 7, June 1895, p. 99. (The title of this entry is mine. L.S.)
177. *Journal of the Society for Psychical Research*, Vol. 7, June 1895, pp. 100-101. (The title of this entry is mine. L.S.)
178. *Journal of the Society for Psychical Research*, Vol. 7, June 1895, pp. 106-107. (The title of this entry is mine. L.S.)
179. *Journal of the Society for Psychical Research*, Vol. 7, June 1895, p. 110. (The title of this entry is mine. L.S.)
180. *Journal of the Society for Psychical Research*, Vol. 7, July 1895, p. 121. (The title of this entry is mine. L.S.)
181. *Journal of the Society for Psychical Research*, Vol. 7, April 1896, p. 244. (The title of this entry is mine. L.S.)
182. *Journal of the Society for Psychical Research*, Vol. 7, May 1896, p. 251. (The title of this entry is mine. L.S.)
183. *Journal of the Society for Psychical Research*, Vol. 7, May 1896, p. 255. (The title of this entry is mine. L.S.)
184. *Journal of the Society for Psychical Research*, Vol. 7, May 1896, p. 259. (The title of this entry is mine. L.S.)
185. *Journal of the Society for Psychical Research*, Vol. 7, June 1896, pp. 271-272. (The title of this entry is mine. L.S.)
186. Seabrook, *Your Soul Lives Forever*, pp. 55-56. (The title of this entry is mine. L.S.)
187. *Journal of the Society for Psychical Research*, Vol. 7, December 1896, pp. 329-330. (The title of this entry is mine. L.S.)
188. *Journal of the Society for Psychical Research*, Vol. 7, December 1896, pp. 332-333, 334. (The title of this entry is mine. L.S.)
189. *Journal of the Society for Psychical Research*, Vol. 7, December 1896, pp. 335-338. (The title of this entry is mine. L.S.)
190. *Journal of the Society for Psychical Research*, Vol. 3, April 1887, p. 83. (The title of this entry is mine. L.S.)
191. *Journal of the Society for Psychical Research*, Vol. 3, April 1887, pp. 84-85. (The title of this entry is mine. L.S.)
192. Harrison, pp. 101-104. (The title of this entry is mine. L.S.)
193. *Journal of the Society for Psychical Research*, Vol. 3, July 1887, pp. 135-136. (The title of this entry is mine. L.S.)
194. *Journal of the Society for Psychical Research*, Vol. 3, January 1888, p. 207. (The title of this entry is mine. L.S.)
195. *Journal of the Society for Psychical Research*, Vol. 3, January 1888, p. 208. (The title of this entry is mine. L.S.)
196. Seabrook, *Your Soul Lives Forever*, pp. 57-58. (The title of this entry is mine. L.S.)
197. Seabrook, *Your Soul Lives Forever*, pp. 52-53. (The title of this entry is mine. L.S.)
198. *Journal of the Society for Psychical Research*, Vol. 3, April 1888, pp. 241-242. (The title of this entry is mine. L.S.)

199. *Journal of the Society for Psychical Research*, Vol. 3, April 1888, pp. 243-244. (The title of this entry is mine. L.S.)
200. *Journal of the Society for Psychical Research*, Vol. 3, April 1888, pp. 244-245. (The title of this entry is mine. L.S.)
201. *Journal of the Society for Psychical Research*, Vol. 3, April 1888, p. 246. (The title of this entry is mine. L.S.)
202. *Journal of the Society for Psychical Research*, Vol. 3, April 1888, pp. 246-247. (The title of this entry is mine. L.S.)
203. *Journal of the Society for Psychical Research*, Vol. 3, April 1888, p. 247. (The title of this entry is mine. L.S.)
204. *Journal of the Society for Psychical Research*, Vol. 3, April 1888, pp. 248-249. (The title of this entry is mine. L.S.)
205. *Journal of the Society for Psychical Research*, Vol. 3, April 1888, pp. 250-252. (The title of this entry is mine. L.S.)
206. *Journal of the Society for Psychical Research*, Vol. 3, April 1888, p. 242. (The title of this entry is mine. L.S.)
207. *Journal of the Society for Psychical Research*, Vol. 3, April 1888, p. 244. (The title of this entry is mine. L.S.)
208. *Journal of the Society for Psychical Research*, Vol. 3, April 1888, p. 246. (The title of this entry is mine. L.S.)
209. *Journal of the Society for Psychical Research*, Vol. 3, April 1888, p. 247. (The title of this entry is mine. L.S.)
210. *Journal of the Society for Psychical Research*, Vol. 3, April 1888, p. 248. (The title of this entry is mine. L.S.)
211. *Journal of the Society for Psychical Research*, Vol. 3, April 1888, p. 252. (The title of this entry is mine. L.S.)
212. *Journal of the Society for Psychical Research*, Vol. 3, April 1888, p. 243. (The title of this entry is mine. L.S.)
213. *Journal of the Society for Psychical Research*, Vol. 3, April 1888, p. 243. (The title of this entry is mine. L.S.)
214. *Journal of the Society for Psychical Research*, Vol. 3, April 1888, p. 244. (The title of this entry is mine. L.S.)
215. *Journal of the Society for Psychical Research*, Vol. 3, April 1888, pp. 245-246. (The title of this entry is mine. L.S.)
216. *Journal of the Society for Psychical Research*, Vol. 3, April 1888, p. 246. (The title of this entry is mine. L.S.)
217. *Journal of the Society for Psychical Research*, Vol. 3, April 1888, p. 249. (The title of this entry is mine. L.S.)
218. *Journal of the Society for Psychical Research*, Vol. 3, April 1888, pp. 249-250. (The title of this entry is mine. L.S.)
219. *Journal of the Society for Psychical Research*, Vol. 3, April 1888, pp. 252-253. (The title of this entry is mine. L.S.)
220. Seabrook, *Your Soul Lives Forever*, p. 53. (The title of this entry is mine. L.S.)
221. *Journal of the Society for Psychical Research*, Vol. 3, April 1888, p. 255. (The title of this entry is mine. L.S.)
222. *Journal of the Society for Psychical Research*, Vol. 3, May 1888, pp. 269-270, 271. (The title of this entry is mine. L.S.)
223. *Journal of the Society for Psychical Research*, Vol. 3, May 1888, p. 272. (The title of this entry is mine. L.S.)
224. *Journal of the Society for Psychical Research*, Vol. 3, July 1888, pp. 292-294. (The title of this entry is mine. L.S.)
225. *Journal of the Society for Psychical Research*, Vol. 3, December 1888, p. 355. (The title of this entry is mine. L.S.)
226. Seabrook, *Your Soul Lives Forever*, pp. 65-66. (The title of this entry is mine. L.S.)
227. Seabrook, *Your Soul Lives Forever*, pp. 60-64. (The title of this entry is mine. L.S.)

228. *Journal of the Society for Psychical Research*, Vol. 3, December 1888, pp. 356-357. (The title of this entry is mine. L.S.)
229. *Journal of the Society for Psychical Research*, Vol. 3, December 1888, p. 358. (The title of this entry is mine. L.S.)
230. *Journal of the Society for Psychical Research*, Vol. 3, December 1888, pp. 359-360. (The title of this entry is mine. L.S.)
231. Finch, pp. 24-26. (The title of this entry is mine. L.S.)
232. Finch, pp. 102-103. (The title of this entry is mine. L.S.)
233. Finch, pp. 113-117.
234. Finch, p. 133. (The title of this entry is mine. L.S.)
235. Finch, pp. 218-221. (The title of this entry is mine. L.S.)
236. Finch, pp. 252-253. (The title of this entry is mine. L.S.)
237. Finch, pp. 372-373. (The title of this entry is mine. L.S.)
238. Mason, pp. 23-24. (The title of this entry is mine. L.S.)
239. Finch, pp. 374-375. (The title of this entry is mine. L.S.)
240. Seabrook, *Your Soul Lives Forever*, pp. 172-173. (The title of this entry is mine. L.S.)
241. Myers, pp. 266-268. (The title of this entry is mine. L.S.)
242. MacKenna, pp. 26-28. (The title of this entry is mine. L.S.)
243. M. B. Wallace, pp. xv-xix. (The title of this entry is mine. L.S.)
244. Lang, pp. 87-88. (The title of this entry is mine. L.S.)
245. Lang, p. 87. (The title of this entry is mine. L.S.)
246. Taylor, p. 241. (The title of this entry is mine. L.S.)
247. Lang, pp. 104-105. (The title of this entry is mine. L.S.)
248. Lombroso, pp. 236-237. (The title of this entry is mine. L.S.)
249. Seabrook, *Your Soul Lives Forever*, pp. 308-309. (The title of this entry is mine. L.S.)
250. Lombroso, pp. 283-284. (The title of this entry is mine. L.S.)
251. Lombroso, pp. 284-285. (The title of this entry is mine. L.S.)
252. Lombroso, p. 287. (The title of this entry is mine. L.S.)
253. Lombroso, pp. 287-288. (The title of this entry is mine. L.S.)
254. Lombroso, p. 289. (The title of this entry is mine. L.S.)
255. Lombroso, pp. 289-290. (The title of this entry is mine. L.S.)
256. Seabrook, *Your Soul Lives Forever*, p. 53. (The title of this entry is mine. L.S.)
257. Lombroso, pp. 290-292. (The title of this entry is mine. L.S.)
258. Lombroso, pp. 293-294. (The title of this entry is mine. L.S.)
259. Lombroso, pp. 294-296. (The title of this entry is mine. L.S.)
260. Seabrook, *Your Soul Lives Forever*, pp. 53-54. (The title of this entry is mine. L.S.)
261. Lombroso, pp. 296-297. (The title of this entry is mine. L.S.)
262. J. A. Hill, *Psychical Investigations*, p. 228. (The title of this entry is mine. L.S.)
263. J. A. Hill, *Psychical Investigations*, p. 270. (The title of this entry is mine. L.S.)
264. Gurney, Myers, and Podmore, Vol. 1, p. 152. (The title of this entry is mine. L.S.)
265. Gurney, Myers, and Podmore, Vol. 1, pp. 152-153. (The title of this entry is mine. L.S.)
266. Seabrook, *Your Soul Lives Forever*, pp. 54-55. (The title of this entry is mine. L.S.)
267. Gurney, Myers, and Podmore, Vol. 1, p. 414. (The title of this entry is mine. L.S.)
268. Gurney, Myers, and Podmore, Vol. 1, p. 416. (The title of this entry is mine. L.S.)
269. Gurney, Myers, and Podmore, Vol. 1, pp. 431-432. (The title of this entry is mine. L.S.)
270. Gurney, Myers, and Podmore, Vol. 1, pp. 435-436. (The title of this entry is mine. L.S.)
271. Gurney, Myers, and Podmore, Vol. 1, pp. 445-447. (The title of this entry is mine. L.S.)
272. Gurney, Myers, and Podmore, Vol. 1, pp. 447-448. (The title of this entry is mine. L.S.)
273. Gurney, Myers, and Podmore, Vol. 1, p. 448. (The title of this entry is mine. L.S.)
274. Gurney, Myers, and Podmore, Vol. 1, pp. 451-452. (The title of this entry is mine. L.S.)
275. Gurney, Myers, and Podmore, Vol. 1, pp. 506-507. (The title of this entry is mine. L.S.)
276. Gurney, Myers, and Podmore, Vol. 1, p. 513. (The title of this entry is mine. L.S.)
277. Gurney, Myers, and Podmore, Vol. 1, p. 515. (The title of this entry is mine. L.S.)
278. Gurney, Myers, and Podmore, Vol. 1, p. 516. (The title of this entry is mine. L.S.)

279. Gurney, Myers, and Podmore, Vol. 1, p. 516. (The title of this entry is mine. L.S.)
280. Gurney, Myers, and Podmore, Vol. 1, pp. 517-518. (The title of this entry is mine. L.S.)
281. Gurney, Myers, and Podmore, Vol. 1, pp. 520-521. (The title of this entry is mine. L.S.)
282. Gurney, Myers, and Podmore, Vol. 1, p. 521. (The title of this entry is mine. L.S.)
283. Gurney, Myers, and Podmore, Vol. 1, pp. 522-523. (The title of this entry is mine. L.S.)
284. Gurney, Myers, and Podmore, Vol. 1, p. 527. (The title of this entry is mine. L.S.)
285. Gurney, Myers, and Podmore, Vol. 1, p. 530. (The title of this entry is mine. L.S.)
286. Gurney, Myers, and Podmore, Vol. 1, pp. 531-532. (The title of this entry is mine. L.S.)
287. Gurney, Myers, and Podmore, Vol. 1, pp. 532-533. (The title of this entry is mine. L.S.)
288. Gurney, Myers, and Podmore, Vol. 1, p. 534. (The title of this entry is mine. L.S.)
289. Gurney, Myers, and Podmore, Vol. 1, pp. 540-541. (The title of this entry is mine. L.S.)
290. Gurney, Myers, and Podmore, Vol. 1, pp. 542-543. (The title of this entry is mine. L.S.)
291. Gurney, Myers, and Podmore, Vol. 1, pp. 544-545. (The title of this entry is mine. L.S.)
292. Gurney, Myers, and Podmore, Vol. 1, p. 548. (The title of this entry is mine. L.S.)
293. Dering, pp. 185-186. (The title of this entry is mine. L.S.)
294. Gurney, Myers, and Podmore, Vol. 1, p. 552. (The title of this entry is mine. L.S.)
295. Dyer, pp. 252-253. (The title of this entry is mine. L.S.)
296. Dyer, pp. 277-278. (The title of this entry is mine. L.S.)
297. Dyer, pp. 127, 128-129. (The title of this entry is mine. L.S.)
298. Dyer, pp. 129-130. (The title of this entry is mine. L.S.)
299. Dyer, pp. 130-131. (The title of this entry is mine. L.S.)
300. Curtin, pp. 178-180. (The title of this entry is mine. L.S.)
301. Harrison, *Rifts in the Veil*, pp. 97-98. (The title of this entry is mine. L.S.)
302. Harrison, *Rifts in the Veil*, pp. 17-22. (The title of this entry is mine. L.S.)
303. Harrison, *Spirits Before Our Eyes*, pp. 27-28. (The title of this entry is mine. L.S.)
304. Harrison, *Spirits Before Our Eyes*, pp. 28-29. (The title of this entry is mine. L.S.)
305. Harrison, *Spirits Before Our Eyes*, pp. 29-30. (The title of this entry is mine. L.S.)
306. Harrison, *Spirits Before Our Eyes*, p. 31. (The title of this entry is mine. L.S.)
307. Harrison, *Spirits Before Our Eyes*, p. 32. (The title of this entry is mine. L.S.)
308. Seabrook, *Your Soul Lives Forever*, pp. 98-99. (The title of this entry is mine. L.S.)
309. Barrett, pp. 118-119. (The title of this entry is mine. L.S.)
310. Flammarion, p. 108. (The title of this entry is mine. L.S.)
311. Flammarion, p. 100. (The title of this entry is mine. L.S.)
312. Carrington, pp. 96-97. (The title of this entry is mine. L.S.)
313. Carrington, pp. 93-96. (The title of this entry is mine. L.S.)
314. Saville, pp. 189-197. (The title of this entry is mine. L.S.)
315. Owen, pp. 231-232. (The title of this entry is mine. L.S.)
316. Owen, pp. 233-235. (The title of this entry is mine. L.S.)
317. Owen, p. 236. See also Crowe, pp. 169-171. (The title of this entry is mine. L.S.)
318. Owen, pp. 237-238. (The title of this entry is mine. L.S.)
319. Owen, pp. 249-250. (The title of this entry is mine. L.S.)
320. Owen, pp. 251-253. (The title of this entry is mine. L.S.)
321. Owen, p. 266. (The title of this entry is mine. L.S.)
322. Owen, pp. 268-270. (The title of this entry is mine. L.S.)
323. Campbell, p. 242. (The title of this entry is mine. L.S.)
324. Crowe, pp. 112-113. (The title of this entry is mine. L.S.)
325. Crowe, pp. 149-150. (The title of this entry is mine. L.S.)
326. Crowe, pp. 150-151. (The title of this entry is mine. L.S.)
327. Crowe, p. 151. (The title of this entry is mine. L.S.)
328. Crowe, p. 168. (The title of this entry is mine. L.S.)
329. Crowe, pp. 168-169. (The title of this entry is mine. L.S.)
330. Crowe, p. 169. (The title of this entry is mine. L.S.)
331. Crowe, pp. 174-175. (The title of this entry is mine. L.S.)
332. Crowe, p. 187. (The title of this entry is mine. L.S.)

333. Crowe, p. 274. (The title of this entry is mine. L.S.)
334. Crowe, p. 277. (The title of this entry is mine. L.S.)
335. Crowe, p. 278. (The title of this entry is mine. L.S.)
336. Crowe, pp. 282-283. (The title of this entry is mine. L.S.)
337. Crowe, pp. 305-307, 313. (The title of this entry is mine. L.S.)
338. Crowe, pp. 329-330. (The title of this entry is mine. L.S.)
339. Crowe, p. 330. (The title of this entry is mine. L.S.)
340. Crowe, pp. 331-332. (The title of this entry is mine. L.S.)
341. Crowe, p. 332. (The title of this entry is mine. L.S.)
342. Crowe, p. 341. (The title of this entry is mine. L.S.)
343. Crowe, p. 342. (The title of this entry is mine. L.S.)
344. Crowe, pp. 414-415. (The title of this entry is mine. L.S.)
345. Crowe, p. 421. (The title of this entry is mine. L.S.)
346. Crowe, p. 421. (The title of this entry is mine. L.S.)
347. Crowe, p. 423. (The title of this entry is mine. L.S.)
348. Crowe, p. 425. (The title of this entry is mine. L.S.)
349. Carrington, *Modern Psychical Phenomena*, pp. 121-122. (The title of this appendix is mine. L.S.)

BIBLIOGRAPHY

And Suggested Reading

Baldwin, Mrs. Alfred. *The Shadow on the Blind and Other Ghost Stories.* London, UK: J. M. Dent and Co., 1895.
Barrett, Harrison Delivan (ed.). *Life Work of Mrs. Cora L. V. Richmond.* Chicago, IL: National Spiritualists Association of the U.S.A., 1895.
Barrett, William F. *On the Threshold of a New World of Thought: An Examination of the Phenomena of Spiritualism.* London, UK: Kegan Paul, Trench, Trübner and Co., 1908.
Blavatsky, Helena Petrovna. *The Secret Doctrine: The Synthesis of Science, Religion, and Philosophy.* London, UK: Theosophical Publishing Society, 1893.
Brougham, Henry. *The Life and Times of Henry Lord Brougham.* 3 vols. Edinburgh, Scotland: William Blackwood and Sons, 1871.
Brougham, W. E. *The Black Cottage, Or, Tom Brace's Picture: A Ghost Story for the Fireside.* London, UK: Tinsley Brothers, 1880.
Campbell, John Gregorson. *Superstitions of the Highlands and Islands of Scotland.* Glasgow, Scotland: James MacLehose and Sons, 1900.
Carrington, Hereward. *True Ghost Stories.* New York: J. S. Olgilvie Publishing Co., 1915.
———. *Modern Psychical Phenomena: Recent Researches and Speculations.* New York: Dodd, Mead and Co., 1919.
Clodd, Edward. *The Question, "If a Man Die, Shall He Live Again?"* London, UK: Grant Richards, 1917.
Crawford, William Jackson. *Experiments in Psychical Science: Levitation, Contact, and the Direct Voice.* New York: E. P. Dutton and Co., 1919.
Crowe, Catherine. *The Night-Side of Nature; Or, Ghosts and Ghost-Seers.* New York: J. S. Redfield, 1850.
Curtin, Jeremiah. *Tales of the Fairies and of the Ghost World: Collected From Oral Tradition in South-West Munster.* Boson, MA: Little, Brown and Co., 1895.
Curtiss, Harriette Augusta, and Frank Homer Curtiss. *The Key to the Universe: Or, A Spiritual Interpretation of Numbers and Symbols.* Washington, D.C.: Curtiss Philosophic Book Co., 1917.
Davis, Andrew Jackson. *Death and the After-life: Eight Evening Lectures on the Summer-land.* Rochester, NY: Austin Publishing Co., 1911.
Dering, Edward Heneage. *Memoirs of Georgiana, Lady Chatterton, With Some Passages From Her Diary.* London, UK: Hurst and Blackett, 1878.
Doyle, Arthur Conan. *The New Revelation* (reprint of the 1918 edition)

Editor: Lochlainn Seabrook. Spring Hill, TN: Sea Raven Press, 2021.
——. *The Case for Spirit Photography*. New York: George H. Doran Co., 1923.
Dresser, Horatio Willis. *On the Threshold of the Spiritual World: A Study of Life and Death Over There*. New York: George Sully ad Co., 1919.
——. *A History of the New Thought Movement*. New York: Thomas Y. Crowell Co., 1919.
Dyer, Thomas Firminger Thiselton. *The Ghost World*. London, UK: Ward and Downey, 1898.
Fanu, Joseph Sheridan Le. *Ghost Stories and Tales of Mystery*. Dublin, Ireland: James McGlashan, 1851.
Finch, Laura I. *The Annals of Psychical Science*. Vol. 4, July-December 1906. London, UK: self-published, 1906.
Flammarion, Camille. *The Unknown*. New York: Harper and Brothers, 1900.
French, Joseph Lewis (ed.). *The Best Ghost Stories*. New York: Boni and Liveright, 1919.
Galloway, George. *The Idea of Immortality: Its Development and Value*. Edinburgh, Scotland: T. and T. Clark, 1919.
Gurney, Edmund, Frederic W. H. Myers, and Frank Podmore. *Phantasms of the Living*. 2 vols. London, UK: The Society for Psychical Research, 1886.
Hall, Granville Stanley. *Jesus, the Christ, in the Light of Psychology*. 2 vols. Garden City, NY: Doubleday, Page and Co., 1917.
Hall, Spencer Timothy. *Days in Derbyshire*. London, UK: Simpkin, Marshall, and Co., 1863.
Harrison, William H. *Rifts in the Veil*. London, UK: self-published, 1878.
——. *Spirits Before Our Eyes*. London, UK: self-published, 1879.
Hill, John Arthur. *Psychical Investigations: Some Personally-Observed Proofs of Survival*. New York: George H. Doran Co., 1917.
——. *Spiritualism: Its History, Phenomena and Doctrine*. London, UK: Cassell and Co., 1918.
Holland, W. Bob (ed.). *Twenty-Five Ghost Stories*. New York: J. Ogilvie and Co., 1904.
Houdini, Harry. *A Magician Among the Spirits*. New York: Harper and Brothers, 1924.
Hudson, Thomson Jay. *A Scientific Demonstration of the Future Life*. Chicago, IL: A. C. McClurg and Co., 1904.
Hyslop, James Hervey. *Life After Death: Problems of the Future Life and Its Nature*. New York: E. P. Dutton and Co., 1918.
James, Montague Rhodes. *Ghost-stories of an Antiquary*. London, UK: Edward Arnold, 1913.
Jarvis, T. M. (ed.). *Accredited Ghost Stories*. London, UK: J. Andrews, 1823.
Journal of the American Society for Psychical Research. 1884-present. York, PA: American Society for Psychical Research (self-published).
Journal of the Society of Psychical Research. 1882-present. London, UK: The

Society's Rooms (self-published).
King, Basil. *The Abolishing of Death*. New York: Cosmopolitan Book Corp., 1919.
Lane, Charles Arthur. *Illustrated Notes on English Church History*. London, UK: Society for Promoting Christian Knowledge, 1888.
Lang, Andrew. *The Book of Dreams and Ghosts*. London, UK: Longmans, Green, and Co., 1899.
Lees, Robert James. *Through the Mists, Or, Leaves from the Autobiography of a Soul in Paradise*. London, UK: William Rider and Son, 1920.
Linskill, W. T. *St. Andrews Ghost Stories*. St. Andrews, Scotland: J and G. Innes, 1921.
Lodge, Oliver. *The Survival of Man: A Study in Unrecognised Human Faculty*. London, UK: Methuen and Co., 1916.
———. *Raymond, Or, Life and Death: With Examples of the Evidence for Survival of Memory and Affection After Death*. New York: George H. Doran Co., 1916.
Lombroso, Cesare. *After Death—What?: Spiritistic Phenomena and Their Interpretation*. Boston, MA: Small, Maynard and Co., 1909.
MacKenna, Robert William. *The Adventure of Death*. London, UK: John Murray, 1916.
Mason, Rufus Osgood. *Telepathy and the Subliminal Self: An Account of Recent Investigations Regarding Hypnotism, Automatism, Dreams, Phantasms, and Related Phenomena*. New York: Henry Holt and Co., 1897.
McComb, Samuel. *The Future Life in the Light of Modern Inquiry*. New York: Dodd, Mead and Co., 1919.
McSpadden, Joseph Walker (ed.). *Famous Ghost Stories*. Chicago, IL: Thomas Y. Crowell Co., 1919.
Middleton, Jessie Adelaide. *The White Ghost Book*. London, UK: Cassell and Co., 1916.
Mulford, Prentice. *The Gift of Spirit*. London, UK: William Rider and Son, 1917.
Mumler, William H. *The Personal Experiences of W. H. Mumler in Spirit-Photography*. Boston: Colby and Rich, 1875.
Myers, Frederic W. H. *Human Personality and Its Survival After Bodily Death*. London, UK: Longmans, Green, and Co., 1939.
Nicoll, William Robertson. *Reunion in Eternity*. New York: George H. Doran, 1919.
O'Donnell, Elliott. *Scottish Ghost Stories*. London, UK: Kegan Paul, Trench, Trübner and Co., 1911.
———. *Animal Ghosts: Or, Animal Hauntings and the Hereafter*. London, UK: William Rider and Son, 1913.
Owen, Robert Dale. *Footfalls on the Boundary of Another World*. London, UK: Trübner and Co., 1860.
Peebles, J. M. *Christ, The Corner-Stone of Spiritualism*. London, UK: James Burns, 1878.
Phelon, W. P. *Healing, Causes and Effects*. Chicago, IL: Hermetic

Publishing Co., 1898.
Rhodes, Daniel Pomeroy. *Our Immortality*. New York: Macmillan Co., 1919.
Rhys, Ernest. *The Haunters and the Haunted: Ghost Stories and Tales of the Supernatural*. London, UK: Daniel O'Connor, 1921.
Rice, Ervin Alvin. *Why Are We Here?: An Answer*. Chicago, IL: P. F. Pettibone and Co., 1913.
Richardson, Cyril Albert. *Spiritual Pluralism and Recent Philosophy*. Cambridge, UK: Cambridge University Press, 1919.
Richardson, John Emmett. *The Great Work: The Constructive Principle of Nature in Individual Life*. Chicago, IL: Indo-American Book Co., 1912.
Richmond, Cora Lodencia Veronica. *Psychosophy*. 6 vols. No location: self-published, 1890.
Savile, Bourchier Wrey. *Apparitions: A Narrative of Facts*. London, UK: Longman's and Co., 1874.
Scarborough, Dorothy (ed.). *Famous Modern Ghost Stories*. New York: G. P. Putnam's Sons, 1921.
Sciens (pseudonym). *How to Speak With the Dead: A Practical Handbook*. London, UK: Kegan Paul, Trench, Trübner and Co., 1918.
Seabrook, Lochlainn. *The Goddess Dictionary of Words and Phrases: Introducing a New Core Vocabulary for the Women's Spirituality Movement*. 1997. Franklin, TN: Sea Raven Press, 2010 ed.
——. *Aphrodite's Trade: The Hidden History of Prostitution Unveiled*. 1998. Franklin, TN: Sea Raven Press, 2011 ed.
——. *Britannia Rules: Goddess-Worship in Ancient Anglo-Celtic Society - An Academic Look at the United Kingdom's Matricentric Spiritual Past*. 1999. Franklin, TN: Sea Raven Press, 2010 ed.
——. *The Book of Kelle: An Introduction to Goddess-Worship and the Great Celtic Mother-Goddess Kelle, Original Blessed Lady of Ireland*. 1999. Franklin, TN: Sea Raven Press, 2010 ed.
——. *UFOs and Aliens: The Complete Guidebook*. Spring Hill, TN: Sea Raven Press, 2005.
——. *Carnton Plantation Ghost Stories: True Tales of the Unexplained from Tennessee's Most Haunted Civil War House!* 2005. Franklin, TN, 2016 ed.
——. *Christmas Before Christianity: How the Birthday of the "Sun" Became the Birthday of the "Son."* Franklin, TN: Sea Raven Press, 2010.
——. *Jesus and the Law of Attraction: The Bible-Based Guide to Creating Perfect Health, Wealth, and Happiness Following Christ's Simple Formula*. Franklin, TN: Sea Raven Press, 2013.
——. *The Bible and the Law of Attraction: 99 Teachings of Jesus, the Apostles, and the Prophets*. Franklin, TN: Sea Raven Press, 2013.
——. *Christ Is All and In All: Rediscovering Your Divine Nature and the Kingdom Within*. Franklin, TN: Sea Raven Press, 2014.
——. *Jesus and the Gospel of Q: Christ's Pre-Christian Teachings As Recorded in the New Testament*. Spring Hill, TN: Sea Raven Press, 2014.
——. *Seabrook's Bible Dictionary of Traditional and Mystical Christian*

Doctrines. Spring Hill, TN: Sea Raven Press, 2016.

——. *Victorian Confederate Poetry: The Southern Cause in Verse, 1861-1901.* Spring Hill, TN: Sea Raven Press, 2018.

——. (editor) *The New Revelation.* Arthur Conan Doyle. Spring Hill, TN: Sea Raven Press, 2021.

——. *Victorian Hernia Cures: Nonsurgical Self-Treatment of Inguinal Hernia.* Spring Hill, TN: Sea Raven Press, 2022.

——. *The Martian Anomalies: A Photographic Search for Intelligent Life on Mars.* Spring Hill, TN: Sea Raven Press, 2022.

——. (editor) *Mysterious Invaders: Twelve Famous 20th-Century Scientists Confront the UFO Phenomenon.* Cody, WY: Sea Raven Press, 2024.

——. (editor) *Your Soul Lives Forever: Documented Victorian Case Studies Proving Consciousness Survives Death.* Cody, WY: Sea Raven Press, 2024.

——. *The Greatest Jesus Mystery of All Time: Where Was Christ Between the Ages of 12 and 30?* Cody, WY: Sea Raven Press, 2024.

Sinnett, Alfred Percy. *The Occult World.* London, UK: Trübner and Co., 1884.

Smith, Hester Travers. *Voices from the Void: Six Years' Experience in Automatic Communications.* London, UK: William Rider and Son, 1919.

Solovyoff, Vsevolod Sergyeevich. *A Modern Priestess of Isis.* London, UK: Longmans, Green, and Co., 1895.

Stead, William Thomas. *Real Ghost Stories.* London, UK: Grant Richards, 1897.

Taylor, John Traill. *The Veil Lifted: Modern Developments of Spirit Photography.* London, UK: Whittaker and Co., 1894.

Taylor, Meadows. *The Story of My Life.* Edinburgh, Scotland: William Blackwood and Sons, 1878.

Wallace, Alfred Russel. *On Miracles and Modern Spiritualism: Three Essays.* London, UK: James Burns, 1875.

Wallace, Mary Bruce. *The Thinning of the Veil: A Record of Experience.* New York: Dodd, Mead and Co., 1919.

Wilcox, Ella Wheeler. *Poems of Pleasure.* New York: Belford Co., 1888.

Wood, J. G. *Man and Beast: Here and Hereafter.* 2 vols. London, UK: Daldy, Isbister, and Co., 1874.

> How ill this taper burns! Ha! who comes here?
> I think it is the weakness of mine eyes
> That shapes this monstrous apparition.
> It comes upon me. Art thou anything?
> Art thou some god, some angel, or some devil,
> That makest my blood cold and my hair to stare?
> Speak to me what thou art.
>
> *Shakespeare, 1599*

INDEX

INCLUDES TOPICS, PEOPLE, KEYWORDS, KEY PHRASES, & SPELLING VARIATIONS
(NOTE: I USE A COMBINATION OF MANUAL AND AUTOMATIC INDEXING, WHICH MAY CAUSE OCCASIONAL LISTING PECULIARITIES.)

Aberdeenshire, Scotland, 271
Aberystwith, Wales, 321
account, 13, 15, 19, 32, 34-36, 43, 46, 52, 58, 64, 69, 70, 74, 77, 78, 85, 101, 102, 105, 109, 113, 115, 117, 118, 126, 127, 129, 130, 132, 140, 146-148, 151, 160, 163, 168, 176, 180, 183, 199, 200, 204, 215-218, 222, 224, 231, 234, 235, 248, 251, 254, 255, 258-260, 269, 274, 275, 278, 280, 282, 283, 295, 311, 326, 343
action, 99, 119, 130, 137, 143, 147, 232, 233, 283
Acton Beauchamp, UK, 210, 216
Adams, J. M. Goold, 65
Aden, Scotland, 271
aeolian harp, 221
affair, 229, 230, 268
Africa, 93, 121, 293
After Life, 11
Aksakof, Sophie, 289
Albany, NY, 172
Alcester, UK, 90
Aldershot, UK, 172
Alderson, Jane S., 204
Alexander, Helen, 235
Alsace, France, 278
alternative health, 365
amalgamation, 146
America, 2, 3, 6, 35, 36, 41, 48, 49, 94, 162, 233, 317
American slavery, 2
Americans, 2
angel, 41, 239, 315, 345
angels, 7, 237, 239, 252, 279
animal, 206, 296, 343
animals, 33, 241, 258, 326, 329
Annecy, France, 249, 250
Antarctica, 365
Appalachia, 365
apparitions, 3, 5-7, 26, 69, 71, 78, 84, 94, 171, 207, 228, 248, 249, 267, 305, 320, 325, 344

Arkwright, Miss E., 141
Armagh Barracks, 205
army, 36, 140, 141, 249
Arras, France, 137
Articles of Confederation, 2
artillery, 185
Ashanti, 143
asleep, 19, 31, 37, 41, 46, 47, 84, 89, 107, 119, 121, 130, 131, 133, 134, 136, 165, 167, 168, 170, 171, 183, 187, 194, 199, 200, 213, 217, 234, 257, 258, 260, 263, 268, 294, 301
astral bodies, 223
astral body, 15, 123, 157, 223, 226, 308
astral light, 220
astral projection, 37, 42, 308
astronomy, 365
atheism, 310
Atkins, Chet, 365
Atkins, H., 121
Atkinson, Miss F., 94
attack, 108, 176, 214, 225, 231, 256, 288
attic stairs, 192
Auchmutz, Helen, 198
aunt, 26, 61, 67, 96, 97, 124, 208, 221, 222, 226, 230, 250, 251, 271, 291, 322
Australia, 64, 89, 218, 273, 274
Austria, 25
Austrian Embassy, 242
Auto Club, London, UK, 244
Av-Meinander, Nicholas O., 169
Ayecroft Hall, 174, 176
Ayrshire, Scotland, 317
Bagot, Mrs. J. W., 170
Bahamas, 161
Bala, Wales, 295
Baltimore, MD, 27, 222
Bancroft House, 258
Bangor, Wales, 235
Banshee, 280, 325
Barber, Reginald, 60

Baring-Gould, Sabine, 281
Barr, Miss L., 256
Basett (marine transport), 89
Bath, UK, 212
battle, 2, 16, 140, 250, 263
Battle of the Lys, 140
Battle of the Piave River, 140
Battle of the Scheldt, 16
Battle of the Somme, 140
beach, 38, 203, 281
beard, 17, 18, 134, 221, 286, 288, 294
Beasley, Miss M. A., 69
bed-curtains, 68, 242
Bedales School, UK, 148
Bedford, UK, 74
bedroom, 15, 19, 33, 34, 38, 40, 41, 46, 52, 53, 55, 70, 77, 84, 91, 101, 103, 104, 107, 108, 117, 119, 124, 131, 132, 136, 137, 152, 157, 161, 170, 182-184, 187-189, 191, 192, 194-196, 205, 207, 210, 213, 216, 224, 242, 255, 256, 263, 273, 293, 294, 314, 318
bedside, 40, 47, 48, 58, 74, 123, 151, 153, 167, 212, 229, 231-233, 235, 253, 255, 258, 261, 286
Belcher, Diana, 16
Belfast, Ireland, 133
bell, 31, 61, 78, 110, 117, 120, 139, 152, 170, 190, 192, 204, 208, 226, 227, 235, 264, 267, 299
bells, 78, 116-118, 120, 121, 187
Benson, Miss M., 86
Bent, Arthur, 161
Bethel, Viner, 161
Better World, 7, 280, 305
Bibby, Ellen, 260
Bible, 3, 22, 56, 95, 271, 331, 344, 365, 367
billiard balls, 67
billiard room, 178
billiards, 178, 179
bilocation, 15, 223, 234
biography, 2, 3, 279, 365
bird, 77, 271
Bird, Isabella, 271
birds, 3
Birmingham Town Hall, 163
Birmingham, UK, 163, 291
birth, 29, 30, 280
Bishop's Frome, UK, 216
Black, Mrs. H. G., 185
Blackheath, UK, 266
Blois, France, 280

blood, 2, 60, 95, 159, 160, 288, 295, 345
Bloomfield, Georgiana, 242
boat, 36, 38, 39, 43, 121, 292, 326-328
bodies, 328
body, 3, 14, 15, 26, 29, 30, 37, 42, 47, 55, 77, 78, 90, 95, 98, 123, 148, 157, 200, 206, 223, 226, 227, 230, 231, 239, 281, 283, 286-288, 303, 305, 308, 311, 312, 321, 322, 325, 329, 366
Boldero, A., 205
Bolland, Mrs. Kate E., 276
Bolland, Theodore J., 174
Bolling, Edith, 365
Bombay, India, 289
Bonchurch, UK, 203, 242
bonnet, 60, 116, 179, 203, 217, 277
bookcase, 66, 117, 118, 184, 185, 225
Boone, Pat, 365
boots, 15, 38, 65, 110, 183, 249
Boston American, 18
Boston Globe, 18
Boston, MA, 62, 139, 295
Boston, Massachusetts, 62
Boulogne-sur Mer, France, 207
Bourke, Australia, 218
Bourne, H. M., 71
Bourne, Louisa, 71
Bournemouth, UK, 141
Bovey Tracy, 269
Bower, Henry, 143
Bowman, Mr. C. H., 66
Bowyer-Bower, Eldred W., 143
boxes, 181, 188, 251
boy, 50, 57, 59, 72, 84, 124, 137, 139, 149, 168, 212, 213, 218, 254, 268, 271, 272, 281, 301, 302, 327, 328
Boyd, Lily, 136, 213
boys, 2, 75, 81, 82, 135, 211, 212, 272
Brasenose College, Oxford, UK, 204
Brazil, 73, 75
breakfast, 17, 23, 42, 141, 147, 180, 210, 212, 214, 229, 261, 265, 271, 290, 301, 322
Breconshire, Wales, 183
Brewster, David, 246
Bridge, G. E. W., 134
Bridgewater, UK, 289
Bridport, UK, 284
Brighton, UK, 70, 218
Bristol, UK, 134, 212

British Isles, 279
British military uniform, 137
British Museum, 249
Bromyard, UK, 216
Bronx County, NY, 19
brooch, 136, 210
Brooke, Mrs. M. A., 257
Broome, Robert, 65
brother, 33-36, 45, 49, 50, 55-57, 61, 75, 77, 80, 89, 92, 93, 95-97, 109, 124-129, 131-133, 136, 137, 143, 146, 155, 161, 162, 169, 170, 172, 205, 210, 212, 213, 216-219, 223-226, 233, 250, 251, 253, 257-260, 263, 272-275, 283, 285, 286, 288, 291-293, 301, 311, 316
brothers, 66, 93, 110, 155, 253, 282, 341, 342
brougham, 110
Broussiloff, Anna N., 169
Brown, Samuel, 174
Brown, William, 87
Browning, Elizabeth B., 306
Buchanan, Patrick J., 365
Buffalo, NY, 172
burglars, 24
Burgundy, France, 293
Bury St. Edmunds, UK, 31
Buxton, Edmund C., 50
Buxton, Thomas F., 50
Buxton, UK, 65, 175, 176
Cabral, Ulysses J. D. C., 75
Cadogan Place, UK, 31
Cahoon, Mrs. E. M., 22
Calcutta, India, 143
calico, 310
California, 211
Cambridge, UK, 117, 118, 185, 233, 255
Cambridgeshire, UK, 304
Camden Town, UK, 115
camera obscura, 21
Camp Independence, 211
Campbell, Joseph, 365
Campbell, R. E. W., 205
Canada, 256, 300
candle, 56, 97, 99, 103, 104, 107, 179, 182, 184, 189, 190, 195, 199, 236, 239, 312, 314, 315, 322
candles, 205
candlestick, 236
candlesticks, 117
Cape Breton, NS, 33
capital, 285

cards, 119
Carlisle, UK, 255
Carmarthen, Wales, 71
Carnton Plantation, 3, 344, 367
cars, 42
Carson, John, 289
Carson, Martha, 365
Cash, Johnny, 365
Cassel, France, 73
castle, 27, 65, 85, 246, 247, 249, 280
Castle of Berry-Pomeroy, UK, 246
Castle Sowerby, 65
cat, 206, 241
Catherine the Great, 239
Catholics, 153
cats, 3
cattle, 326
cavalry, 2
Chaceley Lodge, 260
Chafy, W. K. W., 59
chair, 15, 22, 40, 46, 70, 128, 149, 155, 158, 159, 172, 181-183, 192, 195-197, 201, 206, 209, 219, 234, 240, 272, 275, 281, 300, 307, 308, 314
chairs, 206, 220
Chandler, H. B., 46
chapel, 85, 152, 233, 242
Chaproniere, Sophie, 207
character, 17, 30, 55, 119, 149, 214, 219, 246, 314, 320
Chase, Henrietta M., 18
Chatterton, Georgiana (Lady), 279
Chattisgarh, India, 15
Chedworth, Lord, 290
Chelsea, UK, 31
Cheltenham, UK, 198, 199, 250
chemistry, 19
Chester, UK, 173
Chicago, IL, 292
Chieri, Italy, 273
child, 11, 37, 43, 49, 52, 61, 69, 82, 87, 96, 99, 100, 108, 123, 124, 130, 132, 134, 135, 155, 161, 165, 166, 173, 174, 179, 188, 192, 194, 197, 217, 226, 237, 272, 277, 281, 286, 287, 291, 304, 307, 308, 312, 315, 316, 318, 365
children, 3, 28, 43-46, 66, 69, 80, 89, 92, 110, 134, 135, 152, 173, 232, 237, 242, 248, 249, 261, 277, 291, 294, 301, 304, 307, 308, 315, 319
Children, Richard, 249
China, 119

Christ, 3, 252, 342-345
Christian, 3, 101, 330, 343, 344, 365, 367
Christian mystic, 330
Christiania, Norway, 64
Christianity, 3, 344, 367
Christmas, 3, 107, 155, 185, 193, 194, 219, 278, 283, 344, 367
Christmas Eve, 194
church, 22, 52, 57, 59, 60, 66, 68, 93, 94, 143, 154, 155, 161, 193, 196, 197, 204, 205, 209, 233, 242, 243, 265, 283, 299, 302, 303, 321, 343
Church Lawton, UK, 233
churches, 93, 288, 303, 315
cigar, 300
Cill Challum Chille, Scotland, 311
citizens, 62
Civil War, 2, 3, 344, 365, 367
clairvoyance, 171, 239
Clapham Common, London, UK, 289
Clarke, Margaret, 93
clay, 309
cleaning, 110
Clemes, John P., 219
clergyman, 74, 83, 154, 161, 231, 279, 299, 314, 326, 327
Clevedon, UK, 248
climate, 276, 310
cloak, 38, 39, 112, 113, 126, 192, 226, 227
clothes, 13, 14, 32, 37, 40, 41, 58, 73, 123, 124, 137, 138, 149, 150, 205, 214, 228, 233, 242, 275, 281, 303, 328
clothing, 28, 30, 279
coal, 14, 320
coat, 40, 81, 83, 93, 125, 127, 176, 196, 215, 237, 272, 292, 304
coffin, 62, 89, 157, 171, 185, 305, 322
Cohen, Mrs. Frank, 26
Coldwell, Fanny, 97
collier, 254
Collings, Robert, 268
Combs, Bertram T., 365
communion, 27, 29
Confederacy, 2, 3
Confederate, 2, 3, 345, 365
Confederate flag, 2
Confederate government, 3
Confederate monuments, 2
Confederate States, 2, 3
Confederate States of America, 2, 3
Confederate veterans, 365
confederation, 2
Congress, 6, 125, 126
Congress of Electricians, 125
Conner, Mrs. E. A., 84
consciousness, 3, 27, 29, 40, 160, 166, 168, 232, 238, 260, 288, 345, 367
Constantinople, Turkey, 270
Constitution, 2, 365
Constitution of the Confederate States, 2
conventions, 6
cooking, 51
Cornish coast, 281
Cornwall, 100, 237, 281
corpse, 33, 52, 53, 55, 171, 312, 321
corpse-candle, 312
cottages, 253, 263, 319
cotton, 78
County Cork, Ireland, 65
County Louth, Ireland, 205
Cowpland, Maud, 216
Cowpland, Robert, 210
Cowpland, William, 210, 216
cows, 241
Cox, Anne, 279
Cox, Jane L., 170
Crawford, Cindy, 365
creeds, 310, 365
Cressy, Miss A., 275
cries, 8, 78, 165, 247, 248
crime, 294
Cromer, UK, 50
Cromwell Lodge, 117, 118
Crookes, William, 11, 54
Crowborough, UK, 141
Crowe, Catherine, 312-318, 321, 322, 324-328
Cruise, Tom, 365
Cuba, 62
cupboard, 53, 117, 183, 188, 225, 228, 229
curtains, 66, 68, 119, 144, 158, 172, 192, 242, 253, 260, 268, 294, 317
Curtin, Jeremiah, 283
Curtis, William, 77
cyclist, 99
Cyrus, Miley, 365
Daily News, 15
Darlington, UK, 67
Dauntesy, Alice, 175, 176
Davies, Emma, 14
De Pere, WI, 36, 38, 40-42
death, 3, 16, 23, 32, 33, 35, 36, 45, 46, 48, 49, 52, 53, 55, 58, 59,

62, 66-69, 72, 82, 86, 87, 89-91, 93, 95-97, 100, 101, 115, 123, 125, 128, 129, 131, 132, 136-138, 143, 146, 148, 149, 151, 153-157, 161-163, 167, 169-171, 174, 175, 183, 185, 204, 205, 207, 210, 217-219, 227-233, 235-237, 242, 246, 247, 250-252, 254-257, 259-263, 267, 269-271, 276-280, 282, 287, 288, 291-293, 299, 300, 302-305, 311-316, 321, 322, 324, 325, 328, 341-343, 345, 367
death-bed, 231, 232, 255, 304, 325
death-pact, 279
death-wraith, 16, 49, 101
debunk, 2
delusion, 34, 101, 216, 275
demonstration, 139, 342
Denmark, 31
Depression, 25, 162, 218, 313
Deptford, UK, 326
Derbyshire, UK, 173, 254
Dering, Edward H., 279
Derrihy, Michael, 282
despair, 102, 297, 300
Detroit, MI, 257
development, 122, 175, 239, 342
Devil, 345
Devonpoint, UK, 237
Dewas Kudea, India, 240
dimensions, 11
dining-room, 188, 196, 224, 285
dinner, 31, 33, 118, 122, 138, 176, 187, 213, 216, 249, 254, 267, 270, 299
diphtheria, 216, 217
disease, 132, 217, 246, 273, 304
disorder, 88
Dixie, 3
doctor, 19, 51, 94, 96, 146, 151, 153, 161, 163, 207, 216, 217, 226, 227, 235, 236, 276
doctors, 47
Dodd, Miss C. A., 139
dog, 56, 72, 78, 86, 119, 120, 130, 169, 170, 187, 192, 194-196, 199-201, 241, 324-326
dogs, 72, 85, 107, 181, 189, 240, 241, 247, 270
Doncaster, UK, 147
door, 15, 16, 18-20, 24, 26, 31-34, 36, 38, 46, 51, 53, 56, 59, 60, 63, 65, 66, 72, 74, 77, 79, 87, 91, 92, 94, 97-100, 103, 106,
107, 109, 110, 116-118, 120, 122, 124, 126-132, 136, 138, 139, 149, 150, 152, 153, 160, 165, 166, 169, 170, 172, 174-179, 182, 183, 188-201, 204, 206, 208, 209, 213, 219, 220, 224, 226, 227, 229, 235, 236, 240, 242, 246, 250, 253, 254, 263-267, 269, 272-275, 283, 285, 286, 290, 293, 294, 296, 299, 301, 307-309, 312, 314, 315, 317, 322, 324, 329
doors, 19, 24, 56, 60, 61, 68, 80, 84, 112, 119, 129, 132, 167, 174, 189, 190, 193-196, 198, 201, 209, 249, 261, 317
döppelganger, 207, 313, 314
Douglas, George, 113
Dove, J., 155
Dover, UK, 211, 218
Dow, Moses A., 295
downstairs, 42, 61, 65, 94, 117, 120, 124, 127-129, 131, 132, 176, 180, 183, 189-192, 194, 195, 206, 208, 213, 216
Doyle, Arthur C., 11, 44, 141, 142, 244
Drab Room, 213-215
drawing-room, 66, 128, 185, 195, 213, 224
dread, 122, 157
dream, 18, 21, 24-26, 42, 43, 45, 58, 90, 137, 140, 145, 235, 236, 256, 261
dreaming, 99, 119, 141, 166, 181, 200, 234, 273, 291, 298
dreams, 19, 24, 49, 130, 162, 235, 343
dress, 15, 20, 26, 30, 31, 42, 58, 66, 72, 79, 84-86, 88, 132, 135, 167, 171, 176, 180, 182-184, 189, 191-193, 196, 198, 206, 210, 215, 216, 230, 240, 241, 262, 266, 278, 282, 297, 299, 300, 308
dressing-room, 131
Drewry, Mr. W. T., 290
drowned, 42, 43, 57, 67, 77, 80, 87, 95, 255, 281, 291, 292, 326, 327
drowning, 58, 67, 77, 80, 87, 233, 292, 326
drunk, 33, 47, 110
Dublin, Ireland, 177, 178
Dunn, Edmund, 291
Dunn, William, 211

Dunning, Edward H., 122
Durban, South Africa, 61
dusk, 113-115, 176, 189, 213, 262, 263, 270
Dutch, 123
Duvall, Robert, 365
Dyer, Thomas F. T., 280-282
dying, 30-32, 43, 48, 59, 65, 88, 89, 91, 95, 125, 127, 129, 133, 134, 145, 146, 151, 153, 162, 163, 172, 173, 211, 218, 230, 231, 233, 235, 242, 251, 259, 263, 271, 276, 278, 314
dynamistograph, 123
D'Holbach, Baron, 310
Earl of Oxford, 365
earth, 11, 20, 25, 29, 30, 36, 47, 48, 89, 237, 238, 280, 297, 327
earth-bound ghosts, 249
Easter, 193, 203, 288
Edinburgh, Scotland, 55, 56, 102, 174, 261, 317
Edmonton, UK, 78
educators, 365
Egypt, 256
Ehrhardt, Ferdinand, 23
electric currents, 21
electricity, 21, 125
electrons, 21
Elgin-Crescent, UK, 15
Elizabeth, Queen (I), 52
Ellicott, Bishop, of Gloucester, 66
Ellis, Alice, 218
Ellis, Emma, 117
Ellis, Mary, 218
Ellis, Mrs. Robert, 218, 219
Ellis, Robert, 218
Emmett, M., 89
employment, 101, 251, 296
Enfield, UK, 134, 135
engagement, 86, 132
England, 15, 16, 19, 31-36, 40, 49, 50, 52, 59, 60, 74, 75, 82, 84, 86, 89, 90, 94-98, 112, 120, 121, 131, 134, 135, 138, 139, 141, 145, 155, 156, 161, 163, 168, 170, 171, 175, 176, 184, 185, 187, 194, 196-201, 203-205, 207, 210, 211, 218, 219, 221, 231, 233, 237, 240, 244, 248, 251, 252, 254, 255, 257, 260, 263, 264, 266, 267, 269, 275, 276, 278, 279, 284, 289-291, 304, 311-318, 321, 322, 324-328
English, 25, 41, 48, 103, 157, 168, 187, 231, 242, 271, 280, 298, 306, 327, 343
entertainment, 211, 365
envy, 56
Eritrea, 97
Esher, UK, 309
Essex, UK, 86, 106
Eston-in-Cleveland, UK, 91
eternity, 343
Europe, 23, 240
European royalty, 365
Eurydice (ship), 87
Eustance, Sarah, 233
evil, 56, 67, 89, 114, 200
Exeter, UK, 257
experience, 17, 21, 26, 28, 39, 41, 46, 47, 53, 61, 63, 65, 67, 73, 79, 81, 83, 91, 95, 103-105, 113, 119, 131, 141, 151, 156, 158, 159, 166-168, 172, 175, 176, 198, 204, 217, 221, 223, 227-230, 233, 235, 237, 238, 259, 270, 276, 292, 314, 345
experiences, 26, 27, 46, 48, 67, 70, 79, 81, 83, 87, 95, 103, 106-108, 113, 114, 118, 124, 130, 161, 194, 196-200, 239, 343
eye, 40, 84, 86, 90, 94, 250, 266, 283, 287
eyes, 17-20, 26, 33, 34, 37, 39, 40, 44, 45, 48, 50, 73, 81, 92, 94, 100, 104, 105, 107, 112, 114, 116, 124, 134, 135, 144, 152, 159, 163, 181, 186, 192, 193, 200, 201, 204-206, 210, 213-215, 217, 219, 225, 228, 267, 269, 271, 273, 275, 284, 286, 289-291, 294, 297, 304, 327, 342, 345
fairies, 282, 283, 341
fairy, 280, 282, 283
Fanshawe, Lady, 280, 325
farmer, 13, 281
farmhouse, 13, 249, 312
father, 2, 16, 23-26, 29, 43-45, 52, 55-57, 60, 66-69, 71, 72, 90, 92, 97, 101, 102, 123, 127, 129, 132, 149, 151-153, 161, 167, 172, 173, 181, 183, 208, 211, 212, 218, 229-232, 236, 241, 247, 249, 252, 254, 258, 260, 263, 265, 266, 274, 279, 290, 303, 304, 307-309, 315, 323, 327, 328, 365
fever, 219, 225, 231, 235, 251, 257,

259, 312
field, 47, 50, 71, 81, 90, 237, 281, 297, 319, 323
Firbeck House, 92
fire, 13, 14, 26, 50, 58, 65, 67, 70, 90-92, 103, 131, 132, 149, 158, 159, 173, 181, 182, 199, 200, 205, 206, 213, 234, 240, 242, 245, 265, 266, 272, 279, 281, 293, 315
Fisher, J. Hartman, 161
flannel petticoat, 236
Fleetwood, UK, 133
Fleming, Laura, 84
Flintshire, Wales, 298
float, 82
floating, 17, 26, 221, 274
Florida, 235
flour, 319
folk tales, 110
Folkestone, UK, 254, 255
Foote, Shelby, 365
footfalls, 343
footsteps, 57, 58, 67, 70, 77-79, 87, 88, 94, 113, 115-117, 129, 137, 178, 187, 188, 194, 195, 197, 199, 200, 207, 247, 253, 286, 316, 317
Forbes, Charles, 310
forest, 77
Fort Edward, NY, 171
Fort Hartsuff, 166
Fotherby, Henry A., 221, 233
Fotheringham, W. B., 116
Foy, Emma, 158
France, 121, 134, 137, 141, 143, 205, 207, 231, 233, 273, 280
Friday, 15, 58, 138, 167, 222, 228, 230, 242, 255
Fryer, A. T., 67, 69, 78
funeral, 62, 63, 146, 171, 185, 204, 205, 236, 237, 292, 305, 323
funeral procession, 185, 204, 205
furniture, 68, 70, 97, 120, 130, 139, 190, 195, 220, 243, 247, 249, 251, 261, 315
Galateri, Count, 249
Gansvoort, NY, 171
gardener, 52, 108, 141, 169, 188, 189, 211
garments, 207, 228, 234, 251
gas, 46, 51, 52, 58, 79, 126, 128-130, 132, 189, 191, 194, 198, 219, 264
gastronomy, 365
Gateshead, UK, 134, 135

Gayheart, Rebecca, 365
genealogy, 365
German American Spiritualists' Church, 22
Germany, 20, 314, 325
ghost, 1, 3, 5, 6, 11, 14, 18, 25, 30, 31, 35, 36, 40, 41, 45, 48, 52, 53, 55, 58-60, 62, 64, 66-68, 70, 72, 75, 77-80, 82-87, 92-95, 99, 100, 102, 104, 106, 112-115, 121, 123, 124, 130, 133, 134, 143-146, 154-156, 158, 161, 163, 169, 170, 173-176, 180, 182, 184, 188, 190, 196, 198, 199, 203, 205, 211, 214, 217, 219, 226, 231, 233, 235, 237, 238, 240-243, 245-248, 251, 252, 255-257, 260, 261, 265-273, 275, 276, 278-281, 283, 289, 290, 292-295, 302, 309, 312, 313, 315, 318, 320, 322-329, 341-345, 367
ghosts, 7, 9, 11, 55, 60, 63, 65, 71, 75, 97, 108, 112, 121, 135, 162, 172, 174, 175, 180, 191-193, 198-200, 203, 207, 227, 241, 249, 262, 274, 282, 283, 300, 304, 307, 311, 318, 319, 329, 341, 343
Gibraltar, 87, 275, 276
Gibson, Mr. R., 268
girl, 14, 15, 32, 38, 52, 62, 67, 80, 85, 91, 103, 117, 127, 148, 173, 182, 189-192, 194, 198, 199, 221, 226, 227, 251, 253, 259, 260, 267, 277, 282, 283, 285, 291, 302, 303, 309, 314, 326-328
girls, 13, 31, 32, 51, 52, 81-83, 113, 161, 272
Glasgow, Scotland, 55, 302
Gleason, Adele, 84
gloom, 237, 256
Gloucester, UK, 66
God, 2, 3, 45, 183, 215, 247, 251, 252, 287, 290, 292, 345
Godalming, UK, 32
Godwin, Miss M. E., 87
Goethe, Johann W. von, 240
goffered cap, 229
gold, 2, 124, 215, 250, 365
Good Friday, 255
good health, 23, 56, 61, 71, 93, 156, 218, 226, 255, 260, 276, 313
Goodyear, T. W., 110

government, 3, 285
gown, 88, 127, 182, 191, 198, 222, 236
grain, 47
Grand Island Railway Station, 166
grandfather, 67, 70, 124, 260, 268, 291
grandmother, 110, 111, 143, 171, 229, 230, 260, 280
grass, 47, 302
grave, 27, 28, 88, 238, 289, 312, 313
graves, 321, 365
Graves, Robert, 365
Greaves, Miss C. L., 85
Greenlaw, William, 280
Grey Lady, 177, 179, 241
Greystoke pillar, 65
Griffith, Andy, 365
Grimsby, UK, 254
groans, 40, 215
Groton, MA, 18
growth, 47, 134
Guernsey, British Isles, 279
Gulf of Carpentaria, Australia, 218
gun, 2, 3, 39, 148, 149, 185, 365
gun-carriage, 185
guns, 50
Guthrie, Miss E. E., 82
Hadath, E. G., 120
Hall, Mrs. Conrad, 86
Hall, Spencer T., 174
hallucination, 60, 90, 235, 251, 259, 264, 265, 329
hallucinations, 64, 84, 207, 235
Hamburg, IA, 167
Hamilton County, OH, 307
Hampshire County, UK, 271
Hampton Court, UK, 170
Hampton Roads Conference, 2
happiness, 3, 344, 367
Harbaugh, F. R., 265
harbour, 255
Harding, William G., 365
harmony, 63, 239
Harrington, Lady, 67
Harrison, H. R., 75
Hasted Papers, 249
Hastings, UK, 293
Hastings, Warren, 252
hat, 35, 38, 39, 71, 81, 83, 94, 111, 112, 114, 117, 145, 237, 274, 294, 296, 300, 301, 304
haunt, 65, 86, 97, 281, 319
haunted, 3, 5, 6, 41, 50, 52, 57-59, 68, 70, 77-81, 85, 107, 112-114, 116, 118, 124, 130, 132, 135-137, 165, 177, 179-181, 183, 187, 190, 196-200, 205, 212, 215, 242, 245, 248-251, 293, 316, 318-320, 344, 367
haunted house, 50, 57, 58, 70, 77-79, 107, 116, 130, 132, 180, 181, 187, 196-200, 205, 248, 251, 316, 318, 319
haunted houses, 3, 5, 6, 177, 318
haunting, 183, 283
hauntings, 284, 319, 343
hay, 81
Haye, Shute, 284
healing, 343
health, 3, 23, 31, 41, 52, 55, 56, 61, 69, 71, 73, 75, 84, 92, 93, 156, 157, 163, 167, 177, 178, 207, 210, 211, 216, 218, 226, 250, 254-256, 260, 268, 276, 278, 309, 313, 323, 344, 365, 367
Heanor, UK, 254
heaven, 123, 237, 279, 305
hell, 2, 45
Helvetius, Claude A., 310
Hemmerlé, Agathe, 223
Hemmerlé, Alfred, 225
Hemmerlé, Irma, 225
Hemmerlé, Miss Alma, 226
Henley House School, 98
Henry VIII, King, 212
Heywood, Peter, 16
hills, 47, 319
history, 2, 3, 6, 66, 106, 133, 140, 202, 249, 279, 342-344, 365
Hobday, Alfred, 161
hobgoblin, 251
Hoelger, Richard L., 24
Holiwell, Wales, 298
Holland, Netherlands, 16
Holloway, UK, 173
Holmes, Sherlock, 11, 44, 139
Holt, Frederick, 136
Holy Mother of God, 287
Holy Spirit, 139
Home, Daniel D., 186
honey, 300
Hopkins, John, 72
Horne, Emily M., 61
horror, 19, 39, 90, 99, 112, 120, 183, 206, 240, 268, 272, 294, 300, 317
horse, 59, 65, 71, 84, 110-112, 160, 237, 241, 277, 281, 296-298, 322, 325, 326
horses, 237, 241, 247, 282
Hosmer, Harriet G., 261

hospital, 46, 47, 51, 87, 88, 134, 135, 276, 292
Hotel Interlaken, Switzerland, 271
Houdini, Harry, 244
house, 3, 6, 13-15, 17, 19-21, 24, 25, 31, 37, 41, 43, 45, 50-52, 55-61, 63, 65-70, 72-75, 77-79, 83-86, 89-95, 97, 98, 100, 107-110, 112-120, 124-126, 129-132, 135, 138, 139, 145, 146, 151-153, 156, 171, 173, 175-185, 187-190, 192-201, 203, 205, 207-217, 223, 226, 227, 229, 230, 233, 237, 242, 243, 245-251, 253, 254, 258-260, 262, 265-273, 277, 279, 282-284, 288-291, 293, 294, 299-302, 307-309, 312-322, 344, 367
houses, 3, 5, 6, 23, 33, 38, 57, 63, 64, 66, 75, 78, 177, 281, 316, 318
Hull, UK, 49, 289
Humber River, 254
Hume, Thomas, 102
humor, 3, 365
hunting, 71, 97, 218, 250, 281
Hurry, H.C., 251
husband, 25-27, 29, 30, 38-43, 61, 65, 78, 84, 86, 89, 94, 102, 115, 116, 135, 136, 144, 152, 161, 163, 166, 169, 172, 174-176, 185, 208, 214, 215, 219, 222, 231, 233, 238, 245, 246, 261, 264, 275, 276, 285, 288, 291, 292, 299-302, 304, 305, 314-316, 323, 325
Husk, Cecil, 220
Hyderabad, India, 240
Hyères, France, 273
hypnotism, 75, 343
Hyslop, James H., 222
Hyzer, Mrs. F. O., 30
icy chill, 163
ignorance, 28, 319, 366
ill, 26, 31, 33, 36, 39, 43, 46, 49-52, 67, 84, 91, 93, 95, 100, 102, 115, 122, 124, 126, 127, 129, 132, 133, 151, 155, 161-163, 170-172, 192, 211, 212, 217, 218, 230, 233, 235, 236, 246, 248, 250, 258-260, 262, 271, 272, 274, 276, 289, 304, 309, 310, 317, 322, 324, 326, 345
Illinois, 167
illness, 25, 26, 55, 59, 91, 94, 96, 116, 122, 161, 163, 167, 169, 170, 205, 207, 211, 235, 236, 248, 258, 259, 276, 277, 288, 304
illusion, 72, 102, 115, 136, 157, 229, 265, 273, 324
immortal, 8, 11
immortality, 7, 28, 271, 342, 344
India, 15, 94, 95, 143, 157, 185, 246, 252, 310
Indiana, 300
infant, 282, 304, 305
Ingles, Mary S., 61
intelligence, 28, 35, 55, 65, 72, 102, 137, 174, 316
Interlaken, Switzerland, 271
Ireland, 3, 86, 89, 179, 205, 251, 268, 280, 299, 322, 342, 344
Irish, 65, 86, 107, 133, 205, 250, 260, 268, 280, 282, 299
Irish Channel, 133
Irish fairy tales, 282
iron, 109, 188, 200
Isle of France, 121
Isle of Wight, 203, 242, 247
Isonzo River, 140
Istanbul, Turkey, 270
Italian army, 140
Italians, 140
Italy, 251, 261, 273
Jamaica, 86, 315
James, Richard, 78
Jamieson, Jane A., 173
Jaroslav, Russia, 285
Jefferson Davis Historical Gold Medal, 2, 365
Jenkins, Elizabeth, 64
Jenkins, Sarah, 64
Jenkinson, Lady, 53
Jephson, Mrs. E. J., 118
Jersey, UK, 200
Jerusalem, Israel, 97
Jesus, 3, 342, 344, 345, 367
jewels, 281
Job, 11
Job (Bible), 11
Jones, Ellen M., 135
Jones, John, 298
Journal of the Society for Psychical Research, 15, 16, 50, 52, 53, 57-61, 64-75, 77-80, 82-87, 89, 92-101, 104, 106, 107, 109, 112-118, 120, 123, 124, 126, 130-135, 138, 139, 141, 144-146, 149, 151, 154-158, 161-163, 165-173, 175, 176,

179, 180, 183, 184, 188-192, 194-201, 204, 205, 207, 210, 211, 218, 219
Joy, G. P., 118
Judd, Ashley, 365
Judd, Naomi, 365
Judd, Wynonna, 365
Kansas, 167
Kansas City, MO, 167
Kaye, A. B. R., 205
Kearne, Percy, 161
Kelvedon, UK, 74
Kenford, UK, 257
Kensington Park, UK, 185, 278
Kensington, UK, 59
Kent, UK, 184, 249, 252
Kentucky, 365
Keough, Riley, 365
Ker, Miss Bessie, 271
Kernahan, Coulson, 58
Keynsham, UK, 174
Kherson, Russia, 223
Kiel, Scotland, 311
Kilmarnock nightcap, 318
kindness, 283
Kingsdown, Lord, 97
Kinwarton, UK, 90
Kippenross, Scotland, 246
Kloss, Anna, 19, 23
Klotz, Herman, 23
Krekel, Mattie P., 167
Ku Klux Klan, 2
laborers, 323
Lady and the Lantern, 281
Lady in Black, 241
Lady of the Golden Casket, 281
lake, 29, 44, 77
Lake Hopatcong, NJ, 44
Lakewood, NJ, 165
Lamb, Charles, 78
lamp, 13, 42, 48, 79, 85, 133, 158, 203, 216, 217, 224, 225, 239, 268, 286, 288
lamps, 220, 264, 281
Lancaster Gate, UK, 19
Lancaster, UK, 156
Lang, Andrew, 240, 241
Langley, S. P., 43
Larcombe, Mrs. M. A., 279
Larkin, James J., 146, 151
laughter, 123
law, 3, 6, 55, 56, 75, 84, 92, 106, 109, 129, 135, 136, 138, 156, 176, 210, 214, 216, 233, 258, 285, 286, 288, 301, 344, 367
Law of Attraction, 3, 344, 367

Leebotwood, UK, 13
Leeds, UK, 66
Leeper, R. W., 205
levitation, 30, 100, 186, 341
liberty, 146
library, 6, 70, 174, 226, 227, 274
Liddington, UK, 139
life after death, 342
light, 13, 15, 17, 19-22, 24, 26, 37, 44, 47, 48, 50, 51, 56, 58, 59, 66, 79, 88, 91, 92, 96, 99-101, 105-107, 115, 119, 120, 126, 129, 133, 136, 139, 144, 145, 152, 154, 167, 172, 177-182, 184, 191, 196, 198, 200, 201, 204, 205, 208, 212, 213, 220, 224, 225, 237, 239, 245-249, 256, 264, 266, 269, 281, 284-288, 290, 293, 294, 310, 312, 314, 315, 321, 322, 329, 342, 343
Limerick, Ireland, 268
Lincolnshire, UK, 281
Lincoln's War, 2, 3
Lister, Miss Laura A., 210
Liverpool, UK, 43, 90, 155, 260
Llanwhellyn, Wales, 296
Lodge, Oliver, 11, 228
Lombroso, Cesare, 242, 243, 246-251
London Spiritualist Alliance, 221
London, UK, 15, 16, 36, 82, 94, 96, 98, 112, 115, 121, 143, 170, 185, 205, 221, 233, 244, 249, 263, 266, 268, 278, 279, 289, 290, 292, 304, 311, 317, 326
Londonderry, Northern Ireland, 107
Lord, 35, 97, 155, 235, 268, 283, 284, 290, 291, 297, 298, 341
Loughborough, UK, 85
love, 2, 3, 8, 245, 263, 268
loved ones, 25, 216
Loveless, Patty, 365
Loweswater, UK, 184
Lowrey, George, 221
lumber, 52
lunch, 149, 205
luncheon, 72, 84
Lyons, Louis, 255
MacGowan, A. B., 211, 212
MacGowan, Charles, 211
MacGowan, George, 211
Machynlleth, Wales, 295
MacKenna, Robert W., 238
Macklin, Marian M., 138
Madagascar, 121
Madden, Mary, 88

Madge Figg's Chair, 281
Madras, India, 257
magic, 321
Magna Carta, 2
Maine, 166
Malabar coast, 290
Malvern Wells, UK, 279
Manchester, UK, 120, 175, 176
manhood, 231
Manning, Mary M. C., 166
manor house, 25, 249
mansion, 299
marble, 203
marriage, 3, 23, 49, 101, 163, 285, 327
Martratt, Charles E., 172
Marvin, Lee, 365
Mary, 49, 52, 69, 88, 89, 92, 166, 183, 218, 239, 345
Massachusetts, 16, 62
Massowah, Eritrea, 97
Maxwell family, 246
McCaskill, Agnes, 74
McConnel, David R., Sr., 149
McConnel, David, Jr., 146, 149
McDougall, Mr. A., 65
McGavocks, 3
McGraw, Tim, 365
McLaren, Charles, 78
meadows, 241, 345
medicine, 96, 161, 226, 227, 235, 236
mediumistic powers, 251
mediums, 21, 29, 246
Melbourne, Australia, 64
memories, 11, 131, 231, 237
memory, 48, 49, 60, 61, 93, 119, 228, 230, 237, 240, 256, 275, 276, 313, 343
men, 16, 33, 43, 51, 77, 88, 89, 96, 103, 104, 106, 130, 137, 148, 185, 219, 223, 250, 268, 282, 289, 311, 328
mental impressions, 109
Menton, France, 169
Mentone Infirmary, 163
Meredith, Katharine M. C., 123, 124
Merionethshire, Wales, 295
mesmerism, 213
mess-room, 205
Mexico, 219
Michell, E., 156
Michell, Gwendoline, 155
Michigan, 42, 257, 259
Middleton, Mrs. M., 155
military, 2, 137, 146, 148, 149, 166,

169, 185, 211, 256, 365
milk-maids, 241
mills, 96
Mills, Edmund J., 96
Minehead, UK, 180
miracles, 345
mirror, 79, 80, 129, 240
mirrors, 220
mists, 343
Mitchell, S. Weir, 227
molecules, 21
Monday, 17, 92, 93, 96, 147, 148, 171, 235, 258, 304
money, 35, 93, 102, 193, 248, 250, 296
monks, 65
Monmouthshire, Wales, 71, 72
moon, 3, 58, 152, 228, 230, 268, 300
moonlight, 31, 65, 103, 106, 108, 152, 180, 229, 239, 241, 258, 268, 294, 299, 321
Moore, Miss S., 66
Moray Firth, Scotland, 102
Morgan, Henry, 289
Morland, Mr. W. C., 252
Morris, Mary E., 183
Mortlock, Mary, 52
Morvern, Scotland, 311
Mosby, John S., 365
Moses, Stainton, 231, 234
mother, 3, 26, 32, 37, 41, 45, 48, 49, 55-58, 62, 64, 65, 68-72, 74, 78, 80, 84, 90, 92, 94, 95, 97, 98, 101, 102, 106, 110, 111, 121, 122, 126, 132-136, 138, 143, 147, 148, 155, 161, 162, 167, 169, 170, 172-174, 176, 179, 181, 183, 187-194, 199, 200, 204, 205, 210-212, 223, 226, 229, 230, 235-237, 250, 253-255, 258, 259, 263, 265, 266, 269, 273, 274, 278, 282, 283, 287, 292, 293, 305, 307, 315, 324, 326, 327, 344, 365
mountain, 271, 282
Mountain Jim, 271
mountains, 365, 366
Mulgrave Cottage, 268
Murray, Mr. O., 78
music, 61, 63, 64, 131, 221, 242, 279, 365
musicians, 62, 365
Muskegon, MI, 259
mysterious lights, 280
Napa College, 211
Naples, Italy, 23

Napoleon I, 16
nature, 3, 23, 28, 47, 60, 71, 106, 117, 120, 139, 151, 159, 238, 282, 285, 312, 320-322, 341, 342, 344, 365
Nautical Almanac, 229
navy, 40, 156
Nebraska, 166
neckcloth, 136
negro, 73
nephew, 36, 72, 155, 163, 252
Neues Wiener Tagblatt, 15
New Jersey, 22, 44, 165, 265
New Testament, 3, 344
New World, 341
New York, 19, 22-26, 29, 30, 42, 58, 139, 165, 171, 172, 341-345
New York City, NY, 48
Newenham, E. H., 52
Newfoundland, 42, 43
Newquay, Cornwall, 100
news, 15-17, 24, 31, 32, 42, 56, 58, 67, 90, 95, 137, 149, 153, 162, 174, 185, 219, 233, 242, 252, 257, 259, 260, 262, 263, 270-272, 279, 280, 285, 288, 289, 293
newspaper, 15, 184, 185, 205, 234, 250, 309
newspapers, 90, 184
Newton Abbot, UK, 269
niece, 36, 80, 216, 233, 234, 266, 267, 280, 290
night, 16, 17, 19, 22-26, 28, 31, 32, 36, 37, 40-42, 45-53, 55, 56, 58, 63, 65, 67, 68, 70, 73-75, 77, 79, 85, 88-93, 96, 97, 101-108, 112, 116-122, 125-131, 133, 135-137, 144, 145, 147, 152-154, 157, 161, 163, 165-167, 170-175, 179-183, 188, 190, 192-201, 205, 207, 208, 211-215, 218, 220, 222, 223, 226, 228, 229, 231-236, 242, 245-249, 251, 255-258, 260, 263-265, 268-272, 278, 280-284, 286, 288, 290, 291, 293, 301, 310, 311, 313, 315, 317, 318, 320, 322, 324, 325, 327, 328, 341
nightcap, 318
nightmare, 214
Norfolk, UK, 283
Normandy, 247
Normanton, Australia, 218
North, 2, 3, 31, 52, 55, 72, 230, 254, 271, 290, 307, 318, 319, 365
North Carolina, 365
North Devon, UK, 72
North Finchley, UK, 52
Northern Ireland, 107
Northerners, 2
Northrepps Hall, UK, 50
Northumberland, UK, 328
Norway, 64
Nova Scotia, 33, 35
Novotorjok, Russia, 125
Nugent, Jim, 271
nurse, 14, 47, 57, 61, 78, 85, 108, 123, 136, 151, 153, 163, 177, 216, 231, 235, 242, 248, 286, 287, 299, 317
nursery, 97, 155, 156, 178, 179, 184, 216, 242, 248, 315
nurses, 152, 153
O'Donnell, Elliott, 98-100
O'Donnell, Helena, 100
O'Donnell, Petronella, 101
OBEs, 95
occupation, 81, 183
officers, 16, 33, 35, 121, 137, 147, 150, 240, 311
Ohio, 300, 307
Ohio River, 300
Old South, 2, 3
Olney, UK, 231
omens, 63
onomastics, 365
oppression, 34, 235
Orr, Ada, 146
Oslo, Norway, 64
out-of-body experiences, 95
Owen, Robert D., 249, 303-305, 309
Oxford Phasmatological Society, 204
Oxford, UK, 155, 170
O'Brien, Honor, 325
O'Donnell, Henry, 97
O'Donnell, Red H., 97
pain, 167, 168, 217, 237, 278
Paine, Mrs. Lewis, 77
painter, 22
palace, 170, 239, 270, 299
Palladino, Eusapia, 75
pantomime, 110
Paquet, Agnes, 292
parade, 147
paranormal, 5, 6, 11, 86, 140, 161, 164, 186, 194, 202, 241, 365
paranormal experiences, 161, 194
paranormal history, 202
Paris, France, 231, 233, 242
Parker, T., 121

parlour, 14, 63, 108, 171, 301
Parry, Miss Lucy G., 269
particpatory theater, 110
Parton, Dolly, 365
party, 16, 42, 110, 111, 118, 160, 174, 207, 211, 216, 219, 282, 283, 289, 313, 326
Patrington, UK, 289
peace, 17, 48, 153, 239
Pearson, Emma M., 67
Pederson, Sören, 64
Penge, UK, 263
Penrith, UK, 65
Penzance, UK, 155
Peterburgskaia Gazeta, 126
phantasm, 171, 221, 246
phantasmal form, 308
phantasms, 220, 223, 235, 248, 342, 343
Phasmatological Papers, 70
Philadelphia, PA, 30, 43, 227, 265, 317
Philpot, H., 161
physical body, 37, 95
physics, 19
piano, 61, 63, 128, 131, 193, 199, 200
Piave RIver, 139
pillow, 2, 88, 215, 286
pillows, 68
Piney Point, VA, 303
Pitsea Rectory, 72
plantation, 3, 344, 367
pleurisy, 132
Pluckley, UK, 184
Plymouth, UK, 201
Pole-Carew, F. A., 237
police, 14, 284
politics, 365
Pollock, James S., 291
poltergeist, 6, 13, 66
poltergeists, 3, 5, 6, 70, 77, 117, 248
Poona, India, 157
Porter, Miss Anna M., 309
Portland, Maine, 166
Portland, ME, 166
Portsmouth, UK, 251
Portugal, 36
postillion, 326
potatoes, 67, 68
powers, 23, 130, 186, 251, 310
Powys, May C., 264
pray, 292
prayer, 41, 44, 64, 153, 287, 297, 298
Prel, Carldu, 223

premonition, 139, 212
Presbyterian Church, 265
preservationist, 365
Presley, Elvis, 365
Presley, Lisa M., 365
pride, 227
Pritchard, Maggie E., 235
Probst, Charles, 22
procession, 185, 204, 205, 366
Proctor, Joseph, 248
prophecy, 139, 141, 314
prostitution, 3, 344
protecting spirits, 314, 315
Providence, 298
psychic photograph, 54, 64, 73, 83, 98, 118, 138, 166, 252, 262, 266, 287, 305, 320, 323, 327
psychical phenomena, 306, 329, 341
psychopomp, 126
Purton, Francis A., 90
Putney, UK, 207
Quaker ghost, 86
Quakers, 266
Queenstown, New Zealand, 90
Quitman, MO, 167
R.A.F., 151
R.F.C., 146
R.N.A.S., 146
Radiant Boy, 281
radium rays, 21
Radom, Poland, 169
railway station, 55, 166, 171
Rainham, UK, 283
Ramhurst House, 249
Ramsgate, UK, 86
rappings, 251
rats, 106, 116, 117, 183, 214
Ratzeburg, Germany, 77
Ravensdale Parsonage, 205
Ravensdale, Cassidy, 6
rebellion, 246
Reconstruction, 2
rectory, 31, 57, 68, 69, 72, 85, 154, 210, 216
Red Bank, NJ, 265
Regent's Park, UK, 16
religion, 283, 285, 341, 365
reunion, 343
revenge, 271
Revolutionary War, 365
Revue du Monde Invisible, 233
rice, 344
Richmond, Cora L. V., 76
Richmond, England, 38
Riffold, Mary, 69
Rio, Brazil, 75

river, 29, 30, 36, 38, 39, 139-141, 300, 303, 319
Riverhead, UK, 275
Robert der Teufel (play), 73
Rochas, Albert de, 223
Rochas, M. A., de, 52
Rochester, NY, 165
rocking-chair, 307, 308
Rocky Mountains, 271, 365, 366
Rodrigues, Candido da S., 73
Romanoff-Borrisogliebsk, Russia, 285
Rome, 23, 24
Rome, Italy, 23, 261
room, 13, 15, 19-21, 24, 26, 30-34, 37, 40, 42-48, 51-53, 55-59, 61-64, 66, 72-74, 78, 79, 84-92, 95, 96, 98, 100, 101, 103-108, 111, 117-120, 123, 124, 126-132, 135, 136, 138, 139, 144, 148-153, 156-158, 161, 162, 165, 166, 168-170, 172, 174-185, 187-201, 204-208, 210, 213-220, 222, 224-230, 233-236, 239, 241-243, 245-249, 252, 253, 256-264, 266-269, 271-273, 275, 278, 284-286, 288, 289, 293-295, 300-302, 304, 305, 309, 313, 314, 317, 321, 324-327
rooms, 13, 19, 24, 31, 46, 52, 55, 57, 65, 68, 79, 103, 106, 115, 117-119, 130, 132, 149, 150, 152, 174, 176, 178, 181, 187, 190, 234, 263, 308, 343
Royal Astronomical Society, 229
Royal Bucks Militia, 89
Royal Flying Corps, 146
Royal Irish Fusiliers, 205
Royal Marine Office, England, 121
Royal Naval Air Service, 146
Rucker, Edmund W., 365
Rugby, UK, 170, 260
ruins, 65
Russell, Edwin, 242
Russell, J. G. F., 271
Russia, 169, 223
Rutherglen Road, Glasgow, Scotland, 303
S.P.R., 248
S.S.S.P., 44
sacrament, 152, 204, 232
saddle, 2, 3, 281
Saginaw, MI, 257, 259
sailor, 101, 156, 196, 254, 289, 316
saints, Christian, and bilocation, 223
saloon, 290
Salsbury, T., 121
salt, 8
San Francisco, CA, 242
Sandy, UK, 138
Santos, Silva, 75
Saturday, 14, 15, 92, 93, 95, 147, 165-167, 181, 213, 215, 230, 234, 273
Saunders, Tom, 141
Saxby, Stephen H., 248
Sayce, A. H., 216
Scampton Aerodrome, 146
Scampton, UK, 147, 148
sceptic, 221
sceptics, 55, 202
Schloss Weierburg Castle, Austria, 85
school, 31, 32, 69, 98, 101, 124, 148, 163, 185, 211, 212, 217, 278, 289, 291, 292
Schwartzenberg, Princess, 242
science, 168, 231, 280, 341, 342, 365
Scotland, 102, 113, 245, 246, 271, 281, 302, 311, 312, 315, 341-343, 345
Scott, George C., 365
Scott, Louisa, 113
Scott, Miss M. W., 82, 83, 114, 115
Scott, T. E., 205
scream, 57, 73, 182, 183, 280, 328
screams, 57, 68, 90, 283
sea, 3, 5, 6, 17, 80, 140, 156, 167, 168, 203, 220, 233, 239, 251, 276, 277, 281, 315, 316, 342, 344, 345, 366, 367
Sea Raven Press, 3, 5, 6, 140, 342, 344, 345, 366, 367
Seabrook, Lochlainn, 2, 3, 7, 11, 365
seance, 220, 221
séance, 202, 247, 250, 251, 283
séances, 186, 306
secession, 2
second sight, 133
seed, 68
Semenoff, Alexander, 125
Sengireef, A. F., 285, 286, 288
Sepoy Rebellion, 246
Serboff, M., 223, 224
servant, 31, 36, 51, 52, 59, 61, 80, 101, 109, 120, 125, 126, 137, 170, 171, 175, 181-183, 194, 196, 201, 210, 248, 261-263, 275-277, 282, 285, 299, 302, 303, 309, 315, 316, 321, 322, 327, 328
servants, 13, 24, 67-70, 77, 86, 96, 97, 108, 111, 135, 174, 176,

189, 203, 212, 215, 217, 242, 260, 284, 305, 317
shadow, 65, 74, 96, 128, 139, 169, 172, 175, 179, 262, 281, 341
shadows, 48
Shakespeare, William, 177
sheep, 289, 325, 326
Sheerness-on-Sea, UK, 168
Sheffield Independent, 78
Shelley, Percy B., 240
Sherbrooke, John, 33, 34, 36
Sheridan, Elizabeth, 280
Sheridan, Frances, 280
Sherman, Kate, 259
Shields, UK, 254
ship, 16, 43, 87, 90, 95, 101, 121, 139, 156, 252, 254, 289, 328
ships, 16, 17, 35
shipwreck, 42
shooting jacket, 50
Shrewsbury, UK, 13
shrieks, 67, 215, 280
Shrubsole, W. H., 168
Sidebottom, F., 52
Sidgwick, Arthur, 170
sighs, 8, 215
Simonds, Morse, 248
Sinclair, B. F., 165
sing, 242
singing, 22, 50, 64
Sings, Edward, 254, 255
sister, 23, 26, 27, 30-32, 36, 49, 55-58, 60-64, 66, 71, 72, 75, 77, 79, 81, 86, 91-95, 101, 109, 110, 113-115, 127, 129, 132, 133, 136-138, 143, 153, 155, 156, 165, 166, 178, 181-183, 195, 196, 203, 216-218, 221, 224, 225, 229-231, 233, 234, 236, 242, 251, 253, 255-262, 269, 271-274, 278, 279, 285, 288, 291, 294, 295, 299, 300, 309, 317, 318
sisters, 31, 32, 40, 41, 62, 77, 81, 94, 100, 112, 126, 127, 225, 226, 235, 242, 257, 309, 365
sitting-room, 33, 95, 100, 103, 105, 106, 118, 138, 188, 192
Skaggs, Ricky, 365
skeptic, 49, 220, 244, 290
skeptics, 11
Slade, Henry, 202
slave, 73
slavery, 2
sleep, 11, 17, 19, 23, 25, 26, 28, 31, 32, 39, 40, 42, 46, 47, 49, 51,
59, 74, 88-90, 94, 101, 104, 108, 118-120, 130, 133-135, 139, 144, 145, 152, 166, 167, 170, 171, 180, 181, 183, 188, 192, 194, 200, 201, 212-215, 218, 222, 228, 229, 231, 235, 236, 240, 242, 257, 258, 260, 273, 286, 287, 293, 294, 310, 320
sleeping, 38, 41, 45, 55, 58, 78, 79, 89, 92, 117, 119, 130, 167, 177, 181, 188, 192, 194, 199, 213, 214, 230, 233, 245, 246, 262, 263, 270, 275, 317
Smallbone, Eliza, 72
Smead, Cecil, 222
Smead, George, 221
Smellie, William, 279
Smith, Charles W., 227
Society for Psychical Research, 11, 15, 16, 18, 24, 26, 27, 30, 36, 38, 40-43, 45, 46, 48-50, 52, 53, 57-61, 64-75, 77-80, 82-87, 89, 92-101, 104, 106, 107, 109, 112-118, 120, 123, 124, 126, 130-135, 138, 139, 141, 144-146, 149, 151, 154-158, 161-163, 165-173, 175, 176, 179, 180, 183, 184, 188-192, 194-201, 204, 205, 207, 210, 211, 218, 219, 342
Society for the Study of Supernormal Pictures, 44
Society of Friends, 319
soldiers, 2, 3, 365
Somersetshire, UK, 174
Sons of Confederate Veterans, 365
Sopwith Camel, 146
soul, 3, 7, 8, 19, 31, 32, 40, 42, 43, 45, 47, 49, 57, 59, 69, 72, 73, 80, 84, 89, 90, 95, 96, 102, 110, 115, 121, 123, 134, 136, 163, 174, 185, 205, 212, 216, 233, 235, 238, 239, 242, 248, 251, 255, 290, 292, 298, 343, 345, 367
sounds, 7, 79, 90, 97, 108, 120, 215, 288
South, 2, 3, 25, 61, 87, 93, 94, 228, 229, 251, 255, 266, 299, 307, 341, 365
South Africa, 93
South America, 94
Southampton, UK, 185, 276
Southern Cause, 3, 345
Southern Confederacy, 2, 3

Southerners, 2, 3
Spain, 312
Spearman, Dorothy C., 144
Spechnieff, Anna, 225
spectre, 68, 82, 108, 280, 281, 298
spell-bound, 113
Spencer, Philip, 173
Spencer, R. E. E., 252
Spirit, 3, 8, 11, 17-19, 22, 24, 27, 29, 30, 33-35, 37, 40, 46, 52, 53, 57, 59, 68, 69, 71-73, 83, 84, 87-89, 93, 95, 98, 107-109, 116, 122, 136, 139, 141, 160, 162, 167, 170, 173, 184, 209, 220, 221, 227, 231, 238, 239, 245, 249, 251-255, 260, 263, 270, 271, 273, 275, 282, 289, 291, 293, 295, 297, 302, 303, 311, 320, 328, 342, 343, 345, 366
spirit beings, 238
spirit body, 37
spiritists, 220
spirits, 11, 22, 28, 36, 43, 50, 61, 67, 69, 73, 78, 93, 104, 108, 123, 157, 160, 165, 210, 216, 218, 220, 239, 240, 266, 274, 281, 289-291, 311, 314, 315, 342
spiritual body, 95
spiritual world, 134, 342
Spiritualism, 11, 22, 60, 285, 341-343, 345
Spiritualists, 157, 341
St. Albans, UK, 265, 291
St. Boswells, Scotland, 80, 113
St. Helens, UK, 156
St. Heliers, UK, 200
St. Ives, Cornwall, UK, 281
St. John's Wood, UK, 78
St. Kilda, Scotland, 241
St. Petersburg, Russia, 124, 169
Staffordshire, UK, 210
Staines, Frederick J., 171
Stankewitch, M., 223, 225
statues, 247
Stella, Mrs. I., 273
Stephens, Alexander H., 365
Stevenson, J., 154
Stoke Bishop, UK, 134
strange noises, 175, 213, 246, 320
Stretton, UK, 233
students, 314, 315
suffering, 17, 18, 59, 88, 160, 178, 214, 217, 231, 283, 319
Suffolk, UK, 267
sun, 17, 94, 115, 237, 245, 266, 307
Sunday, 14-17, 22, 58, 82, 93, 95, 122, 161, 171, 178, 191, 196, 200, 203, 205, 207, 214, 215, 235, 238, 239, 259, 278, 323
Sunshine Sisters, the, 365
supernatural, 11, 14, 34, 39, 49, 61, 63, 69, 87, 102, 104, 114, 150, 157, 176, 193, 198, 214, 228, 280, 281, 330, 344
superstition, 69, 250, 318, 325
supper, 14, 65, 90, 129, 131, 160, 216, 258
Surrey, UK, 309
Sussex, England, 141
Sutherland, James, 289
Swansea, UK, 78
Swedenborg, Emanuel, 330
sweets, 237
Swindon, UK, 139
Switzerland County, IN, 300
table-tipping experiments, 306
Tadcaster Aerodrome, 148
Tadcaster, UK, 147, 150
Tandy, George M., 185
Tantum, Francis, 254
Tantum, Richard, 253
Taylor, Jeremy, 241
Taylor, Meadows, 241
tea, 13, 117, 149, 150, 219, 254, 282, 289, 291, 292, 309
teacher, 21, 23, 212, 238, 239
Teddington, UK, 38
Tedworth, UK, 247
telegram, 28, 86, 92, 95, 110, 134, 137, 155, 163, 167, 171-173, 211, 219, 229, 231, 257, 259, 292
telegraph, 173
telekinetic powers, 202
Tellicherry, India, 310, 311
Tennessee, 3, 365
terror, 16, 68, 74, 86, 113, 130, 206, 207, 213, 245, 318
Tewkesbury, UK, 260
Texas, 58
The Crisis, 96
the East, 121, 143, 229, 230
The English Mechanic and World of Science, 168, 231
the Left, 20, 60, 113, 140, 171, 174, 177, 222, 224, 247, 286
The New Revelation (Doyle), 140
the North, 2, 31, 55, 230, 254, 271, 307, 318
The Religio-Philosophical Journal, 27
the South, 251, 255, 299, 307
the West, 230

thieves, 193
Thirsk, UK, 281
Thompson, Margaret, 92
Thompson, Mr. E., 93
Thorne, Emilie, 196, 197
Thursday, 31, 137, 213, 214, 218, 235, 305
timber, 56
Timsbury Ghosts, the, 135, 212
Timsbury, UK, 212
Tinto (British ship), 289
Titanic (ship), 17
tobacco, 15, 159, 220
Tobermory Bay, Scotland, 311
Tomczyk, Stanislawa J., 120
Tommy's kit, 137
Toppington, UK, 13
Torquay, UK, 269
Townsend, Charles, 283
train, 45, 111, 129, 158, 159, 171, 182, 257, 264, 266
trains, 172, 175
travels, 97
Trays, Polly, 195
Trecastle, Wales, 183
tree, 38, 237, 274, 307, 309
trees, 38, 39, 47, 108, 114, 203, 300
Trinity Church, Boston, MA, 62
trousers, 159
truth, 89, 102, 122, 131, 219, 223, 230, 242, 262, 274, 289, 301, 366
Tuesday, 17, 18, 122, 141, 216, 217, 219, 293, 304
Turin, Italy, 251
Tver, Russia, 125
Tweedale, Charles L., 231
Twickenham, UK, 38
Twyford, UK, 271
typhoid fever, 235
typhus fever, 231
U.S.A., 265, 341
uncle, 35, 40, 155, 163, 216, 221, 230, 252, 267, 292, 293, 302, 307, 326
Union, 2, 6, 166
Union Pacific Railroad, 166
United States, 2, 6
United States of America, 2, 6
universe, 28, 341
unseen world, 238
Upcher, Mary, 49
Uppingham, UK, 66
upstairs, 13, 15, 31, 57, 63, 79, 94, 95, 97, 98, 101, 106, 108, 109, 120, 126, 127, 129, 131, 132, 169, 177-179, 182, 183, 187, 189, 191, 192, 194-197, 208, 213, 227, 267, 277, 279, 283
Upton Modsbury, UK, 97
Varennes, Mrs. E. Le Normant des, 233
Vellore, India, 310
Vendome Hotel, 139
Ventnor, UK, 242
vertigo, 292
Vesme, Cesar B. de, 251
Victoria Park, UK, 263
Victoria, Queen, 164
Victorian Period, 164
Victorians, 209
Vienna, Austria, 15, 242
Vincent, Lady Maria, 87
violence, 32, 148, 206, 221
Virginia, 303, 365
vision, 19, 21, 24, 28, 34, 43-45, 49, 59, 84, 88, 95, 96, 129, 135, 143, 157, 163, 168, 172, 173, 185, 205, 217, 220, 222, 235, 237, 239-242, 246, 256, 273, 291-293, 298, 328
visions, 162, 241
visitation, 83, 104
visitations, 19, 81, 104, 157, 320
Vladivostok, Russia, 225
voice, 19, 34, 45, 57, 75, 77, 78, 85, 86, 97, 131, 133, 134, 138, 151, 156, 157, 162, 166, 189, 199, 200, 221, 232, 233, 238-240, 263, 264, 267, 269, 272, 286, 297, 316, 325, 341
voices, 136, 156, 192, 196, 249, 316, 345
Volney, Comte de, 310
Voltaire, M. de, 310
wages, 125
waistcoat, 94, 136, 304
Wake, Charles S., 36
Walcheren expedition, 16
Waldegrave, Lady, 235
Waldegrave, Lord, 235
Walditch, UK, 284
Wales, 72, 183, 235, 295, 298, 321
Walker, Mr. W. A., 85
walking, 24, 35, 38, 50, 60, 64, 66, 74, 79, 82, 85, 87, 88, 107, 109, 110, 113, 114, 122, 126, 149, 155, 161, 175, 177, 178, 183, 187, 188, 192, 194-198, 233, 237, 239, 250, 255, 268, 274, 282, 300, 301, 303, 313, 314, 317, 318, 323

Wallace, Alfred R., 11
Wallace, Mary B., 239
war, 2, 3, 16, 134, 137, 139, 140, 143, 146, 251, 325, 344, 365, 367
War Between the States, 2
War for the Constitution, 365
War Office, 134, 137
wardrobe, 136, 229
wardrobes, 251
Warren, Mabel, 295
Warwickshire, UK, 133, 265
Washington, D.C., 6, 302, 303, 341
water, 29, 30, 42, 80, 94, 128, 131, 172, 215, 218, 255, 266, 282, 303, 319
Watts, Jane, 72
Watts, Mrs. Howitt, 254
wealth, 3, 8, 344, 367
Wedgwood, Hensleigh, 180
Wednesday, 162, 166, 207, 216, 218, 261, 295, 305
Weedon Barracks, 89
Weeford Rectory, 210
Wellesley, Arthur, 310
Welsh, 59, 181, 183, 298
West Leake Rectory, UK, 85
West Virginia, 365
Westlake, Mr. E., 67
Weston Lullingfield, UK, 14, 15
Whepstead Rectory, UK, 31
whip, 56, 69, 254
whips, 251
whisperings, 136
White House, 237
White Lady, 181
White Wood Corner, UK, 138
Whitecar, W. A., 139
wife, 23, 24, 28, 29, 43, 46, 48, 51, 52, 55, 57, 59, 65, 66, 68, 72, 73, 87, 88, 91, 98, 101, 102, 107-109, 111, 116, 134, 136, 154, 165, 169-173, 180, 210-212, 214-216, 230, 233, 246-248, 252, 259, 264, 265, 276, 285, 289, 294, 299, 303-305, 319, 321, 326, 327, 365
Wilcox, Ella W., 8
Williams, Mary H., 92
Williams, Miss M. E., 85
Wilson, Catherine, 49
Wilson, Edmund, 66
Wilson, Mr. D. H., 273
Wilson, Nathan, 310
Wilson, Woodrow, 365

Winchcombe, UK, 86
window, 14, 16, 37, 42, 51, 53, 67, 70, 73, 86, 93, 101, 103, 104, 106, 107, 109-111, 127, 137, 149, 152, 158, 159, 171, 179, 184, 185, 191, 195, 196, 198, 203, 204, 209, 213, 215, 220, 226, 228, 229, 245, 248, 251, 253, 264-266, 273, 280, 291, 301, 316, 320, 321, 324, 325
windows, 13, 34, 51, 66, 91, 92, 178, 190, 258, 280, 315, 325
wine, 33, 250, 254, 260
Wisconsin, 36, 38, 40-42
Witherspoon, Reese, 365
witness, 26, 80, 111, 157, 159, 207, 283
witnesses, 66, 70, 86, 90, 134, 140, 220, 289, 309, 320, 326, 328
Womack, Lee Ann, 365
women, 2, 3, 21, 41, 132, 282, 283
Wood, J. G., 241
Woodham, Eleanore E., 263
woods, 13
Worcestershire, UK, 211
World War I, 134, 137, 139, 143, 146
wounds, 228
Wright, W. Stuart, 49
writing, 3, 27, 72, 83, 88, 93, 109, 112, 134, 140, 144, 146, 148, 149, 169, 176, 184, 185, 195, 271, 273, 287, 290, 365
Wynyard, George, 33-36
Wyoming, 5, 6, 11
X-rays, 21
Yankee myth, 2
Yarmouth, Nova Scotia, 43
yellow fever, 259
Yorkshire, UK, 75, 281

MEET THE AUTHOR EDITOR

NEO-VICTORIAN SCHOLAR LOCHLAINN SEABROOK, a descendant of the families of Alexander Hamilton Stephens, John Singleton Mosby, Edmund Winchester Rucker, and William Giles Harding, is a 7th generation Kentuckian and one of the most prolific and widely read writers in the world today. Known by literary critics as the "new Shelby Foote," the "American Robert Graves," and the "Southern Joseph Campbell," and by his fans as the "Voice of the Traditional South," he is a recipient of the United Daughters of the Confederacy's prestigious Jefferson Davis Historical Gold Medal, and is considered the foremost Southern interpreter of American Civil War history—or what he refers to as the War for the Constitution (1861-1865). A lifelong nonfiction writer, the Sons of Confederate Veterans member has authored and edited evidence-based books ranging in topics from history, politics, science, comparative religion, spirituality, astronomy, entertainment, military, biography, mysticism, and Bible studies, to nature, music, humor, gastronomy, etymology, onomastics, mysteries, alternative health, comparative mythology, genealogy, Christian history, and the paranormal; books that his readers describe as "game changers," "transformative," and "life altering."

One of the world's most popular living historians, he is a 17th generation Southerner of Appalachian heritage who descends from dozens of patriotic Revolutionary War soldiers and Confederate soldiers from Kentucky, Tennessee, North Carolina, and Virginia. Also a history, wildlife, and nature preservationist, the well-respected polymath began life as a child prodigy, later maturing into an archetypal Renaissance Man. Besides being an accomplished and esteemed author, historian, biographer, creative, and Bible authority, the influential litterateur is also a Kentucky Colonel, eagle scout, entrepreneur, screenwriter, nature, wildlife, and landscape photographer and videographer, artist, graphic designer, content creator, genealogist, former history museum docent, and a former ranch hand, zookeeper, and wrangler. A songwriter (of some 3,000 songs in a dozen genres), he is also a film composer, multi-instrument musician, vocalist, session player, and music producer who has worked and performed with some of Nashville's top musicians and singers.

Currently Seabrook is the multi-genre author and editor of nearly 100 adult and children's books (totaling some 40,000 pages and 15,000,000 words) that have earned him accolades from around the globe. His works, which have sold on every continent except Antarctica, have introduced hundreds of thousands to vital facts that have been left out of our mainstream books. He has been endorsed internationally by leading experts, museum curators, award-winning historians, bestselling authors, celebrities, filmmakers, noted scientists, well regarded educators, TV show hosts and producers, renowned military artists, venerable heritage organizations, and distinguished academicians of all races, creeds, and colors.

Of northern, western, and central European ancestry, he is the 6th great-grandson of the Earl of Oxford and a descendant of European royalty through his Kentucky father and West Virginia mother. His modern day cousins include: Johnny Cash, Elvis Presley, Lisa Marie Presley, Billy Ray and Miley Cyrus, Patty Loveless, Tim McGraw, Lee Ann Womack, Dolly Parton, Pat Boone, Naomi, Wynonna, and Ashley Judd, Ricky Skaggs, the Sunshine Sisters, Martha Carson, Chet Atkins, Patrick J. Buchanan, Cindy Crawford, Bertram Thomas Combs (Kentucky's 50th governor), Edith Bolling (second wife of President Woodrow Wilson), Andy Griffith, Riley Keough, George C. Scott, Robert Duvall, Reese Witherspoon, Lee Marvin, Rebecca Gayheart, and Tom Cruise.

A constitutionalist, avid outdoorsman, and gun rights advocate, Seabrook is the author of the international blockbuster, *Everything You Were Taught About the Civil War is Wrong, Ask a Southerner!* He lives with his wife and family in the magnificent Rocky Mountains, heart of the American West, where you will find him hiking, filming, and writing.

For more information on author Mr. Seabrook visit
LochlainnSeabrook.com

Keep Your Body, Mind, & Spirit Vibrating at Their Highest Level
YOU CAN DO SO BY READING THE BOOKS OF

SEA RAVEN PRESS

There is nothing that will so perfectly keep your body, mind, and spirit in a healthy condition as to think wisely and positively. Hence you should not only read this book, but also the other books that we offer. They will quicken your physical, mental, and spiritual vibrations, enabling you to maintain a position in society as a healthy erudite person.

KEEP YOURSELF WELL-INFORMED!

The well-informed person is always at the head of the procession, while the ignorant, the lazy, and the unthoughtful hang onto the rear. If you are a Spiritual man or woman, do yourself a great favor: read Sea Raven Press books and stay well posted on the Truth. It is almost criminal for one to remain in ignorance while the opportunity to gain knowledge is open to all at a nominal price.

We invite you to visit our Webstore for a wide selection of wholesome, family-friendly, well-researched, evidence-based, educational books for all ages. You will be glad you did!

Artisan-Crafted Books & Merch From the Rocky Mountains!

SeaRavenPress.com

LochlainnSeabrook.com
TheBestCivilWarBookEver.com
AmbianceGoneWild.com
Pond5.com/artist/LochlainnSeabrook

If you enjoyed this book, you will be interested in Mr. Seabrook's other popular related titles:

☞ SEABROOK'S BIBLE DICTIONARY OF TRADITIONAL AND MYSTICAL CHRISTIAN DOCTRINES
☞ JESUS & THE LAW OF ATTRACTION: THE BIBLE-BASED GUIDE TO CREATING PERFECT HEALTH, WEALTH, AND HAPPINESS FOLLOWING CHRIST'S SIMPLE FORMULA
☞ YOUR SOUL LIVES FOREVER: DOCUMENTED VICTORIAN CASE STUDIES PROVING CONSCIOUSNESS SURVIVES DEATH
☞ CARNTON PLANTATION GHOST STORIES: TRUE TALES OF THE UNEXPLAINED FROM TENNESSEE'S MOST HAUNTED CIVIL WAR HOUSE!
☞ CHRISTMAS BEFORE CHRISTIANITY: HOW THE BIRTHDAY OF THE "SUN" BECAME THE BIRTHDAY OF THE "SON"
☞ BRITANNIA RULES: GODDESS-WORSHIP IN ANCIENT ANGLO-CELTIC SOCIETY

Available from Sea Raven Press and wherever fine books are sold

ALL OF OUR BOOK COVERS ARE AVAILABLE AS 11" X 17" POSTERS, SUITABLE FOR FRAMING.

SeaRavenPress.com

www.ingramcontent.com/pod-product-compliance
Lightning Source LLC
Chambersburg PA
CBHW020347170426
43200CB00005B/84